COMMODITY CONTROL
IN THE PACIFIC AREA

COMMODITY CONTROL
IN THE
PACIFIC AREA
A Symposium on Recent Experience

EDITED BY
W. L. HOLLAND
Research Secretary, Institute of Pacific Relations

Contributors

JOSEPH S. DAVIS

E. S. HASKELL	CECILE G. H. ROTHE
H. S. PATTON	R. G. HAMPTON
SEIICHI TOBATA	G. L. WOOD
TAIKICHIRO MORI	BARNABAS BRYAN, JUN.
J. B. BRIGDEN	OLIVER LAWRENCE
ROYAL N. CHAPMAN	ROBERT A. MACKAY

*Issued under the Auspices of the Secretariat of the Institute
of Pacific Relations*

STANFORD UNIVERSITY PRESS
STANFORD UNIVERSITY, CALIFORNIA

FIRST PUBLISHED IN 1935

PRINTED IN GREAT BRITAIN
BY THE RIVERSIDE PRESS LIMITED, EDINBURGH

PREFACE

THIS book had its origin in the discussions at the Banff Conference of the Institute of Pacific Relations held in August 1933. The greater part of those discussions had to do with types of economic control in the countries of the Pacific and with the economic or political conflict which so often arose out of the control. Following the characteristic procedure of the Institute conferences the members of the discussion groups spent relatively little time in academic or theoretical debate on the pros and cons of economic control in general. On the contrary it was quickly realized that, in spite of all the arguments for or against control, examples of deliberate interferences with economic tendencies abound in nearly all the countries of the Pacific. It was thus seen that the whole problem could be intelligently appreciated only by careful examination of the principal control schemes already in existence. The record of these discussions has been published in the proceedings of the conference.[1] Readers who consult that record will observe that the term " economic control " was interpreted broadly and not limited to the schemes for the control of staple commodities which form the subject of a greater part of the present book; instead, the discussions ranged over such related problems as the control which is exerted through shipping conferences, tariffs, currency manipulation, cartels and the like. Many of the documents prepared for the conference, however, dealt with specific schemes of commodity control, and many of them either made available for the first time in English a good deal of new information, or else advanced new interpretations of control schemes already described. It was believed that these documents taken together made up a sufficiently valuable and homogeneous collection to warrant separate publication, and the publication committee which considered them recommended that the Institute Secretariat should make the necessary arrangements. The Secretariat has interpreted this mandate broadly, and has arranged not only for extensive revision and enlargement of the conference documents in question, but has also secured seven entirely new essays by competent authorities on other important control schemes in Pacific countries. About half of the present volume is accordingly new material, and the whole constitutes a fairly comprehensive and up-to-date survey of the major commodity controls in the Pacific area.

[1] *Problems af the Pacific, 1933,* edited by Bruno Lasker and W. L. Holland, London and Chicago, 1934.

PREFACE

It does not pretend, however, to deal exhaustively with every known form of commodity control in that area. It excludes the simplest forms, such as the Government monopolies over camphor and tobacco in Japan, and the imperfect Government control of salt in China. It does not consider the Canadian embargoes on pulp-wood, the Chinese restrictions on rice exports, or the British Phosphates Commission under which Great Britain, Australia and New Zealand share in the output of phosphates from Nauru Island. It is not concerned with the meat quotas agreed upon at the Ottawa Conference for the restriction of meat exports from Australia and New Zealand to Great Britain. It excludes the Chilean nitrate control which has had more to do with Europe and the Atlantic than with the Pacific. Moreover, it does not concern itself directly with the many oblique forms of commodity control which are hidden behind national tariff policies, though it is of course recognized that these are often quite as important as an outright restriction scheme.[1]

It may be noted that none of the chapters deal specially with either China or the Soviet Union. China has no important control scheme except the salt control, which is a tax-gathering device, and the restriction on the export of rice, which is seldom operative because of the prevailing necessity for heavy imports. Soviet Russia, on the other hand, is unique in having an all-inclusive system of socialist control, not specifically of commodities, but of all major economic activities. That fact of course does not make it any less interesting to students of the workings of capitalist control schemes, for there are administrative and other difficulties to be overcome in all schemes, whether socialist or capitalist. In the comparison of these difficulties and in the study of the methods the Soviet authorities have evolved to grapple with them, there is indeed room for several books, in addition to the numerous general descriptions of Soviet economic life that appear every year. With the recent establishment of a unit of the Institute of Pacific Relations in Moscow, it is hoped that under Institute auspices there will soon be made available in English some such account of Russian economic control schemes with special reference to the Far Eastern territories of the Soviet Union.

Even with these omissions, the extent and variety of the controls

[1] For a fuller list of control schemes and a discussion of the problems involved see *op. cit.*, chapter i. An excellent account of the Japanese camphor monopoly, the Canadian pulp-wood embargoes and the Chilean nitrate control may be found in Wallace and Edminster, *International Control of Raw Materials*, Brookings Institution, Washington, 1930.

6

described n this book are quite remarkable. The first chapter begins
with wheat; the last ends with whales. Between these extremes are
descriptions of controls exercised over a score of everyday commodities,
the list of which sounds like something the Walrus and the Carpenter
might have sung: cotton and cheese, cinchona and corn, honey and
halibut, pineapples and pigs, rice and rubber, silk and sugar, tea
and tin, butter and seals, frozen meat and tobacco, kauri gum and
salmon. Indeed it is perhaps only when the reader has properly
intoxicated himself in the sound of these names that he can hope
to enter without fear into the economic Wonderland that has produced
this collection of mutually contradictory control schemes. For the
Mad Hatter who presides over this party is named Price-Profit,
and the innocent Alice who asks why consumers must go without
when producers have too much will be rudely answered with the
word " Disequilibrium." And the same answer must suffice for those
who wonder why pigs are encouraged to multiply in England and
destroyed by the million in America, or why Japanese tax themselves
to produce expensive wheat while Canadian farmers burn it for
fuel.

For those who put their trust in economic planning, and still more for
those who advocate such planning within an economic system dominated by price and private profit, there is much of interest in the chapters
of this book. No attempt has been made to secure a uniform point of
view on the part of the contributors. For the most part they are concerned with an accurate description of the various schemes rather than
with passing judgment on them. The reasonably informed reader is at
liberty to draw his own conclusions. Nevertheless it is difficult to
escape the feeling that these control schemes, especially the purely
national controls, fall far short of anything which can properly be
called economic planning. So many of them are marked by the lack
of any underlying social philosophy. They are not co-ordinated with
other parts of the nation's economic life. Like most tariff " policies "
they are not policies at all, but crude compromises between vested
group-interests. They are makeshifts, often devised hastily to meet an
emergency, or to placate a troublesome minority; once established they
often perpetuate themselves because they have themselves created new
vested interests, which governments dislike to break up, even though
the original emergency conditions have passed. Again, even when a
scheme is well conceived, it suffers in the execution because its administration is so often loaded, *faute de mieux,* on the hands of a Government

department quite unfitted for the task and handicapped by the inevitable rigidities of officialdom.

Concrete examples are easily found. Even in Australia, which has had a long history of control and has in recent years gained something of a reputation for systematic planning, there has often been, as Dr Wood points out, lack of co-ordination and positive inconsistency, so that even now after thirty or forty years the general principles of commodity control are largely unformulated. In Japan and New Zealand controls have often been based on no more profound political philosophy than the maxim of " Let George do it "—George being in both cases a paternal Government. It will probably come as a surprise to many Western readers, filled with the common idea of a well-planned and continuing system of governmental assistance to economic activities in Japan, to find even the two classic controls, over silk and rice, so shot through with inherent contradictions and mere conciliatory gestures. One cannot speak as yet with certainty on the vast American program of agricultural control. Among the leaders in the Roosevelt administration there have been many who have tried to co-ordinate this program with other parts of the national recovery plans. Secretary Wallace and his lieutenants have clearly shown their concern with the problem, and the land-withdrawal plans in the Agricultural Adjustment Administration are of course an important indication that practical steps are being tried. Yet the mere technical difficulties in achieving a coherent plan of action are tremendous, and the fundamental inconsistencies in the American commodity controls have evoked severe criticism. Again, even for those who do not criticize, it is difficult to forget that so many agricultural control schemes in the United States have had a political motive, however genuine—an oft-announced desire " to do something for the farmer "—rather than an economic motive of restoring some workable balance between industry and agriculture in the whole American economy.

Control schemes, then, are a far cry from real planning, and the socialist planner rightly objects to the arguments of those critics who point to the difficulties and inefficiencies of such schemes as proof that socialist controls would be doomed to failure. He properly urges that the answer to the ineffective working of some control schemes is not to return to an impossible laissez-faire, but a wider and fully co-ordinated system of controls. He will further urge, with reason, that for many commodities, such controls, to be fully co-ordinated, must come under a centralized international authority.

8

Many will agree with this, and in fact there are many signs to show that capitalists and individualists have, by their actions in reference to some of the existing international commodity controls, come to the same conclusion. The international agreements affecting wheat, rubber, tin and tea are a long way from meeting the desires of the socialist economic planner, but they at least expose the hollowness of the argument that a mere " getting back to the old system " is any longer a workable, much less a desirable, policy. On the other hand, those who regard these agreements as encouraging evidence that nations can work out an intelligent means for the production and consumption of the world's staples, within the framework of capitalist society, may be deceiving themselves just as completely as the most rugged of the individualists. For it is a discouraging fact that these control schemes depend so largely for their success on *restriction*, on the creation of an artificial and unnatural scarcity when there might be abundance. They have overcome some of the stupidities of economic nationalism, but they have still to grapple with deeper problems of producing, to use the stock phrase, for use and not simply for profit.

Yet when all this and much more is conceded, the fact remains that controls, whether set up now or in a future socialist commonwealth or a fascist dictatorship, still have to be put into execution, and to meet similar obstacles. Production must still be adjusted to consumption; alternative or competing uses for goods have to be decided; joint products, such as beef and hides, or cotton and cotton-seed, continue to be produced in proportions fixed within narrow limits by nature; even Soviet Russia has maintained a price system, however radically modified, as an indicator—a kind of economic pressure-gauge. To the extent that this is true, the study of these existing control schemes is valuable. They serve in some measure as test-tubes, as examples of methods of interference with the interplay of supply, demand and price. Some are perhaps unfortunate examples, but a surprising number, especially in their technical or administrative aspects, have been un-doubtedly effective and full of promise for future schemes. This book ends with an account of international co-operation in the conservation of fisheries; it is not perhaps a topic of world-shaking importance, though it plays no small part in the often troubled diplomatic relations between Soviet Russia and Japan, but the chapter aptly ends with a sentence that might well apply to all international controls—" It [the treaty] permits the development of an international technique so badly needed in international affairs; and above all, it permits the development

9

of international institutions according to function rather than according to the outworn canons of national sovereignty."

The Institute of Pacific Relations is an unofficial body for the scientific study of international affairs, and does not itself advocate policies or express opinions. Although this volume is issued under the auspices of the Secretariat, the Institute as such is not responsible for opinions expressed either in the chapters or the Preface. These remain as much the personal views of the writers as if given orally at an Institute conference. The Editor wishes to acknowledge with gratitude the co-operation given by the contributors in supplying new material and in revising old. He is also indebted to Mr Bruno Lasker, of the American Council of the Institute, and Mr Samitaro Uramatsu, of the Japanese Council, for assistance in editing and revising certain chapters.

W. L. HOLLAND.

Tokyo,
October 8, 1934.

CONTENTS

11

CONTENTS

CONTENTS

THE CONTRIBUTORS

JOSEPH S. DAVIS.—One of the three Directors of the Food Research Institute, Stanford University, California; formerly Assistant Professor of Economics at Harvard University; chief economist of the United States Federal Farm Board in 1930; author of *The Farm Export Debenture Plan* and works on the baking industry; at present co-director of an extensive inquiry into the American agricultural recovery program being conducted under the auspices of the Brookings Institution, Washington.

E. S. HASKELL.—Formerly Director-General of Agriculture and Public Domains of Persia; now Senior Agricultural Economist in the General Crops Section of the United States Agricultural Adjustment Administration, Washington.

H. S. PATTON.—Professor of Economics at Michigan State College of Agriculture and Applied Science, East Lansing; author of *Grain Growers' Co-operation in Western Canada.*

SEIICHI TOBATA.—Professor of Agricultural Economics, Tokyo Imperial University; author of *Control of Prices of Agricultural Products* (in Japanese) and other works.

TAIKICHIRO MORI.—Professor at the Sericultural Institute, Kyoto; author of *A History of the Silk Industry in Japan* (in Japanese).

J. B. BRIGDEN.—Formerly Professor of Economics at the University of Tasmania; now Director of the Queensland Bureau of Economics and Statistics, Brisbane.

ROYAL N. CHAPMAN.—Dean of the Graduate School of Tropical Agriculture at the University of Hawaii and Director of the Experiment Station of the Pineapple Producers' Co-operative Association, Honolulu.

CECILE G. H. ROTHE.—Member of the Staff of the Colonial Institute, Amsterdam.

R. G. HAMPTON.—Secretary of the Canterbury Group of the New Zealand Council, Institute of Pacific Relations.

G. L. WOOD.—Associate Professor of Commerce at the University of Melbourne; author of *The Pacific Basin* and *Borrowing and Business in Australia.*

BARNABAS BRYAN, jun.—Consulting Petroleum Geologist, New York.

OLIVER LAWRENCE.—Member of the Staff in the Information Department of the Royal Institute of International Affairs, London.

ROBERT A. MACKAY.—Professor of Government, Dalhousie University, Halifax.

CHAPTER I

PLANNED AGRICULTURAL ADJUSTMENT IN THE UNITED STATES, 1933-1934

by Joseph S. Davis

UNDER the Agricultural Adjustment Act of May 12, 1933, an amazing adventure in national planning and control of agriculture has been launched in the United States. The new program has not yet been revealed or even formulated in all its fullness, but in a single year many far-reaching moves have been made. The measures represent a bold and vigorous effort to pull American farmers out of the worst agricultural depression the United States has experienced, and to develop machinery and procedures for solving old and baffling problems of American agriculture. In his message of March 16, 1933, referring to the bill which developed into " The Farm Act of 1933," [1] President Roosevelt said to Congress:

Deep study and the joint counsel of many points of views have produced a measure which offers great promise of good results. I tell you frankly that it is a new and untrod path, but I tell you with equal frankness that an unprecedented condition calls for the trial of new means to rescue agriculture. If a fair administrative trial of it is made and it does not produce the hoped-for results, I shall be the first to acknowledge it and advise you.

Without pretence at forecasts or premature appraisal, it is pertinent to summarize the principal operations in the first year of the Adjustment Act, against the background of the conditions which they were designed to correct and the philosophy which underlies them.

THE BACKGROUND OF THE ACT [2]

In the five years before the war, American agriculture was fairly prosperous. Though data for adequate comparisons with earlier and later periods are lacking, practically all available evidence supports this

[1] 73rd Congress, *Public No. 10, H.R. 3835.* Title I. constitutes the Agricultural Adjustment Act. Title II. constitutes the Emergency Farm Mortgage Act of 1933, which, together with the Farm Credit Act of 1933 (June 16), the Farm Credit Administration is administering. Title III. comprises five sections (the so-called Thomas Amendment) which confers on the President extraordinary powers with respect to currency and credit.

[2] Materials for this background are drawn chiefly from a large variety of printed and mimeographed publications of the Department of Agriculture, including the Bureau of Agricultural Economics and the Agricultural Adjustment Administration. Among the most important are the annual *Yearbook of Agriculture*; the monthly

generally accepted opinion. The 10-crop index of crop value per acre was about double its depressed level in the middle nineties, and higher than even in the years of currency inflation following the Civil War.[1] Wholesale prices of farm products stood notably higher in relation to the general index of farm prices than ever before. Values of farm real estate per acre, which had fallen slightly in the nineties, rose sharply in the decade 1900-1910, and continued upward; this increase was striking, even after allowance is made for the concurrent upward trend of commodity prices. These trends were accompanied by a notable decline in the volume of our agricultural exports from the high peak to which they had risen in the late nineties.

During the Great War, expansion of foreign demands for American farm products led to notable increases in farm prices and farm income, and considerable increases in volume of output and exports (except of cotton).[2] Before the boom broke in 1920, farm land values had risen sharply and many farms had changed hands at high prices. Incidental to this process, accompanying exceptional prosperity, the farm mortgage debt rose from 3320 million dollars in 1910 to 7858 million in 1920. Owing to these factors, the post-war deflation crisis was the more severe upon agriculture. In the course of the ensuing financial re-adjustment, the farm mortgage debt rose to over 9000 million dollars, while total agricultural capital valued at current rates declined from 78,436 million in 1920 to 58,244 million in 1924, as compared with 45,042 million in 1909-1913; and the index of farm real estate value per acre (1912-1914 average=100) declined from 170 in 1920 to 130 in 1924.

After substantial recovery from the post-war depression, American agriculture experienced a period of reasonably stable prosperity in 1925-1929. The volume of net agricultural production fluctuated within narrow limits, on a considerably higher level than in 1919-1922, or presumably than before the war. Production of dairy and poultry products, of wool, truck crops, and some fruits, showed marked up-trends, while production of grains and meat animals declined somewhat from the level of 1923 and 1924.[3] In these five years, gross income

Crops and Markets; L. H. Bean and A. P. Chew, Economic Trends affecting Agriculture, July 1933; Mordecai Ezekiel and L. H. Bean, Economic Bases for the Agricultural Adjustment Act, December 1933; and Agricultural Adjustment, the A.A.A.'s extensive report on its operations to February 1934, released March 26.

[1] Crops and Markets, December 1931, viii. 542.

[2] See charts in Economic Bases . . ., pp. 7, 9, 33. Current indexes of the volume of production run back only to 1919.

[3] See charts in Economic Bases . . ., p. 38.

18

from farm production averaged 11,745 million dollars as compared with
6602 million in 1909-1913. The 10-crop index of crop value per acre
averaged 19.38 dollars as compared with 15.89 dollars in the late pre-war
period, and more conspicuous increases in value of output occurred in
livestock products and various lesser crops. Annual ratios of index
numbers of wholesale prices of farm products to those prices of non-
agricultural commodities averaged above the 1910-1914 average in this
period, though the same did not hold for the index of purchasing
power of farm products at the farm.[1] Valued at current rates, agricultural capital averaged 57,070 million dollars in 1925-1929 as compared
with 45,042 million in 1909-1913,[2] when land values were high; and the
index of farm real estate value per acre averaged about 23 per cent.
above its 1910-1914 level.[3]

It may be questioned whether history will bear out the prevailing
view that agriculture was still in a depressed condition in 1925-1929,
as compared with a reasonably normal level; and it is inherently difficult
to test the general opinion that farmers were not then getting their
" fair share " of the increasing national income. Indubitably, however,
that share was a declining one [4]; industrial and commercial expansion
far outran expansion in farm output; and in spite of many improvements
in the plane of living and business operations on the farm, non-farm
activities were relatively more attractive. According to the latest official
estimates, the net movement from the farm in most years of the first
post-war decade exceeded the natural increase, so that the farm
population as of January 1 declined from an interim peak of 31,768,000
in 1922 to 30,169,000 in 1930; this was nearly 2 million less than the
estimate for 1910. Land values per acre continued to sag rather than
resume the advance that had characterized the pre-war period. Taxes
on farms kept on rising, and farm mortgage interest charges failed to
decline appreciably; the mortgage debt itself even tended slightly upward,

---

[1] See charts in *Economic Bases* . . ., pp. 7, 27. The latter index has been revised;
see below, p. 21.

[2] Averages of six end-year figures. See *Yearbook of Agriculture, 1934*, p. 698.

[3] Assuming that the 1910-1914 average was 98 per cent. of the 1912-1914 base
figure.

[4] According to estimates of the National Bureau of Economic Research and the
Department of Agriculture, farm income constituted 18·5 per cent. of the national
income in 1919, 14·9 per cent. in 1920, close to 11 per cent. in each year of 1921-1925,
around 9½ per cent. in each year of 1926-1928. Preliminary indications for 1931 and
1932 suggest corresponding figures of about 7 per cent. (*Economic Trends affecting
Agriculture*, p. 33). For various reasons, including the imputation of low valuations to
various items of non-cash farm income, any such percentages understate the farmers'
share in the nation's *real* income.

19

and the estimated total for 1928, nearly 9500 million dollars, was perhaps an all-time peak.[1]

Because of such conditions, pressure for relief and aid for agriculture did not cease with substantial recovery from the post-war depression in 1924-1925. Various major and minor measures were adopted; but President Coolidge vetoed, in February 1927 and May 1928, two successive McNary-Haugen bills that embodied a vigorous policy designed to raise agriculture to " equality with industry." With a device quite different from the equalization-fee feature of these bills, but with the same major price-raising objective, an export debenture plan was strongly urged as an alternative.[2] With substantially the same objective, the Agricultural Marketing Act of 1929 was passed at a special session early in President Hoover's administration. This provided for a Federal Farm Board with broad powers, and put at its disposal a revolving fund of 500 million dollars to use in aid of co-operative marketing and for commodity " stabilization operations." [3]

With the growing industrialization of the United States, each successive census has showed an increasing proportion of the population in the cities and a declining relative importance of agriculture. About the time of the Civil War, agriculture ceased to be the principal occupation of the majority of those gainfully occupied. During the Great War the population first ceased to be predominantly rural.[4] The decade 1910-1920 was probably the first, however, in which the farm population actually decreased, and the decline went considerably further in 1910-1930.[5] In 1930 slightly under one-fourth of the total population were on farms. The same census showed approximately 10 million persons of 16 years and upwards gainfully occupied in agriculture; this was 21·2 per cent. of the total gainfully occupied population of these ages.[6]

In the first three years of the latest depression, however, the gross

[1] No estimates were prepared for 1926, 1927 and 1929. The preliminary estimate for 1930—9241 million dollars—is below those of 1925 and 1928.

[2] The movement for farm relief, the conditions in which it thrived, and the principal proposals up to early in 1929, are discussed in J. D. Black, *Agricultural Reform in the United States* (New York, 1929), published in April 1929. See also J. S. Davis, *The Farm Export Debenture Plan* (Stanford University, 1929).

[3] See Chapter II., by E. S. Haskell. No thorough-going discussion of the Federal Farm Board, beyond that given in its three annual reports, has yet been published.

[4] Counting as rural the population outside of incorporated places with a population of 2500 and over.

[5] No census data on farm population were collected prior to 1920, but a census estimate was made for 1910.

[6] *Recent Social Trends in the United States* (New York, 1933), i. 281. For persons 10 years and over the number reported engaged in agriculture was 10,482,000, and the percentage slightly under 21·3 (*Economic Trends affecting Agriculture*, p. 34).

movement from the farms, which is estimated to have exceeded 2 million persons a year from 1922 to 1929, declined so sharply that the farm population rose to a point on January 1, 1933, above that of 1910. This reflected not the absolute attractions of farming, but the fact that under prevailing industrial conditions few could find jobs in the cities and towns, and food and shelter were less difficult to obtain on the farms. The latest estimate of the farm population, as of January 1, 1934, is 32½ million. The official estimates indicate a net migration from the farms in 1933 for the first year since 1929, but a net increase of 267,000 in the farm population owing to an excess of natural increase in farm population over net migration from the farms.[1]

The world-wide depression of 1930 fell with cruel force upon American agriculture. In the face of this, the bold and costly loan and stabilization operations of the Federal Farm Board alleviated some disasters for a time, but completely failed to prevent drastic declines in prices of farm products, eventually to or below the historic lows of the eighteen-nineties. From a level approaching 12,000 million dollars in each year of 1925-1929, gross income from agriculture declined in 1929-1932—in 1932 to 5331 millions, well below the pre-war average. With taxes, interest charges, rent, wages and operating expenses declining only moderately, net income from farming shrank even more severely.[2] Exports declined in volume, and much more heavily in value. The estimated farm value of exports of farm products had constituted 15·8 per cent. of gross income from farm production in 1919, and averaged 14·1 per cent. of it in 1920-1924 and 12 per cent. of it in 1925-1929; in 1929-1932 the corresponding percentages fell to 10·2, 7·5, 6·7 and 6·5.[3]

The index of crop value per acre declined relatively further from 1929 to 1932 than from 1919 to 1921, and to a point in 1932 lower than any in the record extending back to 1866. Net income from agriculture, which in 1925-1929 had yielded operating farmers around 4 per cent. on their capital in addition to a computed return for their labour at going rates,[4] fell increasingly short of rewarding their labour

---

[1] These estimates take no account of changes in the rural non-farm population; for these there are no available data, but "it is generally conceded that there have been marked increases since 1930 in the number of persons living on plots of land too small to be classed as 'farms' by the census" (U.S. Department of Agriculture press releases of March 27, 28, 1934).

[2] See chart in *Economic Bases . . .*, p. 8; *Crops and Markets*, August 1934, xi. 314-315.

[3] *Economic Trends affecting Agriculture*, p. 22.

[4] *Yearbook of Agriculture, 1934*, p. 697. Competent students in this field are not yet satisfied with the procedures by which such percentages are derived.

even at reduced rates. From the level at which they had appeared to be settling, farm real estate values per acre declined 36½ per cent. in the three years ending March 1933, as compared with a fall of 32½ per cent. in the preceding decade from the exceptional peak in 1920. At the end of 1931, the value of agricultural capital was estimated at 43,316 million dollars, reflecting a drop of nearly 25 per cent. in two years; and the shrinkage continued for more than a year longer. Whatever the train of causes responsible for it, the severe and protracted disaster to agriculture affected all business interests dependent on farmer purchases; and because of extensive farm indebtedness, it contributed toward undermining the financial structure of the nation.

Prices of farm products were generally at their lowest, and farm distress was at its worst, during the summer, autumn and winter preceding the change of administration on March 4, 1933. This contributed heavily to the Democratic landslide in the elections of November 1932. Disappointment with the Federal Farm Board led to demands for new and more potent measures of farm relief and agricultural reorganization. During the campaign Mr Roosevelt had virtually committed himself to the principles of the voluntary domestic allotment plan, as a major device to be employed.[1] This contemplated giving farmers cash payments, in return for their agreements to reduce acreage or production by stipulated percentages, the payments to be financed by processing taxes on the farm products consumed within the country but off the farms.[2]

The new Administration was elected by such large majorities that it had a relatively free hand in trying out measures breaking sharply with tradition and experience. The Farm Act of 1933 was largely drafted by the incoming Administration, in close consultation with representatives of farm organizations, with the aid of several men who were given the task of applying it. These included the new Secretary of Agriculture (Henry A. Wallace), the Assistant Secretary (Rexford G. Tugwell), the first and second Governors of the Farm Credit Administration (Henry Morganthau and W. I. Myers), the first Administrator of the

---

[1] His major utterance on the subject was in his speech at Topeka, Kansas, September 14, 1932.

[2] This plan was analysed, chiefly in the form in which it stood during the presidential campaign, in a study by the present author, " The Voluntary Domestic Allotment Plan for Wheat," *Wheat Studies of the Food Research Institute*, November 1932, ix. 23-62. Professor M. L. Wilson, its leading exponent, discussed it at a later stage in an address at Minneapolis on February 15, 1933: " Farm Relief and the Domestic Allotment Plan," *The Day and Hour Series of the University of Minnesota*, No. 2, April 1933.

Agricultural Adjustment Administration (George N. Peek), his personal legal adviser (Frederick P. Lee), the leading figure in the evolution of the domestic allotment plan (M. L. Wilson), and an assistant chief economist of the Federal Farm Board (Mordecai Ezekiel), who became Economic Adviser to Secretary Wallace.[1]

Nevertheless, the Act as passed represented a compromise between the demands of politicians and farm leaders, who mainly sought quickly-operating farm relief, and the desires of a few far-sighted students of agriculture who sought to provide for more fundamental adjustments of agriculture to changed conditions in the emergency and beyond it.

THE ACT AND ITS PHILOSOPHY [2]

The Agricultural Adjustment Act is not elaborate.[3] It is largely permissive rather than mandatory, and leaves wide discretion to the Secretary of Agriculture. Indeed, unlike the Agricultural Marketing Act, it makes no specific provision for the organization that has been set up to administer it. The substantive provisions chiefly confer authority on the Secretary of Agriculture to apply a cotton option plan and voluntary domestic allotment plans for agricultural commodities designated as " basic," to enter into marketing agreements covering any agricultural commodity or product thereof, and to license processors and handlers of these and competing products. The Act makes provision for processing taxes to be levied on the specified basic products (and for compensating processing taxes on products competing with these), in order to finance land rental and benefit payments to farmers and costs of disposal of surpluses. It also appropriates 100 million dollars to be used for administrative expenses and rental and benefit payments.[4] The Act is

[1] Henry I. Harriman, President of the United States Chamber of Commerce, had played an important rôle in connection with certain features of the allotment plan.

[2] The case for the Act is most elaborately presented in Ezekiel and Bean, *Economic Bases for the Agricultural Adjustment Act*. The present discussion follows closely the corresponding portion of the present author's address on " The A.A.A.," at Minneapolis, December 11, 1933, published by the University of Minnesota Press, in its *Day and Hour Series*, No. 7, March 1934.

[3] As amended up to February 1934, it is conveniently accessible in *Agricultural Adjustment*, pp. 361-368. Relevant executive orders are given in *ibid.*, 369-373.

[4] In practice this appropriation has thus far been drawn upon to only a limited extent, and for administrative expenses only. In addition, the National Industrial Recovery Act of June 16, 1933 (sec. 220), authorized the President to allocate not more than 100 million dollars (the so-called Bankhead Fund) for carrying out the purposes of the Agricultural Adjustment Act. Of this amount the President allocated 60 millions to be used in adjusting accounts between the Secretary of Agriculture and the Farm Credit Administration in acquiring cotton and cotton options for use in making benefit payments, and 37 millions for the corn-hog program.

to expire when " the President finds and proclaims that the national economic emergency in relation to agriculture has been ended " (sec. 13).[1]

The Act designated as " basic agricultural commodities " wheat, cotton, field corn (maize), hogs, rice, tobacco, and milk and its products.[2] All of these except rice are of major importance from the standpoint of a number of producers and amount of farm value. Various other products of lesser importance had as good claims to inclusion as rice, and most of the rice program actually developed would have been equally feasible if rice had not been called " basic." All those listed except milk and its products have been produced in substantial proportions for export, though corn has been exported mainly in hog products rather than as grain. Beef cattle, sheep and wool, and poultry and eggs are also basic agricultural products from certain standpoints; like dairy products, they are produced almost wholly for domestic use. When the bill was before Congress, however, organizations representing the cattle industry vigorously opposed inclusion of cattle in the list, and sheep and poultry interests preferred that their products too be left out.

Recent amendments to the Act have significantly broadened the scope. Late in March 1934, without a record vote, Congress passed an amending bill, which the President signed on April 7.[3] This added to the list of basic commodities, cattle, rye, flax, barley, grain sorghums and peanuts. It further appropriated 200 million dollars to enable the Secretary of Agriculture to finance programs of " surplus reductions and production adjustments with respect to the dairy and beef cattle industries . . . and to support and balance the markets for the dairy and beef cattle industries," not more than 120 million of which was to be used for either of these two industries. An additional 50 millions was appropriated to enable the Secretary to make advances to the Federal

---

[1] " Emergency " is a term so elastic that only a hardy prophet would predict the date of expiration under this limitation. It will not be surprising if, before that time comes, the Act is replaced by another measure ostensibly designed to be permanent.

[2] Three reasons for designating these as basic are mentioned in *Agricultural Adjustment*: " One is that changes in their price strongly influence changes in the prices of other agricultural commodities. Another is that the United States produces an exportable surplus of nearly all of them. Export demand and world price of each had fallen sharply before the Act was passed, and these commodities were generally in a relatively worse economic situation than others that are produced and consumed on a domestic basis. A third reason is that each of these commodities is put through some manufacturing process before it is ready for human consumption, and their production and distribution can be more easily regulated in these processing channels than could the production and distribution of commodities not so processed." These criteria were not strictly applied, and have subsequently been abandoned.

[3] 73rd Congress, *Public No. 142, H.R. 7478.*

Emergency Relief Association for relief purchases of beef and dairy products, and " to eliminate diseased dairy and beef cattle, including cattle suffering from tuberculosis and Bang's disease, and to make payments to owners with respect thereto." The Secretary's power to enter into marketing agreements was broadened by a re-wording in which the italicized words indicate the significant additions:

After due notice and opportunity for hearing, to enter into marketing agreements with processors, *producers*, associations of producers and others engaged in the handling of any agricultural commodity or product thereof, in the current of *or in competition with, or so as to burden, obstruct, or in any way affect*, interstate or foreign commerce.

A separate bill, passed April 27 and signed May 9,[1] designated sugar as a basic commodity, set maximum quotas for domestic beet- and cane-sugar production, and authorized the Secretary of Agriculture to fix quotas for sugar from the island possessions and foreign countries. Under it the President proclaimed a $\frac{1}{2}$-cent. reduction of the tariff-duty, effective June 8, and processing taxes of like amounts have been levied from that date.

In certain respects, the philosophy underlying the Act is essentially the same as that which underlay the McNary-Haugen bills, the export debenture plans, the Agricultural Marketing Act of 1929, and the operations of the Federal Farm Board. It is possibly not too much to say that agriculture is held to be *the* fundamental industry,[2] and farmers a class of peculiar and paramount importance in society. This " agricultural fundamentalism " is a deep-seated doctrine which few are willing to call in question, though many of its far-reaching implications rest upon assumptions rather than upon proved facts. Second, our national policy, in its positive and negative aspects, is held to have operated on the whole to aid other classes more than farmers; consequently it is held that agriculture has not had a "square deal," or farmers a " fair share " in the national income. Third, for a variety of reasons, farmers are regarded as incapable of organizing to secure their " rights " as effectively as industrialists, commercial interests, railways, bankers and industrial employees; hence in a society shot through with organization it is held that farmers tend to get " the short end of the stick " unless the Government steps in to give them special aid in organizing and otherwise. In addition, it is held that a great depression, accompanied

---

[1] 73rd Congress, *Public No. 213, H.R. 8861.*
[2] The seal of the Department of Agriculture bears the motto: " Agriculture is the Foundation of Manufacture and Commerce."

by severe declines in the level of prices, works peculiar hardship upon farmers, since prices of raw materials such as they produce tend to fall sharply and contraction of output is not readily feasible for them, and since their debts and taxes tend to remain fixed while their net income falls; hence it is held that agriculture requires extraordinary governmental aid at such a juncture.

Foremost among the theories expressed in the Adjustment Act itself is " that the present acute economic emergency " is partly due to " a severe and increasing disparity between the prices of agricultural and other commodities, which disparity has largely destroyed the purchasing power of farmers for industrial products, has broken down the orderly exchange of commodities, and has seriously impaired the agricultural assets supporting the national credit structure." It is therefore " declared that these conditions in the basic industry of agriculture have affected transactions in agricultural commodities with a national public interest, have burdened and obstructed the normal currents of commerce in such commodities, and render imperative the immediate enactment of title I. of this Act." Here is a group of theories, in which price disparity appears as the evil cause of sad results.

The word " disparity " implies that " parity " is definable, and the Act proceeds to define it. It is declared to be the policy of Congress:

(1) To establish and maintain such balance between the production and consumption of agricultural commodities, and such marketing conditions therefor, as will re-establish prices to farmers at a level that will give agricultural commodities a purchasing power with respect to articles that farmers buy, equivalent to the purchasing power of agricultural commodities in the base period. . . .

(2) To approach such equality of purchasing power by gradual correction of the present inequalities therein at as rapid a rate as is deemed feasible in view of the current consumptive demand in domestic and foreign markets.

For tobacco the base period is fixed as the ten post-war years ending July 1929, for all other agricultural commodities the five pre-war years ending July 1914. Thus the old slogan " Equality for Agriculture " is given more precision, in a manner resembling the ratio-price plan of Messrs Peek and Johnson of 1922.[1] The ultimate objective of the Act is to raise the income of farmers, and their standard of living; the

---

[1] The two men who in 1933 became administrators, respectively, of the A.A.A. and the N.R.A., published in 1922 and 1923 two editions of a pamphlet entitled " Equality for Agriculture." Mr Peek was subsequently a leader in the long fight for the McNary-Haugen or equalization-fee plan.

intermediate objective is the attainment of "parity prices" for farm products.[1]

The official indexes show that in the first three months of 1933 farm prices of farm products averaged 50 per cent. of the pre-war level, while retail prices paid by farmers for goods used in living and production averaged 101 per cent. of their pre-war level. Practically, therefore, the Agricultural Adjustment Administration was given the task of doubling farm prices as a group, and then raising them by as much more as the index of prices farmers pay actually rises. Not since 1920 has the index of prices received by farmers reached 100 per cent. of the index of prices paid; and only in one year of short crops (1925) has the percentage averaged over 91. Moreover, the Act, sec. 9 (c), is interpreted to mean that the normal or "parity" price of *each* "basic" farm product, its "fair exchange value," is as much above *its* pre-war average as the index of prices farmers pay is above its pre-war average. How much more this implies is suggested by the fact that farm prices of grains *as a group* were only about 35 per cent. of their pre-war level in January-March 1933. For some farm products the standard implies more than trebling the prices of early 1933.

Behind these specific declarations in the Act lie three major assumptions. First, it is assumed that this statistical procedure really shows what can be truly called the "fair exchange value" of farm products. This is in spite of the facts that *wholesale prices* of farm products in the United States were relatively higher in 1909-1914 than in any period of equal length before, at least in more than a century,[2] and that price relationships among various commodities not only fluctuate within a season, and from year to year, but change notably from decade to decade as changes occur in conditions of production, transportation, and demand.[3] Second, it is assumed that farm prices of farm products *can* be raised, through Government or Government-sponsored actions, by the relative amounts indicated. Third, it is assumed that if farm prices are so raised, even by curtailment of farm output at the direct expense

---

[1] The parity-price objective, in spite of its weaknesses, is open to less objection than that of "making the tariff effective," as earlier versions of the plan usually put it, or "giving farmers cost of production," as some farmer groups would have had it. On technical grounds President Roosevelt vetoed, in the spring of 1934, the Shipstead bill providing for re-defining parity prices in such a way as to take account of farm labour costs, interest, and taxes as well as commodities farmers buy.

[2] See chart and tables covering the period 1798-1932 in G. F. Warren and F. A. Pearson, *Prices* (New York, 1933), 24-27; and Leonard P. Ayres, *The Economics of Recovery* (New York, 1934), 77-79.

[3] This matter is briefly discussed by the present author in a paper in *Journal of Farm Economics*, April 1933, xv. 247-254.

of consumers, agricultural prosperity will be restored and general economic recovery enhanced if not ensured.

These important assumptions commonly pass unquestioned, and seem to have been generally accepted as if they were self-evident. Actually, each rests upon no clearly demonstrated foundation,[1] and they are likely to be subjected to severe tests. Perhaps the largest single question is this: If farm production be sufficiently curtailed to ensure farm producers parity prices, will they regard the income from parity prices on the reduced output as satisfactory? If parity prices, an intermediate objective, should be attained without achieving the more ultimate objective—satisfactory income per farmer—will the success be regarded as success or failure? Another pertinent question is: If the restoration of parity prices itself is slow in coming, will farmers await with patience the full achievement of a goal so widely advertised as their due? Leading spokesmen of the A.A.A. have warned that magic and miracles are too much to expect of them, and openly appealed for patience as well as co-operation; but the goal set is relatively so high, so definite, and so widely advertised, that comparison of achievements with objectives is inevitable.

Other features of the philosophy behind the Act and its administration must be summarized more briefly. The view is rejected that time, and the simple operation of economic forces, can be trusted to restore farm prosperity. It is held that something *must* be done to accelerate recovery, and not merely something—a vast series of campaigns under Government leadership is regarded as essential. A grand extension of economic planning and adjustment, to be worked out by a process of trial and error, is held to be necessary not merely to accelerate recovery, but to prevent future crises and prolonged depressions, and to ensure continuously more effective use of our abundant resources. Economic engineering, including currency management and planned agriculture and industry, is held to be essential to temper the cruelty of economic forces and make them serve human ends, just as medicine and engineering have proved invaluable in tempering the cruelty of natural forces and making them serve human ends. The avowed intention of the Secretary of Agriculture is to evolve out of these emergency measures a comprehensive system of planning for agriculture. Early in October 1933 he said: " We are face to face with the necessity for planning our production to fit the needs of all our people, plus what we can reasonably

[1] They are not effectively argued for in Ezekiel and Bean, *Economic Bases for the Agricultural Adjustment Act*, though much of it touches upon them.

expect to export at a fair price," with "a margin of safety to allow for drought, crop failure, or other disaster."[1] And such planning, in the view of its proponents, implies not merely plans but execution, "control." It is held that Government machinery can be developed adequate to these tasks, and that the requisite co-operation of individual farmers, private business interests and technical experts can be enlisted and mobilized.

Over-production of several commodities is accepted as a stark fact, not a mere illusion. Specifically, it is held that the present emergency calls not only for diverting surplus foodstuffs and raw materials to those in dire need, into export, and to lower-value uses, but also for positive steps to contract the output of several farm products. The experience of 1930-1933 is held to have shown conclusively that un-stimulated contraction of production is too slow and too cruel, and the experience of the Farm Board to indicate that mere advice to farmers to reduce production is futile. Moreover, it is held that prices of agricultural products are so depressed that a huge transfer of purchasing power from consumers to farmers is not only just, but necessary to promote national economic recovery, in the interests of consumers themselves. This is the ground on which processing taxes are levied to provide funds for cash rental and adjustment payments, which in turn are being paid to secure contraction of production so that farm and market prices may be raised. At recent levels of prices of farm products on the farm, at wholesale, and at retail, it is held that the trades and consumers can fairly be asked to pay the higher prices that these taxes may entail.

The larger implications of the contraction programs are beginning to be realized, albeit reluctantly, to the effect that productive acreage may need to be permanently reduced by 40 to 50 million acres of average land, or its equivalent in poorer land; and a few spokesmen frankly admit that material reduction in the number of commercial farmers may also be involved or is even inevitable.[2] The A.A.A. does not avow the belief that our agriculture must be readjusted to a basis of national self-sufficiency; but it is pessimistic regarding at least the early prospects for notable expansion of our diminished export trade

[1] *A.A.A. Weekly News Service*, October 14, 1933.
[2] See Rexford G. Tugwell (then Assistant Secretary of Agriculture): "The Place of Government in a National Land Program," *Journal of Farm Economics*, January 1934, xvi. 64-65. Dr Ezekiel was even more outspoken in a less widely available but mimeographed address on October 30, 1933, before the Open Forum, Chicago Sinai Congregation.

in farm products. Secretary Wallace said on November 14: " By reducing acreage we are trying to get off the international market until such time as we can bring about a real increase of foreign purchasing power by tariff reduction and the negotiation of reciprocal tariffs." It is not with enthusiasm but as a warning that he said also: " If we finally go all the way toward nationalism, it may be necessary to have compulsory control of marketing, licensing of ploughed fields, and base and surplus quotas for every farmer for every product in each month of the year." [1] The Secretary does not shrink from envisaging this logical limit of the process of economic planning in a world obsessed by economic nationalism, but he clearly hopes that the road may have a turning toward another and better goal.[2]

The various programs subsequently adopted must be viewed with this philosophy in mind. There are some serious gaps in it, and it has weaknesses as well as strength; but so far as it goes it is reasonably coherent, and it is more clear-cut and comprehensive than our agricultural philosophy has ever been in the past. It is being set forth so boldly, in deeds as well as in words, that its testing may be expected to bring to light such defects and positive errors as it may contain. The success of the new policy will depend in large part upon the soundness of the underlying theories.

THE AGRICULTURAL ADJUSTMENT ADMINISTRATION [3]

The Federal Farm Board formally ceased to exist on May 27, 1933, by virtue of an executive order of March 27,[4] which Congress did not choose to reject or alter. Many of its functions were taken over by the Farm Credit Administration, a new agency simultaneously set up under a single head, independent of the Treasury and Department of Agriculture; this was given far more extensive powers and responsibilities in connection with farm debts, agricultural credits and related matters.[5]

[1] A.A.A. press release, 1067-34, November 14, 1933.

[2] See his widely circulated statement, " America Must Choose," *World Affairs Pamphlets*, No. 3 [February], 1934, published jointly by the Foreign Policy Association and the World Peace Foundation.

[3] This section is largely based on *Agricultural Adjustment*, the A.A.A.'s own extended report to February 1934.

[4] Under authority of an appropriation Act of March 3, 1933: 72nd Congress, *Public No. 428*.

[5] By the Emergency Farm Mortgage Act of 1933 (May 12) and the Farm Credit Act of 1933 (June 16). See *First Annual Report of the Farm Credit Administration*, 1933 (Washington, 1934). Disposal of stabilization holdings of grain was completed by April 29, 1933, and of cotton by June 15 following. The last lot of Brazilian coffee received in exchange for stabilization wheat was sold on May 3, 1934. On December 31,

The basic task of restoring agriculture to prosperity, however, was mainly consigned to the Agricultural Adjustment Administration, which was organized under the Act of May 12, 1933.

Unlike the Farm Board and the F.C.A., the A.A.A. was set up within the Department of Agriculture. Until December 15, 1933, George N. Peek was Administrator, and for part of that period Charles J. Brand was co-Administrator. Chester C. Davis, Mr Peek's former associate in farm organization work and in the A.A.A., succeeded as Administrator. The prime leader in the A.A.A., however, has been the Secretary of Agriculture himself; his Economic Adviser, Mordecai Ezekiel, is also primarily occupied with its problems, and the A.A.A.'s Economic Adviser, L. H. Bean, is closely associated with Dr Ezekiel.[1]

As reorganized on January 2, 1934, the A.A.A. contains a Commodities Division, a Program Planning Division and a Division of Information, each in charge of a Director with the title of Assistant Administrator. The Commodities Division, headed by former Congressman Victor Christgau, contains sections named as follows:

Wheat Production	Dairy
Grain Marketing and Processing	Tobacco
Cotton Production	Rice and Sugar
Cotton Processing and Marketing	General Crops
Corn-Hog	Field Investigation
Cattle and Sheep	Contracts Records
Meat Processing and Marketing	

The Program Planning Division is headed by H. R. Tolley, Director (on leave) of the Giannini Foundation of the University of California. With its Replacement Crops Section, it has the task of correlating the commodity programs, helping to co-ordinate all the economic work of the Department, and shaping " the entire program itself into a coherent whole which will constitute an advance through emergency measures to an established and lasting agricultural industry to the ultimate benefit

1933, the Grain Stabilization Corporation held German Government notes for 3,961,827 dollars due in equal instalments, December 31, 1934-1936. After cancellation of portions of loans in connection with donations of wheat and cotton to the American National Red Cross, under Congressional authorization, the balances due the Farm Credit Administration on December 31, 1933, were 81,817,542 dollars by the Grain Stabilization Corporation and 16,160,768 dollars by the Cotton Stabilization Corporation.

[1] Professor M. L. Wilson, who had been a leader in the evolution of the domestic allotment plan and the Act itself, was the first chief of the Wheat Production Section of the A.A.A.; but in August 1933 he became Director of the Division of Subsistence Homesteads in the Department of the Interior. In July 1934, after Dr Tugwell was appointed Under-Secretary of Agriculture, Dr Wilson succeeded him as Assistant Secretary.

of the whole nation." The Division of Information under A. D. Stedman includes, in addition to the functions implied by its name, the office of Consumer's Counsel (in charge of Frederic C. Howe), by which the interests of consumers are considered and through which publicity efforts are made to meet consumer criticisms and enlist consumer support. In addition, the A.A.A. contains a Legal Division headed by the General Counsel, Jerome N. Frank, which includes a Licence Enforcement and Revocation Division; a Comptroller's Office, under Comptroller John B. Payne; and a Finance Division, headed by Ward M. Buckles.

Within a few months the A.A.A. has grown to be one of the largest agencies in Washington, with an important group of experts obtained from the Farm Board, the Bureau of Agricultural Economics, state agricultural colleges, and elsewhere. Early in 1934 the personnel of the commodity and service sections numbered about 1000, while another 2700 were divided among the Contracts Records Section, Comptroller's Section and Disbursing Section. With the expansion of programs further enlargement of staff is under way. Such expansion is facilitated by the fact that most of the administrative expenses for the work are being met out of revenues from processing taxes imposed under the Act.

For its work in Washington and in the states the A.A.A. has drawn heavily upon the Bureau of Agricultural Economics and its Division of Crop and Livestock Estimates, federal and state extension services, and the state agricultural colleges. Without these well-developed institutions the rapid formulation and application of its various commodity programs would have been impossible. Indeed, the A.A.A. has called the 2200 county agents the " shock troops " of its production control campaigns.

In addition, heavy reliance has been placed on organized participation of farmers themselves, especially in the extensive local work involved in allotment programs. Federal Farm Board measures had aroused severe criticism among farmers on the score that they were developed " from the top down " instead of " from the ground up." Proponents of the voluntary domestic allotment plan, notably Professor M. L. Wilson, stressed the importance of applying it only after a thorough educational campaign reaching to the " grass roots " and a subsequent referendum among the growers of the crop concerned had been undertaken, and of having the local responsibility for applying it devolve upon farmer committees elected by participating farmers in each county and community. Except for omission of the farmer referendum, this

32

has been done; and a large part of the total administrative outlay will be paid to farmer committee-men locally elected, and deducted (on a county or district basis) from the benefit payments made to co-operating producers.

The A.A.A. has been the target of much criticism, particularly from business men having dealings with it, for its poor administration, lack of practical sense, dilatoriness, vacillation, and so on. Considering the rapidity of its growth, the magnitude of the tasks it has assumed, and the extent to which it has been ploughing new ground, it would be astounding if such criticisms had not been made and in large measure earned. The organization and its operations have yet to meet severe tests that time will bring, but its first year's achievements—mostly, of course, of an intermediate rather than final character—are none the less amazing.

The various measures adopted or in process of adoption under the new adjustment policy are summarized below. With few exceptions they are novel in United States experience.

(1) Voluntary domestic allotment plans calling for contractual reduction of acreage or production on individual farms were applied to 1933 crops of cotton and cigar-leaf tobacco, and to 1934 crops of wheat, cotton, corn, hogs, and all six major types of tobacco; and are in contemplation for other products. Under marketing agreements involving types of producer quotas, the pack of cling peaches was restricted in 1933 and the acreage or production of rice was restricted or reduced in 1934. For sugar, a quota scheme for limiting domestic production and imports from various sources, including United States possessions, received Congressional sanction in May.

(2) The United States is a party to the international wheat agreement fixing export quotas for 1933-1934 and 1934-1935, requiring the major exporters to restrict acreage and/or production in 1934 and 1935, and committing signatory importing nations to measures calculated to assist in bringing wheat supplies and consumption into better adjustment.

(3) An emergency pig-sow slaughter operation in August-September 1933 was conducted to reduce supplies for market in 1933-1934, and resulted in eliminating over 6 million young pigs and over 220,000 sows about to farrow; the edible products were used for relief.

(4) Also for relief disposition through the Federal Emergency Relief Administration, market stabilization purchases of hogs and hog products, butter, and a considerable variety of other products have been made,

c

chiefly through an official Federal Surplus Relief Corporation.[1] Such integration of surplus-removal and relief policies (through what are in a double sense " relief purchases ") is designed in part to avoid accumulation of stocks such as Farm Board stabilization operations entailed,[2] and partly to forestall or to meet public condemnation of policies of destruction or contraction of supplies when large numbers are in want of food and clothing.

(5) A marketing agreement providing for subsidized exports of wheat from the Pacific Northwest was in operation for several months in 1933-1934, and two rice marketing agreements permit certain funds contributed by rice millers to be used for facilitation of rice exports.

(6) Domestic marketing agreements designed to raise prices to producers and improve marketing conditions were adopted for fifteen urban milk markets,[3] evaporated milk and dry skim milk; and for 1933 production of cling peaches, flue-cured tobacco, rice, Northwest Pacific tree fruits, California Tokay grapes, citrus fruits in the three chief producing areas, California ripe olives and English walnuts. Additional similar agreements to be effective in 1934 have been adopted for California fresh deciduous tree fruits (except apples), and asparagus, and peanuts; and others are under consideration.

(7) By request of the A.A.A., canners of tomatoes, corn, Lima beans, beets, and cabbage for sauerkraut, agreed to increase prices paid to growers by 20 to $37\frac{1}{2}$ per cent. above those stated in contracts made early in 1933.

(8) Riskless loans on generous terms have been made to growers of cotton and corn of the 1933 crop, and to holders of cotton options given in part payment for contractual reduction of that crop.

(9) Processing taxes to raise funds to cover benefit payments, costs of surplus removal and administrative expenses, have been levied on wheat, cotton, tobacco, corn, hogs and sugar. In addition to import-compensating taxes on these products, compensatory processing taxes have been levied on jute yarns, jute fabric, paper bags, paper towels and gummed paper tape. Up to about October 31, 1934, net collections from these taxes (including taxes on " floor stocks " held at about the

[1] Its board of directors consists of the Secretaries of Agriculture and the Interior, the Governor of the Farm Credit Administration, and the Federal Emergency Relief Administrator.

[2] Under Congressional authorization, large parts of the surplus stocks of wheat and cotton accumulated by stabilization corporations under the Federal Farm Board were subsequently disposed of for relief in 1931-1933.

[3] These were cancelled around the end of 1933, as mentioned below.

34

date of imposition) had materially exceeded the adjustment payments made up to that date.

(10) Codes for grain exchanges, the milling industry, the liquor industry, cotton ginners, and a few lesser trades and industries directly concerned with agriculture have been put in force, and many others are in process.

No compulsory measures were applied in the first year, except those requiring contract signers to comply with their contracts, and those requiring parties not signing approved marketing agreements to operate under licences containing similar provisions. Offers of substantial benefit or adjustment payments have served to bring under contract the producers of the great bulk of the products for which adjustment programs have been put into effect. Preliminary steps were taken, however, to administer the recent Bankhead Act, designed to restrict cotton ginnings from the 1934 crop to 10 million bales exclusive of certain premium varieties.[1] Problems of enforcing marketing agreements and accompanying licences have presented difficult problems, particularly in the case of milk; and early in 1934 these led to radical revision of the dairy program. The Smith bill (s. 3326) was drafted in part to give the A.A.A. much more power in these respects, but failed to pass in spite of vigorous support from the Administration.[2]

Thus far, decisions upholding the constitutionality of the Act on the ground of national emergency have been rendered by a United States District Court in California (cling peach case) and, in three milk cases, by the Supreme Court of the District of Columbia. An adverse decision was rendered on January 30 by a United States District Court in Florida (citrus case), but on April 14 this was reversed by the Fifth Circuit Court of Appeals at New Orleans. The Supreme Court of the United States has not yet rendered any decision under the Act, but the A.A.A. has regarded that court's 5 to 4 decision of March 5, 1934, upholding the price provisions of the New York Milk Control Law in he Nebbia case,[3] as foreshadowing favourable decisions under the federal Act.

Beyond the co-ordination of relief requirements and surplus-removal objectives, several examples of co-ordination between the A.A.A. and other Government agencies deserve passing mention. The Farm Credit Administration has restricted production loans by agencies under its

[1] A similar measure with respect to the 1934 tobacco crop was signed June 28, 1934.

[2] Hearings on this bill, before the Senate Committee on Agriculture and Forestry, May 8-11, 1934, have been published.

[3] *Nebbia* v. *People of the State of New York*, 78 U.S., 563.

authority in such a way as to favour producers participating in commodity programs and to avoid financing production by others in excess of what their limits would be if they were participants. The Federal Alcohol Control Administration has assigned import quotas to foreign countries in part in exchange for agreements to admit certain agricultural exports from this country. Under a marketing agreement with the Secretary of Agriculture signed December 9, 1933, manufacturers of distilled spirits agreed to make them solely from cereal grains (except by special permit from the Secretary), and to pay into the Treasury, for use under the Adjustment Act, the difference between " parity prices " and the current average farm price.[1] The Secretary of Agriculture is a leading spokesman for the policy of removing restrictions upon international trade, partly with a view to promoting recovery in the volume of our agricultural exports; and he and the Assistant Secretary are members of an interdepartmental executive committee that is seeking to reformulate American policy in this field.

The whole problem of land-use planning, which has engaged increasing attention in the past decade, is being attacked with fresh vigour by the Program Planning Division of the A.A.A., which is absorbing most of the Division of Land Economics of the Bureau of Agricultural Economics. President Roosevelt announced in August 1933 the policy of retiring from production land equal in productive power to what is henceforth brought into cultivation under federal reclamation projects. The Federal Surplus Relief Corporation has since been empowered to buy up sub-marginal lands, with an initial fund of 40 million dollars allocated for this purpose. The experiments in establishing " subsistence homesteads," for which 25 million dollars was appropriated by the National Industrial Recovery Act (sec. 208), are conceived of as pointing the way to a method of absorbing those who are no longer " needed " in urban industry or commercial farming, into a type of life in which rural living will be combined with occupations of an industrial, handicraft, or other character.[2]

COMMODITY PROGRAMS

The principal operations of the A.A.A. in its first year can best be discussed under the various commodities for which " programs " have been devised and applied. The most important of these are reviewed

[1] A.A.A. press release, 1346-34, December 9, 1933.
[2] See M. L. Wilson, " The Place of Subsistence Homesteads in our National Economy," *Journal of Farm Economics*, January 1934, xvi. 73-84.

in the following sections, in each case with some essential introductory information.[1]

(1) *Cotton*

Among the commodity situations promptly taken up by the A.A.A., that of cotton was the first to be vigorously grappled with. Cotton is the most important cash crop of the United States. From the standpoint of farm value it tends to rank second only to corn. It ordinarily uses from 10 to 12 per cent. of the total acreage in crops. Farm income from cotton and cotton-seed ranged in 1924-1930 from 8 to 15 per cent. of gross income from all farm production, and roughly equalled the gross income from all grains during this period. It is one of our leading export commodities, and by all odds our chief agricultural export; ordinarily more than half of the crop is exported. Cotton is grown by some two million farmers, chiefly in the southern states west to Texas, but to some extent in California and neighbouring south-western states. The level of income of individual cotton growers is lower than that of most other farm groups, and their standard of living suffers terribly in depressions.

War conditions, post-war devastations by the boll weevil, and expansion in Texas had kept cotton *yields* per acre far below pre-war levels from 1915 to 1930. In the face of supplies thus restricted, increased demand led to high prices for cotton, particularly in 1917-1920 and 1922-1925, which greatly stimulated expansion of acreage at home and abroad. The world-wide depression, on the other hand, caused a great decline in cotton consumption at home and abroad. A high yield in 1931 had more than offset some reduction in acreage, after the Farm Board proposal for ploughing up every third row had been laughed at. Owing largely to these facts, reinforced by Farm Board measures in support of cotton prices here in 1929-1931, the world carry-over of American cotton had risen from 5 million bales on August 1, 1928, to nearly 13 million in 1932.

The outstanding facts of the immediate cotton outlook in May-June 1933 were (1) a prospective world carry-over of American cotton somewhat below the peak of 1932,[2] but still more than double a normal level

---

[1] *Agricultural Adjustment* furnishes much of the material for these sections. More detailed discussions of operations on cotton, wheat, corn-hogs and dairy products are given in a series of pamphlets published by the Brookings Institution, Washington, D.C.

[2] Eventually estimated at 11,597,000 bales as compared with 12,961,000 on August 1, 1932 (U.S. Department of Agriculture press release 733-34, September 29, 1933).

37

and not far short of a year's supply at depression levels of consumption; (2) prospects for high yields on a fairly large acreage, promising a big crop; (3) a prospective supply for 1933-1934, from carry-over and new crop, far exceeding the pre-depression peak of 1926 when consumption was running high, and perhaps above the record peaks of 1931 and 1932; (4) a prospective farm price well below six cents a pound,[1] promising a gross farm value from cotton lint about equal to the average for the three preceding years; this was 522 million dollars as compared with the average of 1374 million dollars for the crops of 1924-1928 and 1245 million for the crop of 1929 when Farm Board operations had supported the price; (5) a further increase in the carry-over in 1934, to perhaps an all-time peak.

To meet this situation the A.A.A. decided that prompt and drastic curtailment of production was essential. It therefore devised a plan for the elimination of about one-fourth of the forthcoming crop before harvest, and subsequently a plan for even more severe reduction of the crop of 1934. These were supplemented by monetary policies designed to lower the exchange value of the dollar and to raise the general price-level, and by loans to enable growers to hold their cotton for higher prices.

In a whirlwind campaign in the month following the announcement on June 19 of the 1933 crop reduction plan, growers were invited to sign offers to enter into contracts calling for ploughing up the growing crop on 25 to 50 per cent. of their acreage under cotton. In return they were offered rental payments based on the productivity of the land, according to the schedule below, (a) at a lower rate plus a non-transferable option to buy, at 6 cents a pound, cotton futures contracts held by the Government in an amount equivalent to that ploughed under; or (b) at a higher rate without this option:

Yield per acre (lb)				Plus option	Without option
100–124	.	.	.	$6.00	$7.00
125–149	.	.	.	7.00	9.00
150–174	.	.	.	8.00	11.00
175–224	.	.	.	10.00	14.00
225–274	.	.	.	11.00	17.00
275 and over	.	.	.	12.00	20.00

---

[1] In the post-war depression, farm prices of cotton did not fall below 9·4 cents, and the huge crop of 1926 did not depress them below 10 cents. They were below 10 cents from September 1930 to December 1933. The weighted average farm price in the 1931-1932 season was 5·7 cents a pound, and a low point of 4·6 cents was reached on June 15, 1932. From November 15, 1932, to February 15, 1933, the farm price was under 6 cents. In view of dollar depreciation here, and some business recovery here and abroad, the average farm price for a full crop in 1933 would probably have been around 7 cents a pound.

On July 31, just before these contract offers ceased to be irrevocable, the Secretary of Agriculture accepted them subject to further investigation and final inspection. Eventually 1½ per cent. of the offers were rejected. Of the 1,026,514 offers accepted and approved for payment of benefits, 55·7 per cent. called for cash benefits plus options. Of the 1933 acreage 73 per cent. was covered by contracts, and 10·4 million acres were ploughed under. This represented about 35 per cent. of the acreage of contract signers, and slightly under 25 per cent. of the total cotton acreage as of July 1.

The scheme of offering options on cotton as an inducement to reduce acreage had been repeatedly urged on the Federal Farm Board by Senator Smith of South Carolina, and was specifically provided for in sections 3-7 of the Agricultural Adjustment Act. About two-thirds of the cotton available for offer represented cotton and cotton futures taken over by the Farm Credit Administration from the American and Staple Cotton Co-operative Associations, to which the Federal Farm Board had made loans that proved excessive[1]; the other third represented cotton pledged by growers to the Secretary of Agriculture for seed and production loans for several years prior to 1933. The Farm Credit Administration took this cotton over at a base price of 9½ cents per pound, sold it to the Secretary of Agriculture for 5 cents a pound, and was reimbursed for the difference from the Bankhead Fund. Cotton option offers, at 6 cents a pound, were accepted to the extent of 2,387,795 bales, approximately the full amount available.[2] These options may be held to May 1, 1935, subject to carrying charges of about ·08 cent. per pound per month after May 1, 1934.[3]

Although the growers' response was gratifying to the A.A.A. and performance of contracts was strictly enforced, Nature kept the reduction of the 1933 crop from reaching the extent intended. With exceptionally favourable weather conditions, the yield per acre proved 22 per cent. above the 1923-1932 average, and inferior only to the bumper yields of 1898 and 1931. At this rate a full crop would have approached the record peak of 1926. Even after eliminating an estimated 4·2 million potential bales, the crop proved slightly larger than the 13-million bale crop of 1932. The world supply of American cotton for 1933-1934 was estimated at 24·8 million

---

[1] See E. S. Haskell, Chapter II.

[2] On January 1, 1934, the Secretary had acquired, by delivery or exchange, actual cotton to the equivalent of 1,869,000 standard bales and 618,300 bales in futures contracts.

[3] Under earlier arrangements, they were to be exercised by May 1, 1934.

bales, as compared with about 26 million in each of the two preceding seasons.

Improving prospects for the crop, together with speculative reactions and business recession after mid-July 1933, led to weakness in cotton prices. In August-September farm prices averaged 8·8 cents per pound as compared with 10·6 on July 15 and a " parity price " of about 14·7 cents. Accordingly, the A.A.A. announced in October a program for cutting the cotton area for harvest in 1934 to about 25 million acres, a figure exceeded ever since 1901 and 5 million acres under the reduced area harvested in 1933. It also arranged in October (through an official Commodity Credit Corporation financed by the Reconstruction Corporation, and agencies that could rediscount such paper with the C.C.C.) to lend growers on unsold cotton in warehouses 10 cents a pound on 4 per cent. notes maturing July 31, 1934, and 4 cents a pound on the options taken by participants in the 1933 program. These loans, riskless to the borrowers (in that if they were not paid the C.C.C. would take over the collateral as payment in full), were granted on condition that the borrower would sign acreage-reduction contracts for 1934. Up to March 6, 1934, approximately 158 million dollars had been so loaned, and about 7 million repaid. These measures [1] contributed to the subsequent firmness of cotton prices, which averaged 11·7 cents per pound at the farm in February-March 1934.

The 1934 cotton program, as revised in December, called for a reduction of the planted acreage by 35 to 45 per cent. from the average planted in 1928-1932, and committed the participant to a reduction in 1935 of as much as 25 per cent. from this average if officially required in January 1935. In return each co-operating grower was offered a cash rental payment at the rate of $3\frac{1}{2}$ cents per pound on the 1928-1932 average yield on his " contracted acreage," [2] up to a maximum of 18 dollars per acre; and an additional benefit payment of not less than 1 cent a pound (more if cotton prices are farther below " parity ") on farm allotments representing the domestic consumption fraction (40 per cent.) of his average crop in 1928-1932. A heavy sign-up was secured in January-March, and preliminary indications were that the desired reduction to 25 million acres might be approached. [3] Many non-signers,

---

[1] Of minor importance were relief purchases of wool and cotton blankets amounting to 1,329,235 dollars up to February 1, 1934.

[2] The ambiguous term " contracted acreage " does not mean acreage covered by the contract, but the number of acres taken out of production of the crop under the contract. M. L. Wilson earlier spoke of this as " released acreage."

[3] Provisional results made public on April 21 indicate 954,766 contracts signed calling for rental of 15,353,646 acres, approximately 40 per cent. of that which signers

however, increased their acreage, and reports indicated that growers were buying fertilizer more heavily than in the three preceding years and taking other steps to raise their yields. To prevent such action from defeating the desired reduction of cotton output, as well as to ensure that non-signers should not gain more than contracting farmers, the Secretary of Agriculture reluctantly [1] approved the principles of the Bankhead bill designed to limit the marketed supply to a maximum of 10 million bales (cotton with a staple of $1\frac{1}{2}$ inches or longer is exempt). Under this bill, finally signed on April 21,[2] each grower will be given a certificate (transferable on conditions prescribed by the Department) entitling him to sell without tax his *pro rata* share of this total; and an almost prohibitive tax (50 per cent. of the average central market price of $\frac{7}{8}$ inch middling spot cotton, as proclaimed from time to time, but not less than 5 cents per pound) will be collected on other cotton except lots of previous crops that are officially tagged as such. This measure is credited with important influence in holding down the harvested acreage, provisionally estimated at $27\frac{1}{4}$ million acres, and the average yield as well.

The cash rental payments made under the 1933 cotton program planted on the average in the base period 1928-1932. The sign-up represents over 90 per cent. of the acreage planted in the base period.

[1] Secretary Wallace first circulated a questionnaire to some 41,000 growers, the returns from which convinced him that the great majority of growers (at least 85 per cent., perhaps 95 per cent.) favoured some such compulsory restriction.

[2] 73rd Congress, *Public No. 169, H.R. 8402*. Under certain conditions, a similar restriction may be applied in 1935-1936. On signing this bill, President Roosevelt stated:

" I am advised that the overwhelming majority of the south's cotton producers desire the enactment of legislation now embodied in the Bankhead bill. It aims to prevent that very small minority which has refused to co-operate with their neighbours and the government from impairing the effectiveness of the current cotton program, which now includes 92 per cent. of the cotton acreage.

" There is nothing new in the sentiment which has resulted in the passage of the Bankhead bill. During the days of the Confederacy methods to adjust cotton production were advocated. Again in 1905, 1915, 1921 and 1927 widespread sentiment was developed for some plan that would prevent the recurring accumulation of cotton surpluses from dragging prices to starvation levels.

" The cotton states have found it impossible to act independently or in unison to achieve this end. They have asked for the use of federal powers. A democratic government has consented. The sponsors of the Bankhead bill say it will not supplant, but will supplement and make even more effective, the present adjustment program.

" It is the purpose to make certain that the splendid progress already made is consolidated into enduring benefits. The objective of the bill is to place the cotton-growing industry on a sound financial and economic basis. I hope our progress already made toward this objective will be facilitated by this legislation."

The Secretary of Agriculture, in an address at Nebraska City, April 23, openly expressed his " abhorrence " of the principle of compulsion, and urged " the farmers of the west and north not to start doing a similar thing . . . until we have at least had an opportunity to benefit by the results of this southern experiment."

amounted to 111·4 million dollars. This was paid, after certification of fulfilment of contracts, chiefly in October 1933. In addition the holders of cotton options have received or will get at least 4 cents a pound on their options, less interest on their loans on this collateral. Including upwards of 48 million dollars on this account, the total direct " benefits " are calculated at 160 million dollars or more. The cash payments, plus the loans on cotton and options made available during the autumn, exerted a striking influence on the spirit and business conditions in the Cotton Belt. Preliminary official estimates (March 1934) of growers' income from the cotton crop of 1933 (including cotton-seed) indicate a total of some 684 million dollars. Inclusive of benefits mentioned above, the total will be around 850 million dollars, nearly 80 per cent. larger than in 1932-1933, and about 60 per cent. of the average in 1925-1929.

Cash rental payments for the 1934 crop are provisionally budgeted at 100·8 million dollars, half of it payable in March-April to take care of demands for production credit, and half in August-September after certification that contract obligations have been met. The 1934 benefit payments payable in December are provisionally estimated at 29·5 million dollars.

In order to finance the cash payments, the Secretary announced on July 14, 1933, a processing tax of 4·2 cents a pound, net weight, effective August 1, on all cotton entering into domestic consumption, and an import-compensating tax at the same rate on the cotton in imported cotton goods. After hearings during the summer and fall, compensatory taxes were imposed from December 1, 1933, on the processing of jute yarns into twines and jute fabric into bags, at 2·9 cents per pound, and on multiwall, coated, and open-mesh paper bags, paper towels, and gummed paper tape, at rates found necessary to offset the disadvantages suffered by cotton in domestic competition with jute and paper. It is officially estimated that the processing tax will net 116 million dollars on cotton consumed in 1933-1934, and that two years' net collections from processing and compensatory taxes will come within $6\frac{1}{4}$ million dollars of meeting the cash payments over the two years, exclusive of an estimated $10\frac{1}{2}$ million for administrative expenses. The net costs to the Government involved in the option offer, however, were absorbed by the Bankhead Fund appropriated under the National Industrial Recovery Act (sec. 220).[1]

The drastic reduction in cotton acreage in 1934, under conditions

[1] *Agricultural Adjustment*, pp. 34, 366n.

preventing the use of the " contracted acreage " in other commercial crops, threatens to create a difficult surplus labour situation in the South, and it does not yet appear how this can be met.[1] Another problem ahead concerns the reaction of cotton growers abroad. Foreign production of cotton rose sharply during the war and after the post-war depression; and after some decline during the present depression, foreign production in 1933-1934 nearly equals the peak of about 12½ million bales reached in 1928. Obviously the contraction of American supplies, with consequent effects on world cotton prices and the relative price of American cotton, will tend to stimulate production abroad. American restriction programs will therefore tend in some degree to restrict American exports of cotton, and contraction here will be somewhat offset by expansion abroad.

Supplementary to the major cotton program, the A.A.A. has sponsored a cotton ginners' marketing agreement fixing maximum rates for ginning in each ginning area, and regulating ginners' practices. Five other marketing agreements and a dozen codes affecting cotton, cotton-seed and its products, and allied commodities are under consideration. The agreements in particular are designed to facilitate adjustments in supplies, raising farm prices toward parity, reducing costs of handling and processing, and improvements in handling and processing services.

(2) *Wheat*

Wheat is the most important grain crop of the United States from the standpoint of cash income. Though it is less important than corn in terms of farm value, it is commonly considered even more truly basic. In the six years 1924-1929 wheat contributed about 7 per cent. of the gross income from all farm production. It is grown, though not every year, on some 1,500,000 farms, and to some extent in all but a few states. The harvested area averaged around 60 million acres in 1926-1930, or about one-sixth of the total crop acreage. It is a major crop in the hard winter wheat belt centering in western Kansas, the hard spring wheat belt stretching from Minnesota to Montana, where macaroni wheat (durum) is also produced, in the Pacific Northwest centering in south-eastern Washington, where chiefly white wheats are raised, and in parts of the Middle West where, as in the East and South, chiefly soft red wheat is grown.[2] The United States has long been a major

[1] See *United States News*, May 7, 1934, p. 12.
[2] Dot maps in the *Yearbook of Agriculture, 1933*, pp. 141-143, show the distribution of the crop according to census data for 1869, 1889, 1899, 1909 and 1929.

exporter of wheat and flour, though Russia outstripped us in the pre-war decade and Canada in the first post-war decade. Prior to the present depression United States wheat exports had averaged for several years about a fourth of our crop and a fourth of the total international trade. In terms of export values of farm products, wheat and flour were usually exceeded only by raw cotton.

The distressed condition of American wheat growers in two crop years following the post-war deflation of prices in 1920-1922 gave rise to vigorous agitation for farm relief. Much higher wheat prices in 1924-1925 and 1925-1926—resulting from a short world crop in 1924, a short crop here in 1925, and much improved European demand—quieted this agitation for a time, but it was renewed as wheat prices declined in the next three years. When the economic crisis broke in 1929, huge wheat stocks had accumulated and the world wheat position was among the most vulnerable elements in the economic structure.[1] Wheat prices fell drastically in 1930, and sagged further in the next two years. Stabilization operations of the Federal Farm Board in 1930 and 1931 served merely to limit the extent of the disaster to wheat growers for a time, at heavy cost to its revolving fund and at the expense of building up carry-overs to record heights. The farm value of the wheat crop, which had averaged 918 million dollars a year in 1921-1928, declined in the next four years to 850, 596, 364, and 282 millions. The drop in cash income from wheat was even more drastic; it fell in 1932 to 195 million dollars, about one-fourth of the corresponding average for 1921-1928. The world wheat situation has continued to be characterized by abnormal surplus and unprecedented price depression. Among the many factors responsible have been the bumper world crop of 1928, high yields in Europe in 1929, 1932, and 1933, European measures restricting consumption and stimulating domestic production, and unexpectedly heavy exports from the U.S.S.R. in 1930-1931 and her liberal exports in two subsequent years.

The wheat situation which the A.A.A. faced in the spring and summer of 1932 was modified by prospects for an exceptionally short crop of wheat in the United States,[2] eventually realized, and by speculative activity based upon this and expectations of a general price inflation. Despite the huge carry-over, these influences led to substantial advances

[1] See J. S. Davis, " Wheat, Wheat Policies and the Depression," *Review of Economic Statistics*, April 15, 1934, xvi. 80-88.

[2] This led to abandoning a project for curtailment of the 1933 crop, such as was carried through in cotton.

in American wheat prices to well above levels (" export parities ") that would permit liberal exports. In the face of these developments and a small crop in Canada, the world wheat surplus condition persisted, in large part because of a record crop in Europe. World wheat prices, as reflected in prices of wheat imported into Great Britain, sagged in 1933-1934 to fresh low levels in terms of gold.[1]

The A.A.A. wheat program, as thus far developed, includes five major elements [2]: (1) application of a voluntary domestic allotment plan involving reduction of acreage for harvest in 1934 and probably 1935, through contracts with individual farmers who are to receive " adjustment payments " in three years beginning with 1933-1934; (2) participation in the international wheat agreement, involving export quotas for the exporting countries and acreage and/or production restriction in the four leading ones, and auxiliary commitments by most of the leading wheat-importing countries; (3) subsidized exports from the Pacific Northwest, reinforced by a loan to China partially earmarked for purchases of wheat and flour; (4) market-supporting wheat purchases for disposition in relief channels; and (5) the adoption of codes for the grain exchanges, country and terminal elevators, millers and other wheat interests. Of these five, all but one are novel, and even the relief purchases significantly differ from the stabilization purchases made under the Federal Farm Board.

The domestic allotment plan was the first to be launched, and wheat, for which the plan had been most carefully worked out, was the first product to which it was applied. The wheat adjustment program, as it came to be called, was announced in broad outlines on June 16, 1933, and ten days later a processing tax of 30 cents a bushel was proclaimed, to go into effect July 9. Individual growers were offered contracts by which they agreed to reduce their average sown to wheat for harvest in 1934 and 1935 by a percentage to be prescribed by the Secretary of Agriculture up to 20 per cent. of the average sown in a base period (typically 1930-1932); in return they were offered adjustment payments proportioned to their average production in 1928-1932, at a rate per bushel determined by the relation of current farm prices to the computed " parity price." County allotments equal to 54 per cent. of the estimated

---

[1] See J. S. Davis, *op. cit.*, " Wheat, Wheat Policies, and the Depression," and *Wheat Studies of the Food Research Institute*, May 1934, x. 267.

[2] Most of the discussion of the wheat program closely follows the author's presentation in his Minneapolis address, referred to above. For a fuller discussion, see Sherman Johnson, *Wheat under the Agricultural Adjustment Act: Developments to April 1934* (Brookings Institution, Washington, D.C., May 1934).

average production in 1928-1932 [1] were announced on July 27, for 2245 wheat-producing counties in 37 states. Three days earlier growers had been informed that on each bushel of their individual " farm allotments " contract signers would receive a first instalment of 20 cents a bushel about September 15, and not less than 8 nor more than 10 cents after fulfilment of the first year's acreage reduction had been certified.

During August, forms, regulations and publicity material were issued, and an extensive educational campaign regarding the plan got under way in all the wheat sections. A central feature of the plan was the formation of county wheat production control associations, with articles of association prescribed by the Secretary (August 11), and with boards of directors elected by communities; an " allotment committee " of this board had the primary responsibility for assigning and adjusting individual quotas and passing on applications and contracts. These associations were organized in August-September, in 1155 counties, and 603 more counties were covered by 189 district associations. Applications for contracts were first invited.[2] On August 28, after delays pending the reaching of the international wheat agreement, the Secretary announced that contract signers would be called on to reduce their acreage sown for harvest in 1934 by 15 per cent. of their average acreage in the base period.[3] All contract applications were supposed to have been received by September 25, but extensions of time were granted in numerous counties. Before contracts could be finally signed, much time was required for making adjustments between county figures on acreage, production, or both, as officiallly estimated and as totalled from individual farmers' data. On October 16 the " County Acceptance Unit " in Washington approved the first batch of county wheat contracts, for Clark County, Virginia, and on October 31 the first checks were mailed to Monona County, Iowa, a centre of the farm strike movement; but the bulk of the checks were delayed until well after Christmas.

In the actual application of the plan innumerable complex problems arose, an enormous burden of work devolved upon the Wheat Section of the A.A.A., the Extension Service, and the local associations, inevitable delays proved irritating, and numerous decisions evoked complaints.

[1] It was computed that the domestic consumption of wheat subject to the processing tax in 1933-1934 (forecast at 460 million bushels) would constitute 54 per cent. of the average production in 1928-1932.

[2] Copies of blank applications and contracts are reprinted in *Agricultural Adjustment*, pp. 335-342.

[3] By August 15, winter-wheat growers had gone far in preparing their land for fall sowing of wheat.

Yet the " campaign " was pushed through, and the A.A.A. was sufficiently impressed with the practicability of the wheat adjustment plan to undertake to apply it, with modifications, to cotton, corn and tobacco for the next harvest, and to hogs as well for 1934, and to consider it for other products.

Speaking of the wheat adjustment program, the Secretary of Agriculture said on September 24 [1]:

. . . It is a program that in the face of need breaks sharply with long-established habits of thought. To sow less wheat at a time when throughout the world people are out of work and hungry—that is not an easy proposal to understand. The facts are harsh and unpalatable. Too much wheat diminishes farm-buying power. Diminished farm-buying power closes factories, and helps throw millions of people out of work. Because these millions of people are out of work they have no money. When in this modern commercial world you have no money, you go hungry, even in the shadow of mountainous surpluses of food.

People on farms and people in cities who fear that our production control program will increase the number of hungry mouths simply do not understand the world situation that exists to-day. Piling up a wheat surplus to three times the normal as we have done in the past four years makes more hungry mouths rather than less. It took the wheat farmer off the market as a buyer of goods, and the depression spread. It spread to all other farmers, then to those whose business depends directly upon farm custom, and finally to Wall Street and the Loop. No business can keep on hiring people and making money when the buying power of the nation is off balance at the base.

Final results of the initial sign-up campaign, announced on April 24, 1934, showed 573,723 contracts signed, representing about 50 million acres of wheat in the base period. The sign-up represented considerably under half of the eligible wheat growers, but about 75 per cent. of the wheat acreage in the base period. Participation was relatively heaviest —in most states over 90 per cent. in terms of acreage—in areas where wheat is a major crop; it was much smaller in diversified farming regions, especially east of the Mississippi, where wheat plays a modest rôle. The size of the allotment payments proved the chief inducement to participation; the inducement was especially potent where, as in many sections, the 1933 crop was seriously reduced.[2] In some other areas many small farmers felt that they could not afford to restrict their freedom of action for the sake of the small payments to which their allotments entitled them. The first instalment of 20 cents a bushel on

[1] U.S. Department of Agriculture press release 649-34, September 25, 1934.
[2] Since benefit payments are in proportion to the grower's average production in 1928-1932, they are of special importance to farmers who, because of crop failure, find their current wheat income heavily reduced.

allotments amounted in total to over 66 million dollars; nearly all of this had been distributed by April 30, 1934. Further payments at 8 cents a bushel on allotments,[1] subject to deduction for local expenses averaging 1 to 2 cents a bushel, will be made after reduction of individual acreage according to contract has been certified.

Since only about three-fourths of the wheat acreage was covered by contracts and some non-participants were likely to increase their acreage, the net reduction contracted for under the first campaign (about 7·5 million acres) promised to fall considerably short of that to which the United States was committed under the international wheat agreement (computed at 10·1 million acres).[2] On February 26, 1934, therefore, a second campaign was launched to get additional signers by May 10, 1934. Applicants who had completed their papers by the end of 1933 will be entitled to full payments. Other new signers will get only the second instalment for 1933-1934, but full payments in the next two years—this constitutes the chief inducement, in view of the wheat price outlook. More liberal terms are offered those who have recently broken land to wheat. Provision has also been made for waiving, under certain conditions, the requirement that contracting farmers must sow at least enough acres to produce, at average yields, the amount of their allotments.[3] Since large numbers of contract signers planted their winter wheat before they knew the adjusted acreage fixed in their final contract, some of these will have to take some planted acreage out of wheat for grain in order to fulfil their obligation. The net reduction in the acreage sown for grain now bids fair to approach or exceed 10 per cent. of the average sown in 1930-1932, whereas in the absence of restrictions an increase might well have occurred.

There is a tendency for the reduction in wheat acreage to be partially offset by increased average yields due to (undetected) elimination of poorer lands, better preparation of the soil with larger cash income, and slight acreage reduction in higher-yield areas; and increased resort to fallowing will make for higher yields in 1935. Nature, however, largely determined the 1934 yield per acre. Drastic deterioration of crop prospects during the spring so radically altered the picture that the 1934 crop turned out only about 500 million bushels. Domestic uses for food, seed, and feed for 1934-1935 may be forecast at roughly

[1] In mid-June it was announced that, in view of disastrous drought, this payment would be 9 cents.

[2] See *Agricultural Adjustment*, p. 43, and A.A.A. press release 2445-34, April 27, 1934.

[3] Extensive drought has led to making this waiver available over large areas.

48

615 million bushels as compared with the revised average crop of 860 million in 1928-1932. The carry-over on July 1, 1934, is estimated at over 290 million bushels (at least twice normal size). With Nature thus supporting the restriction program, the elimination of our surplus wheat carry-over is at hand; and the United States will probably be a small net importer in 1934-1935. Before the severe crop deterioration, reasonable prospects for 1934-1935 included lower wheat prices in the United States, an increase in processing-tax rates, larger allotment payments to contracting growers, and the maximum rate of restriction upon sown acreage (20 per cent. of that in the base period). Under the changed conditions, the processing tax was continued at 30 cents per bushel.

The prospective imposition of the processing tax stimulated wheat milling in the quarter preceding its application on July 9, 1933, and this was followed by a slump in the ensuing months.[1] Broadly speaking, though by no means uniformly and universally, it appears that the tax has been passed on to consumers; and prices of flour and bread have increased because of higher wheat prices and the tax of 30 cents per bushel.[2] The tax represents an addition of about $\frac{1}{2}$ cent. per pound, or around 6 per cent. of the retail price of bakery bread, and a very much larger percentage of the retail price of flour. Reduction of wheat consumption attributable to higher prices of flour was appreciable in the south-eastern quarter of the country, where substitutes (chiefly corn-meal) were much more cheaply available; but the aggregate reduction seems to have proved moderate. In some wheat-deficit areas of the south-east the tax stimulated increased planting of wheat for local consumption, but the net effect on acreage and production was slight. Ordinary commercial milling has been adversely affected to the extent that wheat growers have had grain ground locally tax-free for their own use, and by some illicit grinding. In addition, with wheat prices above export parities and foreign restrictions on flour imports, very little milling for export has been possible except of Canadian wheat.

The processing tax has naturally aroused some criticism,[3] but none

---

[1] *Wheat Studies of the Food Research Institute*, January 1934, x. 158-160.

[2] *Agricultural Adjustment*, pp. 221-229. Baking interests have complained that they have not succeeded in passing on the tax, and that their industry has consequently suffered injury.

[3] For months the *Northwestern Miller* has regularly carried on its editorial page a demand for removal of the tax. In the issue of April 25, 1934 (p. 331), the editor made the following observations:

" Months ago we took our stand on the proposition that the bread tax would have to surrender to common sense and the people's need. We failed much to interest millers, as yet very vigorous or widespread, though the undercurrent of opposition is increasing in strength. Collections, in spite of exemptions and evasions, will probably suffice to finance the program, and contracting farmers are likely to find themselves better off in 1934-1935 than those who did not sign. Substantial enforcement of the contracts for reducing acreage is anticipated. The thorny problem of restricting the use of the land taken out of wheat has not been wholly met, but no surpluses of other products from diversion of this land to them occurred this year.

Major tests of the program have yet to come. Will it be adequate to eliminate " burdensome " surplus carry-overs, and to raise wheat prices to " parity " levels? Will farmers be content to accept continued restriction, however voluntary in form? Can the uneconomic " horizontal " method of restriction be replaced by more discriminating restriction of high-cost acreage? Will producers abroad take advantage of contraction here, and quietly take over our export markets for wheat and flour? These are some of the important questions to which confident answers cannot yet be given.

Other elements in the wheat program can be discussed more briefly. The international wheat agreement (dated August 25, 1933, but fully signed a few days later) must be regarded as an integral part of the A.A.A. program.[1] Argentina took the initiative in proposing the conference that led up to it; but the United States delegation led in winning adhesion to it, and in following it up. It represents a striking adventure into the domain of international planning.

Parties to the agreement include the four major overseas exporting countries, the four normally exporting countries of the Danube basin, and the U.S.S.R. All but the U.S.S.R. agreed, in view of light import requirements in prospect for 1933-1934, to accept export quotas for each of the two crop years ending July 31, 1935. Out of total import demand estimated at 560 million bushels in 1933-1934, quotas were assigned as follows, in million bushels: Canada, 200; Argentina, 110; Australia, 105; the United States, 47; the Danube countries, 50-54; the balance remaining for the U.S.S.R. and others, 44-48. The Danube states anxious not to antagonize the administration while code regulation of industry impended. We failed wholly to interest bakers, whose business was threatened but who saw in the tax and a higher price-level advantage for their industry. Wheat growers, with high hopes in the new deal and expectant of doles for fallow fields, were and are largely inarticulate. Consumers appeared not much to care, but, as will some time appear, have been eating, and will continue to eat, less bread."

[1] What purports to be the text was published by the U.S. Department of State, *Treaty Information Bulletin No. 48*, September 30, 1933. See also U.S. Department of Agriculture, *World Wheat Prospects*, September 30, 1933; and *Wheat Studies of the Food Research Institute*, January 1933 and May 1934, x. 151-152, 253-255.

subsequently agreed on a percentage subdivision of their quota, and Hungary later secured an increase in hers at Rumania's expense. The U.S.S.R. had not accepted a quota, but exported little more than the implied quota proposed for her. Except Hungary, Argentina alone found the quota limitation embarrassing, and eventually exceeded it without permission of other exporters.

Export quotas were also provisionally fixed for 1934-1935, and the four major exporting countries further agreed to ill-defined provisions for restrictions on acreage, production, or stocks as of July 31, 1935. All have taken some steps in this direction, though none has taken such radical steps as the United States.

Also parties to the agreement are all but two (the Netherlands and the Irish Free State) of leading European wheat-importing countries. These agreed to co-operate to eliminate the world wheat surplus, and undertook (a) not to take henceforth any measures to increase domestic acreage or production; (b) to take every " possible " measure to increase wheat consumption; (c) progressively to remove measures tending to lower the quality of breadstuffs, and thus to reduce their consumption; (d) that substantial improvement in wheat prices should be followed by downward revision in tariff duties on wheat; and (e) that such adjustment should begin when prices of British imported parcels have been for sixteen weeks at or above 63·02 gold cents per bushel (12 gold francs per quintal). A few moves in these directions have been made; but since parcels prices have averaged during much of the year only about two-thirds of the price named, barriers to imports have not been relaxed.

This fact registers at least temporary failure of the agreement to contribute significantly to the objectives sought. Attempts in the winter and spring of 1934 to strengthen the agreement, on lines suggested by the Wheat Advisory Committee set up under it, came to naught; and its future is uncertain.

Within the quota limits fixed by the international wheat agreement, the United States is subsidizing exports from Oregon, Washington and northern Idaho. This area constitutes a distinct wheat-surplus region, ordinarily shut off by high freight rates from domestic markets east of the Rockies. It invariably grows more wheat than is needed for the region itself and for shipments to California, Alaska and Hawaii, and normally exports to foreign countries and the Philippines a third of the crop or more. In 1932-1933 the surplus was held so firmly that prices were too high to permit liberal exports to the Orient in competition with Australia and Argentina, or to Europe; hence the carry-over was of record size. Despite heavy winter-killing, the spring wheat turned out so well that the 1933 crop was little below average. The regional surplus was therefore exceptionally large. During the summer and early autumn farmers sold sparingly, under the influence of wheat shortage in the country as a whole, and also of prospects for relief measures. Market prices in Portland and Seattle were further than usual below Chicago prices; but they remained well above export parity, and the wheat did not move out. On June 5, 1933, the Reconstruction Finance Corporation had authorized the Chinese Government to borrow 10 million dollars to buy wheat and flour, but practically no purchases were made. Wheat growers, supported by banking interests, sought effectual relief from the disaster of " export-parity " prices. Exporters, who since November 1932 had been urging some form of export subsidy, pressed their arguments. These were reinforced by complaints of Mississippi Valley farmers and millers that Pacific Coast wheat and flour were invading their domestic markets and threatening their prices.

On July 24, shortly after the wheat market crash, the Secretary announced, under authority of sec. 12a of the A.A. Act, that 2 cents out of the 30-cent. processing tax (then estimated to yield about 9 million dollars) would be reserved to finance wheat exports if opportunity arose. On October 10, after weeks of negotiation, the Secretary of Agriculture signed a marketing agreement with wheat growers' organizations, grain exporters, and millers of the Pacific Northwest. The North Pacific Emergency Export Association was set up to administer the scheme, while permitting the actual trade to be handled by exporting merchants and millers. Two directors were selected by each of four organizations—the Farmers National Grain Corporation, the North Pacific Grain Growers Association, the North Pacific Exporters Association, and the North Pacific Millers Association. The executive committee consists of the directors and a resident representative of the Secretary of Agriculture, who has the last word.

The Association purchases wheat on bids announced daily, and sells for export (or to mills for milling for export of flour) on approved offers from the trade, at lower prices that effectually cover losses on export sales. It seeks to hold up prices to growers, and to keep local market prices as high as possible in relation to Chicago prices; yet it may not be " long " more than 1 million bushels, and must not let its total subsidy exceed the sums available from the processing tax, now figured at about 8 million dollars; it also seeks to give no ground for charges of " dumping " in foreign markets.

Up to May 9, 1934, the Association had purchased 25,758,000 bushels, and had sold for export 25,431,000, of which 4,218,000 were in the form of flour.[1] Nearly half of the sales were of wheat to China under the R.F.C. loan; the rest went to some thirty-nine different destinations, including the Philippines. The average differential or subsidy (less on Chinese Government sales than on others)[2] to that date was slightly under 23 cents a bushel.

In various senses, the agreement has worked well. Wheat prices in the Pacific Northwest have certainly been materially higher as a result of the agreement, though world prices may have been slightly lower. Mild protests appear to have come only from Australia against under-selling her in the Orient, and no country has applied anti-dumping measures. Millers have been disappointed in the volume of flour sales effected, particularly since China, under the influence of opposition from Chinese milling interests, has not yet bought appreciable quantities of flour, though the portion of the loan earmarked for wheat is practically exhausted. At prices thus supported, ordinary commercial exports from the region have been very light. Indeed, the Association's export shipments (about 22½ million bushels up to May 5) constitute the great bulk of American exports during the year, exclusive of flour milled in bond from Canadian wheat. Despite the price support thus given, the domestic flow from the Pacific Northwest to the East, partly by rail, but chiefly by water to the Atlantic seaboard, has continued. This movement would doubtless have been greater in the absence of the arrangement, but it already appears to have exceeded 15 million bushels, setting a record far above that for any previous year.[3] The A.A.A. has approved no other outright export subsidy plan, and has opposed general resort to this device under present world conditions.

A fourth element in the wheat program consists of " relief purchases." Beginning October 17, 1933, when the wheat market had a sinking spell, considerable purchases of cash wheat and futures were made through the Farmers National Grain Corporation on behalf of the new

[1] See A.A.A. press release 2551-34, May 10, 1934.
[2] See *Agricultural Adjustment*, p. 64.
[3] Trade data reported by the *Commercial Review*, Portland, Ore., show wheat and flour shipments to Atlantic and Gulf ports of 13·9 million bushels in July-April 1933-1934; the maximum shipments in any previous crop year was about 6 million, in 1932-1933. No satisfactory data on eastward rail shipments are available, but this movement too has been appreciable during parts of this crop year.

Federal Surplus Relief Corporation. This operation differed from the stabilization purchases under the Federal Farm Board in that, while they were timed so as to support the wheat market, they were limited to needs for relief disposition.[1] At the outset, the trade expected these operations to reach considerable dimensions, and purchases were reported to have exceeded 10 million bushels by December.[2] Actually, they were unimportant except in the initial weeks; net purchases [3] were only $11\frac{3}{4}$ million bushels, of which over 8 million were used for feed.

The formulation of codes for grain exchanges, millers and other groups dealing in and/or processing wheat and its products and by-products represents in part an integral element of the wheat program. In the weeks following the speculative crash late in July 1933, temporary regulations of grain exchange operations were put in force with the approval of the A.A.A. As a more permanent measure, a code for the grain exchanges was approved in March 1934, after months of negotiations, effective from March 31. Among its objectives are the prevention of extreme fluctuations in grain market prices and of major abuses that figured in the speculative crash of July 1933. Under the code, daily price fluctuations are limited,[4] minimum margin requirements established,[5] trading in " indemnities " (" puts " and " calls ") prohibited, and the exchanges will operate under stricter supervision in addition to what the Grain Futures Administration does under existing laws. The Secretary of Agriculture or his representative is to have the right to attend meetings of the Business Conduct Committee that will be set up in each exchange. A Code Authority of seven members, with not more than two from any one exchange, will administer the code.

Of the other codes under consideration, only that for the country grain elevators was approved in the first year (May 8, effective May 21).[6] Its provisions, among other things, prohibit underweighing and over-weighing, require dockage and grading to confirm to the Federal Grain Standards Act, prohibit bribes and other gratuities, and relate to

[1] Further differences lie in the facts that the Federal Farm Board was operating without powers to restrict production, such as are now in use, and in a period of strong downward drift of prices in general, without drastic currency measures designed to raise the whole price-level.

[2] See *Wheat Studies*, January 1934, x. 155, 167.

[3] Part were exchanged for corn, oats, barley and milo for feed use in drought areas.

[4] Until modified these are as follows in cents per bushel: wheat, rye and barley, 5; corn, 4; oats, 3; flax-seed, 10.

[5] Ten per cent. on all open trades up to 2 million bushels, and 15 per cent. additional on larger lines effective August 1, 1934. From these minima *bona-fide* hedging and spreading trades can secure exemption.

[6] A.A.A. press release, 2529-34, May 8, 1934.

storage qualifications and rates. Codes for terminal elevators, the flour-milling industry and the baking industry encountered more serious obstacles, but were subsequently agreed upon. With these, however, wheat growers are less directly concerned.

(3) *Corn-Hogs*

Corn is the outstanding crop of the United States, which usually produces over half of the world crop. It is grown in every state, though most heavily in the Corn Belt centering in Iowa and including all or parts of a dozen states. It ordinarily uses around 100 million acres, or about 30 per cent. of all acreage in crops. In tonnage produced it far exceeds other grain crops, and in farm value at local farm prices it usually tops even hay, cotton and wheat. As a cash crop, however, corn is much less important. Most of the crop is fed to livestock (ordinarily hogs consume over 40 per cent. of it), and most of this on farms where it is grown. Usually less than ten per cent. of the crop is used for food (corn-meal, corn, sugar, etc.), distilled liquor and industrial products. Only a slight fraction of the crop is exported as grain, or in corn products, and in corn the United States ranks among the minor exporters as compared with Argentina. Swine husbandry, for which corn furnishes the principal basis, ranks in importance second only to the dairy industry. Some $4\frac{1}{2}$ million farmers grow corn and/or hogs, and about a third of these produce them as a major farm enterprise. The geographical distribution of hog-raising is similar to that of corn. A substantial fraction of our huge output of hog products goes into export, as pork and lard. Domestic consumption of pork products is heavy; but it responds to price changes, and statisticians have observed that consumer expenditures for them vary closely with the index of industrial pay-rolls. This means that the farm returns from hogs (and in turn from corn) are severely reduced in periods of depression.

During the war, and again in 1922, hog production greatly expanded in response to high prices, resulting mainly from strong foreign demand; and more hogs ate corn released by the domestic decline in number of horses and mules. With the post-war recovery of swine husbandry in continental Europe, foreign demand for hog products fell off, and our exports declined. In 1923-1925 the swine population declined materially. After recovery in 1926-1927, it declined again in 1928-1930. During the latest depression the decline in foreign demand had been greatly accentuated by reduced purchasing power, import restrictions and larger hog populations in Europe. Our peak exports were the equivalent of about 16½ million hogs in 1919 and 13 million in 1923; the corresponding figures for 1929 and 1932 were 8 and 5.[1] In spite of low foreign demand, the swine population rose again in 1931 and 1932. Because of drought the corn crop of 1930 was the shortest since 1901; but that of 1931 was fairly good and that of 1932, after a striking expansion of acreage in 1929-1932, was one of the largest on record.

The immediate situation that confronted the A.A.A. in its early days contained several important elements.[2] Gross farm income from hog production, now estimated at 538 million dollars in 1932, was only about 35 per cent. of what it had been in 1929. In May-July 1933, hog slaughter was running at record levels for this period of the year.[3] The export market was the poorest in many years, and evidently getting still worse. Huge stocks of hog products had piled up; at the record levels of August 1933 packers' stocks were equivalent to 6 million hogs. Heavy hogs at Chicago were selling around 4 dollars per 100 pounds, the lowest since 1879. Spring farrowings had been larger than in 1932, and the June 1 pig survey indicated prospects of a larger increase in fall farrowings. By June and July 1933, owing to severe drought, short feed crops were in prospect. This contributed heavily to sharp advances in farm prices of corn from the record lows of 20 cents a bushel in the autumn and winter; but at 40·2 cents in mid-June 1933 they were only about 60 per cent. of the pre-war average for June. The outlook was that farm income from corn-hogs in 1933-1934 would fall below the low level of the preceding year.

This situation aroused increasingly grave unrest in the Corn Belt. To evolve plans for coping with it, the A.A.A. stimulated organized consideration of the problem by representatives of producers and packers. After various state committees had been set up, a national meeting of corn-hog producers was held at Des Moines, Iowa, on July 18. The National Corn-Hog Producers' Committee of Twenty-five, appointed at this meeting, shortly drew up a seven-point program. This was then considered by representatives of the packers, and joint agreement with the A.A.A. was reached on the outlines of a program. Similar procedures were followed later. Various proposals supported by

[1] *Economic Bases* . . ., p. 18.

[2] On these and the A.A.A. program, see *Agricultural Adjustment*, esp. pp. 94-152, 241-260, and D. A. FitzGerald, *Corn and Hogs under the Agricultural Act* (Brookings Institution Pamphlet Series No. 12, Washington, April 1934).

[3] Slaughter under federal inspection, dressed weight basis, was 30 per cent. above the figure for the corresponding period of 1932 and 5 per cent. above the previous record for these months.

producers or processors have not been acted upon,[1] but the measures adopted included elements strongly urged by the producers, and others are under consideration.

As thus far put in operation, the program has involved four major elements: (1) an emergency pig-sow slaughter campaign for prompt fulfilment; (2) allotment plans for substantial contraction of corn and hog production in 1934; (3) generous loans on corn in farm storage, and (4) extensive purchases of pork for relief. Together these constitute the most strikingly ambitious venture that the A.A.A. has yet made. In addition, vain efforts were made toward securing a marketing agreement with packers, and detailed studies of methods of marketing hogs have been undertaken.

The emergency program, dramatically announced by the Secretary of Agriculture in a speech at the Century of Progress on August 18, 1933, called for the slaughter of 4 million young pigs and a million sows about to farrow, in order to reduce the marketings of hogs that autumn and in 1934 by some 2000 million pounds. Growers were offered (1) premium prices ranging from 9.50 to 6 dollars per 100 pounds, Chicago basis, for normal young pigs weighing between 25 and 100 pounds,[2] and (2) a bonus of 4 dollars per head in addition to the price of packing sows of comparable grade (without the usual dockage), for sows weighing over 240 pounds (275 pounds until September 1) and unmistakably near farrowing—all to be shipped before October 1. During September pig quotas were increased, giving preference to producers in drought areas.

In all, between August 23 and September 29,[3] 222,149 sows and 6,188,717 pigs were delivered for slaughter to some 135 plants at 83 processing points, at a delivered cost of 30,643,102 dollars. The A.A.A. has estimated that producers received for these at least 10 million dollars more than would otherwise have been obtained by sale at prevailing prices. The sows, and pigs weighing over 80 pounds,[4] yielded

---

[1] These included plans for enlarging domestic outlets for hog products, financing exports to Russia or subsidizing exports, and relaxing certain restrictions under the anti-trust laws.

[2] The schedule of premium prices at the base processing point, Chicago, started at 9.50 dollars per 100 pounds for pigs weighing 25 to 30 pounds, and decreased 25 cents for each 5-pound interval to 6 dollars per 100 pounds for pigs weighing 96 to 100 pounds. The base prices applied at Chicago and in Michigan and Ohio, and were 25 cents higher at points east of Ohio and north of Virginia. At other processing points the prices were set at from 10 cents to 1 dollar below the base price. Prices realized by producers depended also in part on their costs for handling and shipping to the processing point.

[3] For one plant, one week more.

[4] For a brief period, pigs weighing 71 to 80 pounds were converted into edible products.

about 100 million pounds of edible salt meat. The live cost of these was 9,283,360 dollars; processing costs were covered out of the lard, edible offal and by-products. This meat was donated to the Federal Surplus Relief Corporation, and by the end of January 1934 most of it had been distributed for relief. The light-weight pigs, 82½ per cent. of the total number, were rendered for inedible grease and the residue given away, or converted into fertilizer tankage, at a processing cost of 1,874,000 dollars. Against a total cost of about 32,517,000 dollars the saleable products netted 604,319 dollars.

The main objectives of the emergency program were to prevent an increase in 1933 farrowings, to adjust production to the extent of the loss of export outlets, and to bring about further contraction of marketings to ensure a rise in hog prices.[1] The Committee urging the program anticipated that it would serve to remove 500 million pounds of pork and pork products before January 1, and to decrease supplies n the year beginning November 1 by a total of 2000 million pounds. Economic advisers of the A.A.A. estimated the net reduction more conservatively, at between 1400 to 1800 million pounds live weight; yet they forecast that such reduction would raise hog prices for the season by 25 to 35 per cent., possibly 40 per cent. (say, 1 to 1.50 dollars per 100 pounds) above what they would otherwise be. Actually, the very disappointing response to the bonus on sows, and the heavy predominance of light pigs, on which premium prices were higher,[2] held down the net reduction in potential supplies for 1933-1934, in spite of the 50 per cent. increase in the pig quota, to about 5 million head or around 1000 million pounds, about 9 per cent. of the annual federally inspected slaughter. The campaign contributed nothing significant to reduction of autumn farrowings. The principal effect on farm prices of hogs presumably occurred in February to March 1934, when these were much higher than a year earlier, but hardly as high as in June to July 1933.[3] It is inherently difficult to check the A.A.A. estimates that gross benefits to hog producers from the operation will exceed 100 million dollars and may reach 150 millions.[4]

While this emergency operation was going forward, ambitious plans

[1] An incidental objective was to relieve hog farmers in drought-stricken areas who, because of feed shortage and urgent need for cash, were being forced to sell pigs and sows at very low prices.

[2] The average live weight of the pigs delivered was slightly under 60 pounds.

[3] Farm prices were adversely affected by the processing tax, which tends in considerable measure to fall on producers.

[4] *Agricultural Adjustment*, p. 150. FitzGerald's calculations (*op. cit.*, pp. 42-47, 100-107) point to considerably lower figures.

were devised (first announced on October 17) for bringing about a substantial reduction in pig-raising and corn production in 1934. According to the final form of the plan, largely perfected by December 5, farmers were offered contracts whereby each corn grower would agree to cut his corn acreage by not less than 20 per cent. below the 1932-1933 average, and each hog raiser to reduce his pig litters and marketings by not less than 25 per cent. of the 1932-1933 average.[1] Co-operating corn growers were offered a cash rental for the " contracted " acreage equal to 30 cents. a bushel on the average yield [2] of their average acreage in 1932 and 1933. One-half of this is payable after preliminary approval of contracts subject to subsequent adjustment, and the adjusted balance (less local administrative costs) after certification of fulfilment of contract, about November 15, 1934. Co-operating hog producers were offered " adjustment payments " of 5 dollars per head on 75 per cent. of the producer's average annual number of hogs farrowed and sold in the base period. Of this 2 dollars is payable when the contract is accepted; 1 dollar on or about November 15, 1934, after certification as to reduction of litters; and the balance (less local administrative costs) on or about February 1, 1935, after certification that the contract has been wholly fulfilled. The maximum cash payment under these two heads was estimated at 350 million dollars.

In October-December the plan was put into definitive form, and contracts, other forms, and administrative rulings were drawn up. State corn-hog committees for nine Corn Belt states were announced on December 22. Educational and sign-up campaigns all over the country proceeded during the following months with the aid of extension services and county and local committees. Blank contracts were sent out to 1,500,000 farmers. In Iowa and some other states the final date for receiving applications was set at March 31, but in other states a later date was set.

The sign-up of producers was heavy, in the Corn Belt states at least; but preliminary indications made it doubtful whether the goals—in corn acreage, a net reduction to about 90 million acres, as compared with 108·7 million in 1932 and 102·2 million in 1933—would be reached. The official survey of farmers' intentions to plant corn, as of March 1, pointed to a reduction of 12·7 per cent. as compared with the 15 per cent. net goal, with increases of nearly a million acres in five southern states.

[1] Strictly the two years ending December 1, 1933. The corn base follows the land, the hog base the farmer.
[2] Under a ruling of January 25, 1934, on the basis of the average of the ten (originally put at five) years.

59

To finance the benefit payments under the 1934 program, and to cover the net costs incurred in " surplus removal " operations,[1] processing taxes went into effect on November 5, 1933, to continue for two years. The hog-processing tax, from which the principal revenue must be secured, was initially put at 50 cents. per 100 pounds live weight, and scheduled to advance 50 cents on December 1, January 1 and February 1. The scheduled advance to 1 dollar was made on December 1, but in view of heavy storage stocks and still heavy marketings, a revised schedule set subsequent rates at 1.50 dollars from February 1, and 2.25 dollars from March 1, 1934. The rates set were much higher than processors favoured,[2] but the highest is only about half the maximum authorized under the Act (4.32 dollars computed as of August 15, and higher in most months since). It is generally conceded that, because of the elasticity of demand for pork products, the hog-processing tax tends mainly to fall on producers' prices. The corn-processing tax was first announced as 28 cents per bushel; this was the maximum rate allowed under the Act, computed as of October 15. After public hearings the rate was lowered to 5 cents to prevent drastic reductions in corn-processing, which prospects of the heavy tax had stimulated. For the same reasons, the scheduled advance to 20 cents on December 1 has thus far been further postponed.

Exempt from the processing taxes are (1) corn ground for feed; (2) corn grindings for producers of 1 bushel per week or less for any purpose; (3) corn or hogs processed by or for a producer for consumption by his own family, employees, or household; and (4) since January 27, 1934, hogs processed by a producer who sells or exchanges not more than 300 pounds of the product during any marketing year.

Because of the delays involved in getting the 1934 contracts out, signed, and approved, and the first benefit payments made under them,[3] and because reductions in corn and hog supplies sought by this plan could not affect market prices for many months, two intermediate measures were devised to bring prompt relief to corn and hog producers.

The first of these, for which sectional pressure was heavily responsible, was the corn loan. Subject to the borrowers' agreement to participate

---

[1] Toward these costs, the President allocated 37 million dollars from the " Bankhead Fund " appropriated in the National Industrial Recovery Act, sec. 220.

[2] Fearing adverse effects on consumption, processors had argued for a very low initial rate, 20 cents per *head*, and a gradual increase to a maximum of 1 dollar per head. This would not have yielded the revenues required for benefit payments, considered necessary to induce producers to participate in the program.

[3] Up to May 12, 1934, payments under corn-hog contracts had reached only 40,380 dollars.

in the reduction program, corn growers were offered the opportunity to borrow at 4 per cent., through the Commodity Credit Corporation or banks assured of the privilege of re-discounting such paper with it, 45 cents a bushel (2½ cubic feet of corn on the cob) on No. 4 or better corn stored on their farms under seal,[1] in states having appropriate legislation,[2] or on No. 3 or better shelled corn in approved bonded public warehouses. Such loans were to mature August 1, 1934; but since it is specifically provided that if the borrower had not repaid his note by that date the C.C.C. will take title to the sealed corn instead (at 56 pounds per bushel), they involved virtually no risk to the borrower.

This opportunity first became available in Iowa late in November, and produced a magical transformation of farmer attitude and spirit. The time limit for borrowing, first set at March 1, was later extended to April 1 and then to May 1. Early in May the combined loans totalled about 113·8 million dollars, representing some 252,450,000 bushels—nearly one-third of the corn on farms March 1, and more than four times the heavy visible supplies of corn; most of the corn collateral was on farms in Iowa, Nebraska and Illinois.

The rate fixed for corn loans was, and remained up to May 1, 1934, well above the terminal market price less shipment costs from most of the corn-surplus area. It was consequently responsible for a most abnormal ratio of prices of corn to prices of hogs and, by making feed relatively expensive, tended to accelerate marketings of live hogs. While this made for reduction in future hog marketings, it depressed hog prices for the time.

With a view to supporting the hog market and reducing future market supplies, as well as to provide pork for the needy, the Secretary of Agriculture arranged with the F.S.R.C. to buy 300 million pounds of pork (representing about 3 million hogs) before July 1934.[3] Bids for the first 75 million pounds were opened on November 17, 1933, on terms calling for medium-weight hogs. The Secretary donates the live cost of the hogs to be covered out of processing tax receipts, while the Relief Administration bears the processing costs. Other purchases have

---

[1] As first announced, on October 25, the loans were to be made on the basis of 50 cents a bushel for No. 2 December corn at Chicago; as next revised, November 8, on the basis of 50 cents on Nos. 2, 3 and 4 corn at fourteen market centres in the Corn Belt. The final revision was announced November 9.

[2] Illinois, Iowa, Minnesota, Nebraska, South Dakota and Colorado already had appropriate farm warehouse Acts. Missouri, Kansas and Ohio soon passed such laws. In Indiana loans were made on farm-stored corn inspected by state officials.

[3] Small purchases of corn for relief have also been made.

been made at intervals since, and some commercial products have also been bought. Up to May 12, 1934, the Corporation had thus purchased about 240 million pounds of pork and pork products. The budget estimate for removal of surplus up to 1933-1934 is 65 million dollars, of which about half represents the net cost of the emergency program. An estimate of 30 million dollars is made for 1934-1935.

Throughout the year after the passage of the Act a marketing agreement for the meat-packing industry has been a subject of conferences and negotiations, on the initiation of the packers. One such agreement was formulated as early as June 1933; a second was submitted to the A.A.A. on August 15, and a public hearing on it was held in September. Thus far, no agreement has been reached, chiefly because the industry is reluctant to concede the Secretary of Agriculture what he considers adequate power to audit and check the packers' books and records.[1]

(4) *Dairy Products*

The most difficult problems of the A.A.A. have arisen with respect to milk and its products, and the first year's efforts have been admittedly least successful in this field.[2]

Dairying is the most important branch of American agriculture. Milk is produced by nearly 4 million farmers, scattered all over the country, with the heaviest production in the North Central, Northeastern, and Pacific Coast states. Dairying differs from many other branches of agriculture in that its most valuable product (fluid milk, also cream and icecream) is distributed chiefly through a large number of urban markets, each supplied mostly from limited tributary " milk sheds." Most of the other dairy products—butter, cheese, evaporated milk, dry skim milk and casein—have much broader markets, regional or national in scope. Exports of dairy products have been relatively negligible, consisting chiefly of condensed and evaporated milk. Butter imports have been relatively small, owing partly to tariff protection; cheese is the principal imported dairy product.

Output of dairy products rose strikingly through the post-war decade, by about 50 per cent. between 1920 and 1929, according to the official index. Farm prices of milk, butter and butter-fat [3] were above the so-

---

[1] See *Agricultural Adjustment*, p. 148, and FitzGerald, *op. cit.*, pp. 95-100.

[2] On these subjects, in addition to *Agricultural Adjustment*, pp. 153-172, and subsequent A.A.A. releases, see F. F. Lininger, *Dairy Products under the Agricultural Adjustment Act* (Brookings Institution Pamphlet Series, Washington, 1934).

[3] Like those of chickens, lambs, wool and cotton-seed, but unlike those of most farm products.

called pre-war parity through most of the period 1919-1929. At its peak in 1929, farmers' gross income from dairy products was estimated at 2323 million dollars, or nearly 20 per cent. of the gross income from all farm production. Increasing *per capita* consumption, sometimes effective tariff duties, and good returns stimulated expansion of milk output prior to the depression, though the number of dairy cows increased very little in 1924-1928. During the latest depression, as in that of 1920-1922, dairying has suffered from heavy reductions in consumer purchasing power; but low feed prices helped until 1933 to make it less unprofitable than most other branches of agriculture. In consequence, dairy herds increased to successive high peaks.[1] On January 1, 1934, there were over 26 million cows and heifers of milking age, reflecting a 17 per cent. increase in five years. Though output per cow has declined during the depression,[2] reduced purchasing power in connection with large output brought farm prices of dairy products far below " parity " levels; and the potential output of the present herds is far above customary consumption of the population even under prosperity conditions.

In April-July 1933 farm prices of dairy products advanced considerably, contrary to usual seasonal tendencies, under the influence of factors that affected prices in general; but disturbances developed in various milk markets, and in August, after the collapse in the speculative markets and under the influence of expanding production, prices of butter and butter-fat fell sharply from their July peak.

The initial plan of the A.A.A. for aid to fluid-milk producers provided for marketing agreements made by the Secretary of Agriculture with producers and distributors in each important milk-shed, reinforced by a system of licences through which non-signatory producers and distributors were also subject to control. Tentative agreements were commonly drafted by producers' co-operatives and a few large distributors. These draft agreements were first submitted to the Dairy Section of the A.A.A. Following a conference of the contracting parties with the Dairy Section, Legal Division and Consumers' Counsel, a public hearing was held in Washington or in the market itself. After

---

[1] The expansion in 1929-1933 was apparently at a more rapid rate than in previous periods of rapid increase, such as 1912-1917 or 1900-1908, though the estimates are not sufficiently trustworthy to permit confident assertion. According to the Department of Agriculture's standing estimates, no such expansion occurred during the depression years of the eighteen-nineties, and the number of dairy cows even declined in 1895-1899.

[2] See chart in Bureau of Agricultural Economics, *The Dairy Situation*, February 20, 1834, p. 17.

receipt of supplementary evidence the agreement was re-drafted by the A.A.A. sections most concerned. After it had passed the heads of the Production and Processing divisions, and the Administrator, it was tentatively approved by the Secretary and sent out for the signatures of the contracting parties. When they had signed, the Secretary signed, issued the licences, and fixed the date when the agreement and licences should become effective.

Such agreements were designed to raise prices to producers, to elevate the plane of competition, and to provide appropriate machinery for adjustment of prices and controversies of other sorts. Among the delicate questions to settle have been those concerning the differential between delivered prices and cash-and-carry prices, and the size of the distributors' spread; both of these were generally reduced in the agreements made effective, and several agreements eliminated the cash-and-carry differential. Usually a system of price differentials for base- and surplus-production was embodied in the agreements. In several instances milk-delivered prices were raised to consumers. In none of the agreements did the parties come to grips with the underlying problems of excess milk-distributing capacity, competitive wastes in milk delivery and excess producing capacity.

The procedure was inherently and inevitably time-consuming, and it also appeared that on various fundamental points the factual basis for wise action was not clear without further research. Out of 205 milk-marketing draft agreements submitted up to November 30, 1933, only 15 were put into effect.[1] National agreements covering evaporated milk and dry skim milk were also approved and made effective September 9 and 16.[2] Progress had been made on others, as well as on amendments to those in effect, when, following the resignation of the Administrator

---

[1] These were as follows, with dates when effective: Chicago, August 1; Philadelphia, August 25; Detroit, August 27; St Paul-Minneapolis, September 2; Baltimore, September 29; Knoxville, Tenn., October 14; Evansville, Ind., October 23; Des Moines, October 28; New Orleans, October 31; Boston, November 3, Oakland, Calif., November 7; Los Angeles and St Louis, November 22; San Diego, Calif., December, 15; Richmond, Va., December 20.

[2] Neither of these has been accompanied by licences, and both are thus regarded as successful. At the annual meeting (April 19, 1934) of the Dry Milk Institute, which was charged with administering the agreements, the chairman of the Dry Milk Committee reported that the agreement was working exceptionally well and that the manufacturers are co-operating wholeheartedly. The Dry Milk Industry Marketing Corporation that has been formed serves as a clearing-house, such as members of the industry had vainly attempted to set up under provisions of the Agricultural Marketing Act. It seeks to prevent unnecessary price fluctuations due to misinformation, and to facilitate exchange of stocks among manufacturers so as to reduce distress sales and excessive price increases.

(Mr Peek) and the chief of the Dairy Section (Dr C. L. King), the policy was altered.

Experience under the effective milk agreements revealed weaknesses in them, serious difficulties of enforcement, and a variety of perplexing problems. Prices of fluid milk were fixed at levels which restrained consumption and stimulated production, and more surplus milk flowed into butter and other processed products. Enforcement of resale price provisions turned out to lead into treating the milk industry of each market as a public utility, for which the A.A.A. was legally and otherwise unprepared. Other problems included the expansion of milk distribution by individual dairymen, territorial delimitation of milk-sheds, competition between wagon distributors and retail stores, the fixation of distributors' margins and the question of production control. On demand of the Chicago milk producers' organization, the Chicago agreement was revoked as of December 31; and early in January the others were terminated as of February 1, to be replaced as soon as possible by others conforming to a new policy.

Meanwhile, unprecedented butter production in the summer of 1933 led to abnormal expansion of butter stocks and to abnormal pressure on butter prices. To meet this situation, made acute by the speculative collapse late in July, and at the urgent demand of butter producers, the Secretary of Agriculture resorted to stabilization purchases for relief use. These purchases were first made through John Brandt of Land o' Lakes Creameries, Inc., from August 17 to October 25; from then until December 16 through a new, industry-sponsored Dairy Marketing Corporation, headed by Mr Brandt; and thereafter through the Federal Surplus Relief Corporation. During the second period, when 32 million pounds were bought, there was virtual price-pegging at five leading markets—New York, Chicago, San Francisco, Portland and Chicago; and butter prices dropped heavily when this operation was terminated.[1] In all, through January 1934, some 61 million pounds of butter were thus " removed from commercial channels of trade." On January 1, 1934, net commercial storage holdings, after deduction of Government holdings and proposed purchases, were down to average levels, though total stocks were still abnormally high. Cheese purchases for relief were also made in January and February 1934. The cost of these purchases,

---

[1] Acute controversy developed over this action. In particular, butter producers and the Secretary both felt that the other did not live up to the understanding that 30 million dollars would be allocated for purchases (of which 11,250,000 dollars was made available), and that the industry would support a feasible plan of production control.

E

as butter in tubs and natural cheese, remains to be covered out of processing taxes; the Federal Surplus Relief Corporation bears the costs of processing and distribution.

The new dairy policy included a revised program for milk-marketing agreements, announced early in 1934, and a proposed " program for adjusting the dairy industry," [1] which was made the subject of fifteen regional conferences in April.

The A.A.A. proposed in new milk-marketing agreements to concentrate on establishing minimum producers' prices in each market, taking into account the competitive value of milk in relation to its value for non-fluid uses at the outer edge of the milk-shed, the history of prices during the pre-depression decade in that milk-shed, and the earning-power index of the locality. It proposed to enforce such agreements promptly and effectively. It contemplated setting up local advisory boards representing producer, distributor and consumer interests. The first licences conforming to this revised policy were issued late in March 1934; and by May 12 they extended to 19 markets, covering 15 per cent. of the fluid milk and cream consumed by the non-farm population. The whole matter is still a subject of much controversy, and the obvious progress made has been far less comprehensive than in wheat, cotton, corn and hogs.

The proposed adjustment program called for contracts with dairymen (open to all producers) by which they would agree to cut their milk production for one year (and two if the Secretary of Agriculture should so require) by 10 to 20 per cent. below their average in 1932-1933 (a period of high production), in return for benefit payments at about 40 cents per pound of butter-fat, or about 1.50 dollars per 100 pounds of " surplus " fluid milk, on the amount by which they reduced their sales below their 1932-1933 quotas as determined. The method of reduction of output was to be left to the individual producer. Payments were to be made one-half on acceptance of contracts and the balance after six months. County production-control associations and local committees were contemplated. To provide the funds, estimated at 165 million dollars for one year, or 300 million for two, there was proposed a processing tax on processed milk, beginning at 1 cent per pound of butter-fat content, and gradually rising to 5 cents, with a compensatory tax on oleomargarine.

The reactions expressed in the different regional conferences varied greatly. While at most of the conferences the majority vote of producers

[1] See the A.A.A. pamphlet under this title, issued March 27, 1934.

was for the program, evidence of dissent was so substantial that the A.A.A. announced late in April the shelving of the proposal for the present at least.[1] In no other field has the A.A.A. aroused such severe criticism or such vigorous opposition from strongly organized producer groups, in this case notably from the National Co-operative Milk Producers Federation.[2] The dairy interests have been largely responsible for recent Congressional action imposing heavy duties on coconut and other imported oils, against the wishes of the Administration.

Additional features of the proposed adjustment program called for appropriations of at least 5 million dollars each for aid in financing distribution of surplus milk to underfed children in cities, for purchase and distribution of healthy cows to needy farmers lacking milk cows, and to speed up the conquest of bovine tuberculosis, with possibly some provision for federal participation in the control of Bang's disease. Under the recent amendment to the Act, some progress has been made on these lines in the absence of a production-control program.

(5) *Tobacco*

After corn, hay, cotton, wheat, oats and potatoes, tobacco is the most important crop in terms of farm value, although the area harvested was only about 2 million acres at its record level in 1929-1931, and gross farm income from tobacco is usually between 2 and $2\frac{1}{2}$ per cent. of that for all crops and livestock. As a cash crop it is relatively much more important. It is raised by over 400,000 growers, in various areas mostly east of the Mississippi. The crop is made up of numerous types that differ in use, conditions of production and value. The Secretary of Agriculture has designated six main classes as separate basic products, of which the relative importance is broadly indicated by the following approximate percentages of the total disposed of for domestic consumption and export in the ten years ending with 1932-1933 [3]: flue-cured, 45·8; burley, 21·2; fire-cured, 13·3; cigar-leaf, 12·9; dark air-cured, 5·3; and Maryland, 1·5. Exports ordinarily account for some 40 per cent. of the total crop, but consist very largely of two types: most of the fire-cured and more than half of the flue-cured go into export. Practically all of the cigar-leaf types, heavily protected by tariff duties, and almost all of the burley and dark air-cured, go into

---

[1] The development of drought reduced milk production and lessened the pressure of supplies for the time being.

[2] See various issues of the *Co-operative Marketing Journal*.

[3] Based on Chart 12 in *Agricultural Adjustment*, p. 71.

domestic use. Computed as of August 15, 1933, or on the basis of the 1932 crop, parity prices of four of the principal types (on the August 1919-July 1929 base authorized by the Act) were as follows: flue-cured, 17 cents; burley, 14·6; fire-cured, 8·9; dark air-cured, 7·4 cents. Parity prices for the different cigar-leaf types varied considerably, but for wrapper types were far higher.

While tobacco growers have had very limited success with co-operative marketing, manufacturing and exporting interests are largely concentrated in a few powerful companies. The maintenance of manufacturers' profits at peak levels in 1930-1932, in contrast with heavy reductions in returns to the growers,[1] gave rise to great dissatisfaction. From a high level of 286 million dollars for the 1929 crop, the farm value of the later crops declined to a low of 107 million dollars for the small crop of 1932.

Three huge crops in succession in 1929-1931 (in spite of a small crop in 1932), coupled with reduced exports in 1931-1932 and 1932-1933 and reduction in domestic consumption of certain types, had led to accumulation of excessive carry-overs of practically all types. The A.A.A. therefore launched programs of contraction of acreage and production, with substantial benefit payments, and supplemented these by several marketing agreements. It sought to reduce the 1934 production of the continental United States to 1000 million pounds, approximately equal to the average for 1909-1913, or the short crops of 1921 and 1932, and about 60 per cent. of the average for 1930 and 1931. To finance benefit payments then estimated to total 40,740,000 dollars with respect to the 1933 and 1934 crops, processing taxes effective October 1, 1933, were imposed as follows in cents per pound, farm sales weight [2]:

Type	First processing	Second processing	
		Stemmed	Unstemmed
Cigar-leaf . . .	3.00	3.75	5.00
Flue-cured . .	4.2	4.7	6.1
Dark air-cured . .	3.3	3.8	5.1
Fire-cured . .	2.9	3.2	4.1
Burley . . .	2.0	2.3	3.1
Maryland . . .	1.7	1.8	2.4

These tax rates were fixed at the full difference between " parity prices " and current farm prices, except on cigar-leaf types; these were fixed at half the difference, on the ground that a larger tax would unduly reduce consumption. Compensating taxes have been imposed on imports

[1] Based on Chart 13 in *Agricultural Adjustment*.
[2] U.S. Department of Agriculture press release, September 14, 1933.

at the following rates per pound: cigarettes, 6·2 cents; cigars, 5 cents; and other manufactures, 3·1 cents.

The first curtailment program was offered to growers of cigar types in the summer of 1933. Stocks of these types were practically sufficient for two years; the price was lowest in relation to the average for the base period August 1919-July 1929; and the growing crop promised to be larger in relation to consumption than in 1932. In a few weeks, ending August 26, each grower in the four districts producing filler and binder types was offered a contract whereby, in return for benefit payments,[1] he agreed to reduce his harvested acreage in 1933 by 50 per cent. of his base-period acreage,[2] and if called upon to reduce acreage in 1934 and 1935 in return for benefit payments at not less than about three-fourths of the rates applied in 1933. Contracts were signed by about 17,650 growers, representing about three-fourths of the total number of growers and about 70 per cent. of the average acreage in 1931 and 1932; but more than 40 per cent. of the signers had planted no tobacco in 1933. Contract-signers took out of production about 32 per cent. of the acreage they had under tobacco in 1933, or about 15 per cent. of the total 1933 acreage. The production was about two-thirds of the current annual consumption—the first year since 1930 to make no addition to stocks. The first payment slightly exceeded 1 million dollars, and total payments under the plan are expected to be about 2½ millions.

Producers of shade-grown cigar-wrapper types in Georgia-Florida were offered contracts to leave unharvested the low-grade leaves of each tobacco plant, in return for two payments of 30 dollars an acre each. About 95 per cent. of the growers participated; the out-turn was reduced about 23 per cent., and benefit payments totalled about 86,500 dollars. This contract also committed signers to acreage control in 1934 and 1935, and an allotment plan for this purpose has since been adopted. In the more important Connecticut Valley area conditions rendered the use of a similar plan impracticable, and a marketing agreement was entered into with 93 per cent. of the handlers providing for

---

[1] The first payment was figured on a per acre basis, uniform for each district, at about 20 per cent. of the " parity price " for the average production of one acre in that district; the second payment was, for each acre retired from production, 40 per cent. of the average market value per acre of the tobacco harvested on his farm in 1933.

[2] On any one of three bases—namely:

    (a) 80 per cent. of his average acreage in 1926 and 1932;

    (b) the 1932 acreage if not above that of 1931;

    (c) the average of 1931 and 1932 acreage, if the 1932 acreage did not exceed that of 1931.

adjustment of marketings and consumption requirements. Beginning with the crop of 1934 production allotments are to be made to growers, and handlers will be required to buy from each producer not more than his allotment.

Of the most important flue-cured types, stocks had accumulated during the depression to record heights in 1932, and the short crop in 1932 caused only limited reductions. The 1933 crop promised to equal a year's consumption, and turned out to be much larger (December estimate, 708 million pounds). Very low prices realized in the Georgia auction markets in August, and at the opening of those in the Carolinas, led to state action closing the Carolina markets. This precipitated action. In a week's campaign in September, over 90 per cent. of the growers signed tentative contracts calling for reducing their output in 1934 and 1935 by not over 30 per cent. of the average in 1931-1933. Following this, a marketing agreement was negotiated (signed October 12), whereby each of eight companies that buy about 90 per cent. of this type agreed to buy between September 25, 1933, and March 31, 1934, at an average price of at least 17 cents a pound (the parity price calculated as of August 15) as much as it had used in manufacture in the United States in the year ended June 30, 1933.[1] Exporters, who usually buy about 60 per cent. of the crop, were sympathetic to the program, but were not urged to become parties to the agreement.

Adjustment programs for 1934 crops have been launched for all of the various types of tobacco, and several marketing agreements have been made. The details are too numerous, varied and complex to be given here. Heavy participation by growers was secured. The budget calls for rental and benefit payments of nearly 40 million dollars during 1933-1934 and 1934-1935; of this total, 5·2 million had been paid up to May 12, 1934, much of it on account of 1933 adjustment programs. A program for adjusting Puerto Rico production of cigar-leaf tobacco has been developed. Considerable progress has been made on codes of fair competition for the tobacco trades and processors, which are regarded as important to tobacco growers. The major results of these various efforts lie in the future, but the programs have thus far won considerable support.

(6) *Other Products*

Rice, though named a basic commodity in the original Act, is a minor crop in the United States. It is important only in two areas: the older

---

[1] They had purchased before September 25 about 75 million pounds.

in Louisiana-Arkansas-Texas, where about 10,000 growers are involved; and the newer (developed since 1912) in the Sacramento Valley of California, where the number of growers is much smaller. Save in 1918-1920, after expansion during the war, the harvested area has never much exceeded a million acres; it averaged about 942,000 in 1921-1930. In this decade the farm value of the crop at December 1 prices averaged about 42 million dollars. Before the war and in two years during the war, rice imports exceeded domestic exports plus shipments to Hawaii, Puerto Rico and Alaska. Since the war imports have been small, and exports plus shipments to possessions have regularly exceeded imports, on the average to the extent of about 45 per cent. of the crop. The American crop is only a small fraction of the world crop, and the United States ranks only among the minor exporters of rice.

High yields on large acreages in 1930 and 1931 and on a reduced acreage in 1932, in conjunction with reduced demand during the depression and big world crops in 1930 and 1931, had led to drastic reductions in rice prices. From an average of about 1.10 dollars per bushel for rough rice at the farm in 1921-1929, prices fell to an average of 39 cents for the 1932 season. Such low prices, with a reduced crop, led to reduction in the carry-over from its 1932 record peak of 220 million pounds, but left it excessive. In 1933 acreage was further reduced to 769,000 acres—the lowest since 1914—and the crop, despite good yields, was the smallest since 1925. Conferences with representatives of rice producers and millers led to the conclusion that, if the acreage could be held down, prices satisfactory to the growers could be maintained.

The problem of the rice growers appeared relatively simple. The industry is small, geographically compact, and well manned; and it had had experience with industry co-operation. Acreage had already been reduced very materially, and yields per acre vary little from year to year. Moreover, growers' ideas of reasonable returns seemed not beyond hope of achievement. Apparently, Southern growers will be satisfied with a gross return of about 27 million dollars, and California growers with around 6 million; this is only about 20 per cent. above the returns from the crops of 1931 and 1933. It was therefore felt desirable to attack the objectives of production control and price enhancement through marketing agreements without resort to a processing tax.

Two such agreements were negotiated, one with the California industry (approved September 25), the other for the Southern (signed September 29), which eventually all the millers signed. Under these the millers agreed to a minimum conversion charge for rice milling, and to pay minimum prices for rough rice fixed by the Secretary of Agriculture. The initial prices were approximately " parity prices." The December 1 farm price was 79 cents a bushel, double that of the preceding year. The Southern millers agreed to set aside 10 cents a barrel, and the California millers an undesignated amount, to create a fund to be used under the supervision of the Secretary to develop market outlets. Parts of these funds may be employed to facilitate exports so as to reduce the carry-over by 60 million pounds during the year; but reciprocal international arrangements in connection with liquor import quotas proved helpful in disposing of the surplus stocks. Millers' and growers' organizations further agreed to apply production-control measures if needed. As developed, the agreements call for with-holding a percentage of the fixed minimum price (30 in California, 40 in the South), and paying this into a growers' trust fund to be re-distributed *pro rata* among growers who co-operate by planting no more than an allotment based on their past production. In California the objective is to limit production to 3 million bags; and in mid-April, 1934, when prospects indicated a crop of 4,404,000 bags, the Secretary of Agriculture authorized the Crop Control Board to institute measures designed to reduce the prospective crop by 1,404,000 bags. In the Southern area preliminary allotment plans called for a 20 per cent. reduction from the average acreage planted in the past five years. This implies only a moderate reduction from the 1933 acreage, as shown below in thousand acres:

Year	Louisiana	Arkansas	Texas	Total
1929–1933 average	439	164	172	775
1933 actual	369	153	141	663
1934 proposed	351	131	138	620

For making individual allotments, according to ascertained preferences, the 1929-1933 average will be used in Louisiana and Arkansas, and the 1931-1933 average in Texas.

Sugar, like rice, is a minor crop in the continental United States as a whole, but sugar cane is important in a limited area in the South, chiefly Louisiana, and sugar beets are important in a number of scattered areas, of which the largest is in north-eastern Colorado.[1] Gross farm income from sugar crops has never much exceeded 100 million dollars in any year, and averaged about 70 million in 1931-1933. Domestic production of raw sugar has been and remains heavily dependent on

[1] See dot map of acreage in 1924, in *Agricultural Adjustment*, p. 190.

tariff protection; the effective rate on Cuban raw (80 per cent. of the rate on other foreign sugar) was raised on June 17, 1930, from 1·76 cents to 2 cents a pound under the Tariff Act of 1930. Under the shelter of this protection domestic production has risen appreciably in recent years; and, much more important, production has notably increased since the war in Puerto Rico and Hawaii, and most spectacularly in the Philippines. This expansion, primarily attributable to the American tariff, has notably contributed to excessive world production of sugar and to consequent severe price depression in spite of production curtailment in several foreign countries under the Chadbourne Agreement of early 1931.

In the years 1922-1929 United States consumption of Cuban sugar averaged 2,887,000 long tons, refined basis, and the great bulk of the increase in total consumption (nearly 1 million tons over this period) was provided by sugar from island possessions. Since 1929 a decline in sugar consumption has accompanied expansion in production and consumption of domestic and insular sugar. American consumption of Cuban sugar has accordingly shrunk from 3,015,000 tons in 1929 to 1,336,000 tons in 1933.[1] Since sugar is Cuba's outstanding crop and the United States has been her leading market, Cuba was extremely hard hit by the joint effects of drastic curtailment in exports to the United States and very depressed prices. Among the consequences were sharp declines in Cuba's imports from the United States, social unrest, political revolution, and serious injury to American investments there.[2]

The sugar problem facing the A.A.A. was unique in its political complications, as well as in the fact that sugar is predominantly an import commodity. Hitherto domestic sugar-beet and sugar-cane producers have looked primarily to the tariff for protection, though in recent years they have vigorously sought limitation of imports from the Philippines and ardently advocated independence for the islands.

After the passage of the Adjustment Act, in which sugar was logically not designated as a basic agricultural commodity, spokesmen for American sugar interests urged a marketing agreement " to stabilize the industry." On September 25, 1933, such an agreement was signed by representatives of the various sugar interests. This the Secretary of Agriculture refused to sign, chiefly on the grounds that the aggregate quotas for the different producing areas exceeded prospective

[1] Willett and Gray data.
[2] See Philip G. Wright, *The Cuban Situation and Our Treaty Relations* (Washington, Brookings Institution, 1931), and article by Winthrop W. Case in *The Annalist* (New York), February 16, 1934, pp. 300, 320.

consumption, that no effective control of production was provided for, and that benefits to farmers would be limited, uncertain, and small in relation to the aggregate cost to consumers, while profits to processors might be large.

The A.A.A. therefore worked out a new program involving the designation of sugar as a basic crop and the application of production-control measures as well as import quotas. On February 8, 1934, the President sent a message to Congress supporting this plan and recommending appropriate legislation.[1] In this he adverted feelingly to consumers' interests, made sympathetic references to Cuba's position, and mentioned among the objectives " to provide against further expansion of this necessarily expensive [domestic] industry." After weeks of discussion, Congress passed the Jones-Costigan Sugar Control Act, which the President signed on May 9.[2]

Under this Act, sugar is declared a basic crop. Domestic beet-sugar producers are assured a quota of 1,500,000 short tons, raw sugar basis—100,000 tons above that proposed by the President, but 200,000 tons less than was assigned them in the abortive stabilization agreement; domestic cane-sugar growers are assured a quota of 260,000 tons, as suggested by the President. The Act fixes the aggregate of quotas for 1934 at the figure proposed by the President, but gives the Secretary of Agriculture discretion (within limits described) in fixing specific quotas other than for domestic producers. Comparisons of announced quotas for 1934 with those earlier proposed are as follows, in thousand short tons:

Source	Announced May 31	President's proposal	Proposed in stabilization agreement
Domestic beet . . .	1550	1450	1750
,, cane . . .	260	260	310
	1810	1710	2060
Hawaii	917	935	975
Puerto Rico . . .	803	821	875
Virgin Islands . . .	5	5	15
Philippines	1015	1037	1100
	2740	2798	2965
Cuba	1902	1944	2000
Grand total	6452	6452	7025
Reserve for other import .	17	..	..

Cuba's quota is considerably above United States imports from the island in 1932 and 1933, but less than in any preceding year since

[1] Quoted in *Agricultural Adjustment*, pp. 192-193.
[2] 73rd Congress, *Public. No. 213, H.R. 8861.*

74

before the war, and only about half the average annual imports from Cuba in 1922-1929.

The President simultaneously proclaimed a reduction in the duty, effective June 8, cutting the duty on Cuban raw sugar by $\frac{1}{2}$ cent; and on the same date a processing tax of this amount was imposed on sugar, domestic and imported, to provide funds for benefit payments to domestic producers under adjustment programs to ensure them " parity prices " for sugar beets and sugar cane. Among the prospective effects of the scheme are to assure domestic producers higher prices than they could otherwise expect, and to give them a preference to a larger part in the American sugar market than they have had hitherto, but to keep their expansion within bounds; to restrict to somewhat lower levels than their recent peak the sugar imports from insular possessions; and to hold out to Cuba the hope of a larger sugar market in the United States than she would otherwise have. The effects on prices to sugar consumers will depend mainly upon how the aggregate quota is fixed from year to year, and not, as heretofore, on the world price plus the tariff duty.

Marketing agreements have been resorted to not only for North Pacific wheat exports, dairy products, tobacco and rice, but for a number of agricultural commodities not yet designated as " basic." The principal ones approved in the first year were as follows [1]:

Commodity	Region	Effective date
Canning (cling) peaches . .	California	Aug. 17, 1933
Fresh deciduous tree fruits, except apples . . .	,,	Sept. 2, 1933
Tokay grapes . . .	,,	Sept. 20, 1933
Walnuts	Pacific Coast states	Oct. 9, 1933
Fresh deciduous tree fruits .	Pacific Northwest	Oct. 14, 1933
Ripe olives for canning . .	California	Dec. 13, 1933
Oranges and grapefruit . .	California, Arizona	Dec. 14, 1933
,, ,, . .	Florida	Dec. 14, 1933
,, ,, . .	Texas	Dec. 26, 1933
Asparagus for canning . .	California	Mar. 17, 1934

In addition, at the request of the A.A.A., canners of tomatoes, corn, Lima beans, beets, and cabbage for kraut, agreed in August and September 1933 to increase prices to growers above those fixed in contracts made earlier in the season, before prices in general had advanced so considerably.

[1] Chiefly from *Agricultural Adjustment*, p. 188. The second agreement listed above was not operative in 1933, partly because it " was not consummated early enough," and partly because a heat wave in California materially reduced the output of several of the fruits concerned.

75

The first agreement for a non-basic product, for the California canning peach industry, was signed on August 15, and licensing was resorted to in order to bring under the agreement canners (representing 20 per cent. of the industry) who did not sign. This agreement was evolved from voluntary agreements used, with variable success, in several recent years except 1932. The pack was limited to 10 million cases (requiring about 218,000 tons of fruit); and growers were assured of 20 dollars per ton for all their No. 1 crop used for canning, as compared with 6.50 dollars per ton obtained for less than half of the crop in 1932; in addition 15 dollars per ton for the rest of the No. 1 peaches left unharvested. Quotas were assigned to the various packers, and canners' prices to the wholesale trade were set at 1.38 to 1.50 dollars per case. It is officially stated that the effect was to yield returns to peach growers of about 5 million dollars as compared with 906,000 dollars in 1932; and to increase these returns by 3 million dollars, and to increase prices to consumers by 2 cents per can, above what they would otherwise have been. In a case under this agreement (*U.S.* v. *Calistan Packers, Inc.*), early in September 1933, Judge St Sure of the Federal District Court of San Francisco upheld the constitutionality of the Act and agreement.

Many other agreements have been drafted and considered, and the Secretary of Agriculture recently set forth " the determination of the Agricultural Adjustment Administration to extend its facilities as rapidly as possible to producers of commodities, principally non-basic, grown in widely scattered states and regions, through marketing agreements and licences." In his statement before the Senate Committee on Agriculture, from which these words are quoted,[1] Secretary Wallace urged the passage of the Smith bill (s. 3326), designed to strengthen the Act in these respects, and to enable the A.A.A. to cope with what he regarded as obstruction to formulation of agreements and their enforcement after adoption, on the part of large processors and distributors. He submitted a long list of special crops for which the agreement-licence procedure is considered appropriate.

The agreements already adopted, like others yet to be made, vary greatly in their character. In general, they seek to raise returns to producers by limiting the marketed supply, involving a moderate increase in prices to consumers; often provision is made for diverting

---

[1] Dated May 8, 1934, for release when the statement is given. This was accompanied by an A.A.A. release, 2528-34, giving " Detailed Explanation of A.A.A. Amendments."

surpluses to lower-value domestic outlets or into export. An cfficial statement runs thus [1]:

Agreements may extend from the producer to the consumer, and may touch every point in the chain of distribution. Trade agreements made under the Adjustment Act do not come under the anti-trust laws. They may regulate practices as to prices, production quotas, supply areas, and relationships among various branches of trade. They are designed to prevent " cut-throat " competition and to assure fair treatment for producers, distributors, and consumers of farm products or goods made from farm products.

Other adjustment programs, in some cases supplemented by marketing agreements, are in process of formulation for commodities newly declared as basic under the amending Act of April 7, 1934. The most important of these is the beef-cattle industry. On April 26 the A.A.A. held a preliminary conference at Chicago, attended by about 1000 people representing the cattle industry of the nation, for discussion of the cattle situation and the advisability of an adjustment program. Almost all agreed that the industry needed Government aid, in contrast to the general conviction held a year earlier; and while much opposition to a processing tax on beef was voiced, the conference authorized the A.A.A. chairman to appoint a committee of 25 to meet A.A.A. officials with a view to developing a program for subsequent consideration by the industry.

CONCLUDING OBSERVATIONS

Celebrating the first anniversary of the passage of the Adjustment Act, Administrator Chester C. Davis reported that in all 3 million adjustment contracts with individual farmers were filed with or on the way to the A.A.A., representing " more than 90 per cent. of this country's cotton and tobacco, 80 per cent. of its wheat, and most of the corn and hog production that is significant "; and that in addition about 800,000 producers were favourably affected by marketing agreements.[2] From the standpoint of administrative achievement, this is a remarkable record for this country, surprising even to farm leaders and the A.A.A. itself,[3] as well as to sceptics who had regarded the proposals as administratively unworkable. Of the major programs proposed, only that for control of dairy products has been shelved, because of dissent

[1] U.S. Department of Agriculture, *The Agricultural Adjustment Act and its Operation*, October 1933, p. 11.

[2] A.A.A. press release 2533-34, May 13, 1934.

[3] See Secretary Wallace's statement in A.A.A. press release 2532-34, May 13, 1934.

77

on the part of an important fraction of the producers. The scope of operations is still undergoing expansion.

The experiments thus far appear to show that it is administratively feasible, by offering liberal benefit payments, to get a substantial proportion of farmers (particularly in terms of volume produced) to agree to reduce their acreage of major crops, and to secure a net reduction in acreage of those crops in spite of maintenance or increase of acreage by non-signers.

The question of voluntary or enforced compliance with these contracts largely remains to be answered. Substantial compliance was secured in the 1933 cotton and tobacco programs, and the A.A.A. anticipates similar success with others. To what extent, if at all, contraction of acreage will be offset by improvement in yields, resulting from the farmers' efforts, remains to be seen. Some tendencies in this direction are in evidence, with various crops; and these have contributed to the introduction of supplementary compulsory restrictions on marketings under the Bankhead Act for cotton, and under the Kerr-Smith Act for tobacco. Also of major importance is the use that farmers make of the " contracted acreage "—the acres taken out of production of crops under contracts. The objective is to prevent contraction in major crops from leading to expansion and resulting surpluses of other crops. Regulations restricting the use of such contracted acres—in the main to fallowing, soil-improvement crops, erosion prevention and production for home consumption—have given the A.A.A. serious concern, and their enforcement may not be easy. For 1934, drought prevented expansion of acreage in crops not subject to contracts.

To a considerable degree, the new program is " self-financing." Through the Bankhead appropriation of 100 million dollars, the general funds of the Treasury have borne the financial burden of the cotton option plan, covered the costs of the emergency hog-reduction campaign, and contributed something more to the corn-hog program. Relief operations have also been financed by the general Treasury funds; these have amounted directly to between 50 and 60 million dollars, and indirectly to considerably more. Rental and benefit payments of 186,380,000 dollars made up to May 12, 1934,[1] had been approximately covered by receipts from processing taxes paid in by that date. According to the Bureau of Internal Revenue, collections of processing and other taxes under the Adjustment Act up to April 30, 1934, were as shown in the Table opposite, in thousand dollars. Budgets for the various programs,

[1] A.A.A. press release 2530-34, May 13, 1934.

drawn up by the A.A.A., point to approximate coverage of administrative costs as well as adjustment payments during the period ending July 1, 1935.[1] Under the recent amending Act the general Treasury appears destined to bear a share of the cost of relief measures for the dairy and cattle industries.

Commodity	Date first imposed	Total	Processing	Import compensatory	Floor Stocks	
					Retail Dealers	Others
Wheat	7-9-33	94,989	81,517	17	2,607	10,848
Cotton	8-1-33	122,640	64,386	854	11,487	45,913
Paper and jute	12-1-33	6,221	2,841	537	63	2,780
Tobacco	10-1-33	14,028	11,850	131	242	1,805
Field corn	11-5-33	3,355	2,285	13	81	976
Hogs	11-5-33	43,854	37,578	21	116	6,139
Total		285,087	200,457	1573	14,596	68,461

The A.A.A. has pointed to increases in estimated farm income in 1933 as compared with 1932, and of estimated cash farm income in the twelve months ending May 1, 1934, as compared with the corresponding year preceding. The one showed an increase of about 1200 million dollars (or 23 per cent.), the other an increase of about 1560 million (or about 36 per cent.).[2] Of the latter figure, benefit payments represented 185 millions (most of it for cotton and wheat). The rest represented increased returns due primarily to higher prices per unit of nearly all farm products, in most cases more than offsetting reductions in volume marketed.

It has been occasionally asserted, and frequently implied, that the price increases are the result of adjustment programs and marketing agreements. This view is not warranted, except in limited degree. While no precise allocation of credit can be made, it is safe to say that, thus far, most of the price increases in most farm products have been due to a combination of other factors. Chief among these were (1) short crops in 1933 resulting from adverse weather; (2) currency depreciation and accompanying speculative activity; (3) a substantial measure of increased business activity and consumer purchasing power; (4) corn and cotton loans, and (5) relief purchases, relief expenditures, and public works outlays on a large scale.

[1] *Agricultural Adjustment*, pp. 277-323.
[2] A.A.A. press release 2530-34, May 13, 1934.

The first two of these factors call for a little elaboration. All of the major food and feed crops in 1933, and most of the minor ones, were well below the average for 1926-1930.[1] Yields of all the cereals except buckwheat and rice were far below normal. Of other field crops only five—tobacco, dry beans, sugar cane and beets, and hops—had yields above average. Of the fruits and nuts, yields for apricots alone were above average. The 1933 index of the mass of crop production, based on ten crops that constitute about 96 per cent. of the total farm value of crops, combined on the basis of pre-war average farm prices as of December 1, was 86 per cent. of the average for 1910-1914 as compared with 105 in 1932 and averages of 106 for 1928-1932 and 105 for 1919-1932.[2] This represented an unprecedented decline, for which Nature was very largely responsible. In the absence of any other factor, this would unquestionably have led to a substantial increase in crop prices and a material increase in income from crops. This year Nature outdid the A.A.A. in its efforts to restrict production.

The depreciation of the dollar in terms of gold and the foreign exchanges directly helped to raise prices of crops of which there are substantial exports or imports. It was an important factor in respect to cotton, wheat, rice, tobacco, sugar, and several of the fruit crops. Indirectly, prices of other crops were also affected. Though it is difficult to measure the influence of this factor on farm prices of individual crops, and much more difficult to estimate its influence on total farm income, there is good reason to believe that, in the year under review, its influence on dollar returns to the farmer was second only to that of crop shortage.

The first year's operations of the A.A.A. as a whole contributed substantially to increase farmers' income from cotton, but in much smaller measure to increase their income from corn, wheat, tobacco, rice, dairy products, hogs, and some other products, in addition to benefit payments supplementary to returns from sale of farm products. At least apart from cotton, the chief influence of adjustment programs on farm prices is yet to be exerted; and benefit payments also will be much larger in the second year.

It is impressive that, thus far, contraction of output has received by all odds the major emphasis under A.A.A. programs. The immediate objectives were, in the main, restraint or reduction of crop acreage and output, and reduction in livestock and output of animal products, as a

[1] *Crops and Markets*, December 1933, p. 455.
[2] Unpublished data of the Bureau of Agricultural Economics.

means of reducing supplies so as to promote price enhancement. The A.A.A. has not seen its way clear to make significant progress with schemes for promoting increased consumption, except in limited degree through relief purchases, or increased exports, except under the North Pacific wheat subsidy.

In the year ending April 15, 1934, the index of farm prices rose from 53 to 74, the index of prices farmers pay from 101 to 120, and the " parity ratio " from 52 to 62. The index of farm real estate value per acre rose only from 73 to 76 per cent. of the 1912-1914 average, in the year ending March 1, 1934. Despite undoubted gains by farmers during the first year under the A.A.A., the goal of " price parity " lies far ahead, and the more important goal of farm prosperity as well. It remains for the future to tell whether the extraordinary measures in hand, as they may be expanded and modified, will prove adequate to the task set.

The declaration of policy in the Adjustment Act includes the following objective:

(3) To protect the consumers' interest by readjusting farm production at such level as will not increase the percentage of the consumers' retail expenditures for agricultural commodities, or products derived therefrom, which is returned to the farmer, above the percentage which was returned to the farmer in the pre-war period, August 1909-July 1914.

Actually, the spread between farm prices and consumers' prices has widened considerably since before the war, with increases in wages, distances, freight rates and service of many sorts. There is at present no prospect that this declaration will interpose any practical limitation upon the efforts of the A.A.A. to raise prices to producers of farm products, and apparently no effort has been made to calculate what limits this provision might impose. Restriction programs and processing taxes are, however, subject to continuous attack as contrary to the interest of consumers. Through the Consumers' Counsel and speeches by the Secretary of Agriculture and others, the A.A.A. is alert to discover instances of " unwarranted " increase in consumers' prices, and to persuade consumers that the adjustment programs are reasonable from their standpoint.

The A.A.A. is doing its utmost to profit by the experience of the Federal Farm Board, to take a realistic view of world conditions, to co-ordinate its various programs, and to proceed with due recognition of powerful economic forces. It is not yet clear whether it can adequately take all those forces into account. It is clear that several markets have been disturbed by A.A.A. operations. It is clear that horizontal reduction of acreage is not in the interest of economical production. It is not clear how far the processing-tax device can be carried with public approval, or how far Congress will approve drafts upon the Treasury for farm relief and adjustment. Serious and intelligent efforts are under way to make the transition from emergency programs, of a largely restrictive character, to far more comprehensive measures of agricultural planning that will involve expansion as well as contraction [1]; but it remains to be seen whether these can be successfully matured and implemented, and whether the degree of governmental direction that they will entail will be acceptable to the American farmer and the general public.

ADDENDUM

DEVELOPMENTS IN JUNE–OCTOBER 1934

To the foregoing discussion of the first year under the A.A.A. a few words can be added to summarize outstanding developments from June through October 1934.

The dominating, overshadowing fact was the drought—" the most widespread and most devastating . . . ever experienced in this country." " Never before, in the weather history of the United States, has so little rain fallen over so wide a territory throughout the growing season as this year." Per acre yields of thirty-three leading crops averaged only about 79 per cent. of the corresponding 1921-1930 average, and yields equal to or above average were obtained only on seven crops, including rice, sugar cane, cotton and tobacco. A new index of production of twelve leading crops, on a 1910-1914 base, stood at 89 for 1933, the lowest since 1903, and for 1934 at about 66, the lowest since 1890, or possibly 1894. Available records show no previous case of two years in succession of wheat yields per harvested acre so far below average, or of very short yields of all grains in the same year. In cotton and tobacco A.A.A. measures were important factors in reducing output, but in other crops and on the whole the influence of the drought was overwhelmingly more important. The wheat carry-over, though reduced in 1933-1934, appears ample to supplement the 1934 crop except in durum; but according to a survey by the Bureau of Agricultural Economics published in October, " The nation's total feed and forage

[1] See the address by H. R. Tolley, at Columbus, Ohio, January 31, 1934, on " The Problem of Long-time Agricultural Adjustment," A.A.A. press release 1762-34.

supply is only sufficient to provide a little more than a subsistence ration for livestock in drought areas and rations below normal in other states if the present reduced numbers of animals are maintained."

Such a catastrophe radically altered the agricultural adjustment problem. It presented a peculiar emergency, with which the A.A.A., the Farm Credit Administration, and the Federal Emergency Relief Administration collaborated in grappling. The A.A.A. drew upon funds appropriated by the amending Act of April 7, 1934, for a cattle adjustment program, to buy 7 to 7.5 million head of cattle in drought areas, send most of them to slaughter for relief, and pay for pasturing others where pasture was available. Less extensive purchases of sheep and goats have also been made. The railways were persuaded to grant reduced rates on cattle movements out of deficiency areas and on feed shipments into such areas. Restrictions on use of " contracted acres " under wheat and corn programs were relaxed so as to encourage provision of pasture and feed. Steps were taken to accumulate seed for the next planting. To encourage conservation of feed-stuffs, the A.A.A. offered to pay farmers seven to nine dollars a ton for corn stover and fodder in quantities within specified allotments remaining on farms April 1, 1935. Wheat sales for export under subsidy from the Pacific Northwest have not been made since May, and even flour sales were suspended on August 9; and plans for buying up to 16 million bushels of export wheat in the Pacific Northwest, for shipment to deficiency areas for feed use, are held in reserve.

Some features of the A.A.A. policy have risen in favour among farmers, and in other circles, as a result of this experience. Benefit payments, made on the basis of past production, have proved life-savers in drought-stricken areas. The event seemed to justify the diversion of some wheat and corn acreage into pasture and forage crops under these 1934 control programs. The corn loan policy, which had grave possibilities of embarrassment, resulted in giving borrowers the advantage of good markets for their corn in the summer and autumn of 1934, or of saving them the expense of buying high-priced feed then. This favourable experience has led to much talk of employing the loan policy much further in future, so as to maintain an " ever-normal granary."

Pressure of current domestic surpluses of food and feed crops has been suddenly removed, and forced liquidation of livestock has drastically reduced the animal population. Some have urged that all restrictions on acreage and output should be removed now that Nature has crudely done in one year what the A.A.A. sought to do with less disturbance over several years, and that processing taxes added to enhanced prices unduly burden consumers. The A.A.A., however, is already committed to payments calling for the use of processing-tax revenues; and it holds that dangers of excessive production persist, that the principle of production control and organized adjustments must be adhered to, and that relaxation of restrictions rather than abandonment of " control " is appropriate. In view of experience that increased corn acreage and high corn yields have followed crop failure in the past, plans for restraints on corn acreage for 1935 are being made. Wheat growers under contract are required to restrict their wheat acreage sown for harvest in 1935 to 90 per cent. of their base acreage as compared with 85 per cent. for the past crop. Other two-year programs are to be continued with only minor changes. Plans for some form of " unified contract " per farm covering several crops, with a view to simplifying administration and affording greater flexibility in farming operations, are expected to be matured for application in 1935-1936.

The second campaign for signers of wheat contracts last spring was not actively prosecuted, and the results were almost negligible. According to preliminary estimates the total acreage seeded for 1934, including increased acreage of non-signers, was about 11 per cent. below the average for 1930-1932 and about 10 per cent. below the average for 1931-1933. The check on compliance was carefully made, though late; except in crop-failure areas, field men made measurements from which office calculations of individual acreages in wheat and " contracted acres" were computed and checked against the contracts. In a few counties in Washington and Oregon, airplane photography was used with excellent results. Relaxations of restrictions on account of the drought rendered compliance in many areas easy, yet many cases of small amounts of excess acreage were found. Growers were generally allowed to make amends by cutting excess acres for hay, ploughing wheat under, or (if harvest had been completed) diverting the excess grain to feed or relief uses. Only in a few cases of flagrant violation were contracts cancelled.

Extremely heavy abandonment in spring wheat states reduced the harvested wheat acreage to about 44 million acres, apparently the lowest since 1904 and some 18 per cent. below the average for 1931-1933. The crop, reduced far more by drought than by contractual restrictions on acreage, is now estimated at about 500 million bushels, the smallest since 1890 and about a third less than the average crop of 1931-1933.

Wheat prices have been close to levels permitting imports of bread wheats from Canada and Argentina duty-paid, and durum is being imported. Exports seem likely to consist almost wholly of flour milled in bond from imported wheat, plus delayed shipments of subsidized sales from the Pacific Northwest.

Sales of wheat and flour under the North Pacific Emergency Export Corporation since its inception have totalled 28,383,600 bushels, including 6,537,307 in the form of flour.[1] Of this total about 45 per cent. was sold to the Chinese Government under its loan. The subsidy cost averaged 22 cents a bushel. Operations were greatly curtailed, and shipments suspended during the port tie-up from May 9 to July 31. After June 30 the only important sales were of flour to China under the loan, and all purchases and sales were suspended on August 9. Pacific Northwest wheat and flour have continued above an export basis and have moved east in fair quantities; but this movement has been restrained pending the A.A.A. decision on the proposed purchase of the regional surplus for feed use in the interior.

The 1934 cotton crop was officially estimated in October at 9,443,000 bales, the smallest since 1922, and well below the aggregate amount of 10·46 million bales on which tax-exemption certificates have been issued. The Bankhead Act is credited with having restrained expansion of acreage by non-signers and larger use of fertilizer by many growers, but drought radically reduced yields in the western part of the Cotton Belt. Growers with a crop in excess of their quotas may buy pooled certificates of those with deficit crops, at 4 cents per pound, and with these market their excess crop without payment of the tax; such purchases are serving to augment somewhat the income of growers with light yields who have certificates to sell. Very small growers are being issued certificates beyond their quotas or in the absence of any.

The maturity of loans on cotton was extended, and early in September the policy loan was continued and the loan basis raised from 10 to 12 cents a pound. On September 15, loans outstanding on the old basis were 42,058,290 dollars. On November 2, loans outstanding on the old and new basis stood at 135,861,672 dollars, with totals rapidly increasing as cotton prices have fallen below the loan basis. This policy is helping to restrict grower sales and cotton exports, and threatens to cause an

---

[1] Operations to June 30 are analysed in J. S. Davis, " Pacific Northwest Wheat Problems and the Export Subsidy," *Wheat Studies of the Food Research Institute*, August 1934, x. 353-426.

embarrassing accumulation such as occurred under Farm Board operations. Serious concern is expressed in business circles lest A.A.A. policies cause enduring losses of cotton export markets. While this problem is receiving consideration in the A.A.A. and crop restrictions will be somewhat relaxed in 1935, continuation of the control program into 1935 is assured; only the degree of restriction to be asked for and the amount of benefit payments to be paid have not yet been decided.

Great difficulties were experienced in getting finally adjusted contracts in the corn-hog campaign, so greatly did farmers' statements regarding hogs marketed in the base period exceed standing official estimates. Most of these difficulties were eventually ironed out, but not without much dissatisfaction. One result was to delay sending out the first benefit payments until late summer and autumn. The drought cut down the corn crop to the smallest since 1894, and extreme shortage of feed is causing reductions in hogs. Even so, farm prices of corn as well as hogs have not reached " parity " levels; barley and oats, for which no control programs had been adopted, were up to " parity " on September 15. After a referendum among corn-hog growers in September, it was decided to offer growers another one-year adjustment program in 1935, broadly similar to the one in use this year.

As in the case of cotton, the corn pledged as security for loans to growers by the Commodity Credit Corporation was not taken over at the scheduled maturity. The maturity dates were first extended. Out of total loans made at the rate of 45 cents a bushel on 271 million bushels, loans were outstanding on about 100 million bushels on September 18. On September 22 corn borrowers were offered the option of having part or all of such grain reinspected, re-sealed, insured (special policies at low rates were made available), and if in suitable cribs used as collateral for new loans at 55 cents per bushel, maturing June 30, 1935, but callable when the price is at or over 85 cents a bushel, Chicago basis. New crop corn was made eligible for loans on the same terms. A month later farmers were offered outright an additional 20 cents for options on corn suitable for seed, with assurance of a price of 1 dollar a bushel (later raised to 1.25 dollars) for corn on which this option should be exercised before May 1, 1935.

There was a very high percentage of grower participation in the A.A.A. tobacco programs, and participants have generally viewed the outcome with enthusiasm. With some revisions in details, the programs are to be continued under existing contracts in 1935, but marketing agreements seem unlikely to be renewed. Under the Kerr-Smith Act of June 28, 1933,[1] a tax of 25 per cent. of the sale price is imposed on sales of most types of tobacco harvested in 1934 in excess of individual growers' production quotas. Non-transferable warrants exempting from the tax are issued to contracting growers in accordance with their allotments; and further warrants to not more than 6 per cent. of the aggregate allotments, county by county, are given growers for whom no equitable allotments were possible under the program. Under regulations issued by the Secretary of Agriculture applicable to flue-cured tobacco, of which the crop promised to be less than equal to the demand at satisfactory prices, growers with less tobacco than their allotments are permitted to use their surplus warrants with the sale of tobacco produced by growers who had more than their allotments. The principal effect of the Act in operation is to penalize production by eligible non-signers and excess marketings by contract signers, but in flue-cured areas it is moderating somewhat the variations in fortune among individual growers.

The A.A.A.'s efforts in the dairy industry continue to be ill-starred. Experience with the modified licences under which many fluid-milk markets are operating has been unsatisfactory. State milk-control boards are now in operation in most states. No new broad control program has been formulated, and in view of the drought none is under consideration.

The sugar quotas, fixed under the Jones-Costigan Act of May 9, are generous for domestic producers, in the case of beet sugar exceeding the amount marketed even in the year of maximum production, 1933. The various processors have been assigned quotas for the current season. The balance of estimated consumption was distributed according to percentages entering into domestic consumption in 1930-1932 for Hawaii and in 1931-1933 for Cuba, the Philippines, and Puerto Rico. The tariff on Cuban sugar was reduced by 40 per cent., effective September 4, to 0·9 cents a pound under the reciprocal trade agreement signed August 24. In each island possession the governor has been appointed Administrator for a Sugar Control Plan there, with responsibility for submitting plans for a control program to Washington, and executing this when approved. Allotment programs with benefit-payment features for growers in domestic sugar-cane and sugar-beet areas were

[1] 73rd Congress, *Public No. 483, H.R. 9690.* The Act also authorized the Secretary to fix and readjust import quotas on cigar-leaf tobacco, and to allot these equitably among importers, excess imports to be subject to a special import tax at a rate determined by the Secretary.

announced on October 2, and growers are virtually guaranteed " parity prices " for their 1934 crop.

Effective October 1, 1934, a processing tax of one cent per pound was imposed on peanuts except on nuts crushed for oil. The rate was set well below the statutory maximum of 2·8 cents, and the exemption made, after evidence indicated that this procedure was necessary to prevent decreases in consumption such as to aggravate the peanut situation. With the exception of peanuts and the sugar crops, no programs have been announced for basic agricultural commodities added to the original list under amendments to the Act.

Rates of processing tax have thus far been continued at the rates previously established, though in most instances current farm prices plus the processing tax per unit exceed the computed " parity prices." In June 1934 compensating taxes were removed from some jute and paper products, including jute grain sacks, and rates were readjusted downward on others. Gross proceeds of floor stocks, processing and compensating taxes through October 1934 totalled 550 million dollars while, after heavy disbursements of rentals and benefit payments under corn-hog and cotton contracts, payments to all participating growers had reached a total of only 472 millions. The original plan of the A.A.A. was to make benefit payments run well ahead of collections of taxes imposed to meet them, and thereby to stimulate general economic recovery. Unforeseen administrative complications so delayed establishing the contractual basis for benefit payments that this objective was not attained. Before the end of 1934, however, total payments are likely to exceed total collections.

The official index of prices farmers receive has been extensively revised. For recent years and months the revised index, published in September 1934, stands several points higher than the older one. When plotted with the index of prices farmers pay, it shows distinctly less " price disparity " or " farmers' disadvantage " than had previously been indicated. The average ratio between the two indexes for 1932 was 53 on the old basis, 61 on the new. Between March 15, 1933, and September 15, 1934, under the combined influence of dollar depreciation, drought, and curtailment measures, the new index of prices farmers receive rose from 55 to 103 per cent. of the pre-war average, while the index of prices farmers pay rose from 100 to 126, and the ratio between them from 55 to 82. This ratio was the highest in four years, but is lower than any annual average ratio between 1910 and 1930 except that of 1921, which also was 82.

PLANNED AGRICULTURAL ADJUSTMENT IN U.S.A.

The A.A.A. is busily engaged on plans for continuation of its adjustment efforts after 1934-1935, on a more permanent basis adapted to changed conditions, with a view to " achieving a balanced agriculture "; and its leaders express confidence that farmers, after this experience with production control, will not again be willing to return to an " unplanned agriculture." While the November elections were highly favourable to the " New Deal," the precise attitude of the new Congress toward the A.A.A. cannot yet be forecast.

CHAPTER II

STABILIZATION OPERATIONS OF THE FEDERAL FARM BOARD

by E. S. Haskell

THE AGRICULTURAL MARKETING ACT

THE control of agricultural surpluses has been a subject for continuous and widespread discussion, and for much proposed legislation in the United States during recent years, the tangible result of which was the Agricultural Marketing Act, approved June 15, 1929, establishing the Federal Farm Board, with a revolving fund of 500 million dollars.

In the Agricultural Marketing Act it is the declared policy of Congress " to protect, control and stabilize the currents of interstate and foreign commerce in the marketing of agricultural commodities and their food products." The Federal Farm Board is authorized to accomplish this " by aiding in preventing and controlling surpluses in any agricultural commodity, through orderly production and distribution, so as to maintain advantageous domestic markets and prevent such surpluses from causing undue and excessive fluctuations or depressions in prices for the commodity." [1]

The Board interpreted the intent of Congress to be the minimizing of such " undue and excessive " price fluctuations as are injurious to the producers, and to eliminate the causes of such fluctuations. " Not stabilization, in the sense of rigid fixation or levelling of prices, but stabilizing, in the sense of limiting fluctuations, is regarded as the objective. Even this end is to be sought only in so far as it promises real benefits to farmers, not only for the time being but over a period of years." [2] The Act provided the Board, within its discretion, with a choice in the methods and machinery for attaining these ends.

The Farm Board recognized several groups of measures which have a stabilizing effect upon the production and the marketing of farm products and upon farm prices and incomes. It believed that the normal development of co-operative marketing associations should contribute much towards these ends. It considered its major task to be

---

[1] See Appendix for provisions of the Agricultural Marketing Act pertaining to stabilization.

[2] *First Annual Report*, p. 24.

the rendering of assistance towards strengthening and extending the scope of " producer-owned and producer-controlled " co-operatives, strengthening their financial position, and improving their efficiency. This phase of the Board's activity, though less publicized than the operations of the stabilization corporations, and hence less in the public eye, was nevertheless foremost on its program.

In the Agricultural Marketing Act the provisions for stabilization operations appear as second in importance only to those measures intended to build up effective co-operative marketing associations. The two groups are closely linked. The Act provides that the Board shall invite the co-operative associations handling any agricultural commodity to establish an advisory commodity committee consisting of seven members, of whom at least two shall be " experienced handlers or processors of the commodity." Whenever the Board finds a marketing situation that requires the establishment of a stabilization corporation in order effectively to carry out the declared policy of Congress previously referred to, it is authorized, upon the recommendation of the concerned advisory commodity committee, to recognize a stabilization corporation. Such a corporation must be organized under the laws of a state or territory, and all of the outstanding voting stock or membership interests must be owned by the co-operative associations handling the commodity in question.

Under this authority but two stabilization corporations were set up, dealing respectively with wheat and cotton. A few other stabilization operations were conducted directly by co-operative associations, with the assistance of loans from the Board's revolving fund. But these were comparatively minor in scope and duration.

The Board at all times regarded measures for the prevention of surpluses, through the control of excessive production, as indispensable to the stabilizing of farm prices and incomes. This point was constantly stressed by the Board in its reports and its contacts with the co-operatives, with Congress and with the public. In its judgment the operations of co-operative associations and stabilization corporations might suffice in dealing with " temporary or occasional surpluses. But none of these, nor all together, nor any Government agency can protect farmers from the consequences of repeated or continuous production in excess of market requirements. Adjustments of production to market requirements are indispensable, in agriculture as in industry, to the solution of surplus problems." However, the Agricultural Marketing Act contains no provisions, other than through voluntary agreements, for regulating production to market demands. The Board conducted numerous and widespread campaigns through the Press, extension forces, and all other agencies at its command, to induce growers to reduce their production in conformity with the lessening effective market demands for their products. The facts of the existing and prospective situations were presented clearly and in detail, and numerous specific proposals for adjustments of acreage and production were urged upon co-operators and non-members alike. These voluntary measures proved quite ineffective in accomplishing the reductions sought. The inevitable result—in the face of a drastic, prolonged and world-wide depression, with the accompanying curtailments in consumer purchasing power—was a final breakdown in the effectiveness of the stabilization efforts to accomplish the initial objectives. The Board clearly foresaw such an end to stabilization efforts if extended to long-time operations unaccompanied by adjustments in production. What the Board did not foresee, in common with practically all elements in the country, was the extent and depth of the business depression which later developed.

WHEAT STABILIZATION

The first step looking to the stabilization of wheat prices was taken by the Farm Board on September 5, 1929, less than two months after the approval of the Agricultural Marketing Act. On that date the Board announced that qualified grain co-operatives could obtain supplemental commodity loans on unsold wheat on the basis of 10 cents per bushel, or 90 per cent. of the current market price. However, only a few co-operatives were yet in a position to take advantage of such loans.

During the stock market crash of mid-October wheat prices declined sharply in sympathy with securities. To the Board this " appeared to be due to purely temporary factors unconnected with the supply and demand situation for the year as a whole, which continued to point to higher levels of wheat prices.[1] . . . The Board, therefore, on October 26, announced the important offer to lend to co-operatives up to stated values on the different grades in the principal terminal markets." [2] The values stated were substantially the closing prices of the preceding day, October 25.

[1] *First Annual Report*, p. 27.
[2] These values were, for No. 1 Northern Spring, 1.25 dollars per bushel, basis Minneapolis, with the customary differentials for other grades and markets. These

For a time this move appeared to be successful. Wheat prices improved during the rest of October, declined during November, in sympathy with stock prices, and again recovered. When prices again weakened in December, the Farmers National Grain Corporation,[1] on December 19, offered unsuccessfully to buy wheat at the loan value. In January some wheat was thus purchased.

The World Situation

At the time the policy of lending up to stated values was adopted the stress of the existing market situation, in the judgment of the Board, seemed to justify unusual measures, especially in view of the then available information on the world wheat situation. The 1929 world crop was expected to be 500 million bushels under the large crop of 1928. Carry-overs in exporting countries were known to be large, but European countries were expected to import heavily. Both official and trade sources generally anticipated higher prices than those prevailing.

Subsequent developments showed the error in this forecast. It was found that the European carry-overs were unusually large, that the excellent crops of all cereals in Europe reduced the wheat imports, and that the European countries imposed milling regulations, higher tariffs, and other restrictive measures designed to discourage imports. Also, the Argentine export supplies proved to be larger than expected, while China's imports were reduced by civil war and the depreciation of silver. In consequence of these unforeseen contractions in import purchases, the international wheat trade for the year was reduced by more than 300 million bushels.

loans, like most of the commodity loans made by the Farm Board to the co-operatives, were supplemental to primary loans from the commercial banks and the Federal Intermediate Credit Banks.

In announcing this basis for loans, it was stated that: " The Federal Farm Board believes that, based on known world supply, the present prevailing prices for wheat are too low. The Board believes that this unsatisfactory price-level is chiefly due to the rapid or disorderly movement which is putting a large part of the year's supply of wheat on the market within a short time. . . .

" The Board is confident that, considering the soundness of underlying conditions which affect the price of wheat, the plan described above furnishes a completely safe basis for making loans from the Board's revolving fund. The Board places no limit on the amount of Government money to be so loaned. Nearly 100 million dollars is available for this purpose, and, if necessary, the Board will ask Congress to appropriate more."

[1] The central marketing agency for the grain co-operative associations. It is a Delaware corporation, incorporated October 29, 1929. As was the practice with most other commodities, the Farm Board loaned only to the central marketing organization, the stock of which was owned and controlled by the regional and local member associations.

Grain Stabilization Corporation

Wheat prices weakened during January and February of 1930 under the pressure of record visible supplies and a lessening export demand. The Farmers National Grain Corporation continued to support the market by purchasing country-run wheat. But this proved insufficient, and on February 11 the Grain Stabilization Corporation [1] was recognized by the Farm Board, upon the recommendation of the Wheat Advisory Committee. The Stabilization Corporation continued the policy of purchasing country-run wheat, with the dual objectives of stabilizing the wheat market and of extending the benefits of the loan basis to farmers not in a position to borrow through a qualified co-operative. But it was soon found that others than producers were taking advantage of this type of buying to make a profit by selling to the Stabilization Corporation wheat purchased earlier from the farmer. This general purchasing was then discontinued, and until March 1 country-run wheat was purchased only from qualified co-operatives and their members. But the Stabilization Corporation undertook to support the market by buying cash wheat and May futures at market prices.

The accusation was frequently made that through these transactions in futures the Corporation was speculating in the grain market. This the Board denied, stating, on March 6, " The Stabilization Corporation is prepared, and expects, to take delivery of all grain purchased on futures contracts and merchandise it as the market conditions will permit."

These actions appeared to check a threatened severe break in wheat prices in the United States during February and March, Liverpool prices dropping to a new low point by the middle of March. But from that time until late in April world prices advanced in response to market news pertaining to the new crop. The Stabilization Corporation

[1] " The Grain Stabilization Corporation is composed solely of qualified Capper-Volstead grain co-operatives, and its membership is open to all such co-operatives. The various members have waived all rights or claims to any profits which may accrue from its operations, to the end that all profits or losses will fall upon the revolving fund provided in the Agricultural Marketing Act.

" This is simply another step in the program of the grain co-operatives and the Farm Board for a unified national system for marketing grain, and has been under consideration by the Board for several months " (Farm Board *Press Service*, No. 1-26, February 11, 1930).

The management of the Farmers National Grain Corporation was closely interlocked with that of the Grain Stabilization Corporation—*e.g.* the Vice-President of the former was also President and General Manager of the latter. The Stabilization Corporation, however, was much more directly and strongly subject to control by the Farm Board, especially in matters of policy.

took advantage of this advance to reduce its holdings (see Figures Nos. 1 and 2). This was accomplished principally through export channels, and was of sufficient volume to permit the Corporation to reduce its Farm Board obligations by approximately one-fourth.

When wheat from the new crop began to move to market in June, however, prices declined sharply to new low levels. At this time, June 26, the general manager of the Stabilization Corporation made the following announcement of policy:

The Grain Stabilization Corporation discontinued the sale of wheat when the new crop began moving, with the exception of a few small lots to millers who were unable to take care of their immediate needs from any other source. . . .

The grain trade need have no apprehension of competition from the wheat held by the Grain Stabilization Corporation during the coming months when farmers will be moving the 1930 crop to market, unless in the meantime prices rise to the level at which purchases were made. In no event will this 1929 stabilization wheat be thrown on the market in a way to depress prices.

The operations of the Stabilization Corporation during the less than five months from the date of its incorporation to the end of the fiscal

FIGURE 1.—WHEAT PRICES AT KANSAS CITY, LIVERPOOL, AND WINNIPEG, WEEKLY, 1929-1930 TO 1932-1933 [1]

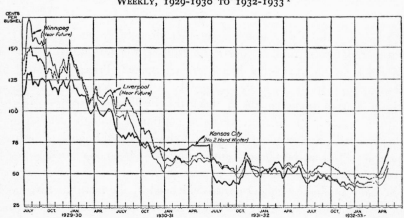

year resulted in holdings of 65,545,201 bushels of cash wheat and futures contracts on June 30, 1930.

In accordance with the policy just referred to, the net holdings of the Stabilization Corporation were not reduced during the 1930–1931

[1] This Chart shows weekly average prices of cash wheat at Kansas City, compared with corresponding averages of the prices of the nearest future delivery at Winnipeg and Liverpool (*Courtesy of Farm Board*).

fiscal year. Small amounts of wheat favourably situated for milling, export, and drought-relief purposes were sold, but these were immediately replaced by contracts for future delivery.

During July prices continued to decline, reaching pre-war levels, under pressure from carry-overs of record proportions, both in the United States and abroad. The new crop, too, added to these unwieldy

FIGURE 2.—SPREAD BETWEEN KANSAS CITY AND LIVERPOOL WHEAT PRICES, AND GRAIN STABILIZATION CORPORATION HOLDINGS, MONTHLY, 1929-1930 TO 1932-1933 [1]

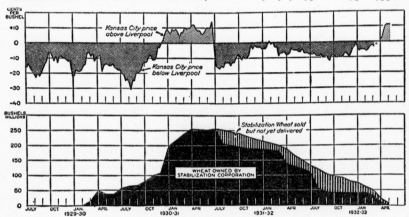

stocks. Nor did the disastrous summer drought, which reduced the corn crop by 500 million bushels, result in the feeding of wheat to livestock on the scale that had been anticipated. Prices continued to show a downward tendency during August and September, in spite of the Corporation's efforts to check this by limited purchases in the futures market. The market weakness continued through October and the first half of November, in spite of the increased buying of futures contracts. These purchases, amounting to 28,300,000 bushels from August through October, did appear, however, to have a steadying effect on the domestic markets, as evidenced by the fact that Liverpool prices declined much more than did prices in the United States during this period.

In November wheat prices weakened still more rapidly. World wheat stocks reached new records of high levels. Shipments to importing European countries were large from the Danube countries, Australia

[1] As stabilization holdings increased, domestic prices rose in relation to foreign prices until they actually exceeded them. Even in the 1931-1932 season, when stabilization stocks were gradually being liquidated, domestic prices were maintained closer than is usual to foreign prices (*Courtesy of Farm Board*).

and Russia, resulting in heavy accumulations in the European ports. Much of the grain, especially that from Russia, was shipped on consignment and remained unsold, to exert tremendous pressure on the market. Several of the European importing countries raised their tariffs and increased milling restrictions. The result was a serious crisis in world and domestic wheat prices.

Emergency Purchases of Wheat

This virtual collapse of wheat prices was reflected in financial conditions in the United States, particularly in the grain-growing states, where there were many important bank failures. Wheat pledged against loans from banks and other lending agencies was beginning to be forced on the market. The co-operative associations holding wheat were faced with bankruptcy. In the judgment of the Farm Board, an acute emergency existed which could be met only by heavy stabilization purchases. Increased purchases during the week ending November 15 failed to be effective in holding the market. Drastic action appeared to be necessary to save the domestic market from collapse in sympathy with world markets. Accordingly, on November 15, 1930, the Board authorized the Stabilization Corporation to purchase as much wheat as was necessary to prevent further declines in the price of the 1931 crop. In announcing this program the Board stated: " Demoralization in world grain markets has made it necessary for the Grain Stabilization to again enter the wheat market in order to stop panicky selling, and to prevent further unwarranted declines in domestic prices. Comparatively, wheat is lower in price than other agricultural commodities. . . . While the visible supply of wheat is large, there is no congestion in any of the terminal markets. . . . Further price declines would be in sympathy with foreign markets and not justified by domestic conditions."

Stabilization operations were extended to eight principal markets; and price differentials between markets maintained in a way to prevent congestion at the terminals and to avoid uneconomic movements of the grain so far as possible.

From the beginning of these extended stabilization purchases until April, the domestic prices of cash wheat and futures from the 1930 crop were held within a narrow range of 2 to 3 cents per bushel, whereas Liverpool prices declined about 15 cents during the first part of this period and remained near that level. This brought Liverpool wheat prices actually below those of Chicago and Kansas City, reversing the usual differentials between foreign and domestic markets. During this period wheat prices in the domestic wheat markets were maintained at 15 to 30 cents per bushel higher than the comparable prices in the principal foreign markets, such as Liverpool and Antwerp.[1] Naturally, exports of both wheat and flour virtually ceased. In an effort to minimize this handicap to mills that customarily grind wheat for export, as well as to help reduce domestic wheat stocks, the Stabilization Corporation on January 20, 1931, announced a plan whereby mills near the seaboard could buy stabilization wheat and, after the flour therefrom had been exported, return wheat of the same grade and quality from purchases of the 1931 crop, and have their money refunded. Under this plan, 9,056,490 bushels of wheat were exported as flour, 70 per cent. of it being taken by Pacific Coast mills for export to the Orient.[2]

On February 26, the Stabilization Corporation announced that it would offer from its stocks in the ports an amount not to exceed 35 million bushels of wheat to be sold in export markets during the following four months, the prices not to be lower than those of other principal exporting countries, the customary differentials considered. Under this special export plan, 21,458,809 bushels were sold up to June 30, 1931, resulting in a substantial saving in carrying charges.

Only cash wheat and futures from the 1930 crop were purchased under the stabilization plan. Since futures for the 1931 crop were not handled, these reflected world market prices, and declined considerably below prices for the 1930 crop. For the information of the grain trade, the Farm Board announced on March 23 that it would authorize no stabilization purchases from the 1931 crop, and that the stocks on hand would be disposed of in a manner to impose the minimum burden upon domestic and world prices. The Stabilization Corporation shortly thereafter issued a schedule of selling prices to be effective during May and June. These prices were to be those of the current market at the beginning of the period, with one-half cent per bushel to be added every ten days thereafter to cover carrying charges.

During May, domestic wheat prices for the old crop remained virtually unchanged. Early in June, sales of the new crop began, whereupon stabilization purchases were stopped. Prices of cash wheat at first declined, regained the former levels by the middle of the month, and thereafter declined again as the new crop appeared in the markets.[3]

---

[1] See Farm Board *Press Service*, No. 3-4, November 21, 1931.
[2] *Ibid.*
[3] See Figure 1.

Limitation on Sales

On June 30, the Farm Board issued a further statement of policy for the disposal of the stabilization wheat stocks.[1] It was announced that the Stabilization Corporation would " limit its sales of wheat from July 1, 1931, to July 1, 1932, to a cumulative maximum of 5 million bushels per month." But it was declared that, " This limitation, however, shall not apply to sales to foreign governments or their agencies now being considered. Any sales for the purpose of clearing trade channels, or for other efficient merchandizing purposes, will be promptly replaced by purchase of an equal quantity of wheat." It was further stated that, " The sales program will be conducted in such a fashion as not to depress the movement in prices. It is not the purpose of the corporation to make any immediate sales, even of these limited amounts, at the present range of prices."

The Farm Board had been repeatedly urged to fix specific prices below which the Stabilization Corporation would not sell its holdings. But this the Board did not consider to be in the interests of the growers, since if a high price were fixed the holdings would not be disposed of, and would continue to overhang the market, and if a moderate price were announced this would automatically become the maximum price for the market.

By the end of the fiscal year, June 30, 1931, the first half of the wheat stabilization operations was completed. The period of accumulation was over. The Farm Board had concluded that it had extended to the wheat growers all of the assistance through stabilization operations that its limited resources would permit. The disposal of these supplies now remained to be accomplished. During the year the net stabilization purchases amounted to 192 million bushels. The gross purchases of wheat from the inception of the Corporation totalled 329,641,052 bushels, accumulated at a total cost of 270,204,503·78 dollars, or an average cost price of 81·97 cents per bushel. Disposals through export and other channels equalled 72,504,481 bushels, leaving 257,136,571 bushels on hand on June 30, 1931. These holdings amounted to 80·6 per cent. of the total carry-over in all positions on July 1, as estimated by the United States Department of Agriculture.

The beginning of the crop year 1931-1932 faced world wheat markets still weak, and gradually working lower. The domestic markets, with the stabilization support removed, declined rapidly

[1] Farm Board *Press Service*, No. 2-65, July 1, 1931.

210435

from the artificial levels at which they had been sustained to approximately the customary shipping differentials below world markets.

In carrying out the announced policy of limiting the sales of wheat through commercial channels to a total of 60 million bushels during the year 1931-1932, and of marketing this amount in the manner least disturbing to domestic markets, the Stabilization Corporation endeavoured to restrict sales in domestic markets to the smallest feasible proportions, especially during the first half of the season. Approximately two-thirds of the sales through commercial channels were disposed of for export. This wheat was offered to exporters at the seaboard at the strictly competitive prices prevailing in the world markets, but somewhat under the current prices in the interior, plus the transportation costs to the ports. This procedure relieved domestic markets of the pressure of his amount of grain and tended to keep domestic prices from falling to the parity of world markets. As evidence of the success of this policy it is pointed out [1] that Kansas City and Chicago spot prices averaged during the crop year 7 cents and 5 cents per bushel respectively, below Liverpool, whereas the customary differentials previously had been 20 cents and 15 cents when supplies had been as heavy as they were the previous year.[2] In making this comparison, some allowance must be made for decreased ocean freight rates available during 1931-1932.

Figure 2 shows the decreases in the unsold stocks held by the Stabilization Corporation. The heavy decline in July 1931 was due to sales to foreign governments; and the declines during March and July 1932 represent allocations of wheat to the American Red Cross. During the first four months of the crop season, July to October, inclusive, when domestic marketings are heaviest, the net sales of stabilization wheat totalled the full quota of 20 million bushels. These sales nearly all either were for export or represented sales of hard spring wheat of which there was an acute shortage even after the new crop had been marketed. Net sales during the November to February period were restricted to 7 million bushels. But during the last four months of the season, when domestic marketings are lightest, 33 million bushels, or the balance of the 60 million bushel quota, were disposed of.

The scarcity in the market of certain types of wheat during the year, especially of high-protein hard spring wheat early in the season, enabled the Corporation to dispose of 36 million bushels of cash wheat in excess of the announced quota. These sales to domestic millers in the spring-

---

[1] Farm Board, *Third Annual Report*, p. 67.
[2] See Figures 1 and 2.

wheat territory were at once replaced by an equal amount of futures contracts. Such replacements were made in futures rather than cash wheat in order to help maintain a better balance between the cash and hedging markets.

Sales to Foreign Governments

The Grain Stabilization Corporation, with the approval of the Farm Board, on August 21, 1931, announced the sale of 25 million bushels of wheat to the Government of Brazil, agreeing to take in payment 1,050,000 bags of coffee. The wheat was to be shipped in instalments, beginning in September or October 1931. It was agreed that the coffee would be withheld from consumption until the fall of 1932, and then sold through established trade channels and delivered in monthly allotments of 62,500 bags. This provision was to avoid disturbance of the coffee trade and to conform to the Brazilian Government's export program.

The Government of Brazil, on its part, entered into an agreement with the Bush Terminal Company of New York to grade, handle, and store the coffee and to give certain guarantees to the Grain Stabilization Corporation.

Brazil normally imports comparatively little wheat from the United States, but this country is the largest importer of coffee from Brazil.[1]

The sale of 15 million bushels of wheat to the Chinese Government " exclusively for charitable purposes in the flooded areas of China " was announced by the Farm Board on September 26, 1931. The Stabilization Corporation contracted to deliver No. 2 Western white wheat at Pacific Coast ports, reserving the right to furnish not more than one-half of the quantity in the form of flour at a corresponding price. The schedule of deliveries called for 90,000 tons by the end of October, 75,000 tons monthly during November to February inclusive, and 60,000 tons during March. The price for each shipment was to be the current market price on the day of issue of ocean bills of lading at port of loading. Payment was to be made in obligations of the Chinese National Government, bearing 4 per cent. interest, payable semi-annually, and maturing in three equal instalments at the close of each of the years 1934, 1935 and 1936. It was agreed that shipments would be made on vessels under the American flag if available on competitive terms.[2]

---

[1] Farm Board *Press Service*, No. 2-96, August 21, 1931.
[2] *Ibid.*, No. 2-83, September 26, 1931.

The Grain Stabilization Corporation, with the approval of the Farm Board, concluded on September 11, 1931, the sale of 7,500,000 bushels of wheat to the Deutsche Getreide Handelsgesellschaft of Berlin, payment to be made in obligations bearing $4\frac{1}{2}$ per cent. interest, maturing December 31, 1934, and guaranteed by the German Government. The sale was made at current market prices of September 10, deliveries to be entirely of No. 2 Ambur Durum, No. 1 Dark Hard Winter or No. 1 Hard Winter of the crop of 1930, and at the rate of 833,333 bushels per month.[1]

These three sales to foreign governments, totalling 47,500,000 bushels of stabilization wheat, were looked upon as representing an enlarged use of American wheat by countries which had heretofore imported relatively small quantities of either wheat or flour from this country. They therefore were to only a slight extent in direct competition with the domestic crop. The sale to China proved of marked value to the wheat growers of the Pacific Northwest. It removed practically the entire surplus from that region and resulted in an immediate and sharp improvement in wheat prices in the Northwest, virtually placing that region on a domestic basis.[2] The stipulation that up to one-half of the deliveries might be made in the form of flour was inserted to protect the millers from a loss of export business.

The total sales of stabilization grain for export during the fiscal year 1931-1932, including sales to foreign governments and those through commercial channels, amounted to 87,500,000 bushels, of which 79 million bushels had been shipped by the close of the year. These shipments represented almost two-thirds of the 123 million bushels net exports of wheat and flour from this country during that year.

Disposal through Donation for Relief

In addition to the $87\frac{1}{2}$ million bushels sold for export during the year, the net sales in domestic markets amounted to 20 million bushels. In March, Congress directed the Farm Board to release 40 million bushels of stabilization wheat to the American Red Cross for charitable uses.[3]

---

[1] Farm Board *Press Service*, No. 2-92, September 11, 1931.

[2] See *Hearings before a Subcommittee of the Committee on Agriculture and Forestry, U.S. Senate, April 5-8, 1932*, pp. 243-247 and 273-276.

[3] Congress provided that the Farm Board should credit the account of the Grain Stabilization Corporation with an amount equal to the current market value of this wheat at the time of delivery. When Congress in July directed the Farm Board to deliver an additional 45 million bushels of stabilization wheat to the Red Cross, funds were provided only for paying off outstanding bank loans and meeting the carrying charges until actual delivery of wheat had been completed. No provision was made to reimburse the Board's revolving fund for its equity.

Thus a total of 147,500,000 bushels were sold, leaving 108,000 unsold on July 1, 1931. This consisted of 72 million bushels of cash wheat and 36 million bushels in future contracts. There remained on hand, sold but undelivered, about 9 million bushels still to be delivered to the Brazilian Government and 15 million still due to the Red Cross.

This year of liquidation of stabilization wheat stocks, therefore, resulted in sales equal to 57 per cent. of its holdings at the beginning of the year. The Farm Board expected to complete the remaining liquidation during the following year.

In July, Congress further reduced the stabilization stocks by directing that 45 million bushels be made available to the American Red Cross. This brought the total donations of wheat to the Red Cross to 85 million bushels.

On September 6, 1932, it was announced that the stock of unsold wheat amounted to less than 3 million bushels, and that this remainder would not be reduced before January 1, 1933, except for export to countries not otherwise important buyers of American wheat. It was also stated that remaining holdings of futures would not be reduced before the end of the calendar year.[1]

By March 7, 1933, the Grain Stabilization Corporation had disposed of all its cash wheat, and by April 29 all of its wheat futures had been sold. The Farm Board announced on the latter date that as soon as all of the wheat donated by Congress to the Red Cross had been delivered the offices of the Grain Stabilization Corporation would be closed, and that " the Farm Board would not undertake any more stabilization deals in any commodity." [2] The Red Cross agreed to take the balance of the stabilization relief wheat by August 1.

Summary

The total purchases by the Grain Stabilization Corporation, from May 1930 to March 3, 1933, amounted to 370,278,449 bushels of cash wheat and 538,337,000 bushels of wheat futures, making a total of 908,615,449 bushels. In disposing of its wheat, 237,204,468 bushels were sold through regular domestic and foreign channels, 47,500,000 bushels were sold or exchanged to foreign governments, and 85 million bushels were donated to charity.[3]

[1] Farm Board *Press Service*, No. 3-38, September 6, 1932.
[2] *Ibid.*, No. 3-69, April 30, 1933.
[3] The difference of 573, 981 bushels between purchases and sales of cash wheat is due to shrinkage and a small amount retained for making adjustments.

Up to March 31, 1933, the Grain Stabilization Corporation had borrowed 579,658,617.47 dollars from the Farm Board, and repaid 364,386,653.02 dollars. Assets and claims yet to be realized were estimated to total 31,118,732.05 dollars, leaving an estimated net loss to the revolving fund from the entire wheat stabilization operations of 184,153,232.40 dollars. This estimated loss to the revolving fund was divided as follows:

Loss on stabilization operations	.	. .	160,334,489.41 dollars
Loss on Red Cross donations:			
First 40 million bushels .	.	. .	21,304,939.25 „
Equity in 45 million bushels .	.	. .	2,513,803.74 „

These determined losses to the revolving fund would be substantially lessened if the fund were credited with the full current market values of the wheat donated to the Red Cross at the time these donations were ordered by Congress.

Offsetting these losses to the Farm Board's revolving fund there were undoubtedly considerable gains in prices to wheat growers, both to non-members and to members of the co-operatives, at least during the accumulative period of the stabilization operations. Thus the Board concludes from a comparison of domestic and foreign market wheat prices that: " Stabilization purchases in the fall of 1930 and thereafter apparently supported prices by about 10 cents per bushel in September and October, and by 25 to 35 cents from November 1930 until June 1931. In addition, the world market level of wheat prices during the marketing of the 1929 and 1930 crops was probably somewhat higher than it would have been had stabilization not kept the pressure of United States sales off world markets." [1] It is conceded that allowances must be made for reductions in ocean freight rates, that increases at terminal markets frequently are not fully reflected in local prices to growers, and that, even without stabilization, growers would probably have restricted their marketings when prices were rapidly falling, thus lessening the effect of foreign price declines upon the domestic markets. But after allowing for these factors, the Board felt that " it seems conservative to estimate that the grain stabilization operations increased cash incomes of wheat producers by at least 100 million dollars during the period from August 1929 to June 1931, on their sales of the 1929 and 1930 crops of wheat."

The Board concluded further that during the fiscal year ending June 30, 1932, " if grain stabilization had not assumed the burden of

[1] *Third Annual Report*, pp. 72-73.

export movement during the season " domestic wheat prices would have been materially lower than they were, and much nearer the usual parity with world prices. This was in spite of the fact that stabilization wheat was in process of liquidation, and after making allowances similar to those outlined above. Thus during the year Kansas City prices averaged but 7 cents per bushel below Liverpool, whereas had stabilization not been undertaken the weight of domestic stocks would have forced domestic prices to an average of at least 17 cents lower than Liverpool. It is contended, therefore, that wheat growers profited by at least 10 cents per bushel on wheat sold during this year, or a total in excess of 60 million dollars. The total cash gains to wheat growers resulting from stabilization operations up to June 30, 1932, are estimated to amount to at least 160 million dollars. " And in addition, the entire economic structure was saved from the crash which would have resulted had wheat prices been allowed to drop as precipitously as they otherwise would at the beginning of the decline," in the opinion of the Board.

Another estimate of the cash value of grain stabilization to wheat growers was presented in detail before a committee of the United States Senate by a grain co-operator. It was based on data prepared in the Grain Futures Administration, United States Department of Agriculture.[1] During the years 1923 to 1928, inclusive, the combined averages of all Chicago wheat futures quotations were, respectively, 16½ cents, 15⅛ cents, 16⅛ cents, 16¾ cents, 18 cents and 14½ cents per bushel below the average prices of all Liverpool futures, or a six-year average spread of 16⅛ cents. This represented the approximate total of transportation and other costs between these two markets. During the last four months of 1929, following the inauguration of the Farm Board's policy of lending to co-operatives, the average Chicago-Liverpool spread was 5.3 cents per bushel. For the whole year of 1929 it was 7 cents. For 1930 the average spread was 5⅝ cents, and for 1931 Chicago averaged 1½ cents higher than Liverpool, or an average of about 16½ cents above world parity, after allowing for reduced freight rates. Over the three years 1929 to 1931 the spread averaged 3.7 cents, which, deducted from the assumed normal of 15 cents, left an average price at Chicago of approximately 11 cents above world parity. Ascribing this price difference wholly to stabilization operations, and applying it to the amount of wheat sold from farms during the three-year period, it was deduced

---

[1] *Hearings before a Subcommittee of the Committee on Agriculture and Forestry, U.S. Senate, 62nd Congress, 1st Session, April 5-8, 1932,* pp. 230-242.

that the gain to wheat growers was in excess of 200 million dollars. It was further pointed out that the higher domestic wheat prices in turn sustained prices of other grains and livestock.

COTTON STABILIZATION

The story of wheat stabilization is virtually a record of the operations of the Grain Stabilization Corporation. But cotton stabilization was to a very large extent shared jointly by the Cotton Stabilization Corporation and the co-operative associations more directly through their central marketing organization, the American Cotton Co-operative Association.

On August 10, 1929, following a weakening tendency displayed by the cotton market, resulting from the forecast of a cotton crop larger than expected, the Farm Board announced its initial loan policy to qualified cotton co-operatives. The Board offered to make advances on cotton up to 90 per cent. of its market value when a definite value had been fixed by sale or hedging. On September 5 the Board announced further that supplemental commodity loans would be made to bring the total up to 75 per cent. of the market value on cotton on which the value had not been fixed.

Loans to Co-operatives

Following these actions, however, prices continued to weaken; and on October 21 the Board announced its policy to make advances to qualified cotton co-operative associations in amounts up to 16 cents per pound, basis middling $\frac{7}{8}$-inch staple, average of ten designated southern spot markets. The Board considered that the prevailing prices were too low, due to " developing weakness in the stock market and unusually rapid marketing of cotton, which was favoured by open weather in the South." Confidence was expressed that, " considering the soundness of underlying conditions which affect the price of cotton, the plan . . . furnishes a completely safe basis for the making of loans from the Board's revolving fund." [1]

At the time of this announcement, the 16-cent limit for advances amounted to 92$\frac{1}{2}$ per cent. of the current price on the designated markets. Supplementary loans totalling 18,500,000 dollars were made to thirteen co-operative associations on the basis described.

Cotton prices held above the 16-cent. level until the end of January

[1] *First Annual Report*, p. 38.

1930, when a long market decline commenced, carrying prices well below the levels of the advances made by the Farm Board. On February 3, by arrangement with the Farm Board, the American Cotton Co-operative Association became the central marketing agency for the co-operatives which borrowed from the Board against short-staple cotton.[1] The Staple Cotton Co-operative Association, with headquarters at Greenwood, Mississippi, continued to be the marketing agency for long-staple cotton.

Cotton Stabilization Corporation

The Cotton Advisory Committee, set up by the co-operatives in February, met on May 16 and 17 to consider the market situation. By this time it seemed apparent that an early substantial recovery in cotton prices could not be expected; also that a forced liquidation of the co-operatives' cotton supplies against which the Farm Board had made advances would further depress the market, result in heavy losses to the Board's revolving fund, bankrupt the co-operatives, and seriously injure as well all non-member cotton growers and the cotton trade. The Committee, therefore, reported to the Board that an emergency existed in the cotton market, and recommended the setting up of a stabilization corporation as provided for in the Agricultural Market Act. The Cotton Stabilization Corporation, a non-stock organization, was incorporated in Delaware on June 5, and recognized by the Farm Board.

On June 30 the Board extended a loan of 15 million dollars to the Corporation, and authorized it to purchase and withdraw from the market the unsold cotton held by the member associations of the American Cotton Co-operative Association, amounting to 1,241,509 bales. This included both spot cotton and futures.

The futures contracts had been acquired by the co-operative associations principally in two ways. When the market had declined to a point where the cotton could not be sold for enough to repay the advances against it, plus the accumulated charges, it was still necessary for the associations to deliver cotton to meet the demands of their customers. Under the conditions this could be done only by hedging. Also, the co-operatives had acquired futures contracts in the handling of optional pool cotton.

---

[1] This marketing agency was owned by eleven affiliated co-operative associations functioning over the thirteen cotton states and representing a total farmer membership of about 248,000. Its headquarters were in New Orleans.

Holding of Permanent Surplus

It soon became evident that in view of the continued reduced demand there was ample cotton outside of the stabilization stocks to meet all requirements. It was therefore decided to continue to withhold the stabilization cotton from the market during the 1930-1931 crop year. On September 23, 1930, the general manager of the Cotton Stabilization Corporation announced that holdings of the Corporation would be maintained until July 31, 1931, unless the price should advance to or above the purchase price. If any cotton should be sold for special reasons, he stated, it would immediately be replaced by a like number of bales. This policy was adhered to.

By the close of the fiscal year, June 30, 1931, the Cotton Stabilization Corporation had purchased 1,319,809 bales at a total cost of 107,533,244 dollars, or an average of 16·3 cents per pound. Net sales amounted to 9020 bales, leaving 1,310,789 bales on hand. This completed the accumulation period for the Stabilization Corporation (see Figure 3 and Table II.).

The decline in cotton prices under way when the holdings of the American Cotton Co-operative Association were taken over by the Stabilization Corporation in July 1930 continued. It was accelerated in August, when the size of the new crop became known, nearly reaching the 10-cent level, compared with 18½ cents a year earlier.

Advances to Cotton Growers

On August 25 the Farm Board announced that it would lend to the co-operatives on a basis to enable them to make commodity advances to their grower members up to 90 per cent. of the value of the cotton in the seasonal pool, and up to 80 per cent. on cotton in the optional pools. On the latter further margin was to be required should the market decline. Proportionally smaller advances were to be made if prices advanced above 12 cents per pound. Recognizing the hazard in advances so close to market values, the Board agreed to carry these loans if necessary for three years, or until July 31, 1933.

At the time these high advances were authorized it was expected that July and August 1930 would mark the low point in the depression. But the business situation failed to improve, and prices continued to decline. When prices reached such levels that the cotton would not repay the loans against it the co-operatives faced the choice of three courses: they could sell the cotton and sustain losses that would mean insolvency; they could refuse to sell cotton and thereby lose their mill customers, both in this country and abroad; or they could sell to the mills and buy futures contracts to maintain their net position. With the approval of the Board they adopted the last-named course, with the expectation that within the three-year period of the loan they would be able to liquidate the cotton with profit to their grower members.

In authorizing 90-per-cent. loans for a three-year period the Farm Board had in mind two objectives. It felt that so large an advance, and the temporary withholding of so large a quantity of cotton, would strengthen the price structure in the South and encourage cotton growers to market the crop in an orderly manner over the season. Further, it thought that these operations would strengthen and expand the co-operative marketing movement in the South. One result of these operations was temporarily and in part to convert the co-operatives, in effect, from marketing organizations into cotton-holding organizations.

By the end of the fiscal year, June 30, 1931, the co-operative association's holdings, spots and futures represented 2,073,178 bales of cotton. Added to the stabilization stocks of 1,310,789 bales, a total of 3,383,967 bales were being held from the market with the aid of loans from the revolving fund (see Figure 3 and Table II.).

In the handling of the 1930 crop the cotton co-operatives borrowed from the Farm Board 64,435,398.65 dollars, and by June 30, 1931, had repaid 25,680,013.10 dollars. Other loans to the cotton co-operatives amounted to 6,095,553.74 dollars, leaving a total of 44,850,939.29 dollars owing the revolving fund on the date given.

Further Withholding of Stocks

The fiscal year 1931-1932 was one of withholding from the market the cotton stocks on hand. The Stabilization Corporation purchased no more cotton, and the co-operative associations did not add to the stocks of unhedged cotton already on hand. The extraordinarily large crop of 1931, the excessive carry-over, and the heavy early marketings combined to force cotton prices to new low levels. To meet this situation the Farm Board and the Southern bankers entered into an agreement, announced October 12, 1931, to withhold from the market until the end of the season all cotton financed by them. The Southern banks agreed to finance through new loans or renewals not less than 3,500,000 bales. The Farm Board, on its part, agreed to maintain intact the stabilization holdings of 1,300,000 bales, and to continue to finance the 2,100,000 bales held by the American Cotton Co-operative

Association and the Staple Cotton Co-operative Association until July 31, 1932, unless cotton prices should rise above 12½ cents.

FIGURE 3.—COTTON WITHHELD FROM SALE BY CO-OPERATIVE ASSOCIATIONS AND THE COTTON STABILIZATION CORPORATION, MONTHLY, FROM JULY 1929 TO APRIL 1933 [1]

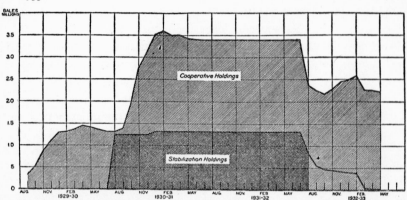

The announcement of this agreement was followed by an immediate small improvement in cotton prices, all or a part of which was retained until the following June.

By November 23 the bankers' committee had received pledges covering 3,100,000 bales, and the Farm Board stated that it would proceed to carry out its part of the agreement.

The removal of so large a quantity of cotton from the market for the season tended to relieve the pressure of the combined record accumulations of stocks and a near-record current crop.

The Farm Board assisted the co-operatives to finance the marketing of the 1931 crop through loans to the American Cotton Co-operative Association. But this was done in a manner to ensure that all of the cotton received from that crop would be disposed of by the end of that season. Therefore, no additions were made to stocks being withheld from the market by the means of loans from the Farm Board.

Liquidation

The fiscal year 1931-1932 marked the end of the holding period for stabilization cotton stocks. Looking to the early liquidation of these

[1] The stocks of unsold cotton which the co-operative associations and the Stabilization Corporation held on June 30, 1931, were continued without significant change until June 1932, after which disposal began. The drastic drop in the Stabilization Corporation's stocks during July and August was due principally to donations to the Red Cross by direction of Congress (*Courtesy of Farm Board*).

accumulations, the Farm Board announced on May 2, 1932, that the Stabilization Corporation would be authorized to sell not more than 650,000 bales of its holdings during the year commencing August 1. It was stated that these sales of half of the Stabilization Corporation's stocks would be distributed throughout the season in order to minimize the effect on markets and prices. This program was in accordance with recommendations of the Cotton Advisory Committee.

In July 1932, Congress directed that the Farm Board make 500,000 bales of stabilization cotton available to the American Red Cross as needed for use by the needy. No provision was made to reimburse the revolving fund for the Board's equity in the cotton. The donation plus the 650,000 bales to be sold during the season accounted for 88 per cent. of the cotton held by the Stabilization Corporation. Further action by Congress brought the total stabilization cotton donated to the Red Cross for distribution to the needy to 844,063 bales.

At the close of the crop year, July 31, 1932, the Cotton Stabilization Corporation held 1,308,732 bales of cotton. Loans secured on this cotton totalled 124,051,298.40 dollars, of which 102,042,735.70 dollars was from the Farm Board, the balance being financed from banks. Other net liabilities of the Stabilization Corporation amounted to 3,524,091.34 dollars. The total liabilities exceeded the current market value of the cotton by 85,051,477.73.

On the same date the co-operatives withheld from sale 1,825,202 bales of 1929 and 1930 cotton, spots and futures, against which loans from the Farm Board amounting to 70,433,346.23 dollars were outstanding. The total investments in this co-operative cotton, from all sources, equalled 120,959,319.40 dollars, which exceeded the then market value by 62,934,211.81 dollars.

The disposal of stabilization cotton in accordance with the announced schedule was begun in August 1932. Cotton prices then rose markedly, though later this improvement proved to be temporary. To help maintain the higher prices and to lessen the competition with the new crop, arrangements were made with the Reconstruction Finance Corporation partially to re-finance the cotton holdings until March 1933. Under this arrangement the Farm Board announced on September 5 [1] that of the 650,000 bales to be marketed by the Cotton Stabilization Corporation more than 300,000 bales had already been sold; and that the remainder would be withdrawn from sale until March 1, with the exception of some small amounts then on consignment abroad and any

[1] Farm Board *Press Service*, No. 3-39, September 5, 1932.

cotton that might be sold for not less than 12 cents per pound. The announcement further stated that the American Cotton Co-operative Association would maintain its existing stocks of 1930 cotton until July 31, 1933, with exceptions similar to those just stated.

On March 21, 1933, it was announced [1] that the Red Cross still owned 548,643 bales of spot cotton, and that on October 31 it would take over and sell the undelivered balance of all cotton donated to it. It was also stated that the Cotton Stabilization Corporation as of February 28 owned 28,875 bales of spot cotton, of which all but 450 bales were on foreign consignment to be disposed of immediately. As of February 28, 1933, the Cotton Stabilization Corporation owed the Farm Board 97,530,235.40 dollars; and it was estimated that upon liquidation of the Corporation 94 million dollars would remain unpaid. This would represent the final loss to the Board's revolving fund from the Corporation's operations. This does not, however, allow any credits for the 844,063 bales donated by Congress to the Red Cross. The primary loans, from banks, against this cotton had been paid from Board funds.[2]

On March 21 the Chairman of the Farm Board stated to the Press that he " will certainly recommend the abolition of section 9 of the Agricultural Marketing Act," [3] which would mean the end of Farm Board Stabilization operations in all commodities.

The President and General Manager of the Cotton Stabilization Corporation announced to the Press on May 16 the acceptance of bids on all but 2800 bales of the Corporation's cotton, stating that disposal of the latter would end the work of the Stabilization Corporation.

The Board also stated on March 21, 1933, that the American Cotton Co-operative Association held 1,352,619 bales of cotton of the 1930-1931 season, against which there was due the Farm Board a net balance from that season's operations of 60,424,979.72 dollars as of February 28, 1933. It was estimated that upon liquidation the indicated deficit to the Board would be about 57 million dollars.

On the same date the Staple Cotton Co-operative Association held 214,800 bales from the 1930-1931 season, against outstanding net loans of 7,776,549.55 dollars chargeable thereto. Upon liquidation the estimated deficit would be 5,576,606.41 dollars. Liquidation of the amount due from the 1929-1930 operations would add a further deficit of 2,677,743.66 dollars to the unpaid balance due the Farm Board.

[1] Farm Board *Press Service*, No. 3-54, March 22, 1933.

[2] Also, the Stabilization Corporation did not have a salary roll, its work being performed by employees of the American Cotton Co-operative Association.

[3] Farm Board *Press Service*, March 23, 1933, p. 8.

The estimated losses to the Farm Board funds from these three groups of cotton stabilization operations would total, therefore, about 129 million dollars, without allowing credit for the 844,063 bales donated to the Red Cross.

Summary

The developments of the cotton stabilization operations beginning with their inception to May 1, 1933, by which date the liquidation of

FIGURE 4.—PRODUCTION, WORLD CONSUMPTION, CARRY-OVER AND PRICE OF AMERICAN COTTON [1]

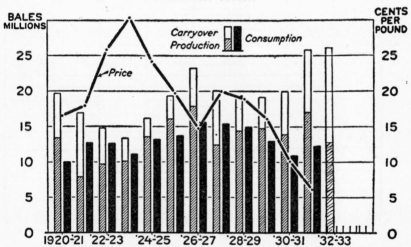

the strictly stabilization stocks had been completed, are shown in Figure 3. This chart shows separately and for each month the unhedged holdings of the Stabilization Corporation, and the similar combined holdings of the American Cotton Co-operative Association and the Staple Cotton Co-operative Association.

The development of the supply situation for American cotton since 1920 is shown in Figure 4. Since 1926-1927 production has not been unusually large, with the exception of the near-record crop of 1931-1932. On the other hand, the total world consumption of American cotton declined steadily during the five seasons ending with 1930-1931. In 1931-1932 there was some improvement over the low level of the previous season, but consumption was still below that of the preceding

[1] When cotton production was low in comparison with consumption, carry-over dropped, cotton prices advanced, as from 1921 to 1924. When production was high and consumption low, carry-over increased and prices declined, as from 1929 to 1932. The supply for 1932 to 1933 was the largest on record (*Courtesy of Farm Board*).

H

four years. During each of the three past seasons consumption has run substantially below production, resulting in the piling up of record carry-overs, the weight of which has been the major factor contributing to the prolonged and drastic decline in cotton prices. The reduction in consumption was, in turn, due primarily to the business depression. Cotton goes to a large extent into industrial uses; and its consumption, therefore, is closely linked with the business situation.

FIGURE 5.—CONSUMPTION OF AMERICAN COTTON, MONTHLY SEASONAL RATE [1]

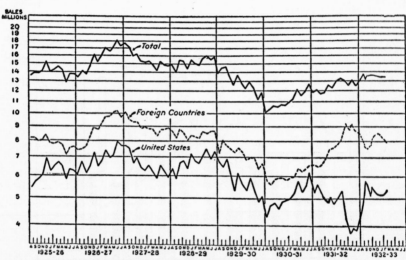

The changes in cotton consumption, both here and abroad, are shown by months in Figure 5. During the 1931-1932 season consumption of American cotton abroad increased markedly, due to short crops in India and China, and aided by the remarkable rise of the cotton textile industry in Japan.

Japan, as a consumer of cotton, has risen during the past few seasons to the point where she is now the largest purchaser of American cotton. During 1931-1932 Japan imported 2,396,000 bales of American cotton, or 26·6 per cent. of our total exports of cotton to all countries that year. This was slightly more than double the amount of Japan's average takings of American cotton over the preceding four years. Not only have

---

[1] World consumption of American cotton has tended steadily upward from a low seasonal rate of about 10 million bales in August 1930 to a rate of about 13 million bales in the spring of 1932. Consumption abroad has gradually worked higher since the fall of 1930, while in the United States the severity of the business depression forced consumption downward during the season 1931-1932 (*Courtesy of Farm Board*).

Japan's total cotton imports increased rapidly in recent years, but an increasing proportion of these imports has been supplied from this country. In 1931-1932 two-thirds of Japan's imports of 3,628,000 bales were of American cotton, compared with an average of 44·5 per cent. during the previous four seasons. India and China are Japan's other principal sources of cotton supplies.

In the face of the continuous accumulation of cotton stocks to such huge figures, it was not to be expected that stabilization operations could do more than soften the price decline. During the three years that the Farm Board financed the withholding of about 3,500,000 bales from the market, lessened consumption resulted in the addition to the supplies of approximately 10 million bales. This was nearly three times as much as the limited resources available from the revolving fund could handle. Nevertheless, it is felt by those associated with the stabilization operations that the actions taken did check the price declines temporarily, and resulted in materially better returns to the growers than they would otherwise have received.

Cotton offers no such fairly definite or tangible means of estimating the benefits probably derived by the growers from the stabilization operations as was the case with wheat. The President of the Cotton Stabilization Corporation has stated that in his opinion the 16-cent loans on cotton, commencing October 31, 1929, sustained the market to the extent of 4 cents per pound during the remainder of that marketing season, resulting in higher prices to that extent on 6 million bales marketed by both non-members and members of the co-operatives. This would amount to about 120 million dollars. He also believes that the 1930-1931 operations sustained the market on the 13,250,000 bales produced that year by from $1\frac{1}{2}$ to 3 cents per pound, or a saving to all cotton growers of about 132,500,000 dollars. It was conceded, however, that these sustainings of prices to some extent acted as deterrents to the acreage reductions, and to that extent added to later surpluses.[1] These views are commonly shared by those associated with the co-operatives. But it is only an opinion, not susceptible of definite proof or disproof. It is violently disputed by many persons in the cotton trade not favourably disposed toward the co-operatives or to the stabilization undertakings.

To influence the price of cotton by any form of stabilization

[1] *Hearings before the Committee on Agriculture and Forestry, U.S. Senate, 62nd Congress, 1st Session, November 24-28, 1931,* pp. 309-311. See also Farm Board *Press Service,* March 23, 1933, pp. 2-3.

operations is inherently a more difficult undertaking than is presented by such operations relating to wheat. In this connection it must be borne in mind that ordinarily approximately one-half of the cotton production is annually exported, whereas only about a fifth or a sixth of the wheat crop must be marketed abroad. On the other hand, our exports of cotton constitute a far larger proportion of the international trade in the commodity than do our exports of wheat. The withholding of a substantial proportion of the cotton supply destined for export might, therefore, have a much greater influence on world prices than would similar withholdings of wheat.

CONCLUSIONS

In reviewing the stabilization undertakings of the Federal Farm Board, it is now quite clear that coming, as they did, at the outset of so drastic and prolonged a business depression they could not but be foredoomed to failure in the major objectives. Undertaken under the conditions and the manner that they were, the only possibility of avoiding heavy final losses to the revolving fund lay in limitating operations very strictly, since carrying charges, particularly in the case of so bulky a product as wheat, would have rendered the avoidance of large eventual losses all but an impossibility. Such large accumulations, inevitably carried " in the show-window " of visible supplies, are always a depressing factor on prices, no matter how skilfully handled.

The Board clearly foresaw this, as already discussed. But the Board, at the outset and through the entire period of accumulation, was under tremendous and widespread pressure, alike from producers, members of Congress, and many elements in the trade, to make use of the stabilization machinery provided in the Agricultural Marketing Act. The Board was constantly urged to extend these operations to even larger proportions than was done. Had the Board not used this machinery put at its disposal it would have been as severely condemned by many of these same elements as it was later criticized for the actions taken. Once the operations were launched, it is difficult to see how they could have been withdrawn in a markedly different manner or with widely different final results. The proportions of the wheat and cotton surplus crops and supplies, extended over a period of years such as these, are quite beyond the capacity of a fund of even 500 million dollars.

The principal mistake of the Board, if it may be called such, was in not foreseeing a depression such as developed. But it could hardly be blamed for this, in the light of the experiences and losses subsequently sustained by every line of business in the country. The real errors of judgment by the Board were in making the initial loans on the commodities up to the high stated values, and later loans on such high percentages of the current prices. Ninety-per-cent. loans are always hazardous, and at the beginning of a price decline they can hardly be other than fatal. It should be remembered, too, that most of these commodity advances were supplemental to primary loans from banks. These marginal loans by the Board were, therefore, extra-hazardous. They involved risks which banks would not assume even in more normal times than these.

Finally, the conclusion is inescapable that the impelling motive in the setting up of the stabilization corporation was to save the co-operative associations from the insolvency which they faced as a result of the high-basis loans or advances to their members. The forced liquidation of these associations, had the stabilization corporations not taken over many of their obligations, would have been disastrous to the whole program which the Farm Board had before it. Such liquidations would have meant a severe set-back to the whole agricultural co-operative marketing movement which the Farm Board was created to foster. In view of the later development, and the present financial status of many of these associations, it may well be questioned whether the associations were, or will be, in the end aided by the stabilization efforts.

In summary, the principal conclusion derived by the Farm Board from its stabilization operations may well be cited: " The Board recognizes that there are rigorous limits as to what can be accomplished by stabilization operations. Successful stabilization means keeping prices from going unduly low in periods of large supplies or poor demand. It also means keeping prices from becoming unduly high during periods of short supplies or of inflation. Prices cannot be kept artificially high over long periods by such methods. The experience . . . shows it is futile to engage in stabilization purchases for any product over a period of years in the face of a constantly accumulating surplus of that product.

" Stabilization involves selling as well as buying; producers must face this fact. Many people have thought ' stabilization ' means to hold the price permanently higher than it would otherwise be. This cannot be done without control of production. The experience of the Board shows that with the existing organizations and legislation it is not yet possible to control agricultural production . . . so long as farmers do not make the necessary readjustments, emergency stabilization measures can give only temporary relief.

" The very act of purchasing supplies and maintaining prices in surplus years tends to encourage farmers to continue production, and so to prevent the deficit years, in which the supplies could be sold without loss, from ever arriving. In the long run stabilization thus tends to perpetuate the very situation it is aimed to relieve." [1]

TABLE I.—STABILIZATION WHEAT

(In millions of bushels)   (Total quantities)

	Wheat owned by Stabiliza- tion Corporation	Holdings end of month	Sold but not delivered		Wheat owned by Stabiliza- tion Corporation	Holdings end of month	Sold but not delivered
1930				**1932**			
January .	0	..	..	January .	185	208	23
February	15	..	..	February	183	201	18
March .	50	..	..	March .	138	189	51
April .	38	..	..	April .	129	166	37
May .	38	..	..	May .	120	150	30
June .	58	..	..	June .	108	132	24
July .	65	..	..	July .	56	121	65
August .	67	..	..	August .	42	101	59
September	80	..	..	September	41	96	55
October .	100	..	..	October .	41	91	50
November	108	..	..	November	41	79	38
December	199	..	..	December	41	73	32
1931				**1933**			
January .	219	..	..	January .	41	64	23
February	240	..	..	February	32	49	17
March .	206	..	..	March .	12	21	9
April .	254	..	..	April .	0	5	5
May .	252	..	..	May .	..	..	..
June .	257	257	0	..	..	..	..
July .	205	252	47	..	..	..	..
August .	200	247	47	..	..	..	..
September	196	241	45	..	..	..	..
October .	190	231	41	..	..	..	..
November	188	222	34	..	..	..	..
December	187	215	38	..	..	..	..

[1] *Third Annual Report*, pp. 61-62.

TABLE II.—COTTON HELD BY CO-OPERATIVES AND STABILIZATION CORPORATION

(In thousands of bales)

Date	Co-operative combined holdings	Stabilization Corporation holdings	Total holdings
1929—			
Aug. 31	333	..	333
Sept. 30	521	..	521
Oct. 31	866	..	866
Nov. 30	1108	..	1108
Dec. 31	1295	..	1295
1930—			
Jan. 31	1315	..	1315
Feb. 28	1367	..	1367
Mar. 31	1451	..	1451
Apr. 30	1412	..	1412
May 31	1365	..	1365
June 30	1319	..	1319
July 31	70	1242	1312
Aug. 31	144	1242	1386
Sept. 30	689	1242	1931
Oct. 31	1524	1242	2766
Nov. 30	1880	1242	3122
Dec. 31	2198	1321	3519
1931—			
Jan. 31	2271	1321	3592
Feb. 28	2172	1321	3493
Mar. 31	2184	1321	3505
Apr. 30	2105	1321	3426
May 31	2082	1321	3403
June 30	2074	1321	3395
July 31	2072	1321	3393
Aug. 31	2072	1321	3393
Sept. 30	2069	1321	3390
Oct. 31	2069	1321	3390
Nov. 30	2069	1321	3390
Dec. 31	2068	1321	3389
1932			
Jan. 31	2068	1321	3389
Feb. 29	2066	1321	3397
Mar. 31	2067	1321	3388
Apr. 30	2067	1321	3388
May 31	2065	1321	3386
June 30	2057	1321	3378
July 31	1571	808	2379
Aug. 31.	1707	541	2248
Sept. 30	1692	475	2167
Oct. 31	1843	443	2286
Nov. 30	2006	424	2430
Dec. 31	2082	400	2482
1933—			
Jan. 31	2181	398	2579
Feb. 28	2231	28	2259
Mar. 31	2229	26	2255
Apr. 30	2182	24	2206

TABLE III.—PRODUCTION, WORLD CONSUMPTION, AND CARRY-OVER PRICE
OF AMERICAN COTTON

Season	Production in the United States (1000 478-pound bales)	World carry-over beginning of season (1000 running bales)	Total supply (1000 mixed bales)	World consumption (1000 running bales)	Season average spot price at New Orleans (cents per pound)
1920–1921 .	13,440	6,338*	19,778	10,030	16·55
1921–1922 .	7,954	9,179	17,133	12,757	17·92
1922–1923 .	9,761	5,130	14,892	12,666	25·94
1923–1924 .	10,140	3,284	13,424	11,107	30·33
1924–1925 .	13,628	2,664	16,292	13,256	24·21
1925–1926 .	16,104	3,306	19,410	13,730	19·71
1926–1927 .	17,977	5,357	23,334	15,780	14·74
1927–1928 .	12,956	7,845*	20,801	15,407	19·98
1928–1929 .	14,478	5,079	19,557	15,076	18·98
1929–1930 .	14,828	4,460	19,288	13,023	16·16
1930–1931 .	13,932	6,243	20,175	10,907	10·08
1931–1932 .	17,096	8,838	25,934	12,319	6·20
1932–1933† .	12,994	13,228	26,222	..	..

Source: United States Department of Agriculture, Bureau of Agricultural
Economics. For supporting data for Figure 4 see *Third Annual Report* of Federal
Farm Board, p. 78.

* New York Cotton Exchange estimate.
† Preliminary.

NOTE.—It will be noted that consumption cannot be subtracted from supply to
arrive at the carry-over for the beginning of the next season; this is due to the fact
that consumption is counted in running bales while production is in statistical
478-pound bales, and also due to the fact that the consumption as recorded is usually
too low, due to the non-inclusion abroad of use outside cotton mills.

(Monthly seasonal rate in thousands of running bales)

Season	Aug.	Sept.	Oct.	Nov.	Dec.	Jan.	Feb.	Mar.	Apr.	May	June	July
In the United States												
1925–1926	5,424	5,677	5,864	6,055	6,882	6,217	6,468	6,678	6,472	5,810	6,291	6,234
1926–1927	6,043	6,720	6,124	6,482	7,217	6,473	6,766	7,351	6,928	7,066	7,924	7,646
1927–1928	7,649	7,466	6,633	6,920	6,385	6,239	6,516	6,159	5,853	6,514	6,190	5,924
1928–1929	6,334	5,851	6,655	6,782	6,348	7,143	6,778	6,667	7,068	7,488	6,899	7,306
1929–1930	6,700	6,460	6,881	5,952	5,329	6,116	5,609	5,331	5,888	5,282	4,861	5,078
1930–1931	4,286	4,708	4,813	4,614	4,832	4,877	5,000	5,323	5,748	5,293	5,557	6,178
1931–1932	5,247	5,602	5,107	4,821	5,043	4,755	5,016	5,265	4,182	3,778	3,949	3,808
1932–1933	4,968	5,975	5,537	5,675	5,354	5,167	5,179	5,342	5,386	...	...	...
In Foreign Countries												
1925–1926	8,133	8,127	7,961	8,022	8,365	7,812	7,774	7,874	7,706	7,067	7,500	7,591
1926–1927	7,356	7,422	7,599	8,124	8,874	8,753	9,266	9,655	9,738	10,085	10,188	9,689
1927–1928	10,088	9,595	9,309	9,258	8,863	8,953	8,831	8,800	8,329	8,764	8,756	8,873
1928–1929	8,622	8,173	8,805	8,506	8,057	8,353	8,271	8,183	8,616	8,497	8,656	8,653
1929–1930	7,243	8,058	7,719	7,472	7,251	7,553	7,226	6,841	6,982	6,994	6,382	6,645
1930–1931	5,764	5,630	5,866	5,944	5,936	5,823	5,958	5,998	6,384	6,218	6,382	6,554
1931–1932	6,579	6,473	6,601	6,977	7,476	7,565	7,786	7,981	8,903	8,424	9,158	8,627
1932–1933	8,283	7,734	7,697	7,809	8,305	8,435	8,197	8,076	8,316	...	...	...
In the World												
1925–1926	13,560	13,842	13,833	14,080	15,236	14,034	14,249	14,575	14,189	12,879	13,778	13,799
1926–1927	13,396	14,117	13,722	14,602	16,082	15,218	16,020	17,000	16,634	17,133	18,098	17,315
1927–1928	17,736	17,076	15,956	16,182	15,260	15,172	15,336	14,931	14,153	15,269	14,937	14,832
1928–1929	14,956	14,057	15,467	15,284	14,401	15,517	15,055	14,862	15,690	15,998	15,542	15,919
1929–1930	13,937	14,523	14,589	13,420	12,588	13,078	12,833	12,172	12,881	12,270	11,234	11,785
1930–1931	10,050	10,334	10,678	10,557	10,762	10,712	10,965	11,253	12,154	11,517	11,927	12,676
1931–1932	11,824	12,064	11,711	11,806	12,551	12,287	13,019	13,207	12,978	12,150	13,123	12,564
1932–1933	13,258	13,723	13,244	13,489	13,688	13,563	13,345	13,483	13,656	...	...	...

Source: Bureau of the Census and New York Cotton Exchange Service.

APPENDIX

PROVISIONS OF THE AGRICULTURAL MARKETING ACT PERTAINING TO
STABILIZATION OPERATIONS BY THE FEDERAL FARM BOARD

Section 1. (*a*) That it is hereby declared to be the policy of Congress to promote the effective merchandizing of agricultural products in interstate and foreign commerce. . . .

(4) By aiding in preventing and controlling surpluses in any agricultural commodity, through orderly production and distribution, so as to maintain advantageous domestic markets and prevent such surpluses from causing undue and excessive fluctuations or depressions in prices for the commodity.

(*b*) There shall be considered as a surplus for the purposes of this Act any seasonal or year's total surplus, produced in the United States and either local or national in extent, that is in excess of the requirements for the orderly distribution of the agricultural commodity or is in excess of the domestic requirements for such commodity.

Section 3. (*b*) The Board shall invite the co-operative association handling any agricultural commodity to establish an advisory commodity committee to consist of seven members, of whom at least two shall be experienced handlers or processors of the commodity, to represent such commodity before the Board in matters relating to the commodity. Members of each advisory committee shall be selected by the co-operative associations from time to time in such manner as the Board shall prescribe. . . . Each advisory committee shall be designated by the name of the commodity it represents, as for example, the "Cotton Advisory Committee."

Section 5. The Board is authorized and directed . . .

(4) To investigate conditions of over-production of agricultural commodities and advise as to the prevention of such over-production.

Section 9. (*a*) The Board may, upon application of the advisory commodity committee for any commodity, recognize as a stabilization corporation for the commodity any corporation if—

(1) The Board finds that the marketing situation with respect to the agricultural commodity requires or may require the establishment of a stabilization corporation in order effectively to carry out the policy declared in Section 1; and

(2) The Board finds that the corporation is duly organized under the laws of a State or Territory; and

(3) The Board finds that all the outstanding voting stock or membership interests in the corporation are and may be owned only by the co-operative association handling the commodity; and

(4) The corporation agrees with the Board to adopt such by-laws as the Board may from time to time require, which by-laws, among other matters, shall permit co-operative associations not stockholders or members of the corporation to become stockholders or members therein upon equitable terms.

(*b*) Any stabilization corporation for an agricultural commodity (1) may act as a marketing agency for its stockholders or members in preparing, handling, storing, processing, and merchandizing for their account any quantity of the agricultural commodity or its food products, and (2) for the purpose of controlling any surplus in the commodity in furtherance of the policy declared in Section 1, may prepare, purchase, handle, store, process, and merchandize, otherwise than for the account of its stockholders or members, any quantity of the agricultural commodity or its food products whether or not such commodity or products are acquired from its stockholders or members.

(c) Upon request of the advisory committee for any commodity the Board is authorized to make loans from the revolving fund to the stabilization corporation for the commodity for working capital to enable the corporation to act as a marketing agency for its stockholders or members as hereinbefore provided. Not less than 75 per centum of all profits derived by a stabilization corporation each year from its operations as such a marketing agency shall be paid into a merchandizing reserve fund to be established by the corporation. No such payment shall be required whenever the fund is in such amount as, in the judgment of the Board, constitutes a sufficient reserve for such operations of the corporation. Out of the remainder of such profits for the year the corporation shall repay any outstanding loan made under this subdivision and the accrued interest thereon, or if all such loans and accrued interest have been fully repaid, then it may distribute a patronage dividend to its stockholders or members. Such patronage dividend shall be paid to each stockholder or member on the basis of the total volume of the commodity or its products for the year marketed for his account through the corporation.

(d) Upon request of the advisory committee for any commodity the Board is authorized to make loans from the revolving fund to the stabilization corporation for the commodity to enable the corporation to control any surplus in the commodity as hereinbefore provided and for meeting, carrying and handling charges and other operating expenses in connection therewith. The Board shall require a stabilization corporation to establish and maintain adequate reserves from its profits from its surplus control operations before it shall pay any dividends out of such profits. All losses of the corporation from such operations shall be paid from such reserves, or if such reserves are inadequate, then such losses shall be paid by the Board as a loan from the revolving fund. Any amounts so loaned for payment of losses shall be repaid into the revolving fund by the corporation from future profits from its surplus control operations. Any stabilization corporation receiving loans under this subdivision for surplus control operations shall exert every reasonable effort to avoid losses and to secure profits, but shall not withhold any commodity from the domestic market if the prices have become unduly enhanced, resulting in distress to domestic consumers. Stockholders or members of the corporation shall not be subject to assessment for any losses incurred in surplus control operations of the corporation.

(e) A stabilization corporation shall keep such accounts, records and memoranda, and make such reports with respect to its transactions, business methods and financial condition, as the Board may from time to time prescribe; shall permit the Board to audit its accounts annually and at such other times as the

Board deems advisable; and shall permit the Board, upon its own initiative, or upon written request of any stockholder or member, to investigate the financial condition and business methods of the corporation.

(*f*) No loan shall be made to any stabilization corporation unless, in the judgment of the Board, the loan is in furtherance of the policy declared in Section 1.

CHAPTER III

THE CANADIAN WHEAT POOL IN PROSPERITY AND DEPRESSION

by Harold S. Patton

GENESIS OF THE CANADIAN WHEAT POOL

THE Canadian Wheat Pool System which came into existence in 1924 was the outcome of four convergent movements or situations. These were: first, the progressive experiences in co-operative grain marketing acquired by the prairie farmers' grain and elevator companies during the preceding decade and a half; second, the persistent desire of Western wheat growers for restoration of the system of compulsory pool marketing as conducted under the federally created Canadian Wheat Board in 1919-1920; third, the disastrous decline in world wheat prices between 1920 and 1923; and fourth, the post-war development in the United States of the contract pool method of marketing farm commodities.

The way of entry into large-scale pool merchandizing had been paved by a long and successful experience in co-operative grain marketing, dating from the appearance in 1906 of the puny but belligerent Grain Growers' Grain Company as a farmers' commission agency upon the Winnipeg Grain Exchange. Within half-a-dozen years this upstart farmers' company had taken over the bankrupt country elevator system of the Manitoba Government, and placed it on a paying basis. In 1917 it amalgamated with the Alberta Farmers' Co-operative Elevator Company to form the United Grain Growers, Limited. In the meantime, by special Act of the Saskatchewan Legislature in 1911, the Saskatchewan Co-operative Elevator Company had entered the field as a centralized, province-wide organization, in which the stock was subscribed by farmers, and 85 per cent. of the cost of elevator construction advanced by the provincial government through twenty-year mortgage loans. At the close of the World War the United Grain Growers and the Saskatchewan Co-operative Elevator Company had become the two largest companies operating on the Winnipeg Grain Exchange. Between them they handled annually 20 to 25 per cent. of

---

[1] For early history of these co-operative companies see H. S. Patton, *Grain Growers' Co-operation in Western Canada*, Harvard Economic Studies, vol. xxxii., chaps. iv.-viii.

all the grain marketed in Western Canada. Together they maintained country elevators at one out of every two grain shipping stations in the prairies, and owned or leased nearly 40 per cent. of the terminal elevator capacity at the Head of the Lakes, while each operated important export subsidiaries. Through these companies, prairie farmers not only gained a knowledge of the technique of grain marketing, but also acquired confidence in their capacity to compete successfully with the regular trade. Although the co-operative companies succeeded in eliminating many of the former abuses of the grain trade, and although their earning record permitted the accumulation of large surpluses and the payment of substantial stock as well as cash dividends to their 63,000 farmer shareholders, neither company found it practicable to carry out the co-operative principle of patronage distribution of earnings, and sporadic complaints began to arise that the companies had adapted themselves too closely to the established practices of the regular grain trade.[1]

The creation by the Federal Government, under war-time emergency powers, of the Canadian Wheat Board, as an exclusive agency for the handling of the short 1919 wheat crop on a pooling basis, had been undertaken primarily to protect consumers against speculative excesses and as a counterpart of inter-governmental wheat purchasing by the European Allies. To the Western wheat growers, however, it afforded an impressive demonstration of a method of marketing, under which future trading was suspended, internal competition was eliminated, handling margins and grade differentials were narrowed, and the grower was paid on the basis, not of current market prices at time of delivery, but of the average returns realized from the entire crop. The initial payments plus the liquidated value of growers' participation certificates were equivalent to 2.65 dollars per bushel, basis No. 1 Northern at Lakehead position. When, therefore, the decision of the Dominion Government not to continue the Wheat Board operations was accompanied by a price debacle on the reopened grain futures markets that carried No. 1 Northern below 1.50 dollars, as the crop began to move, it was not surprising that the Western grain growers' organizations should have united in strenuous demands for a re-established Wheat Board.

The agitation was continued throughout the period of deflated grain prices (1921-1923), but when, despite federal enabling legislation for

---

[1] *Op. cit.*, chaps. xiii. and xviii.

the establishment of provincial wheat boards, it was found impossible to set these up on an effective basis, the grain growers' organizations turned to the alternative of voluntary contract pools.[1] This system was at that time at the height of its favour in the United States, under the dynamic advocacy of Aaron Sapiro, of California, who was brought into Alberta and Saskatchewan in the summer of 1923.

Sponsored by the provincial farmers' associations, and aided by organizational loans from the provincial governments and co-operative elevator companies, wheat pool contract " sign-up " campaigns were conducted as a veritable crusade in the three Prairie Provinces. The Alberta Pool was the first to get under way, in the late fall of 1923, followed the next season by the inauguration of the Saskatchewan and Manitoba Pools, and by the co-ordination of the three through an inter-provincial selling agency, incorporated as the Canadian Co-operative Wheat Producers, Limited. The fortunate conjuncture of a marked rise in world wheat prices in the short-crop year of 1924-1925 gave a great impetus to the movement, and by the end of the second year approximately three out of every five wheat growers between the Lake of the Woods and the Rockies had signed five-year pool contracts.

THE POOL ELEVATOR SYSTEM

At the outset the provincial pools were dependent on contracts with the private and co-operative line elevator companies for the physical receiving, storage and forwarding of the wheat delivered by their members. The growers' contracts contained provision, however, for maximum deductions of two cents per bushel from each member's final returns for elevator reserve purposes (as well as 1 per cent. of gross sales for commercial reserve). Beginning with Saskatchewan in 1925 each of the pools decided to apply this provision with a view to acquiring elevator facilities of its own. It was felt that this would ensure more economical, expeditious and more directly controlled movement of pool grain from point of members' delivery to terminal position, and that pool elevator managers would function as permanent contact agents between pool headquarters and locals at country shipping points. Negotiations were entered into between the three pools and the two established farmers' co-operative companies for the acquisition of the facilities of the latter by the former. The United Grain Growers, Ltd.,

---

[1] For discussion of events of this period see *op. cit.*, chap. xiii.

which operated some 380 country elevators throughout the three Prairie Provinces, finally voted to reject a joint offer of purchase from the three pools, mainly on the ground that it was desirable to preserve the company's facilities for the use of farmers who did not choose to sign pool contracts as well as for pool members. The company undertook, however, to continue to handle pool grain at special rates.

In Saskatchewan, where the majority of stockholders in the Saskatchewan Co-operative Elevator Company had become pool members, the company voted in August 1926 to sell its entire assets to the Saskatchewan Pool, at a price subsequently fixed by arbitration at 11,061,269.[1] This transaction, which at a stroke added 451 country elevators and three large modern terminal elevators to the Saskatchewan Pool Elevators, Ltd., represented a victory of the principle of making capital investment in handling facilities subsidiary to contract control of the commodity itself. By purchase, lease, or new construction the three pool organizations had by 1929 acquired 1642 country elevators, approximately one-third of all those in the Prairie Provinces. As the total number of elevator stations in these provinces is under 1800, there are thus comparatively few shipping points where a pool elevator does not exist. In addition to their country systems the three pools own or lease seven modern terminal elevators at the Head of the Lakes, and four on the Pacific Coast, with a combined capacity of over 36 million bushels, or more than a third of the total terminal storage on the eastern and western fronts of the Canadian grain belt.

The capital financing of this, the world's largest elevator system, which was built up during a period of five years, was accomplished without any selling of securities and without any Government loans. The funds were obtained entirely from the annual deductions from growers' returns, on elevator and commercial reserve accounts, which by 1929 had reached a cumulative total of nearly 29 million dollars. Each member received certificates to the amount of his deductions, with interest, generally at 6 per cent., paid or credited on his elevator reserve fund. His individual equity in pool capital assets was thus directly proportionate to the extent of his grain deliveries to the pool. Operating under the double advantage of assured patronage and of centralized and integrated management, the pool elevator subsidiaries

---

[1] A 2-million-dollars cash payment was made at the time of purchase by the Saskatchewan Pool, which assumed outstanding mortgage obligations of 2,091,565 dollars owed by the company to the Saskatchewan Government. The remaining 6,969,704 dollars of the purchase price was payable to the liquidators of the company in seven annual instalments.

were able not only to reduce handling charges and street grain spreads, but also to realize excess earnings which permitted patronage distributions in cash or credits to members of over 6 million dollars between 1925 and 1929. The development of the pool elevator systems up to 1929 is summarized in the following Table:

TABLE I.—STATISTICS OF THE POOL ELEVATOR SYSTEM, 1925-1929

Pool	Elevator Reserves, cumulative totals, 1928-1929	Commercial Reserves, cumulative totals, 1928-1929	No. of country elevators, 1929	No. of terminal elevators, 1929	Rebated excess elevator earnings, 1925-1929
Manitoba	$1,897,333	$932,860	155	3	$427,977
Saskatchewan	12,195,488	6,572,706	1048	6	4,268,934
Alberta	4,496,680	2,436,511	439	3	1,470,214
Three Pools	$19,039,503	$9,942,077	1642	12	$6,164,125

Source: *Canadian Wheat Pool Yearbook*, 1930.

THE POOL MOVEMENT AT ITS CREST

The Canadian Wheat Pool attained the peak of its prestige in 1928-1929, the fifth year of combined operation. At that time the three western organizations boasted 140,779 wheat pool contracts, and 67,532 coarse grain contracts, while the Ontario Grain Pool (formed in 1927) accounted for an additional 13,200 members. The total handlings through the Central Selling Agency for the first five years exceeded a billion bushels of grain. This represented approximately

TABLE II.—DELIVERIES OF WHEAT TO CANADIAN WHEAT POOL, 1924-1930

Crop Year	Pool Deliveries (bushels)	Total Deliveries in Western Inspection Division (bushels)	Per cent. Pool Deliveries
1924–1925	81,668,348	219,241,130	37·3
1925–1926	187,364,999	358,715,990	52·2
1926–1927	179,933,435	338,936,053	53·1
1927–1928	209,908,536	410,617,091	51·1
1928–1929	243,929,491	475,711,628	51·3
1929–1930	121,655,589	236,967,251	52·0

Source: *idem.*

I

52 per cent. of the total wheat deliveries by farmers in the Western Inspection Division. Of the record wheat crop of 1928 the Canadian Pool handled over a quarter of a billion bushels. As Canada contributed in this peak year 42 per cent. of the total international shipments of wheat, and wheat equivalent in flour, the Pool was thus responsible for fully a fifth of the greatest amount of wheat (943 million bushels) that had ever moved into international trade in a single year.

During this five-year period the Central Selling Agency distributed in cash repayments and reserve credits over a billion dollars to the provincial pools, as shown in the following Table:

TABLE III.—WHEAT POOL PAYMENTS, 1925-1929

Pool Year	Price basis (wheat) *	Amount distributed to Members †	
		Wheat	Coarse Grains
1924–1925 . . .	$1.66	$123,398,955	
1925–1926 . . .	1.45	256,943,806	
1926–1927 . . .	1.42	230,767,037	$15,946,357
1927–1928 . . .	1.42½	246,976,260	14,004,668
1928–1929 . . .	1.18½	232,175,545	21,149,660
Total		$1,090,261,603	$51,100,685

Source: *idem.*

* Basis No. 1 Northern, Fort William.
† Including reserve fund deductions.

The Pool marketing system represented co-operative uniformity and centralization on an unprecedented scale. While the contracts of each of the 150,000 or more members ran with their respective provincial Pools, no selling was undertaken by the latter. Their business was to secure members and maintain patronage, to acquire, finance and operate elevators through appropriate subsidiaries, to supervise the delivery of members' grain, to forward it to Pool terminal elevators, and to turn over the terminal storage certificates to the Central Selling Agency. The latter, in which the capital stock was jointly and equally held by the three provincial Pools, was responsible for all sales through its wheat and coarse grain divisions. It also made arrangements with banks for the financing of initial payments to growers upon delivery through Pool elevators or elevators under contract. As sales were made, the Central repaid the banks' advances, and pro-rated the additional proceeds to the respective pools, which made interim and final payments against growers' participation certificates, retaining the contractual elevator and commercial reserve deductions.

Two distinctive features of the Pool marketing system are deserving of special note. These were its methods of risk-bearing and of direct selling. Inasmuch as the pools did not buy the farmers' grain outright, but merely made an initial scheduled delivery payment, substantially below the market price, they did not undertake to hedge their receipts by making immediate sales on the futures market. The United Grain Growers and the Saskatchewan Co-operative Elevator Company had followed the regular practice of the trade in thus protecting themselves on their country purchases. Under the pool system, however, the risk of price fluctuations was spread over the entire membership. Each grower agreed to accept a deferred and undetermined final settlement, knowing that he was assured of receiving the average price realized over the pooling period. The same principle had been applied under the Canadian Wheat Board in 1919-1920, when future trading was suspended.

The second distinctive feature in pool merchandizing was the policy of establishing direct sales connections with the principal wheat-importing countries. By 1927 the Pool had twenty-seven agency connections with grain-importing houses in fifteen countries on four continents; with a branch of its own in London for the purpose of dealing directly with the great British millers' market, and of maintaining closer contacts with Continental agencies. In 1927 two Pool officers were sent to Japan and China with a view to developing export outlets in the Orient, with the result that for the crop year 1928-1929 two-thirds of Canada's trans-Pacific wheat shipments were supplied by the Alberta Pool. During this period from two-thirds to three-quarters of the total business of the Central Selling Agency represented direct sales to domestic and foreign millers and overseas importers. The considerations underlying this policy were that it would not only secure a greater volume of export business, but also enable the grower to receive a larger share of the price in final markets. Each day the head office in Winnipeg cabled its quotations to its London office and Continental agencies, and as orders were confirmed chartered the necessary ocean tonnage through its Montreal, New York and Vancouver offices. The common Argentine practice of making export shipments on consignment was strictly avoided, and in 1928-1929 the lowest Canadian standard grade, No. 4 Northern, was frequently sold in London at a premium over Rosafe, the premier Argentine wheat. Due to the huge volume of its turnover, and to the savings in brokerage fees through its seaboard and London offices, the Central Selling Agency was able to carry on its ramified operations in 1928-1929 at a unit administrative expense equivalent to only $\frac{1}{25}$th of a cent. per bushel of Pool wheat delivered.

THE CRISIS OF 1920-1930

The spectacular success of the Canadian Wheat Pool movement had, not unnaturally, engendered a defensive hostility on the part of the private grain trade abroad as well as at home, which impending developments in the international wheat situation were about to afford an egregious opportunity of converting into open attack. The establishment of the Pool's office in London and its " direct selling " policy were not regarded with favour by the British grain trade in general. To have an overseas farmers' agency in control of half of Canada's wheat supply, quoting its daily selling price directly to British buyers, was, in the eyes of the larger importers and millers, something of an interference with that keen competition among exporters to which they had been long accustomed. Thus George Broomall, writing in the London *Times* in 1927, had stated:

Before the Pools were in existence merchants were sometimes heard to say that wheat was being flung at them, but it is not so now. The Pool's aim is to feed the market.

The fact that the base prices realized by the Pool for the three crop years 1925-1926, 1926-1927 and 1927-1928 had been 1.45, 1.42 and 1.42$\frac{1}{2}$ dollars, respectively (Table III.), would appear to indicate considerable success in stabilizing returns to its members at a high level. To attribute this result, however, solely to the Pool's merchandizing policy is to give undue credit, or blame—according to the point of view—to the influence of an agency controlling less than a fifth of wheat export movement in probably the most highly competitive of world markets. The truth would appear to be that the Canadian Wheat Pool had come into existence under a favourable international conjuncture in which the gold price-level was relatively stable, in which international loans and investments were being made in unprecedented peace-time volume, in which European wheat imports attained record proportions, and in which Canada had assumed first rank as a wheat-exporting nation (see Table IV.). While the Pool had indeed endeavoured to realize the full competitive value of its holdings on world markets through " orderly merchandizing," this had not implied any undue withholding of its stocks, since the end of the 1927-1928 Pool year found the Central Selling Agency completely sold out.[1]

A different situation existed at the end of the 1928-1929 crop year. In 1928 Western Canada produced the largest wheat crop in its history —545 million bushels. This occurred in conjunction with a record world yield of 3945 million bushels (exclusive of Russia and China), an amount 464 million bushels in excess of the average production for 1924-1927. Although international wheat and flour shipments in 1928-1929 also established a record of 943 million bushels, the carry-over in the four principal exporting countries on August 1, 1929, amounted to 554 million bushels. This was 187 million more than at the corresponding date in 1928, and 313 million greater than in 1926. The unsold stocks in the hands of the Pool Selling Agency at the end of the 1928-1929 Pool year (August 31) were 48 million bushels, making it necessary to defer final payments to members.

At the opening of the 1929-1930 crop year the statistical position outwardly appeared somewhat easier, and was reflected in rising prices on the speculative markets; Winnipeg prices being carried above the 1.50 dollar mark in September. Severe drought conditions in Western Canada indicated a crop of only about one-half of the record harvest of the preceding year, while world production for 1929 was expected to be some 500 million bushels under the 1928 crop year. Under these conditions the Pool announced for 1929 deliveries the same initial basis of payment, 1 dollar a bushel, as for the 1924 to 1927 crops. In the event it was extremely unfortunate that the initial payment basis of 85 cents for the 1928 crop was not adhered to. Prices began to decline with the movement of the 1929 crop, and the New York Stock Exchange crash of October was transmitted to the grain markets, the December future falling to 1.20 dollars in Winnipeg in early November. While some recovery occurred towards the end of the year, the downward course was resumed in January 1930 and, by June, Winnipeg prices fell below the level of the Pool's initial payment.

The situation was seized on by interests unfriendly to the Pool, as

---

[1] " Our policy last year, in view of the comparatively low intrinsic value of the crop and the possibility of a high-quality crop being harvested, was to keep well sold up. Nothing happened during the year to make us alter this policy, and as a result we go into the new crop year with no carry-over " (Canadian Co-operative Wheat Producers Ltd. Directors' *Report*, 1927-1928).

well as by the " hindsight fraternity," to discredit its policies and methods. Particularly in England the Pool was blamed for its attempts to hold back supplies in the vain hope of stabilizing wheat prices. A series of lectures on " Canada and her Wheat Pool," given by Mr S. S. Gampell in October 1930, at the City of London College, was promptly reproduced and circulated in pamphlet form by the *Grain Trade News* of Winnipeg. The tenor of this " friendly criticism " may be judged by the following excerpt:

A Pool whose method of bettering the conditions of its members has been to halve their share in the world trade, pile up stocks fourfold at enormous cost for less than no return, stimulate its competitors to increase their acreage by amounts like 22 and 83 per cent., and its consumers to reduce their requirements by about 44 per cent., is clearly an authority on what constitutes short-sighted policy such as no man may controvert.

To ascribe such momentous international consequences to a single co-operative marketing agency, which entered the 1928-1929 crop year with no carry-over whatever, is to reveal a complete lack of proportion and economic understanding. The truth is the Canadian Wheat Pool, like all other competing wheat exporters, was the victim of circumstances beyond its own creation or control. The wheat price debacle of 1929-1931 was the outcome of such multiple factors as post-war international economic disequilibrium, meteorological caprices in 1928 and 1929, the drying-up of the international flow of capital, the collapse of the 1929 speculative bubble, maldistribution of gold, the onset of a major cyclical depression, and the excesses of economic nationalism.

The World War, the Russian Revolution and the post-war agrarian revolution in Danubian Europe had completely upset the pre-war equilibrium in the world's wheat trade. During the 1910-1914 quinquennium Russia and the Danubian countries had supplied over 40 per cent. of the wheat and flour shipments from the principal exporting countries, India 7·5 per cent., the United States and Canada 30 per cent., and Argentina and Australia 21 per cent. The failure of Russia and south-eastern Europe to recover their pre-war status as grain exporters, together with increased domestic consumption in India, meant that the wheat-importing countries of north-western Europe had to depend primarily on North America and the Southern Hemisphere countries to supply their import requirements. Between 1924 and 1929 these two regions supplied 93 per cent. of the world's direct wheat and flour imports, whereas before the war they had contributed 50 per cent.

TABLE IV.—CHANGES IN WORLD EXPORT TRADE IN WHEAT [1]

Average of crop years 1909-1914			Average of crop years 1924-1929		
Order	Net exports in millions of bushels	Percentage share	Order	Net exports in millions of bushels	Percentage of bushels
Russia . . .	164·5	24·5	Canada . .	309·5	38·8
United States .	110·0	16·4	United States .	178·5	22·4
Danubian countries	109·0	16·2	Argentina . .	154·6	19·4
Canada . . .	95·6	14·2	Australia . .	96·6	12·1
Argentina . .	84·7	12·6	Danubian countries	36·7	4·6
Australia . .	55·2	8·2	Russia . . .	12·8	1·6
India . . .	49·8	7·5	India . . .	8·3	1·1
Chile . . .	2·4	0·4			
Total . .	671·2	100·0	Total .	797·0	100·0

This redistribution of demand, and the twofold effect of the great international flow of capital, especially from the United States during 1925-1928, in supporting European importing power, and in accelerating mechanized agricultural development in the younger exporting countries, was reflected in a notable expansion in overseas wheat acreage. Thus in 1926 the acreage harvested in Canada was nearly two-and-a-half times the pre-war average, in Australia it was double, in Argentina and in the United States about one-quarter greater. In Europe, excluding Russia, wheat acreage in the same year, was still slightly below the pre-war average.

TABLE V.—CHANGES IN WHEAT ACREAGE IN PRINCIPAL EXPORTING COUNTRIES

Country	Average acreage 1909-1913 (millions)	Acreage 1928 (millions)	Per cent. increase
Canada . .	9·95	24·12	143
United States .	46·89	58·27	24
Australia . .	7·60	14·84	95
Argentina . .	16·05	20·08	25

Source: U.S. Department of Agriculture Yearbooks.

[1] *The Wheat Situation, 1931*, Imperial Economic Committee, 1932, p. 49.

A complex of circumstances in the years 1928 to 1930 profoundly disturbed the new equilibrium in the world's wheat trade which had been developing since 1915. Two successive years of exceptionally favourable crop conditions in Europe resulted in wheat harvests yielding 167 and 223 million bushels more than the 1923-1927 average. Although the 1928-1929 exports of the four overseas countries attained the record figure of 892 bushels, the very size of these exports, in combination with the bumper European crop of 1929, resulted in a shrinkage in exports from the same four countries for 1929-1930 to 544 million bushels. Canada, Argentina and Australia had all harvested record-breaking crops in the phenomenal year 1928, and, despite greatly reduced yields in 1929, were burdened by unusually large carry-overs in view of Europe's drastically curtailed imports.

TABLE VI.—RATIO OF JULY STOCKS OF WHEAT TO CROPS OF FOUR
LEADING EXPORTING COUNTRIES

(July wheat stocks as percentage of total crop)

Crop of	Canada	U.S.A.	Argentina	Australia
1926	11·6	15·9	28·1	22·1
1927	16·3	16·2	31·0	33·6
1928	18·8	28·2	35·0	28·1
1929	37·1	34·1	45·0	41·3

Source: Canadian Wheat Pool, Dept. of Statistics and Publicity, 1930.

Other factors than physical supply conditions developed to force down world wheat prices. Mounting foreign debt charges, no longer offset by new loans from America, compelled Germany to minimize imports as a means of protecting her external balance of payments, while other Continental countries, especially France, took steps to protect their cereal farmers from the pressure of overseas selling efforts. Abnormally high grain tariff duties (the German basic rate on wheat was lifted during 1930 from an equivalent of 48 cents to 1.62 dollars per bushel), and drastic milling restrictions (French millers were required in December 1929 to use 97 per cent. of domestic wheat in their grind), import quotas and even Government grain import monopolies, were resorted to on a scale which involved a cumulative strangulation of the world's wheat trade.[1] In 1929-1930 the wheat imports of France,

[1] U.S. 73rd Congress, 1st sess., Senate Doc. No. 70: *World Trade Barriers in Relation to American Agriculture*, chap. vii. and pp. 372, 381.

Germany and Italy were 100 million bushels below that of the previous year. Only the great British market remained unrestricted, and into this the wheat surplus of the Argentine (more lacking in storage facilities and marketing organization than the other three competing exporting nations) was dumped on consignment for what it would fetch on a demoralized market.

THE POOL MARKETING POLICY IN 1929 AND 1930

The widely circulated charge that the Canadian Wheat Pool pursued a speculative holding policy during 1929 and 1930, in opposition to the judgment and practice of the private grain trade in Canada, has been a highly controversial issue. In a published reply to the Gampell charges [1] the chief statistician of the Pool presented the following figures to demonstrate that the Pool's proportion of the total Canadian wheat carry-over was less than its share of total marketings.

TABLE VII. (A).—POOL'S PROPORTION OF TOTAL CANADIAN WHEAT CARRY-OVER, 1926-1930

(millions of bushels)

July 31	Total carry-over Canadian wheat	Unsold Pool wheat	Grain trade percentage of carry-over	Pool percentage of carry-over	Percentage of crop handled by Pool
1926 . .	39	20	48·6	51·4	52·2
1927 . .	53	39	26·4	73·6	53·1
1928 . .	72	12	86·5	13·5	51·1
1929 . .	127	52	59·0	41·0	51·3
1930 . .	130	67	48·6	51·4	51·3
Total .	441	190	Average 56·8	43·2	51·4

Source: Canadian Wheat Pool, Statistical Dept.

It appears, however, that the figures given above of "unsold Pool wheat" do not include stocks held by the Pool against outstanding "open market contracts." While the sale of futures (acquired by the Pool in exchange for wheat sold to millers) was in the nature of price protection, the stocks so covered constituted part of the visible Canadian supply. Taking such holdings into account Mr Holbrook Working of the Food Research Institute of Stanford University arrived at the

[1] *A Defence of Canada's Wheat Pool*, issued by Alberta Wheat Pool, February 1931.

following estimate of the Pool's share of the Canadian carry-over for these years.[1]

TABLE VII. (B).—POOL'S PROPORTION OF CANADIAN WHEAT CARRY-OVER

(Millions of bushels. Estimate of Food Research Institute)

August 31 *	Pool stocks		Total Canadian carry-over	Ratio of total Pool stocks to total carry-over
	Unsold	Total		
1926 . .	10·3		22·3	46·2
1927 . .	7·4	10·6	33·3	31·8
1928 . .	0·0	15·0	45·2	33·2
1929 . .	48·4	80·0	87·0	92·0
1930 . .	43·3	50·0	87·1	57·4

* August 31 is taken as end of Pool accounting year.

The above calculation would indicate that while the Pool's proportion of the carry-over from the 1926 and 1927 crops was substantially less than its share of total marketings, the gross holdings (covered and unsold) accounted for the bulk of the carry-over in August of 1929, but that by the end of the 1929-1930 year its share of the carry-over was only slightly in excess of its proportionate crop handlings. Mr Working concludes: " For the year 1929-1930 as a whole the Pool cannot be alleged to have taken less than its share of Canadian sales of wheat." [2]

The maintenance of Winnipeg wheat futures substantially above the customary parities with Liverpool futures during the greater part of the 1929-1930 season has been widely attributed to a holding policy and speculative support by the Pool.[3] Officials of the latter have acknowledged purchases of futures by the Central Selling Agency to the extent of 5 million bushels in the spring of 1929, and of 6,500,000 bushels early in 1930, with a view to " stabilizing a demoralized market and bringing back alarmed buyers to purchase our wheat." [4] Pool participation on these two occasions was of course quite inadequate in itself to

---

[1] *Wheat Studies*, vol. vii., p. 142.

[2] *Ibid.*, p. 143.

[3] Between 1922 and 1928 Winnipeg October wheat futures generally ranged about 20 cents under the corresponding Liverpool future. From June to October 1929, October futures were maintained in Winnipeg at an average spread of 13 cents above the Liverpool price. Not until July 1930 did the two markets regain their normal relationship (*Wheat Studies*, vol. vii., p. 141).

[4] According to a public statement in April 1931 by J. H. Wesson, a director of the Central Selling Agency, the latter organization entered the futures market as a supporting buyer on three occasions during its seven years of operation, the first in the spring

account for the persistent maintenance of Winnipeg futures above world parity throughout the year, which reflected general opinion of the Canadian grain trade. In its *Review of the World Wheat Situation in 1929-1930*, the Food Research Institute made the following appraisal:

There was in Canada an overvaluation of the prospective European imports of wheat and flour generally, an overvaluation shared alike by the pools, private traders, millers and speculators. There was likewise an overvaluation of the proportion of Canadian wheat required in the European mill mix during that crop year, since the high quality of European wheat and the adaptability of millers and bakers was not fully appreciated. These overexpectations provided a basis for confidence in high wheat-price levels, and more particularly for confidence that prices on the unusually short Canadian crop might be held high relative to the prices of other wheats. . . . In the sense that the maintenance of high prices in the face of unusually slow movements of wheat may be regarded as a holding policy, there was a holding policy participated in by practically all factors trading in Canadian wheat, but most significantly by traders in Winnipeg wheat futures.[1]

The situation during 1929-1930 was one of great difficulty for the Central Selling Agency. If sales had been made freely, irrespective of price, the Pool would have been blamed for depressing the market and for failing to secure maximum returns for its members. On the other hand if it held back its supplies in anticipation of improved prices, it had to assume the risk of mounting carrying charges, of embarrassing carry-overs and of imperilling its margin with the banks. The course actually followed was one of compromise. In an address at Regina, in March 1930, Mr A. J. McPhail, president of the Central Selling Agency, stated that by May 1929 the Pool had disposed of 174 out of its total holdings of 225 million bushels, but that thereafter, " we found that Argentine prices simply kept falling away from ours . . . and if we were to have taken such an attitude as to force our prices to a parity with Argentina, no one could have predicted to what level prices would have declined." It was later asserted by the Pool that, during the three months preceding the country movement of the abnormally light 1929 crop, it had offered wheat for export, on fifty-two of the seventy-six market days, at from 1 to 13 cents below Winnipeg quotations, but that this did not avail to prevent an excessive carry-over.[2]

of 1925, the second in 1929 and the third early in 1930, the total purchases involving some 16,500,000 bushels. It was claimed that the first two operations proved financially profitable, that in 1930 the reverse, the result of the three involving a net loss of some 500,000 dollars. See also Alberta Wheat Pool Broadcast of March 26, 1931.

[1] *Wheat Studies*, vol. vii., p. 140.
[2] *A Defence of Canada's Wheat Pool*, p. 22.

On the basis of private information it appears that during the summer of 1929 the directors of the Central Selling Agency were divided as to the policy to be pursued with respect to the 1928 carry-over. In view of the fact that the Pool had already a substantial final settlement in hand for its members, one group favoured disposing of the balance of the stock for what it would bring. This would have seriously depressed exchange prices about the time farmers were making early 1929 deliveries, but would not have particularly affected Pool members, since their returns were on a pooled yearly basis. The other group, influenced by an optimistic interpretation of the statistical situation and by considerations of market sentiment, favoured a holding policy, which on the whole seems to have prevailed. Monthly figures of Pool sales indicate a definite restriction during late January and February of 1930, but a marked reversal in April and May. For the 1929-1930 crop year as a whole the proportion of Pool sales to total Canadian wheat movement was exactly the same as in 1928-1929—namely, 55·9 per cent.[1]

On the whole, therefore, the chief criticism that may be brought against the Pool is that its leaders failed to judge the future and the international situation with greater discernment than the Canadian grain trade in general and the Federal Farm Board in the United States, and that in setting its initial payment for the 1929 pool and in marketing its stocks it allowed itself to be influenced more by the experience of the preceding years and by the purely statistical position, than by an appreciation of the unbalanced international economic and financial situation and of the reactions of nationalistic psychology in European countries. Probably no one could foresee the depth, violence and duration of the ensuing world depression in which wheat prices in exporting countries were borne down to the lowest level in trade history, amid the general collapse of all values except that of gold. While most of the charges made as to the responsibility of the Pool for the wheat debacle after 1928 have been grossly exaggerated or distorted, it must nevertheless be recognized that a pooling system, involving large initial payments on borrowed funds, without hedging protection, is peculiarly vulnerable under persistently falling prices, and that Pool officials were therefore under special responsibility for pursuing a policy of greater safety and liquidity than that which actually prevailed.

[1] " The record of Pool sales of wheat (during 1929-1930) gives clear evidence of a holding policy, other than the usual moderate restriction of sales in September-December, only in the months of January and February 1930 " (*Wheat Studies*, vol. vii., p. 144).

THE CANADIAN WHEAT POOL

The most disastrous action taken by the Pool proved to be the setting of the initial payment for the 1929 pool on the basis of 1 dollar instead of 85 cents as in the preceding year. The announcement of this figure was based in part upon the importance of a substantial initial payment to members, in view of the abnormally light crop of 1929. With the October future on the Winnipeg Exchange ranging between 1.50 and 1.70 dollars during August and September, the figure appeared a reasonably conservative one, and it was approved by the banks financing the C.S.A. As previously noted, however, Winnipeg futures were at this time considerably out of line with Liverpool quotations, and it was not until the opening of 1930 that the international wheat situation began to be adequately reflected on the Winnipeg market.

Under its arrangements with the banks the C.S.A. was required to maintain at all times a 15 per cent. margin between the amount of its borrowings and the market value of the documents held as collateral. In January 1930 when this margin became jeopardized the banks threatened to liquidate their collateral. In order to avert the disastrous results of dumping such large quantities of wheat on a declining market, the Pool leaders appealed to the governments of the three Prairie Provinces for assistance. Realizing the issues at stake and believing that the embarrassment was only temporary, the three premiers agreed to enter into an agreement on behalf of their respective governments to guarantee the lending banks against any ultimate loss resulting from their loans to the Pools.

Experiencing the greatest difficulty in disposing of the light 1929 deliveries, and confronted by ever sinking prices, the Pool leaders held anxious conferences concerning the initial price basis for the 1930 pool. A temporary initial price of 70 cents was decided on early in the summer, then reduced to 60 cents at the commencement of the season, and finally, at the insistence of the bankers, dropped to 50 cents. As values continued to decline, the support of the Federal Government was invoked. An arrangement was finally consummated whereby the banks agreed to continue the financing of the Central Selling Agency, under a Federal Government guarantee, on condition that Mr John I. MacFarland, an able and trusted grain dealer, should be installed as manager of the Agency, with the disposal of the 1929 carry-over and the 1930 pool placed entirely in his hands. In effect, the Pool had been put under receivership.

One of the first acts of the new controller was to close the Pool's overseas sales offices. In a statement issued on December 4, 1930, Mr MacFarland announced that this was undertaken as an experiment " to demonstrate beyond possibility of doubt the truth or otherwise of the statement frequently made that the maintenance of direct representation overseas has militated against the sale of Canadian wheat." The move was greeted with satisfaction by British importers and millers, who, there appears little reason to doubt, had extended a definite buying preference during 1929 and 1930 towards Argentine and Russian wheat, in protest against the direct selling and controlled marketing policy of the Pool.

The international wheat price situation during 1930-1931 presented an extraordinary picture. On the one hand, many European continental countries, through the application of extreme tariffs, milling restrictions and other measures of governmental control, were maintaining domestic wheat prices at about 1928 levels. Thus in May 1931, when domestic wheat prices in Great Britain averaged 75 cents, they stood in France at 1.84 dollars, in Germany at 1.85 dollars, and in Italy at 1.60 dollars. On the other hand, among the principal exporting countries, wheat quotations in Argentina, Australia and Canada reflected directly the price situation in the free British market, the average price of No. 3 Northern on the Winnipeg Exchange being 53 cents in the same month. In the United States the stabilization operations of the Federal Farm Board held the price of No. 2 Hard Winter (Kansas City) at 76 cents. Canada was thus exposed to the full brunt of international competition (with Argentina and Australia marketing crops exceeding by 43 and 77 per cent. respectively their 1929-1930 production), and to the full pressure of European import restriction. Despite the fact that Canada forced her exports of wheat and flour during 1930-1931 to the amount of 258 million bushels, equivalent to 40 per cent. of the total shipments of the " big four " exporting countries, she entered the new crop year with a record carry-over of 140 million bushels in all positions.

Under these disastrous conditions Pool leaders had to decide whether or not they should seek to continue the contract methods in the marketing of the 1931 crop. With the Central Selling Agency no longer under their control, and its functions limited to the liquidation of the 1929 carry-over and the 1930 pool on behalf of the Pool's creditors, with the Federal Government unwilling to establish a national wheat board, and with the realization that initial payments would have to be on such a desperately low basis that most contracts would be unenforceable, representatives of the three Pools decided in June 1931 that they should operate henceforth as separate units, and that their members should be released from their contracts and given the option of delivering their grain on a pooling basis or of selling on the open market through Pool elevators.

Thus step by step, under the stress of international circumstances, the impressive Pool system which had attained such a commanding position in the world's grain trade during the late twenties, was stripped of its most distinctive features. Direct selling abroad had been abandoned, the Pool's powerful Central Selling Agency had been converted into a liquidating agency, their elevators had been pledged to secure their obligation on account of 1929 overpayments, and their growers' contracts, on which the whole system had been based, were now declared non-effective. The " deflation " of the Canadian Wheat Pool appeared to be complete.

READJUSTMENTS BY THE PROVINCIAL POOL ORGANIZATIONS

Although the centralized pool structure had been wrecked, the underlying co-operative organizations of the prairie grain growers were not extinguished. The three provincial pool associations resolutely set themselves to maintain a producer-controlled marketing system for their members, while adjusting their organization and operations in accordance with the dictates of their formidable liabilities and with the exigencies of the calamitous world wheat situation.

Although their growers' contracts were no longer operative, each of the provincial Pools possessed valuable and tangible assets in their respective elevator systems, which had originally developed as a mere auxiliary to pool contract marketing. The acquisition of these properties had been financed entirely through elevator and commercial reserve deductions from members' pooled returns, so that the equity in this extensive—and for the most part highly modern—elevator system had been acquired by the growers as a by-product of pool marketing. It was on these tangibles that the Pools now depended, both to secure their obligations to the guaranteeing governments and to save their co-operative organizations. The extent of the 1929 initial overpayment, as established by the final accounting of the wheat and coarse grains pools, was found to exceed 22 million dollars. As the outcome of protracted negotiations among the three Pools, the seven creditor banks and the three guaranteeing governments, the latter issued to the banks special 4½ per cent. bonds (at a discount of 2 per cent.) to cover their proportionate liabilities on account of the unpaid bank loans. The provincial Pools in turn deposited with their respective governments bonds for corresponding amounts, payable with interest at 5 per cent. on a 20-year amortization basis. These were secured by pledge of Pool country and terminal elevator properties. The obligations of the three Pools to their respective provincial governments were established as follows: Alberta, 5,649,000 dollars; Saskatchewan, 13,752,000 dollars; Manitoba, 3,491,611 dollars.[1] Except in the case of Manitoba, these formidable obligations were more than covered by the free assets of the Pools. The balance sheet of the Alberta Pool, as of July 15, 1932, showed its net free assets to exceed by 3,814,000 dollars its capital liability to the provincial treasury. In the case of the Saskatchewan Pool the corresponding figure was in excess of 7 million dollars.

While Manitoba's liability was the smallest of the three Pools, it was relatively the most burdensome, owing to the extreme losses sustained on the coarse grains pool, to which its deliveries had exceeded those to the 1929 wheat pool. Furthermore the Manitoba Pool elevator system was based on a complicated plan which sought to combine centralized operation and trusteeship (through Manitoba Pool Elevators, Ltd.) with contractual ownership through individually incorporated local co-operative elevator associations.[2] It now became evident that the Manitoba Pool, as such, would have to be liquidated, and Manitoba Pool Elevators reorganized. Under the existing arrangement the province agreed to absorb 1,400,000 dollars of its bank guarantee liability, and to accept the remaining 2,100,000 dollars in the form of stock in the reorganized Manitoba Pool Elevators, on whose board the Government was given minority representation. The Government's stock is to be redeemed over a period of twenty years, through annual payments of principal and interest out of elevator income credited to each of the constituent local elevator associations, whose own stock in Manitoba Pool Elevators is to be increased in proportion as that of the Government is retired.[3]

In Saskatchewan and Alberta the Pools worked out a detailed plan

[1] Special legislation was enacted in the three provinces in 1931 to validate agreements given by the respective governments to guarantee repayment of the bank's advances, and to provide for the taking of security from the Pools.

[2] See H. S. Patton, *Grain Growers' Co-operation in Western Canada*, pp. 254-255.

[3] The arrangements between the Manitoba Pool, Manitoba Pool Elevators, the hundred and fifty local elevator associations, and the Manitoba Government are set forth in a " Four-Party Agreement " authorized by the Manitoba Legislature on May 4, 1932.

of individual adjustment with members who had participated in the 1929 initial overpayment. Thus in the former province it was agreed that against each grower's established individual overpayment there should be credited (*a*) such sum as might be due him on account of the final 1928 pool settlement; (*b*) interest due him on previous elevator reserve deductions; (*c*) his patronage share of excess elevator earnings. Adjustment of any remaining liability might be finally made by cancelling an equivalent amount of commercial or elevator reserve certificates standing in his name. Overpayments exceeding 18 cents a bushel on any variety or grade of grain were to be absorbed through the operation of a sinking fund to be set up from pool elevator earnings.

It will thus be seen that the main reliance of the Pools for the liquidation of their unforeseen liabilities, and for the preservation of their organization, rests upon the potential earnings of their elevator systems. In giving their members the option of participating in voluntary pools or of selling their grain on the open market, the Pools appealed to their loyalty to put their grain through Pool elevators, and to use the Pool's sales departments. They have had their elevators licensed as public instead of private warehouses, as formerly, and have made strong bids for non-member as well as member patronage.

The results to date have been noteworthy. The Saskatchewan Pool Elevators handled 40·5 per cent. of all grain marketed in the province in the 1931-1932 crop year; and 43 per cent. in the 1932-1933 crop year. In August 1933 the company completed its final purchase payments of 2,085,065 dollars on account of the acquisition in 1926 of the properties of the Saskatchewan Co-operative Elevator Company, thereby extinguishing within the seven contractual years its entire purchase commitments of 11,061,289 dollars, plus interest payments of 2,150,331 dollars. In addition the Saskatchewan Pool met in full its instalment of 1,128,589 dollars to the provincial treasury on account of the 1929 overpayment. The Alberta Pool likewise met its provincial obligation of 452,950 dollars on similar account, leaving a net elevator operating profit of 179,055 dollars from its 439 elevators during 1932-1933. In Manitoba the reorganized Manitoba Pool Elevators showed a net operating profit of 300,835 dollars for the year ending July 31, 1933, out of which accrued interest and principal obligations to the Manitoba Government amounting to 230,813 dollars were discharged, leaving approximately 70,000 dollars as addition to operating reserve. In all cases provision was made for depreciation of elevator properties at the regular rate of 5 per cent. The operations of the three provincial pool elevator systems for 1932-1933 are summarized in the following Table:

TABLE VIII.—OPERATIONS OF POOL ELEVATOR SYSTEMS, 1932-1933

	Manitoba	Saskatchewan	Alberta	3 Pools
No. of country elevators *	153	1,067	439	1,659
Grain handled (bushels) .	13,816,534	91,370,045	48,390,660	153,577,239
Payments to provincial governments *re* 1929 pool overpayment . .	$230,813	$1,128,589	$452,950	$1,812,342
Additions to operating reserve . . .	$70,021	$714,030	$179,055	$973,106

* In addition to their country elevator systems, the three Pools own or operate under lease 12 terminal elevators at the Head of the Lakes and on the Pacific Coast, having a combined capacity of 37 million bushels.

The depression record of the Pool elevator organizations affords an impressive demonstration, on the one hand, of efficiency and adaptability of organization and management, and on the other hand, of patronage loyalty and of financial integrity of the membership in fulfilling contractual debt obligations, however burdensome. The record would also appear to vindicate the wisdom of the system of elevator and commercial reserve deductions under the pooling contracts. But for the substantial equity thereby acquired in grain-handling facilities the Pool organizations would have been inevitably extinguished through the collapse in 1930 of the value of grain collateral against commercial bank loans.

Although the designation " Pools "—because of its association and convenient brevity—is still applied to the provincial co-operative wheat producers' organizations, it has been, strictly speaking, a misnomer with respect to the status of these concerns since the 1930-1931 crop year. As stated above, each organization decided in 1931 to release its members from the second series wheat and coarse grains contracts, while continuing to provide for pool handling on a voluntary basis. Voluntary pool deliveries of the 1931 and 1932 crops were, however, of insignificant proportions. With basic initial payments for the 1931 wheat crop of only 35 cents per bushel (basis, No. 1 Northern, Fort William), and with the smallest harvest since 1924, few farmers could afford to await deferred payments, especially as market prices continued generally to decline. In Saskatchewan only a little over 1 million bushels were delivered to the voluntary pool. In Alberta slightly more than

5 million bushels were so marketed in 1932-1933—less than an eighth of total wheat handlings through Alberta Pool Elevators. In both provinces it was found expedient to announce " cut-offs " at various dates during the crop year, in order that the average returns of farmers who had made early pool deliveries should not be unduly reduced by later deliveries when prices were at lower levels. The situation reveals the limitations of the pool method of payment under the conditions of a persistently declining market.

Since 1930 the provincial " Pools " have, in fact, been operating on substantially the same basis as the older farmers' co-operative elevator companies—the United Grain Growers and the old Saskatchewan Co-operative Elevator Company.[1] Each of the three " Pools " maintains its own commission and sales department, operating on the Western grain exchanges, each arranges its own line of credit with the banks, each hedges its country purchases on the futures market, and each bids at country points for non-member as well as member patronage.[2] The 1928-1933 (second series) pool contracts having expired, membership in the Saskatchewan Co-operative Wheat Producers, Ltd., and in the Alberta Co-operative Wheat Producers, Ltd., now rests simply on subscription to one share of stock of one dollar par value. While the stock in the Saskatchewan Pool Elevators and Alberta Pool Elevators is held by the respective parent Pool organizations, individual interests are represented by the elevator reserve certificates standing to the credit of members (subject to hypothecations to the provincial governments). A structural simplification might be effected through reorganization as provincial co-operative elevator companies (as in Manitoba), in which certificate holders would receive preferred stock to amounts corresponding to the difference between the face of their certificates and their adjusted individual 1929 overpayments.

STATUS OF THE CENTRAL SELLING AGENCY

As previously stated, the control of the Central Selling Agency was divorced from the provincial pool organizations in November 1930 when,

---

[1] The United Grain Growers has succeeded in weathering the grain crisis without suspending in any year cash dividend payments to its farmer shareholders, although it sustained substantial operating losses in 1929-1930.

[2] In contrast to the former direct export sales policy of the Central Selling Agency, the provincial pool elevator companies make their sales as a rule on the open market. It appears, however, that the Alberta Pool Elevators do a certain amount of direct export business through Vancouver, while Saskatchewan Pool Elevators during 1932 entered into contracts for the export of some 4 million bushels of wheat through the new grain port of Fort Churchill, on Hudson Bay.

as a condition of continued bank financing under federal guarantee, the disposal of the 1929 pool carry-over and of the 1930 pool[1] was placed entirely in the hands of Mr John I. MacFarland, acting as manager of the Agency on behalf of the Pools' banker and governmental creditors. The situation was one of extreme difficulty. The Canadian wheat crop of 1930 was 38 per cent. larger than the abnormally low crop of 1929.[2] Continental European import restrictions were intensified. Although the wheat stabilization operations of the Federal Farm Board eased export pressure from the United States, Russia reappeared in 1930-1931 for the first time since 1913 as a significant wheat exporter, with shipments of 114 million bushels. Although no official accounting of the 1930 pool has as yet (April 1934) been rendered,[3] it appears that the liquidation of pool stocks was subordinated by Mr MacFarland (with the approval of the Federal Government) to considerations of price support on the Winnipeg market. Cash sales by the C.S.A., it is understood, were gradually replaced by purchases of futures.

As wheat prices continued to decline during the 1931-1932 crop year,[4] and as speculative support for hedging contracts by cash buyers was found to be almost completely lacking, the Dominion Government entered into an informal arrangement with Mr MacFarland to purchase grain futures through the C.S.A. when considered necessary to stabilize prices on the Winnipeg market. While no report of these operations has been made public, it is understood that the Agency's holdings of futures reached substantial proportions towards the end of 1932.[5] The sharp advance in grain prices in the summer of 1933 raised hopes of a substantial distribution on account of the 1930 pool. Although the

[1] Approximately 127 million bushels of wheat and 15 million bushels of coarse grains were delivered to the 1930 pool.

[2] The Canadian wheat crop of 1930 amounted to 421,700,000 bushels; that of 1929 was 304·5 million.

[3] In appearing before the Alberta Wheat Pool delegates in November 1933, Mr MacFarland stated that at no time had the Central Agency been in a position to sell its wheat at a price sufficient to equalize (with carrying charges) the initial payments on the 1930 pool deliveries. The latter had been on a basis, first of 60 cents, and then of 50 cents.

[4] Weighted average prices on the Winnipeg market were 1.26 dollars (U.S.) for the 1929-1930 crop year; 66 cents for 1930-1931, and 50 cents for 1931-1932 (*Wheat Studies*, vol. ix., p. 134).

[5] Commenting on these operations in its " Review of the World Wheat Situation, 1932-1933," the Food Research Institute stated: " The trade has inferred that holdings of the Agency in cash wheat were more than 75 million bushels at the end of 1930; that by the end of April 1931 the cash wheat had been transferred to futures; that substantial additional purchases of futures, designed to support the market, were made in July 1932, and still more in September-November; and that holdings of futures approximated 125 million bushels in mid-November 1932 " (*Wheat Studies*, vol. ix., pp. 80-81).

C.S.A. sold futures freely (to the extent of some 40 million bushels, it is said) at this time, the subsequent sharp break in prices made it necessary to repurchase most of these to support the market.

The Dominion Government, it will be observed, has utilized the former Pool Central Selling Agency in much the same way (although on a smaller scale and with less directness and publicity) as the Grain Stabilization Corporation was employed under the Federal Farm Board in the United States to support wheat markets after 1929. There is a certain irony in the fact that the Pool Central Agency, which was created as an alternative to organized speculation, should have been destined to become the instrument of speculative support to the futures market, and in the further fact that what was established as a co-operative substitute for a Government wheat board should continue to operate under the sponsorship of the Federal Government.

REVIVAL OF DEMAND FOR COMPULSORY WHEAT BOARD

The breakdown of the voluntary system of interprovincial pool marketing appears to have intensified rather than to have dispelled among the majority of prairie grain growers the demand for an all-inclusive wheat-selling agency. As stated at the beginning of this paper the Western wheat pool campaigns of 1923 and 1924 were resorted to only after all efforts to bring about the re-establishment of a compulsory wheat board after the 1919-1920 pattern had proved unavailing. Despite enabling legislation passed by the Dominion Parliament and by the legislatures of Saskatchewan and Alberta in 1922, the premiers of the latter provinces had found it impossible to obtain for the management of such a revised board—in view of certain legal limitations and of the uncompromising opposition of the private grain trade—the services of men commanding the requisite experience and confidence.[1] Notwithstanding the notable results achieved by the co-operative pool movement, it became evident by 1928 (when second series contracts were offered for signature) that no appreciable extension of grower participation on a voluntary basis could be expected.[2]

In Saskatchewan, where Wheat Board sentiment had always been strongest, the leaders of the United Farmers of Canada (Saskatchewan

---

[1] See H. S. Patton, *op. cit.*, pp. 203-209.

[2] At the end of 1926 the pools claimed to have 70 per cent. of Western wheat acreage under contract (79 per cent. in Saskatchewan). In no crop year, however, did pool deliveries exceed 53 per cent. of total wheat inspections. (See above, Table II.)

Section) [1] initiated an educational campaign for a " compulsory wheat pool," and at the 1928 meeting of the organization a resolution was carried, urging the enactment of legislation providing that, when 75 per cent. of the wheat acreage of the province should be shown to be under voluntary pool contract, all growers should be required to deliver their wheat to a reconstituted pool agency. The majority of the Saskatchewan Pool directors and delegates were at first opposed to the " 100-per-cent. pool " plan. The wheat crisis of 1929-1930, with its accompanying embarrassments to the Central Selling Agency, served, however, to strengthen sentiment in favour of a legislative pool, and in August 1930 an official ballot of Saskatchewan Pool members was taken on the issue. The result disclosed a majority of 70 per cent. in favour of formally requesting the Saskatchewan legislature to authorize a " 100-per-cent. Compulsory Grain Pool," to become effective by proclamation, if two-thirds of the grain growers of the province voting on a Government-conducted referendum should declare themselves in favour of such plan. In response to the representations of the Saskatchewan Pool the provincial legislature in 1931 passed two companion measures, an enabling Grain Marketing Act and a Referendum Act.[2] In view of a decision rendered about this time by the Supreme Court of Canada declaring the Produce Marketing Act of British Columbia to be *ultra vires*,[3] the Saskatchewan Government decided, before submitting the referendum under its Grain Marketing Act, to obtain an opinion from the provincial Court of Appeals as to its jurisdictional competence to enact such legislation. The Court held that, in so far as the Act contemplated control of interprovincial and foreign trade in grain, it involved an encroachment upon the field of federal legislative powers. The Act was thus rendered abortive and no referendum was taken.

The Manitoba Pool, at a delegate meeting in November 1930, had gone on record in favour of a legislative pool for that province, and the Alberta Pool, without committing itself officially, authorized a

[1] This name had been adopted under the amalgamation in 1926 of the old Saskatchewan Grain Growers Association and the newer and more radical Farmers Union of Canada.

[2] The former provided for a body to be known as the Saskatchewan Grain Co-operative, control of which should be vested in all grain growers of the province and to which the assets and liabilities of the Saskatchewan Wheat Pool should be transferred. Subject to approval by referendum, all grain grown in the province would be marketed by this body on a pooling basis.

[3] Under this Act, which came into effect in 1927, all extra-provincial movements of tree fruit had been subjected to licensing and control by a statutory Interior Committee of Direction.

ballot of its membership on the issue in the summer of 1931. The Saskatchewan Court decision, however, compelled abandonment of action along provincial legislative lines. This led in turn to renewed demand for a federal wheat marketing board—a demand to which the continued ruinous course of wheat prices gave the support of desperation. The passing of the British Agricultural Marketing Act in 1931, with the far-reaching provisions for legislative commodity marketing boards,[1] was hailed by Western pool members as a vindication of their principle in the country of traditional *laissez-faire* towards agriculture, and as a model to which Canada should conform.

THE POOLS AND THE INTERNATIONAL WHEAT AGREEMENT

Although united in their demand for a national wheat board, Pool leaders were fully aware that, with Canada dependent on export outlets for something like three-quarters of its normal wheat crop, not even the most complete and competent national marketing control could in itself be effective in controlling price. The experiences of the Central Selling Agency had fully brought home to the Pool organization the cogent realities of competition among wheat-exporting countries,[2] of the defensive and nationalistic forces behind import restrictions, and of the price-determining significance of mounting world carry-overs. They had not been impressed by the spacious advantage of a British tariff preference on Empire wheat, as established under the Empire trade pacts of the Ottawa Conference of 1932.[3] In their joint memorandum to the Dominion Government on the Imperial Economic Conference the three Western pools had declared:

Inasmuch as in our judgment trade restrictions and tariff barriers in foreign countries have been particularly effective in disturbing the marketing of Canadian grain we cannot view with favour the extension of this principle in

---

[1] The Act provided, alternatively, for regulatory boards or exclusive marketing agencies. Any marketing scheme before becoming effective must be approved both by referendum of producers concerned and by Parliament (see H. J. Wadleigh, " The British Agricultural Marketing Act," *Journal of Farm Economics*, October 1932).

[2] Largely under the initiative of the Canadian Wheat Pool, international wheat pool conferences had been held in 1926 at St Paul and at Kansas City in 1927, attended by representatives of several States of the U.S.A., Australia and Soviet Russia, as well as of Western Canada. At the latter gathering a resolution was adopted urging that " as soon as practicable the wheat producers of the chief exporting countries of the world should look forward toward co-ordination of their co-operative program," with a view to giving " wheat producers the same control over the marketing of their crop already possessed by other industries " (see H. S. Patton, *op. cit.*, pp. 402-404).

[3] Under the Ottawa pacts Great Britain agreed to impose a duty of two shillings per quarter on non-Empire wheat.

Empire countries. . . . We believe that the only hopeful and permanent solution of the grain marketing problem is for wider and freer markets as the bulk of our surplus must continue to be sold outside the Empire.

As an outcome of conferences towards the end of 1932 among the Western wheat pools and the prairie governments, formal representations were made to Premier Bennett, urging that Canada should take the initiative in convening a conference of the principal wheat-exporting countries with a view to arriving at an international agreement for the regulation of wheat exports.[1] The steps leading to the International Wheat Agreement, signed by twenty-two nations at London in August 1933, need not be reviewed here.[2] The pact is notable in that it represents the first international commodity agreement to involve participation by importing as well as by exporting nations, with the former undertaking to relax import restrictions and encourage consumption, in consideration of the imposition of concerted export restrictions by the latter group. Under the terms of the agreement, Canada is allotted for 1933-1934 an export quota of 200 million bushels of wheat (and wheat equivalent of flour), or 35'7 per cent. of the global figure of 560 million bushels accepted as the measure of world import demand for that year.[3] Under the formula applicable to export allotments for 1934-1935 (15 per cent. less than the average production of the average acreage sown during 1931-1933, less normal domestic requirements), Canada's quota would amount to approximately 265 million bushels.

The principles of the International Wheat Agreement were strongly endorsed by the Canadian pool organizations at their 1933 annual meetings, which gave special consideration to the measures by which Canada should implement its commitments under the pact. To this end the three provincial Pools have united in support of the following three-point policy:

(1) The establishment of a national wheat-marketing board as the exclusive agency for handling Canada's wheat exports.

(2) Adjustment of Canada's exports to the level permitted for 1934-1935, to be effected, not by compulsory limitation of acreage, but by the assignment of marketing allotments to individual growers.

(3) The fixing of a minimum price for all wheat consumed in Canada.

---

[1] Such proposals had been mooted at the conference of wheat-exporting nations at London in May 1931, but no formal action was taken at that time.

[2] For details see *Foreign Crops and Markets*, September 5, 1933.

[3] For 1932-1933 world export shipments amounted to 615 million bushels. For the five preceding crop years they had averaged 778 million bushels. Canada's exports for 1929-1933 averaged 229 million bushels.

In support of this program pool leaders assert that Canada's international commitments as to quantitative limitation of wheat exports afford an additional warrant for the realization of their cherished plan of a national grain-marketing board, as a more direct and effective agency for regulating export shipments than a mere licensing board. In respect to the second point, they maintain that the pro-rating of the national wheat quota for 1934-1935 to growers in the form of individual marketing allotments, based on past delivery records, would be a more effective and more readily enforceable method of limiting market supplies than any attempt to bring about a given reduction in planted acreage, as under the wheat adjustment plan in the United States. The wide variations in seasonal wheat yields in the Prairie Provinces make acreage control an uncertain indicator of the size of market supplies in any given year. Wheat harvested in excess of any grower's individual allotment and seed requirements would be retained or consumed on the farm. In the event of any supplementary quota being allotted to Canada through improvement in world import demand, or failure of supplies elsewhere, these farm reserves could be drawn upon. The third point in the Pools' platform was supported by appeal to the precedent of England's Wheat Guarantee Act of 1932, and of the parity price principle of the domestic allotment plan for wheat in the United States, and on the ground that the protective tariff principle should in equity be applied to wheat producers as well as to manufacturers. Supplementary payments for domestically consumed wheat would be derived, as in Great Britain and the United States, from a tax on milled wheat.

CANADIAN AGRICULTURAL MARKETING LEGISLATION OF 1934

For several months after the signing of the London Agreement no definite intimation was given by the Dominion Government as to the measures by which it proposed to implement Canada's commitments under the pact. Premier Bennett had made it evident on various occasions, however, that he did not favour the Pools' demand for a national wheat-marketing board, superseding private operations on the Western grain exchanges. As the 1933-1934 crop year advanced it became apparent that, in the face of Europe's abundant crops, Canada would have difficulty in realizing its export quota of 200 million bushels,[1] and that control machinery would probably not be required for that season.

[1] Canadian wheat exports for the first eight months of the 1933-1934 crop year amounted to only 133 million bushels.

As an outcome of consultations between the Federal Government and the Western premiers during the winter of 1933-1934, it was decided to introduce concurrent legislation in Parliament and the legislatures of the Prairie Provinces, to ratify the London Agreement and to provide for the control of wheat movements during the 1934-1935 crop year. The nature of the provincial measures is indicated by the Control and Marketing of Wheat Act as passed by the Saskatchewan legislature in April of this year. It provides that the Lieutenant-Governor in council may, if deemed necessary for carrying out Canada's obligations under the London Agreement, establish a provincial " Emergency Wheat Control Board " or enter into an agreement with other provinces and the Government of Canada for the establishment of a joint board. Such Board should have power (a) to control, by licence or otherwise, the total quantity of wheat which each owner or occupant of land may sell within the province during the 1934-1935 crop year; (b) to require that any wheat marketed in Saskatchewan shall be delivered or sold in accordance with regulations of the Board; and (c), at the discretion of the Lieutenant-Governor in council, to require that all wheat shall be delivered to the Board or its order. The provincial acts thus provide for growers' marketing quotas and compulsory marketing boards, in accordance with the Pools' policy. Control over interprovincial and export movements of wheat is dependent, however, on federal enabling legislation and administrative action.

Towards the end of March 1934 the federal Minister of Agriculture, the Hon. Robert Weir, introduced in Parliament a Natural Products Marketing Bill, providing for the creation of a Dominion Marketing Board with broad powers to regulate the marketing and export of any product of agricultural, forest or fishery origin which the Government by order in council may declare to be a " regulated product." The Board would have authority " to regulate the time and place of marketing the regulated product, to determine the manner of distribution, and the quantity and quality of the product that shall be marketed by any person at any time," and to regulate price spreads. It shall have power " to co-operate with any marketing board or agency established under the law of any province," and to impose charges or tolls in respect to the marketing of a designated product for " the pooling of returns, the creation of reserves, or for necessary operating or capital expenditures."

The bill embodies in principle the resolutions adopted at a conference of Western agricultural producers' organizations (including the Wheat Pools) held at Regina in connection with the World Grain Show in

154

July 1933, and of a subsequent conference of Eastern producers' associations at Toronto in November 1933.[1] This Canadian analogue of the British Agricultural Marketing Act and of the United States Agricultural Adjustment Act was strongly attacked by the Liberal opposition in Parliament on constitutional and public policy grounds, and complaints were registered by farmers' organizations that the bill did not contain adequate provisions for consultation of and participation by producers. In response to these criticisms the Government has introduced amendments providing, as in the British Act, for the submission of petitions by producers to have their product put under a scheme, and for the taking of a poll of producers concerned before a board is set up to regulate a commodity.[2] While the measure is still under debate at the present writing (May 1934), its passage appears assured. In the meantime supplementary legislation providing for provincial co-operation has already been enacted or introduced in the legislatures of the Prairie Provinces and British Columbia.

THE FUTURE OF THE WHEAT POOLS

Although the Natural Products Marketing Bill does not specifically provide for a national grain-marketing board, as demanded by the Wheat Pool organizations, it would appear that this comprehensive federal enabling measure, in conjunction with the supplementary legislation of the Prairie Provinces, provides the requisite constitutional authority for the creation and effective functioning of provincial or inter-provincial wheat-marketing boards. Whether or not such machinery shall be installed, or internal wheat-marketing quotas shall be applied during the forthcoming crop year, will doubtless be dependent upon such contingencies as the size of Canada's 1933 carry-over[3] and its 1934 crop in relation to its 1934-1935 export quota under the International Wheat Agreement; the adherence of the signatory countries to the pact[4];

---

[1] The resolution of the Toronto Conference had called upon the federal Minister of Agriculture to prepare " a farm products marketing measure which will enable the producers of agricultural products in any part of Canada to take advantage of legislation embodying the principles of the British Agricultural Marketing Act of 1931."

[2] Determination of the proportion of producers of a commodity who must vote in favour of a scheme before it is made compulsory is left to the Minister.

[3] The Canadian visible supply of wheat on April 28, 1934, was reported by the Board of Grain Commissioners as 203 million bushels, as against 216 million bushels for corresponding date in 1933.

[4] Argentina's insistence upon an enlarged quota for 1933-1944, and the collapse of the minimum price plan at the London meeting of the Wheat Conference delegates in May of this year, appear to make continuance of the agreement uncertain.

the movements of wheat prices; the tactics of the private grain trade; and the play of political forces. Whether a wheat board, if constituted, shall be national, provincial, or interprovincial, and whether it shall function in a marketing or in a merely regulatory capacity, is also dependent on circumstances.

The fact remains that the International Wheat Agreement and the Canadian federal and provincial agricultural marketing legislation of 1934 provide at least the conventional and legal basis for the realization of the cherished objective of the majority of prairie grain growers for an inclusive national wheat-marketing agency, resting on partnership between producers and Government, and co-operating with similar agencies in other wheat-exporting countries. Should such prove to be the outcome, the Canadian Wheat Pool movement of 1923 to 1930 would represent, in historical perspective, a voluntary co-operative precursor to the system of " compulsory co-operation." From another viewpoint it might be regarded as a transitory phase between the war-time expedient of the Canadian Wheat Board and the development of a definitive national plan for the marketing of Canada's major export commodity. In any event it is unlikely that wheat pool marketing on a voluntary basis will be resumed in Western Canada on any such scale as prevailed between 1924 and 1929.

Whether or not the Canadian Wheat Pool becomes absorbed in a national or interprovincial wheat-marketing board, the grain growers of Western Canada have built up under prosperity, and retained under adversity, a producer-owned system of grain-handling facilities which will be of substantial advantage to its far-flung membership, whatever plan of marketing may prevail. The 1660 Pool elevators that dot the Canadian prairies and the great Pool terminals that rise over Thunder Bay and Burrard Inlet are physical symbols of a co-operative faith and solidarity which the world depression has not extinguished, but only intensified in the broader struggle for a co-operative commonwealth.

CHAPTER IV

THE JAPANESE RICE CONTROL [1]

by Seiichi Tobata

ECONOMIC FEATURES OF RICE

BEFORE describing the methods employed for controlling the price of rice in Japan the writer will give, as a background, an outline of the economic features of rice production and consumption.

Rice Consumption

The Tokugawa Era, which extended from the beginning of the seventeenth century to the middle of the nineteenth, is sometimes called the " period of rice economy," since rice was found to be at the root of practically all the economic problems of that time. To-day, although rice is still the most important staple food in the Japanese diet, the term " period of rice economy " is no longer applicable; the importance of rice in the economic life of the people has been much reduced by the increased consumption of a greater variety of foodstuffs.

Of the total amount of rice used in Japan, 86 per cent. is for daily consumption, 5 per cent. is for " mochi," or rice-cakes, 5 per cent. is for *sake*, or rice-wine, and the remaining 4 per cent. is for other purposes.

The rice consumed in Japan is almost all *Japanese* rice, or home-grown rice, for which there is a great demand. Rice from Rangoon, Siam and Saigon is also consumed in Japan, and until ten years ago constituted more than 5 per cent. of the total consumed in Japan. But this imported rice was simply to make good a shortage, and because of its cheapness was consumed mainly by the poorer classes, or used as material in certain industries. Of late, however, this foreign rice has come to be replaced by imports from Chosen and Taiwan.

The following Table gives the varieties of rice and the quantity consumed in Japan proper:

AVERAGE ANNUAL RICE CONSUMPTION (1928-1932) [1]

(In 1000 *koku*)

Rice produced in Japan proper	.	.	.	59,279	85·138	per cent.
Chosen rice	.	.	.	.	.	6,487	9·317	,,
Taiwan rice	.	.	.	.	.	2,578	3·702	,,
Foreign rice	.	.	.	.	.	1,283	1·843	,,
Total	.	.	.	.	.	69,627	100·000	,,

---

[1] All statistics given in this paper are based upon the reports of the Department of Agriculture and Forestry, unless otherwise stated.

1 *koku*=about 5 bushels; 1 *cho*=about 2·45 acres ;1 gold *yen*=about 50 gold cents.

Rice produced in Chosen and Taiwan used to be treated as foreign rice, since in taste and quality it was quite different from the rice grown in Japan proper, but as a result of the experiments encouraged by the Government, the rice produced in these parts has come to differ little from that grown at home. As may be seen from the Table on p. 157, Taiwan and Chosen now make up the shortage of rice in Japan by supplying 13 per cent. of the total consumption, and this increase from the colonies allays, at present, the fear of a shortage.

The following Table shows how rice produced in the colonies has come to supplement home-grown rice, and has in price approached by degrees the price of rice produced in Japan proper:

QUOTATION AT TOKYO AND OSAKA RICE EXCHANGE
(per one koku)

	Quotations (in yen)			Percentage		
	Japanese Rice	Chosen Rice	Taiwan Rice	Japanese Rice	Chosen Rice	Taiwan Rice
Average, 1903–1907 .	14.09	12.00	9.98	100·00	85·17	70·83
Average, 1908–1912 .	15.88	13.37	11.86	100·00	84·19	74·69
Average, 1928–1932 .	25.41	24.13	21.95	100·00	94·96	86·38

The annual consumption of rice per person, according to calculations made by the Department of Agriculture and Forestry on the basis of the estimated population at the end of April in each year, is as follows:

ANNUAL RICE CONSUMPTION PER PERSON

Crop Year [1]	koku	Crop Year	koku
1911	0·980	1922 . . .	1·000
1912	1·068	1923	1·153
1913	1·057	1924	1·122
1914	0·981	1925	1·128
1915	1·111	1926	1·131
1916	1·083	1927 . . .	1·095
1917	1·126	1928 . . .	1·129
1918	1·143	1929	1·100
1919	1·124	1930	1·077
1920	1·118	1931	1·128
1921	1·153	1932	1·014

As a result of investigations on family budgets carried out by the Statistical Bureau of the Government over a year, beginning in

[1] The crop year begins on November 1 of the previous year.

September, 1931, the monthly rice expenditures of labourers and salaried men were found to be as follows:

EXPENDITURE FOR RICE PER FAMILY (1)

	Less than	Less than	Less than	Less than	Less than	Less than	More than
	Yen	Yen	Yen	Yen	Yen	Yen	Yen
Monthly Income Class .	50	60	70	80	90	100	100
No. of Families investigated . . .	15	78	251	254	287	258	374

Monthly Average per Family

No. of Actual Members .	3·80	3·86	3·86	4·04	4·10	4·16	4·21
No. of Unit Consumers .	2·90	3·05	2·90	2·99	3·02	3·11	3·16
	Yen	Yen	Yen	Yen	Yen	Yen	Yen
Total Expenditure .	46.04	51.73	59.31	66.74	75.65	82.13	97.13
	Yen	Yen	Yen	Yen	Yen	Yen	Yen
Total expenditure for food	19.87	20.66	22.26	23.94	25.96	27.85	30.04
for rice . . .	7.14	7.00	7.02	7.01	7.14	7.28	7.01
for wheat . . .	0.09	0.15	0.08	0.08	0.06	0.04	0.06
for housing . .	7.69	9.49	10.73	12.13	13.95	14.51	17.12

Percentages

Total expenditure (%) . .	100·00	100·00	100·00	100·00	100·00	100·00	100·00
for food (%) .	43·16	39·94	37·53	35·87	34·32	33·91	30·93
for rice (%) .	15·51	13·53	11·84	10·50	9·44	8·84	7·22
for wheat (%) .	0·19	0·29	0·13	0·12	0·08	0·05	0·06
for housing (%)	16·70	18·35	18·09	18·17	18·44	17·67	17·63

The above Table shows that the smaller the family the larger is the percentage of payment for rice in the total of expenditures: it is nearly 16 per cent. of the total expenditures among the poorest classes. In families with the smallest incomes there is no other item of expenditure so large as that for rice, except rent, which shows a slightly higher percentage.

The above statistics show the average figures for the families of both labourers and salaried men combined, but when the two classes are considered separately it will be seen that the expenditure for rice becomes far greater in the families of labourers than in the families of salaried men. This may be seen in the following Table:

EXPENDITURE FOR RICE PER FAMILY (2)

Income Class	No. of Family	Salaried Class		No. of Family	Labourers	
		No. of Unit Consumers	Expenditure for Rice		No. of Unit Consumers	Expenditure for Rice
Yen			Yen			Yen
Less than 50 .	1	1·90	5.75	14	2·94	7.24
,, 60 .	7	2·86	5.88	71	3·04	7.11
,, 70 .	57	2·76	6.31	194	2·95	7.22
,, 80 .	74	2·89	6.35	180	3·04	7.29
,, 90 .	103	2·82	6.30	184	3·13	7.61
,, 100 .	106	2·96	6.52	152	3·21	7.81
More than 100 .	177	3·00	6.37	197	3·30	7.60
Total or average	525	2·91	6.37	992	3·12	7.46

Because of its unique place in the Japanese diet, rice is an indispensable article of food. The consumption of wheat, wheat-flour, fruit and vegetables is increasing annually, but this does not mean that they will replace rice. Probably there is no Western nation which spends so large a proportion of its income on wheat as the Japanese do on rice.

Production of Rice

Because of their characteristic preference for Japanese rice, the Japanese people cannot buy their staple food in the world markets, but since about 1900 Japan has become a rice-importing country, the quantity imported varying from year to year. This importation has been made, however, simply to fill a shortage and not to replace home-grown rice. The increasing population has made necessary an increase in the area cultivated for rice. Great efforts have been made to acclimatize the Japanese variety of rice to Chosen and Taiwan since they were annexed to Japan. It is not going too far to state that, without the present development in rice cultivation in Chosen, Japan would never have been able to support the large population which she does to-day.

Although Japanese rice is cultivated over the entire country, the area which produces rice, as compared with the Asiatic continent, is, relatively speaking, so small that climatic conditions vary little over the whole area. Consequently, in any year when weather conditions have been favourable good crops are harvested over the entire country, and when weather conditions have been adverse the whole country is apt to suffer from a poor harvest. If the area of production were wider a poor harvest in one district might easily be offset by a bumper crop in another; and if this were the case, production as a whole would show fewer fluctuations, and changes in price would be minimized.[1] But for Japanese rice such equalizing factors are absent, and fluctuations in the price of rice due to climatic conditions can hardly be prevented. This being the situation, the control of the price of rice in Japan presents certain peculiar difficulties.

As an instance, the rice crop in the autumn of 1930 showed an increase of 12 per cent. over the average crop in Japan proper. In Chosen and Taiwan, in the same year, the crop was larger than that of the previous year by 40 per cent. and 10 per cent. respectively. But for this record crop, the price of rice would not have fallen so rapidly as it did towards the end of 1930. The average monthly price of rice per koku fell from 30.53 yen in August, to 28.70 yen in September, 19.13 yen in October, 18.13 yen in November, and 18.04 yen in December.

Rice cultivation plays an important part in Japanese agriculture. The total cultivated area in Japan proper is about 5,920,000 cho, and is divided into upland farms and paddy-fields. Paddy-fields are solely for the cultivation of rice, and can be satisfactorily used to that end only when they have sufficient irrigating facilities. In 1931 the total area of rice-fields was about 3,200,000 cho, larger than the total area of all the upland farms. These rice-fields are cultivated by about 5,500,000[2] small farmers, and are exclusively devoted to the cultivation of rice (wheat, clover, timothy and other green manure crops being cultivated as second crops only when the climatic and drainage conditions are favourable).[3] Upland farms are utilized for producing various cereals, vegetables, beans, fruits and other products. The existence of two kinds of farm-lands in Japan has caused many agricultural problems in the country.

The cultivation of rice has been continuously and universally carried on in Japan proper from very early times, but the methods of production and marketing, which were handed down by tradition, have not

[1] Cf. A. C. Pigou, *Industrial Fluctuations*, 2nd ed., p. 223, London, 1929.
[2] This is the total number of farming families. We cannot calculate the number of individuals who are engaged in cultivating rice.
[3] Cf. S. Nasu, *Land Utilization in Japan* (Tokyo, 1929): a report to the Kyoto Conference of the Institute of Pacific Relations.

L

been much improved upon so far. Upland farming, however, has begun to make progress under the stimulus of new demands for its products created by the development of industry and commerce, and the growth of urban districts. Since the World War the production of vegetables and fruits has rapidly increased. Taking the cultivated area for principal vegetables and fruits in 1920 as 100, we find an increase to 144 in 1929 for the entire country, and an increase to 291 in the main producing districts. The volume of production of vegetables and fruits also increased from 100 to 165 throughout the country, and to 355 in the main producing districts. Furthermore with the increased demand for silk, the area for the planting of mulberry-trees increased from 100 in 1920 to 134 in 1929. Because of this extensive cultivation of agricultural commodities other than rice, room for increasing the cultivation of rice has become extremely limited.

The tenant system prevails to a considerable degree in Japan. At the end of 1931 the following figures were given:

Rice-fields	(1000 *cho*)
Cultivated by owners	1497
Cultivated by tenants	1715

Upland Farms	
Cultivated by owners	1649
Cultivated by tenants	1093

On the upland farms rent is usually paid in cash, or in money value represented by a certain quantity of produce, and only where grain is raised is the rent paid in kind. In rice-farming the rent is paid in rice. While in many upland farming districts the tenants cultivate and market their crops themselves, rice-field tenants pay their rent in kind, and seldom market their own rice. It is the landowner who does so. Thus, the cultivator of rice and the seller of rice are separate persons, and the rice planter seldom knows anything about the processes for marketing his produce. On the other hand, the tenant of the upland farm is more likely to know how agricultural products are put on the market. In addition, sericulture has played an important part in giving the small farmer a knowledge of commercial dealings. To sum up, in studying the rice price control policy we must not fail to note that the landowner who engages in the marketing of rice is extremely interested in the fluctuations in the price of rice, whereas the tenant is more concerned with the changes in the volume of his crop.

Needless to say, apart from small tenants and small owner-cultivators, there are quite a number of peasants who market their own rice. All who are informed on rural conditions know well how greatly in need of cash these farmers are. They put their rice on the market as soon as it is harvested, causing thereby a glut in the market, and consequently find that they must sell their products at a terrible discount.

According to an estimate made by the Department of Agriculture and Forestry (an estimate based upon the quantity of rice sold in each month of a certain year between 1925 and 1929, when the crop approximated to the average for the said five years), the quantity of rice sold each month was as follows [1] :

	Rice (1000 koku)			Per cent.		
	Sold by Landowners	Sold by Cultivators	Total			
	(A)	(B)	(C)	(A)	(B)	(C)
November .	704	3,309	4,013	5·70	15·86	12·09
December .	1,550	4,773	6,322	12·56	22·88	19·04
January . .	1,461	2,860	4,321	11·84	13·71	13·01
Total .	3,715	10,942	14,657	30·10	52·45	44·14
February . .	1,060	1,664	2,724	8·59	7·98	8·21
March . .	983	1,258	2,241	7·96	6·03	6·75
April . .	996	1,045	2,042	8·07	5·01	6·15
Total (3 months)	3,039	3,967	7,007	24·62	19·02	21·10
Total (6 months)	6,754	14,909	21,664	54·72	71·47	65·24
May . .	996	946	1,924	8·07	4·54	5.85
June . .	892	851	1,743	7·23	4·08	5·25
July. . .	955	810	1,765	7·74	3·88	5·32
Total (3 months)	2,843	2,607	5,450	23·04	12·49	16·41
Total (9 months)	9,597	17,516	27,113	77·76	83·96	81·66
August . .	1,096	909	2,005	8·88	4·36	6·04
September .	883	1,045	1,928	7·15	5·01	5·81
October . .	767	1,392	2,159	6·21	6·67	6·50
Total (3 months)	2,745	3,346	6,082	22·24	16·04	18·35
Grand Total	12,342	20,862	33,204	100·00	100·00	100·00

As can be seen in the above Table, the totals for every quarter of the year, when compared, show that the quantity sold by landowners

[1] Figures are given to the nearest thousand koku and the nearest ·01 per cent. respectively.

is more or less evenly distributed over the whole year, the percentages for each quarter being 30·1, 24·6, 23 and 22·2, whereas the quantity sold by cultivators in the same periods shows very uneven percentages of 52·5, 19, 12·5 and 16 respectively. We can thus see that more than half of the total amount of rice sold by cultivators is marketed from November to January. This fact alone would account fully for any great seasonal fluctuations in the price of rice.

An important step toward controlling the price of rice would be the granting of loans to the cultivators of rice at the time of harvesting in order to enable them to store new crops. The Government does make low-interest loans every year to that end, and furthermore co-operative warehouses exist for the storing of rice (in 1931 these warehouses numbered 2800, their storage capacity reaching 6,500,000 koku, or about 12 per cent. of the rice produced in the country), but the benefits of the loans are not yet widespread.

Problem of the Price of Rice

Assuming the total rice crop to have been sold in every year, the value of the rice sold would have been 1584 million yen in 1929, 1118 million in 1930, 913 million in 1931 and 1200 million in 1932. In corresponding years the sale of silk cocoons amounted to no more than 655 million, 304 million, 276 million and 297 million yen. These figures, however, do not necessarily establish the greater importance of rice as a source of income for the rural population; for though the sale of cocoons is represented by smaller figures, the rice *actually* sold brings in far less than the above figures indicate, as those figures serve only to show the value of rice if the entire crop in each year had been sold out.

We shall next examine the importance which the rice price has in relation to the different classes of the rural population.

Small tenants who pay their rent in rice do not possess surplus rice to sell; some have to buy rice to meet their own needs, or are obliged to sell their high-priced rice in order to buy foreign rice which is cheaper. When, in 1930 and 1931, Professor S. Nasu of the Tokyo Imperial University conducted a survey in twenty villages of different prefectures, the following facts were revealed: out of the 487 peasant households investigated, about 68 per cent. supplied their entire need for rice, 6 per cent. purchased the entire amount needed, 10 per cent. purchased what corresponded to less than a three months' supply, 7 per cent. less than a three to six months' supply, 7 per cent. less than a six to nine months' supply, and 2 per cent. more than a nine months' supply. With the specialization in agriculture and upland farming, toward which there is a strong tendency, there must necessarily be an increase in the number of households which must purchase their rice. The fact that so many farmers have to buy their own rice is contrary to the common belief that the farmer consumes the rice which he cultivates.

Basing its estimates upon the statistics of a standard year between 1925-1929 when the rice crop approximated to the average for the said five years, the Department of Agriculture and Forestry computed that of the rice produced in Japan proper the quantity sold was as follows:

				1000 koku	*Percentage*
Total production	.	.	.	60,269	100·0
Quantity sold	.	.	.	33,204	55·1
Sold by landowners	.	.	.	12,342	20·5
Sold by cultivators	.	.	.	20,862	34·6

The area of the rice-fields cultivated by tenants is 1,497,000 cho, or about 47·8 per cent. of the total area of rice-fields in Japan. The crop from these tenant rice-fields is about 29,230,000 koku, and, incredible as it may seem, the rent of a tenant rice-field in Japan amounts to half of the total crop. Thus the aggregate rent of tenant rice-fields in Japan must reach about 14,615,000 koku. When compared with the quantity sold by landowners (12,342,000 koku) we find that landowners sell as much as 85 per cent. of the crop which they collect as rent. Cultivators —both the owner-cultivator and tenant—sell 20,862,000 koku, or 45 per cent. of 45,654,000 koku, which is the total of the rice cultivated less the quantity paid by tenants to landowners.

To the medium and small landowners rice provides the only source of money income, and it is therefore not surprising that they show much concern over the price of rice. The cultivator, however, as he does not sell so much of his rice, is not so interested as the landowner in the price of rice; the tenant, in particular, is always interested in an abundant crop rather than in a high price, as the volume of rice left on hand after the rent is paid is of greater importance to him. From this we can understand why landowners have continued to give their support to political movements which aimed at keeping up the price of rice.

Speculators and rice merchants are opposed to measures which aim to control and stabilize the price of rice, for they profit chiefly by the fluctuations in the price of rice. Naturally, they were opposed to the promulgation of the Rice Control Act of 1921, and have continued to

165

raise objections to revisions of the Act which would give the Government greater control over the price of rice. According to a census taken in 1920 the total number of rice merchants in Japan proper was about 79,000, and the number of their employees about 70,000.

In Chosen and Taiwan, where phenomenal progress has been made in the cultivation of rice, the rice merchants, unlike the rice merchants of Japan proper, undertake not only the marketing of rice, but also attend to the husking of it. Although in Japan proper the farmer husks his own rice before marketing it, the farmer in Chosen and Taiwan lacks both the time and the proper tools for husking it, and sells his rice unhusked.

The farmer in Chosen and Taiwan has few supplementary sources of money income, for he does not engage in sericulture or horticulture, and at harvest time is usually obliged to sell his rice at a heavy discount, and with even greater losses than the Japanese farmer, or, if he is short of cash, sells out his expected crop before harvest time at a ridiculously low price. The financial difficulties of the farmer have added a special feature to the rôle which the rice merchants play, in that the rice merchants have become moneylenders, as in those countries where a farmers' co-operative movement has not yet developed.

Rice merchants in Chosen and Taiwan are mostly Japanese, and those who import rice into Japan are usually prominent rice merchants in Japan. They are unanimous in their objection to a controlled rice price, and to the importing of colonial rice. Their objection has proved a great obstacle in the way of effecting a system for controlling the price of rice in Japan.

A SHORT HISTORY OF PRICE CONTROL

System of Price Control

Under the present economic system of free competition it is not in the power of an individual to fix the price of a commodity; the individual simply adapts his economic activities to the existing price system, and it can, for this reason, be said that man does not control prices, but that prices control the economic activities of man.

In recent years, however, there has appeared to be a growing interest in the active control of prices, and attempts have been made to divert prices from what has seemed to be their natural and inevitable course. Complete control of prices can be attained only by giving an absolute monopoly to some group of sellers, but partial control may be exercised through groups, such as the co-operative associations in Japan. These organized groups, however, often compete more fiercely with each other than do individuals outside this system. Since the control of prices cannot be effected through measures in the economic field only there has been an increasing tendency of late to employ political measures. This form of control may be called the " political control of price "; it aims at substituting the " political price " for the " automatic price."

The forms of control carried on in Japan may be classified thus:

1. Political control:
   (a) Government action in the market.
   (b) Tariff policy regarding rice.
   (c) Storing of rice and control of production favoured by the Government
   (d) A monetary policy.
2. Economic control through producers or consumers:
   (a) Control initiated by local co-operative associations.
   (b) Control initiated by federations of co-operative associations.

Control through co-operative associations has met with signal success, and the National Federation of Co-operative Marketing Associations was recently established in order to effect this kind of control. This paper, however, will deal only with problems relating to the control of the rice price by the Government, and the Government activities in the rice market.

History of Government Control

It was not until 1921 that the Government adopted for the first time a system for controlling the price of rice. The events leading up to the tariff policy of this year will be traced from the Tokugawa Era.

In the Tokugawa Era the control of the price of rice was a Government policy of great importance. It may be said that the national economy of that period was based upon rice, and the saying " Rice price rules commodity price " suggests the importance which rice held in the life of those times.

The control of the price of rice in the Tokugawa Era was not necessarily or primarily concerned with preventing an advance in its price. In those days, when the cultivation of rice was limited to a small area, the size of the harvest immediately affected the price of rice, but the Government was more concerned with securing a supply of rice sufficient for the needs of the people; it encouraged the storing of rice when there was an abundance of it, even promoting the cultivation of other grains as a provision against lean years. In short, the control of rice in those days was a measure to provide against famine.

The Meiji Restoration brought about a significant change in the economic life of the nation. Within ten years of its establishment the new Government changed the land tax from a tax in kind to a tax in money; until then the land tax had been paid in kind and the Government revenue came from the sale of the rice collected as tax. Landowners were obliged to sell their rice in order to pay their taxes. The Government was now able to draw up its budget without considering the fluctuations in the price of rice, and within ten years was able to complete this reform of the taxation system.

The Government then had to face several new problems. First, since the land tax was to be paid in money, it was necessary to prevent a fall in the price of rice, and thus ensure a source of Government revenue. Secondly, the collecting of a uniform land tax was difficult, for with undeveloped communications local markets rather than the central market were of greater importance, and the price of rice varied according to the locality, fluctuating within short periods of time. Under such conditions it was necessary that the Government should exercise control over the price of rice. Thirdly, the Government had to resort to exporting rice in order to improve the finances of the country, out of which a large amount of gold specie had been taken by traders at a time when a confused monetary system had permitted this exporting of gold.

The Government established the Rice Control Bureau (1872-1882), which was authorized to purchase, sell and export rice, and promulgated the Act for the Storage of Rice (1875) in order to stabilize the price of rice. Between 1876 and 1889 the rice exported by the Government annually was from 1,500,000 to 2 million bushels. Such were the measures taken by the Government to raise the price of rice, but with the improvement in the finances of the Government, after 1890, the importance of the measures for price control gradually decreased. Revenue from taxes other than on land rapidly increased with the development of industry and trade. Of the various kinds of tax on land, tax on upland farmland and residential land contributed to a further increase in revenue. From 1875 to 1879 the revenue from the land tax constituted on the average 81 per cent. of the total of the state revenue, but in the following periods, 1880-1884, 1885-1889, 1890-1894, 1895-1899, 1900-1904, and 1905-1909, the percentage changed to 60, 69, 73, 58, 32, and 28 respectively.

After 1890 the demand for agricultural products greatly increased as a result of industrial development and a rapid increase in population. Under such a stimulus, and with the encouragement given by the Government, agriculture made great progress, but the demand for food still remains greater than the supply. The food problem became quite acute, so that by the end of the nineteenth century Japan, instead of being a rice-exporting country, became a rice-importing country.

Inasmuch as the importing of rice became necessary, Japan's dependence on Oriental countries for her food-supply increased. Under the first Customs Tariff Law of 1897 rice was not dutiable, although import duties were levied on wheat, flour, barley, and other cereals. During the Russo-Japanese War, in order to increase the state revenue, the Government imposed an import duty of 64·1 sen per 100 kin on rice, and the law became effective on July 1, 1905. Since that time the duty rates have been revised many times. The following is a table of the tariffs on imported rice:

IMPORT DUTIES ON RICE (per 100 kin)

	Yen
July 1, 1905–Sept. 30, 1906 . . .	0.641
Oct. 1, 1906–July 16, 1911 . . .	0.64
July 17, 1911–July 28, 1911 . . .	1.00
July 29, 1911–Sept. 30, 1911 . . .	0.64
Oct. 1, 1911–May 27, 1912 . . .	1.00
May 28, 1912–Oct. 31, 1912 . . .	0.40
Nov. 1, 1912–Oct. 31, 1918 . . .	1.00
Nov. 1, 1918–Oct. 31, 1920 . . .	..
Nov. 1, 1920–Nov. 21, 1921 . . .	1.00
Nov. 22, 1921–Oct. 31, 1922 . . .	..
Nov. 1, 1922–Sept. 11, 1923 . . .	1.00
Sept. 12, 1923–July 31, 1924 . . .	..
Aug. 1, 1924–Jan. 25, 1925 . . .	1.00
Jan. 26. 1925–Oct. 31, 1925 . . .	..
Nov. 1, 1925–Feb. 13, 1927 . . .	1.00
Feb. 14, 1927–Aug. 12, 1927 . . .	..
Aug. 13, 1927–Nov. 19, 1930 . . .	1.00
Nov. 20, 1930–Dec. 31, 1934 . . .	2.00

We may note that—

(a) The import of Chosen rice to Japan proper has been increasing in recent years. Up to 1913 (Chosen was annexed in 1910) the duty on Chosen rice was at the same rate as the duty on foreign rice, but since that year Chosen rice has been entering free of duty.

(b) The import duty on foreign rice was lifted on five different occasions in the past; the period during which foreign rice was admitted free of duty being in all fifty months. In such times of emergency as after violent earthquakes and fires, when the price of rice had to be kept at a low level, foreign rice was not dutiable.

Since 1921 the Government has been given the power to control the customs duty on rice whenever it is deemed necessary; in this way the tariff policy has served as one of the measures for controlling the price of rice.

PASSAGE OF THE RICE CONTROL ACT

During the quarter of a century before the Great War, rapid progress was made in Japanese agriculture; the cultivation of rice progressed side by side with the cultivation of mulberry-trees and horticulture. Both mulberry-tree planting and horticulture were carried out on upland farms and did not encroach upon the rice-fields—that is to say, they did not compete with the cultivation of rice. Although importations of foreign rice had been made, the imported rice was merely to fill a shortage, for Japanese rice had a kind of natural protection due to the fact that the demand was exclusively for Japanese rice.

With the outbreak of the Great War, however, the whole situation was changed. The economic disturbance caused by the war affected international trade. In Japan there was a sudden fall in the price of raw silk, Japan's most valuable export, 80 per cent. of which went to the United States. The prices of most farm products fell, especially the price of rice. The abundant crops of 1914 and 1915, which were both about 12 per cent. larger than the average, further spurred the falling tendency in prices. Then, in January 1915, the Government passed a bill called the " Rice Price Control Act," by which it endeavoured for a time to check the falling price by buying up rice. Between March and May 1915 the Government purchased about 1,500,000 bushels and held it off the market. This was the first price-control measure adopted by the Government since the Meiji Restoration. It is doubtful, however, whether the Government purchase had any telling effect, for the annual production of rice at that time was calculated at around 250 million bushels, of which one-half was sent to the market. The Government, moreover, found it very difficult to store the purchased rice, and the greater part was allowed to decay or spoil.

A rise in prices was, however, a more important result of the European War. Japanese manufacture received a great impetus toward expansion and for the first time acquired the strength to enter into competition with the other nations of the world. The total currency in circulation was increased from only 416 million yen in 1914 to 1336 million yen in 1918, and then to 1844 million yen in 1919. The prices of all commodities advanced by leaps and bounds, and industrialists and agriculturists alike were given the full benefit of the war boom. But consumers, and in particular the salaried classes, suffered acutely. The following Table of wages will serve to show the stress under which the wage-earner lived.

WAGES IN THIRTEEN CITIES (1900=100)

		Nominal Wages	Real Wages
1913	. . .	161.6	111
1914	. . .	160.1	120
1915	. . .	160.2	129
1916	. . .	169.2	117
1917	. . .	194.9	99
1918	. . .	257.7	92
1919	. . .	355.1	108
1920	. . .	461.3	138
1921	. . .	459.6	167
1922	. . .	495.2	194

The unsound situation which existed found expression in the notorious Rice Riot of the summer of 1918. In a small provincial town a group of fishermen's wives raided the shops of rice merchants, and this was the beginning of the Rice Riot, which spread to practically all the cities and towns of the country within the brief period of two or three weeks. The houses of rice merchants were set on fire, and demonstrations were carried on in protest against the high price of rice. The Government and local authorities had great difficulty in checking the disturbances, and in many cases the aid of troops was required to check the movements of the angered mobs. With the Rice Riot began the labour movements which developed in later years.

When the Riot broke out the Government, which had no fixed price policy, adopted a number of emergency measures in an attempt to cope with the situation. These measures, unsystematic though they were, sanctioned the importation of 18 million bushels of foreign rice and its sale below cost, as well as the sale at low prices of Japanese, Chosen and Taiwan rice; they prohibited the export of rice, wheat and wheat-flour, abolished the import duty on cereals, encouraged the improvement of transportation, applied an ordinance prohibiting excessive profits, encouraged the use of substitute foodstuffs, and supervised the cereal markets by controlling the movements of the Rice Exchange. Despite these and other measures, the price of rice continued to rise until 1920. The rice question now presented itself with a new significance, for the Government had begun to realize that the production of Japanese rice was no longer sufficient to meet the demand of an increasing population. It became apparent that production must be increased, both intensively [1] and extensively, to prevent a further great rise in price, and to avert the possibility of future riots.

Since the Rice Riot a movement was begun toward the reclamation of virgin lands, especially in Hokkaido. Not only were various facilities and subventions offered to this end, but also the home colonization policy in Hokkaido was systematized. The most extensive plan for increasing production was the creation of rice-fields, and the improvement of the existing fields in Taiwan and Chosen. These measures, of course, did not have immediate results.

Two years after the Rice Riot the post-war depression set in, totally dislocating world economy. This, with the world-wide deflation, sent the price of rice in Japan reeling downward in March 1920. The abundant crop of that year further aided the downward trend. Between the March of 1920 and the March of the following year the price per koku of rice fell from 54 to 25 yen. The Government, which had been alarmed previously by the high price of rice, was now dismayed by the low price. In the autumn of 1920 the National Federation of Agricultural Associations [2] began a country-wide movement to prevent the dumping of rice by producers and landowners, incidentally providing the starting-point for the producers' co-operative movement later on.

Since extreme fluctuations in prices, although advantageous to merchants and speculators, would always give much difficulty to producers and consumers, the Government realized that there was a need for some permanent and systematic price control, and in 1921 adopted the Rice Control Act. By tracing the operation and revisions of this Act, the rice price policy during the ten years following its adoption will be described.

---

[1] The average crop of Japanese rice per tan (0·245 acres) is as follows, and in recent years it has shown little increase:

Crop Year	Koku	Crop Year	Koku	Crop Year	Koku
1912	1·703	1919	1·996	1926	1·799
1913	1·689	1920	2·056	1927	1·993
1914	1·920	1921	1·794	1928	1·923
1915	1·862	1922	1·980	1929	1·908
1916	1·934	1923	1·800	1930	2·102
1917	1·810	1924	1·869	1931	1·733
1918	1·807	1925	1·926		

[2] The National Federation of Agricultural Associations (TeikokuONokwai) is the central organization of cultivators and landowners. Every village has its own Village Association (in 1932 there were 11,371); Village Associations constitute Township Associations (560), the latter constitute Prefectural Associations (47), and these finally constitute the National Federation.

JAPANESE RICE CONTROL

Since its adoption in 1921 the Rice Control Act has undergone revision from time to time, and consequently its application has varied as often. A general outline of the rice problem will be presented along with a description of the circumstances which made the revisions necessary.

First Period (1921-1931)

April 1921-*March* 1925.—The Rice Control Act in its original form was extremely ambiguous, for the text of the Act was very much abbreviated. Article I. said, " in case it is found necessary to adjust the supply and demand of rice, the Government may purchase, sell, exchange, polish or store rice." It did not refer to the price of rice. What exactly was meant by " adjusting the supply and demand of rice " without any reference to the price of rice? Obviously, any intervention of the Government in the supply of rice must necessarily cause changes in its price.

When the bill was submitted to the Diet, the landed interests of the country pointed out this ambiguity in the law, and insisted that the Rice Control Act should aim explicitly at controlling the price of rice. It is possible that this ambiguity was purposely adopted for such reasons as the following. As has already been said, at the time the Rice Control Act was adopted the price of rice had fallen sharply, so the aim of the Act was to raise the price, but any expression of that aim in the text of the law would have been criticized as a neglect of the interests of the consuming public and of the commercial and industrial classes; furthermore, the memory of the Rice Riot was still fresh in the minds of the drafters of the bill. Thus, the Government which proposed the bill strongly objected to including in the text " the control of the price of rice." Both the representatives of the farming interests and those of the commercial and industrial interests expected that the ambiguity of the Act would result in an interpretation favourable to itself.

Apart from this ambiguity in the text, the methods themselves by which the Government would act upon the law were clearly defined. First, the Government was empowered to purchase or sell rice, and to use funds for that purpose up to 200 million yen. This fund was included in the special accounts of the Government. For that portion of the fund which was used for the above purpose, a certain fixed interest was to be paid. Secondly, the tariff on rice could be raised, lowered or abolished freely by the Government. Thirdly, the Government had a free hand in restricting the importation and exportation of rice.

It is to be especially noted that the principles by which these methods were to be applied were not specified. For instance, it was not clear upon what basis the adjustment of the supply and demand of rice would be made. This gave the administrators a great deal of latitude in the application of the Act; as an instance, the political party in power would be able to raise the price of rice by using the Government's power to purchase rice, and attempt to gain the support of the farming classes at election time. If we remember that in Japan the election of the members of the House of Representatives generally takes place in February, that the Diet session opens from January to March, and that the marketing of rice takes place largely during the winter, we can see that the Rice Control Act was open to the danger of political abuse because of the lack of a principle for its application.

April 1925-*June* 1931.—Since the passing of the Rice Control Act the price of rice showed an upward trend, the average price for one koku moving from 29.20 yen in 1921 to 36.85 yen in 1922, 31.57 yen in 1923, 36.64 yen in 1924, 41.95 yen in 1925, and 38.44 yen in 1926. There was no longer a demand from the farmer " to adjust the supply and demand of rice " in a way which would advance its price. The quantity of rice actually purchased by the Government was very small; notwithstanding, the Government at the time of the 1923 earthquake bought and distributed a great deal of foreign rice among the refugees.

Whenever a purchase of rice was to be made the Government each time announced the price at which it would buy rice, but when the price showed an upward trend there was unwillingness on the part of the holders of rice to sell to the Government. For instance, in June 1921, and from February to March 1923 the Government expected to purchase a total of 5 million bushels, but actually could purchase only one-third of what it expected on the first occasion, and about one-fourth on the second. Thus it came about that the mere announcement of purchase by the Government fully served the purpose of the Act. A minor revision in the Act was effected in April 1925, when it was explicitly stated that the aim of the Act was to bring about " the adjustment of the quantity and the market price of rice." This amendment did not, however, effect any substantial change. When speaking of the adjustment of the quantity and the price of rice, it is to be remembered that the chief cause of the fluctuations in the price of Japanese rice is the state of the harvest. In order, therefore, to regulate the quantity of rice on the market, so as to nullify the effects of an over-abundant or poor harvest, there must be some measure for con-

174

trolling the price of rice. Hence, it is important that beside the general " adjustment of price " there should be an " adjustment of quantity."

New Problems of Rice

Since the spring of 1930 the farming communities in Japan began to feel the effect of the world-wide economic depression; silk quotations fell, the price for cocoons declined, the demand for agricultural products decreased, and the price of rice went down. To add to all this the rice harvest of 1930 was the largest ever known. That autumn the rice in Japan proper showed a yield of 66,880,000 koku, or an increase of about 112 per cent. over the crop of the previous year. Moreover the farmers who suffered from the fall in the prices of silk and vegetables made haste to sell out their rice. As a result, the price of rice fell from 28.70 yen in September 1930 to 19.13 yen in October, 18.13 yen in November, and 18.40 yen in December. The average price of rice during 1930 (November 1929 to October 1930) was 27.34 yen, during 1931 was 18.46 yen, showing a fall of about 33 per cent. By this time the general agricultural depression in Japan had set in.

So far, in discussing the rice problem, we have spoken only of Japan proper, but Chosen and Taiwan play an important part in this problem and cannot be ignored. Since the average consumption of rice in Japan proper is about 70 million koku a year, it can be seen that even with the bumper crop of 1930 there would have been a shortage of over 3 million koku but for the rice supplied by Chosen and Taiwan. Actually, the supply from Chosen and Taiwan was far greater than the demand. In 1930 the rice crop in Chosen and Taiwan showed an increase of about 40 per cent. and 10 per cent. respectively over the crops of the previous year. This increase was due partly to the favourable climatic conditions, but was in great part due to the fact that the rice acreage had been increased considerably, and the methods of production improved. These factors undoubtedly played an important part in bringing down the price of rice in 1930.

The cultivation of rice in Chosen has long received the attention of the Government, which, since the Rice Riot of 1918, has endeavoured to increase the output of Chosen rice. A plan to increase the output of rice in Chosen was drawn up and adopted in 1920. This plan was expected to be completed by 1940. In outline it was as follows.

First, it provided for the irrigating and draining of 200,000 cho of rice-land which hitherto had had no irrigation system, and depended for water mainly on the rain. The development of new rice-fields, to the extent of 150,000 cho, was also included in the plan. Second, artificial fertilizer was to be used on the 350,000 cho of rice-land mentioned above, as well as on the 390,000 cho of rice-fields already existing. The cultivation of manure crops was also to be encouraged. Third, Japanese rice was to be introduced and cultivated instead of the native rice.

This large agricultural program was expected to require 330 million yen. The Government General of Chosen gave about 80 million yen as subventions to this plan, while the remainder was to be obtained through low-interest loans of the Japanese Government, or through long-term debentures of the Chosen Industrial Bank and the Oriental Development Company. With the completion of this program, it is expected that the production of rice in Chosen will be increased by about 8 million koku, and estimating the demand for rice in Chosen to increase by 3 million koku, the surplus exported to Japan will be increased by about 5 million koku. Calculating from this, the importation of rice from Chosen, which was 5 million koku in 1926, will increase to about 10 million koku in 1940. The irrigation, the application of artificial fertilizers, and the improvement of the quality of different varieties of rice, have been carried out successfully, and far more quickly than the program demanded. With the program only half completed, the importation of rice from Chosen to Japan has already increased, as in the following Tables:

QUANTITY OF RICE IMPORTED FROM CHOSEN TO JAPAN [1] (1000 *koku*)

Crop Year	(A) Production in Japan proper	(B) Shipment from Chosen to Japan proper	Percentage of (B) to (A)
1918 . . .	54,568	1733	3·2
1919 . . .	54,400	2805	5·1
1920 . . .	60,819	1653	2·7
1921 . . .	63,209	2905	4·6
1922 . . .	55,180	3136	5·7
1923 . . .	60,694	3453	5·7
1924 . . .	55,444	4548	8·2
1925 . . .	57,170	4428	7·7
1926 . . .	59,704	5213	8·7
1927 . . .	55,593	5910	10·6
1928 . . .	62,103	7069	11·4
1929 . . .	60,303	5378	8·9
1930 . . .	59,558	5167	8·7
1931 . . .	66,876	7992	12·0
1932 . . .	55,215	7198	13·0
1933 . . .	60,340	7531	12·4

[1] Each figure in column (A) shows the amount of harvest in the autumn one year previous to the denoted year.

The chief cause of the fall in the price of rice is the increased import of rice from Chosen, and the question arises as to what course will be taken in the future regarding the importation of rice from Chosen.

In studying the problem the following points must be considered. First, Chosen rice, at least that which is sent to Japan, is of the same quality as Japanese rice. Secondly, the average crop per cho in Chosen is at present about 50 per cent. of that in Japan proper, but the total output of the existing fields can without difficulty be increased by using artificial fertilizer. Thirdly, the cost of production in Chosen is much lower than in Japan. Although we have fairly reliable figures for the cost of production in Japan there are none for Chosen; estimates made by the author on the scanty data available are here given for comparison, although these figures are not to be considered as exact:

COST OF PRODUCTION PER KOKU [1]

	(A) Japan proper	(B) Chosen	(B)/(A) Per cent.
	Yen	Yen	
1923 . . .	38.25	21.78	56·9
1924 . . .	37.53	27.16	70·7
1925 . . .	32.97	23.02	69·8
1926 . . .	33.79	29.18	86·3
1929 . . .	26.56	24.68	92·9
1931 . . .	22.70	17.32	76·3
1932 . . .	19.98	15.82	79·2

From this we can see how Chosen rice, from merely supplying a shortage of rice in Japan, has come to compete with Japanese rice. Fourth, the commercial advantages of dealing in the few varieties of Chosen rice are far greater than in dealing with the seventy-four varieties of Japanese rice. Fifth, since Chosen rice is husked and polished by the merchant who sells the rice, a larger quantity of rice is held by one merchant when marketing it than is held by a rice broker or by a co-operative society in Japan. That is to say, the quantity of rice handled by the rice broker or by the co-operative society is very small, for the rice broker usually purchases from small, local producers or landowners, and the co-operative society rarely goes beyond one village for its rice. Naturally, as compared with the dealers in Chosen rice, the small dealers in Japan are not in a position to compete. Sixth, the consumption

[1] Cost of rice production in Japan proper compiled by the National Federation of Agricultural Associations. 3 per cent. of the land value is included in the cost for Japan proper and 8 per cent. in the case of Chosen.

M

177

of rice in Chosen is decreasing, whilst the production of rice is on the increase. To the Chosen farmer rice is not an indispensable foodstuff, and it is his one source of money income. Therefore the Chosen farmer tries to sell larger and larger quantities of rice, purchasing substitute foodstuffs like millet, sorghum and kaoliang, which are far cheaper than rice.

As long as such substitute foodstuffs can be bought, the quantity of rice imported from Chosen will probably increase. In order, therefore, to check the importation of rice from Chosen, it will be necessary to force the consumption of rice in Chosen by limiting production, or else by raising the price of substitute foodstuffs. Measures toward controlling the price of rice have already been taken by restricting the import of millet, sorghum and kaoliang into Chosen, and by the imposition of an import duty on them. (See Table at the end of this chapter.) The annual consumption of rice is shown in the following Table:

ESTIMATE OF RICE CONSUMPTION IN CHOSEN

(*Koku per capita*)

1912	.	.	.	0·699	1922	. . . .	0·635
1914	.	.	.	0·684	1924	. . . .	0·605
1916	.	.	.	0·665	1926	. . . .	0·533
1918	.	.	.	0·682	1928	. . . .	0·541
1920	.	.	.	0·636	1930	. . . .	0·459

In Taiwan a situation somewhat similar to that in Chosen exists. Taiwan rice was formerly put on the market of Japan as foreign rice, but after twenty years of painstaking research a variety of Japanese rice known as " Horai rice " has been acclimatized and is being cultivated extensively. In Taiwan, where there are two harvests a year, in 1932 the area of fields used for the first crop was 283,000 cho, and that for the second crop 370,000 cho, making altogether a total of 653,000 cho. The total of the two harvests in that year reached 7,480,000 koku. The area on which Horai rice was cultivated was 147,000 cho, or 22·5 per cent. of the total area of rice-fields, and the crop yield was 1,909,000 koku, or 25·5 per cent. of the total rice crop. This increase is rather remarkable if one considers that in 1922 the area for Horai rice was only 400 cho. This phenomenal increase has been brought about by several factors, such as—

First, the encouragement given by the Government General for the cultivation of Horai rice (corresponding to the plan of increasing rice production in Chosen); and the developing of an irrigation system through independent corporations which sell water to cultivators. Second, facilities for exporting rice to Japan have been increased.

Third, in Taiwan rice and sugar cane compete for land, although the cultivation of sugar cane has already reached the saturation-point.

With all these advantages in favour of Taiwan rice, the export of rice from that island to Japan has increased as shown by the following figures (in 1000 koku):

Crop Year	Rice Production in Japan proper (A)	Rice Production in Taiwan (B)	Export from Taiwan to Japan proper (C)	Percentage of (C) to (A)
1920 . . .	60,819 *	4,629	663	1·08
1921 . . .	63,209	4,890 †	1,034	1·93
1922 . . .	55,180	4,976	741	1·25
1923 . . .	60,694	5,202	1,132	2·39
1924 . . .	55,444	5,311	1,658	2·95
1925 . . .	57,170	5,246	2,522	4·34
1926 . . .	59,704	6,271	2,187	4·02
1927 . . .	55,593	6,101	2,638	4·36
1928 . . .	62,103	6,637	2,431 (1,064) ‡	4·14
1929 . . .	60,303	6,841	2,253 (1,013)	3·83
1930 . . .	59,558	6,451	2,185 (1,060)	3·25
1931 . . .	66,876	7,111	2,699 (1,663)	4·03
1932 . . .	55,215	7,516	3,419 (2,257)	6·19
1933 . . .	60,390	8,073		

* The figure for each specific year shows the amount of harvest in the autumn of the immediately preceding year.

† The figure includes the second harvest of the preceding year and the first harvest of the year.

‡ The figure in parentheses represents the quantity of Horai rice.

The Government General of Taiwan plans to increase the exportation of rice to Japan to 7 million koku, or to double the present volume, in twenty years. At present the average yield per cho in Taiwan is smaller than in Japan proper: 12 koku for the first harvest, and 10 koku for the second, which is 50 to 60 per cent. of the yield in Japan. However, the cost of production is lower in Taiwan than in Japan, being from three-fifths to two-thirds of the cost in Japan, according to calculations made so far. Thus there are prospects of a further increase in the production of rice in Taiwan.

The above is an outline of the new rice problems which Japan faces as a result of the agricultural developments in the colonies. The points may be summarized as follows. First, the importation of rice from Chosen and Taiwan into Japan has now increased to 20 per cent. of the amount produced at home, and there is a possibility of a further increase. Second, the rice produced in the colonies, with the help of Japanese capital and methods of production, is not inferior in quality, yet is cheaper than home-grown rice, and this fact has only helped to lower the price of rice in Japan. Third, the problem of attaining self-sufficiency in the supply of rice has been solved through the development of rice-fields in the colonies, but the question of price control remains unsolved. If the imports from Chosen and Taiwan were to be prohibited, in order to advance prices in Japan, the colonies would suffer from low prices. The control of the price of rice has been made even more complicated and difficult by the unforeseen development in rice cultivation and the increased acreage. The bumper crop of 1930 emphasized the central problem of price control.

Second Period (after July 1931)

July 1931-*October* 1932.—The Rice Control Act was revised during the agricultural panic of March 1931, and came into force in July of the same year. This revision was more in the nature of a new law than a revision. The revised Act was scarcely an adequate answer to the changed situation outlined above, but it included such new features as:

(*a*) Instead of controlling, as in the past, the import of foreign rice by a restriction on volume, or by tariff regulations, the exporting and importing of rice was to require Government permission. This revision was of little importance when applied to Japan proper, since rice is not generally imported from foreign countries.

(*b*) A *standard for price control* by the Government was definitely set. According to Article IV. " the purchase or sale of rice by the Government within the Empire is restricted only when the price of rice is above the maximum or below the minimum price announced by the Government." For the first time since 1921 the ambiguity concerning price control was removed.

According to the Act three factors determined the maximum and minimum prices: the cost of production of rice, the " price payable by the consumer " of rice, and the " calculated trend price " of rice. The method of computing the maximum and minimum prices is as follows. *Minimum price* should be set at a point not lower than the cost of production and not higher than 80 per cent. of the " calculated trend price " of rice. *Maximum price* should be set at a point not higher than the " price payable by consumers " and not lower than 120 per cent. of the " calculated trend price " of rice.

The three factors mentioned above may be briefly explained. The " calculated trend price " of rice is the price calculated for any particular year by the Government, and is to indicate the relation of the price of rice in the general price-level. In making the calculation all necessary statistical information will be drawn from the " Bank of Japan Index Number of Wholesale Prices." [1] The " calculated trend price " of rice for each crop year is to be expressed by: (a) the coefficient of the ratio of the rice price to the general commodity price in the past multiplied by (b) the index number of the rice price in November of the previous year multiplied by (c) 11.18 yen. As to (a), the ratio of the rice price to the general commodity price varies for different years; the coefficient of the ratio in every year is calculated by the method of least squares, the base being October 1900.

As to (c), the 11.18 yen is the price of rice for October, 1900, which is taken as the base month by the Bank of Japan Index Number.

According to Professor Y. Yagi, of Kyoto Imperial University, the " calculated trend price " of rice for each year is as follows:

	Calculated Trend Prices	(a)
	Yen	
1922	34.53	1.03204
1923	31.00	1.05585
1924	34.52	1.05199
1925	35.86	1.07086
1926	34.29	1.11063
1927	30.78	1.14885
1928	31.12	1.18244
1929	32.13	1.18781
1930	29.47	1.18201
1931	22.86	1.19313
1932	20.39	1.17450

In order to determine " cost of production," the Government took 615 tenant-farmers and 15 owner-farmers (these numbers will be increased to 2000 in 1933), who lived mainly by cultivating rice of average quality, on fields of average size, with crops of average size per cho, and established how much these farmers paid for seed, fertilizer, labour, cattle, tools, machinery, materials, barns, taxes, interest on land value, and rent. Certain stipulations were made in estimating the money value of the farmers' labour, and materials supplied by themselves. By such means the Government sought to obtain the average cost of rice per koku prevailing throughout the country. It was natural that the landed interests attempted to make the figures as large as possible, and in the Parliamentary debate of 1933 they succeeded in including in the

[1] See *Index Numbers of Wholesale Prices in the United States and Foreign Countries*, U.S. Bureau of Labor Statistics, Bulletin No. 284, 1921.

item of cost the expenses for transporting rice from the producers to the central market, and the fees which the agricultural associations demand. However, the cost of production computed in this manner presents many statistical difficulties. This problem, which the Rice Control Act involves, of expressing a theory in concrete figures, may yet prove a valuable stimulus to econometrics in Japan.

The highest price which the public can pay is supposed to indicate the maximum price, or the " price payable by the consumer." This is obtained by finding the average annual expenditure of 2000 labourers and salaried men whose incomes range from 50 to 100 yen, and whose staple food is polished rice. The expenditures are differentiated into two kinds: expenditure for rice, and expenditure for supplementary foodstuffs, fancy goods, entertainment, amusement, travel and savings. An estimate is made of the largest percentage of the latter expenditure which can be sacrificed to the former. (Let K represent this percentage; this is unofficially estimated at from 5-10 per cent.) Then the highest price of polished rice which these people can pay for is expressed by the fraction:

$$\frac{\text{Expenditure for polished rice} + K \text{ (expenditure for supplementary foods, etc.)}}{\text{Quantity of polished rice consumed}}$$

This price is converted into that of unpolished rice and becomes the " price payable by the consumer " for the year.

The three factors so far explained serve as the legal standard for the application of the Rice Control Act. But, as the calculations for the cost of production and the " price payable by the consumer " of rice could not be made immediately, the Government estimated only the " calculated trend price " of rice, and published for temporary reference two prices at 20 per cent. above and 20 per cent. below the " calculated trend price " as the maximum and minimum prices.

When the Act is examined several points come up for criticism. First, what will be the legal price which will be worked out from the three main factors determining the price of rice? Putting aside some doubtful technical points in connection with computation, we can see that the three standards adopted by the Government include almost all the factors which influence the market price of rice. Is not then the price which the Government proposes to set the price which will appear without any deliberate action on the part of the Government for price control? If this is so, then the complicated calculations are obviously of little use.

Secondly, the maximum and minimum prices, as they are stated above, appear in the following Table:

	Max. Price	Min. Price	Market Price
	Yen	Yen	Yen
1925 . . .	43.03	28.69	41.95
1926 . . .	41.15	27.43	38.44
1927 . . .	36.94	24.62	35.93
1928 . . .	37.34	24.90	31.38
1929 . . .	38.56	25.70	29.19
1930 . . .	35.36	23.58	27.34
1931 . . .	27.43	18.29	18.46
1932 . . .	24.47	16.31	20.69

When we compare these prices with the actual market prices we find that the latter seldom vary beyond the prices of the former; from this we may conclude that there has been little occasion for the Government in the past to exercise any price control, and should this tendency of the market price to fluctuate within the limits set by the " maximum and minimum prices " continue, there will be even less necessity for Government control of prices.

Thirdly, the Rice Control Act attempts to calculate the cost of production for one year, and upon that basis to work out the price of rice for the following year. This method presumes that there will be little change, or none at all, in economic conditions during the consecutive years.

Fourthly, the " Bank of Japan Index Number of Wholesale Prices," upon which the Government bases its calculations, has various technical defects and may not offer an altogether accurate statistical standard for determining any specific economic question. In particular it is unsuited to be a guide to any agricultural policy, as it does not give much consideration to the burden of taxes. Many of the agricultural taxes are far more inelastic than industrial taxes and are levied with little attention to the fluctuations in agricultural prices. The " calculated trend price " would necessarily give rice the disadvantage in the general price system. The rise and fall of the actual market price of rice is of greater importance to the farmer than the " calculated trend price." Knowing this the farmer has consistently been opposed to the system of the " calculated trend price."

Fifthly, in computing a " calculated trend price " there seems to have been no reason for making October 1900 the base month, other than that the Bank of Japan Index Number begins then. If one considers the development made by industries since 1900, and also considers how little corresponding progress has been made in the methods of producing rice, the great discrepancy in prices existing between industrial products and agricultural products is not to be wondered at. Assuming that the index number of prices coincides in the long run with the cost of production, we may observe the following discrepancies between agricultural and industrial products:

INDEX NUMBER OF WHOLESALE PRICES
(Average 1926–1928) (October 1900 = 100)

Agricultural Products		Industrial Products from Agricultural Raw Materials		Industrial Products	
Rice	293	Paper	206	Steel	105
Barley	258	Raw silk	183	Foreign nails	119
Naked barley	259	Silk tissue	148	Copper	151
Wheat	234	Cotton fabric	157	Cement	133
Soya beans	224	Mousseline	179	Plate glass	135
Small red beans	338	Matches	215	Ammonium sulphate	130

The year 1900, therefore, cannot serve as an adequate basis for obtaining the " calculated trend price " of rice.

After October 1932.—The extraordinary session of the Diet in August 1932 was almost entirely given up to the discussion of relief measures for the agricultural depression; it was even known as the " Farmers' Relief Session." The question of a revision of the Rice Control Act naturally came up, and certain modifications were adopted.

First, the application of the " calculated trend price " of rice was partly suspended. The average price of rice for the period covering November 1931 to October 1932 was 20.69 yen, which was within the maximum and minimum prices (26.87 and 17.91 yen) announced by the Government [1] in April 1932. No governmental control of price was necessary. On the other hand the cost of production of rice,[2] made public at that time by the National Federation of Agricultural Associations, was 22.99 yen (1931), and the opinion that the price of rice was below the cost of production gained strength. This and several other deficiencies in the Act led to the suspension of the " calculated trend price " as the basis of a minimum price.

Second, cost of production was adopted as the basis of a minimum price.

---

[1] The figures are different from those mentioned above, the reason being that the figures were calculated in March, using the general index number of February 1932 instead of that of November 1931.

[2] The result was obtained by investigating the cost of production of 772 owner-farmers; 4 per cent. of land value is included.

Third, the fund for the Rice Control Act was increased to a maximum of 480 million yen.

The 63rd session of the Diet lasted for only one week, and, after heated discussions of the rice problem, closed with the understanding that the Government would submit at the next session a principle for price control.

THE RECENT REVISION

The Government having promised that it would introduce measures which would go to the root of the problem, prepared several bills to that end, while various organizations representing agricultural interests made proposals of their own. In the autumn of 1932 the problem of rice became one of the most discussed issues. In the course of discussion it became increasingly clear that there were certain points which could not be overlooked. First, it was generally recognized that some sort of restriction on the importation of rice from Chosen and Taiwan would be necessary, in order to prevent a fall in the price of rice in Japan. Second, to maintain a high price on rice over a long period of time was realized to be impossible. Third, to reduce the seasonal fluctuations in the price of rice it was deemed necessary to do away with the seasonal variations in the supply of rice. Fourth, agricultural distress could be partially relieved by keeping the price of rice on a level with the cost production. All these points, except for the first, apply essentially to Japan proper.

Various Proposals.—The following is a summary of the various proposals which have been put forward for Japan proper:

(A) Plan for Price-fixing:
1. Fixing of price: the maximum and the minimum price to be fixed by the Government.
2. Restriction on sales: to prohibit sale or purchase at a price higher than the maximum or lower than the minimum price.
3. Sale and purchase by the Government: the Government shall upon request purchase rice at the minimum or sell rice at the maximum price.
4. Inspection of rice: this shall be conducted by the Government.
5. Producers' control: encouragement of agricultural co-operative societies, agricultural storehouses, etc., in order that they may co-operate in controlling the price of rice.
6. A committee shall be appointed to deal with matters concerning the fixing of price.
7. A special account shall be opened.
8. Compensation to private operators: compensation shall be made to the Rice Exchanges and members thereof.

(B) Plan of Sales Control:
1. The country shall be divided into ten districts of control.
2. The transportation of rice from one district to another shall be regulated.
3. A surplus in one district shall be purchased by the Government to be sold to other districts where there is a shortage.
4. The Government shall at any time purchase or sell rice at a fixed price.
5. Inspection of rice shall be conducted by the Government.
6. Producers' control: agricultural co-operative societies, storehouses, etc., shall be encouraged, in order to gain their co-operation in controlling the sale and purchase of rice within their respective districts.
7. Machinery for control: a Rice Control Board shall be established as an auxiliary body of the Department of Agriculture and Forestry, and a committee appointed to discuss such matters as the prices at which the Government sells and buys, etc.
8. A special account shall be opened.
9. Compensation shall be given to private operators.

(C) Plan of Government Monopoly:
1. Extent of monopoly: all the rice produced, excepting that for the cultivators' consumption, shall be a monopoly of the Government.
2. Organizations for collecting rice shall be established.
3. Price at which rice is bought shall be fixed in December every year, on the basis of the average cost of production throughout the country, taking the general level of prices into consideration.
4. Sale of rice: polished rice shall be sold and its price shall be such as will cover the cost of buying up, storing, polishing and distributing it.
5. Machinery for monopoly: a Central Rice Board, attached to the Department of Agriculture and Forestry, shall be established. Local Rice Boards in ten districts of control, with branches in all prefectures, as well as Hokkaido, shall be established. A Committee to deal with matters concerning the enforcement of the monopoly shall be appointed.
6. A special account shall be opened.
7. Compensation shall be given to private operators.

Every one of these proposals is practicable under present-day political, economic and financial conditions in Japan, but the following points need to be considered further.

There is first the financial question should the monopoly plan be adopted. Presuming that the quantity of rice to be monopolized will be equal to that which is now actually put on the market, the quantity of rice would be 40 million koku, which includes home, colonial and foreign rice, the total value being estimated at about 1000 million yen at 25 yen per koku. The expenditure for carrying on the monopoly would be about 100 million yen, and the compensation to merchants, members of the Rice Exchanges and others would amount to about 101 million yen. It is doubtful, however, whether the present financial situation would permit the carrying out of a plan which entails so large a burden.

In any of the three proposals which have been made it would be difficult to set a limit to the quantity of rice to be held back by the cultivator for his own use and that which is to be collected by the Government, and consequently there would be every opportunity for carrying on illegal transactions. Every one of these proposals made above would, moreover, affect merchants and speculators unfavourably, who, as we have said, have always been raising objections to the Rice Control Act.

Restrictions on Importations from Chosen and Taiwan.—If restrictions on the importation of rice from Chosen could be enforced, the control of the price of rice—the raising of the price for the present—would not be difficult. This system of control has been advocated by a large number of writers on the subject, but the objections which have been strongly voiced against this scheme are not inconsiderable, and may be restated here.

The governments for the colonies, in the first place, have not yet completed their plans for increasing the production of rice, and naturally they cannot be expected to agree with any scheme which would place restrictions on the export of colonial rice. Moreover, the governments would be unwilling to burden the Chosen and Taiwan farmers for the sole purpose of giving aid to the landowners and farmers in Japan proper. Any policy of restriction would be most unsatisfactory to the colonial farmers, whose sources of income are few. Not only are the interests of the colonies involved, but Japanese interests are directly involved in rice cultivation in Chosen and Taiwan, since Japanese dealers in rice and Japanese landowners have put their money into the plan for increasing production in these two regions. It is, therefore, not surprising that they should oppose all measures which would threaten the marketing of colonial rice.

The New Rice Control Act.—The Rice Control Act passed at the 1933 session of the Imperial Diet was a measure by which it was hoped to overcome those difficulties mentioned above. In November of the same year the Act came into effect. According to its provisions, the minimum and maximum prices shall be fixed by law, and the

Government, upon request, shall purchase from the producers any quantity at the minimum price and sell to the public any quantity at the maximum price. Heretofore the purchase and sale of rice by the Government had been made at the current market price.

In order to reduce fluctuations in the monthly supply of rice, the Government is to purchase a certain amount of rice from November to February inclusive, when rice is generally put on the market, and sell it later. In this case the Government would be expected to announce the maximum quantity beyond which it will not buy. According to the Act such purchases must be made at the current market price, and it is clear from the discussion which took place at the time the bill was passed that this market price would be a controlled price somewhere between the minimum and maximum prices. This fixing of prices will also apply to Chosen and Taiwan.

The standard for fixing the minimum and maximum prices is to remain the same as the one set before, only with some revisions in the calculations for setting the standard.

Thus, to the item of cost of production have been added the costs for transporting rice from the farms to the central market, and several minor costs, which formerly were not included in the cost of production fixed by law. These additional costs were included as a result of the claims made by the landed interests. The minimum price is to be fixed at some point between the cost of production and within 80 to 90 per cent. of the calculated trend price. The maximum price is to be fixed at some point between the " price payable by the consumer " and within 120 to 130 per cent. of the calculated trend price. The Government is to have discretionary power to revise the minimum and maximum prices. The Government fund for carrying out the measures is also to be increased to 700 million yen.

Thus far no specific provisions have been made regarding the importation of Chosen and Taiwan rice, although indirect measures have been taken to reduce the quantity of rice imported to Japan by encouraging the consumption of more rice in Chosen and Taiwan and by placing prohibitive duties on such substitute foodstuffs as millet, sorghum and kaoliang. It is understood, too, in regard to price control, that the Government will encourage landowners and producers to co-operate in controlling prices, and by the joint control exercised by the Government and agriculture will aim at stabilizing prices.

JAPANESE RICE CONTROL

THE NEW DEAL

Before November 1, 1933, when the revised Rice Control Act was to become effective, a new situation developed, making it clear that the Act was no longer adequate to meet the changed set of circumstances. The rice crop in Japan proper in the autumn of 1933 was a bumper crop, which exceeded by 8 per cent. the average of the crops during the preceding five years; a bumper crop was also expected for Chosen. This meant that to the existing surplus there would be a further addition, and that the quantity of rice carried over at the end of the 1934 crop year would be unprecedented.

The following is a Table of the quantity of rice carried over at the end of several crop years, beginning in 1927:

1927	.	.	.	.	5·8 million koku		
1928	.	.	.	.	7·8	,,	,,
1929	.	.	.	.	7·0	,,	,,
1930	.	.	.	.	5·7	,,	,,
1931	.	.	.	.	9·1	,,	,,
1932	.	.	.	.	8·9	,,	,,
1933	.	.	.	.	10·0	,,	,, (Estimated)
1934	.	.	.	.	15·0	,,	,, (,,)

In 1933, in expectation of recovery in the United States, the general price-level showed an upward trend which the price of rice reflected. The price of rice rose until the above-mentioned situation brought a sudden fall, with indications that it would continue even further. Meanwhile the Government, in a temporary measure, resorted to fixing the minimum and maximum prices according to the provisions of the revised Act. A month later, in December 1933, the Government, in order to prevent a further fall in the price of rice, fixed the official minimum and maximum prices, which were slightly higher than the market price at that time.

As political control will not cover the entire problem, and as, moreover, there is a definite limit to what the Rice Control Act can finance, the Government is attempting to control the price of rice by inducing producers to limit either their production or the amount which they put on the market. As an example of a method which this policy advocates, we mention the fact that the storing of unhusked rice is being encouraged. Unhusked rice which has been dehydrated can be preserved in good condition for a long time. About 10 million koku of unhusked rice (or 5 million koku when husked) was stored in the autumn of 1933, in the following percentages: Japan proper, 60;

Chosen, 30, and Taiwan, 10. This rice could not be brought out and sold until the price of rice had reached a certain point, but the Government lent financial aid to those who had stored their rice. Another method which has possibilities of being realized is the limiting of the production of rice. According to a plan suggested by the Government in the autumn of 1933, surplus rice-fields were to be given over to other crops, and compensation given to the cultivators who followed this method of limiting production. However, the difficulty of this plan lies in determining the acreage which shall be considered surplus. According to an estimate made by the Government, the amount of rice which will be carried over into the following year from the crop of 1934 will be 15 million koku, and it was then estimated that production should be reduced to half this amount, or 7,500,000 koku. This plan caused consternation among the farmers, who had always been encouraged to increase their production of rice. Apart from the deficiencies in the plan itself, the idea of limiting production was in itself enough to defeat the plan, for the belief that the national interest lies in increased production is too deeply imbued in the people. Whether or not the Government succeeds in deliberately limiting production, the limitation will come inevitably as the result of economic forces.

Still another plan has been to utilize rice as material in industries, as for example distilling alcohol from rice, but at present the product cannot be commercialized.

The Rice Control Act must be still more comprehensive to bring any solution to this problem. Considering the financial side alone, it can be said that in some years' time the Act will be totally impracticable owing to the fact that the Government must continue buying up rice without being able to sell it.

The following Table shows the changes in the Rice Control Act:

[TABLE—

CHANGES IN THE RICE CONTROL ACT

Period	April 1921–March 1925	April 1925–June 1931	July 1931–September 1932	October 1932–October 1933	After November 1933
Aim	Adjustment of the supply and demand of rice	Adjustment of the quantity and market price of rice	„	„	(Control of rice added)
Methods:					
Direct control	Purchase, sale, exchange, manufacture and storage of rice by the Government	„	„	(Also loans of rice to prefectures)	(Storage of unhusked rice)
Import duty on rice	Raising, lowering, or abolition of it by the Government (for Japan proper only)	(Later applied to Taiwan, Chosen and Saghalien)	„	(Also on millet)	(Also on sorghum and kaoliang)
Import and export of rice	Restriction by the Government (for Japan proper only)	„	Permission by the Government (later applied to Taiwan, Chosen, Saghalien)	„	(Restriction of the import of millet, sorghum and kaoliang). Importation of rice from foreign countries permitted
Standards for control prices	Not explicitly given	„	Announcement of the highest and lowest prices according to the "calculated trend price of rice"	Announcement of the lowest prices calculated from the cost of production	Announcement of the highest and lowest prices calculated from cost of production, cost of living, price-level and other factors
Prices of purchase or sale by Government	Market price	„	„	„	Buying at the announced lowest price and selling at the highest
Maximum Government fund	200 (million yen)	270 „ (March 1929)	350 „	480 „	700 „
Districts where the Act is enforced	Japan proper	„	„	Japan proper (Taiwan and Chosen partly)	„

The ditto sign (,,) means the contents same as preceding column.

COMMODITY CONTROL IN THE PACIFIC AREA

The sales and purchases undertaken by the Government are as follows:

	Purchase		Sale	
	Volume 1000 koku	Average Price per koku	Volume 1000 koku	Average Price per koku
		Yen		Yen
1921 . . .	923	21.88	205	20.09
1922 . . .	490	31.85	452	17.48
1923 . . .	450	26.70	530	17.36
1924 . . .	1330	28.82	550	30.91
1925 . . .	407	39.39	458	33.25
1926 . . .	178	34.28	108	22.41
1927 . . .	1749	32.41	560	15.26
1928 . . .	494	29.62	644	19.69
1929 . . .	1468	29.70	595	21.75
1930 . . .	3040	18.84	1828	13.19
1931 . . .	1027	17.97	1315	14.06

A glance at this list shows that the sale prices are lower than the purchase prices. This is contrary to the principle of profit-making in private economy, but the nature of this measure is such that profit is not its purpose.

Any attempt to estimate by means of statistics the effects of the Act is accompanied by difficulties, for, in the first place, an announcement by the Government that it will purchase rice is in itself sufficient to influence the market price. Moreover, in the past, the amount actually purchased by the Government often fell far short of the amount it had announced it would buy, and where this has happened it is difficult to tell whether the statistical study should be based on the amount actually purchased, or the amount the Government had announced it would buy. In the second place, during the past ten years there have been significant changes in the conditions under which the supply of rice is carried on, and it would be difficult, when studying the effects of the Act, to measure the influence of those forces which have effected these changes. Furthermore, in particular cases the objectives and standards of governmental control have changed.

The following Table gives the price of rice during two periods, the one before, and the other after, 1921, the year when the Rice Control Act was put into force. In these figures the influences of commodity prices as well as harvest variations are not included.

	Average Price per koku	Standard Deviation	Coefficient of Variability
	Yen	Yen	Per cent.
Oct. 1901–Sept. 1910 . .	11.37	1.76	15·48
Oct. 1911–Sept. 1920 . .	10.34	2.27	21·95
Oct. 1921–Sept. 1930 . .	10.29	1.35	13·12

From these figures we may infer that over the period of ten years since the promulgation of the Rice Control Act the price of rice has been more or less stable, although it would not be altogether safe to assume that this stability was a result of the Act alone.

A study of the variations in the price of rice over shorter periods leads us to the following two entirely separate conclusions:

(1) The monthly variations in the " deflated price " of rice according to Professor Yagi's calculations:

	1911-1920	1921-1930
January	98·8	95·7
February	97·3	96·5
March	97·4	97·4
April	97·6	99·4
May	97·8	100·1
June	99·7	101·2
July	103·0	103·3
August	106·1	105·4
September	103·1	104·2
October	101·3	102·6
November	99·0	98·9
December	98·9	95·3
Average	100·0	100·0

(2) The difference between the highest and the lowest monthly average of the nominal price of rice in Tokyo during a year, divided by its yearly average:

Crop Year	Per cent.	Crop Year	Per cent.
1912 . . .	32·3	1922 . . .	24·8
1913 . . .	7·5	1923 . . .	24·3
1914 . . .	39·1	1924 . . .	18·2
1915 . . .	33·8	1925 . . .	14·2
1916 . . .	11·3	1926 . . .	7·6
1917 . . .	43·3	1927 . . .	10·2
1918 . . .	68·2	1928 . . .	11·2
1919 . . .	55·7	1929 . . .	10·2
1920 . . .	35·8	1930 . . .	41·7
1921 . . .	46·8	1931 . . .	16·7
		1934 . . .	24·5

The above two sets of figures permit of various interpretations. We may observe from a study of the first that since the promulgation of the Rice Control Act in 1921, the monthly variations have increased, although we may at the same time observe that, but for the Act, the variations might have been much greater as a result of changed conditions of supply. From the second we may conclude that the Rice Control Act has served to reduce the monthly variations in the nominal price of rice. The problem is, which of the two observations shows the actual economic relation between the price of rice and the producer, as well as the consumer?

We come now to the question of Government expenditure. The fund drawn upon for rice price control is borrowed by the Government every fiscal year at a fixed rate of interest, usually at from 4 to 5 per cent. Out of this fund must come all the expenses for operating the Act, including the cost of administration. Interest on the losses sustained in past years must also be covered. If the working of the fund, which is essentially of a public and non-commercial nature, is considered in purely commercial terms, we have the following figures (in 1000 yen):

	Profit	Loss	Total of Accumulated Loss
1921	1225		(−) 1,225
1922		8,283	7,058
1923		7,797	14,856
1924		1,461	16,316
1925		6,366	22,682
1926		11,079	33,760
1927		15,969	49,729
1928		25,331	75,060
1929		28,946	104,006
1930		43,907	147,912
1931		18,843	166,756
1932		18,668	185,424

Because of the " losses," the available fund has gradually diminished, so that, for instance, at the end of 1932 the total amount of the fund was 480 million yen, but when the losses listed above are subtracted from the total, and the estimated value of the stored rice which the Government has purchased is subtracted also, the remainder will be somewhere around 190 million yen. Therefore, the amount available for future use is not more than 410 million yen despite the fact that the maximum limit of the fund was raised to 700 million yen by the latest Act.

Undoubtedly, the Rice Control Act has entailed a heavy financial burden. Can we find any " prudent waste " after considering on the one hand the financial burden, and on the other the good results of the Act? It is a question of how much longer the Government will be able to bear the losses caused by the control of rice, for it should not be forgotten that, apart altogether from the expenditures for the operating of this Act, there are other policies which entail expenditures that increase yearly.

FUTURE PROBLEMS

This paper, being merely a description of the history of the Rice Control Act, does not arrive at any specific conclusions, but the writer would like to indicate here a few problems which have yet to be studied, in view of the fact that the Act has produced results suggesting material for further study in economic planning. First, the price control of rice has been unsuccessful primarily because it constituted only a sort of interference in the trading and distributive processes of rice, instead of being a measure whereby production could be regulated and controlled. An effective and lasting price control can be achieved only by this control of production. Second, production in agriculture at present is practically left to the free initiative of producers, so that when price control is exercised with any degree of efficiency, and the price of rice raised, not only will existing producers increase their production, but new producers will appear in order to take advantage of the high price. Thus, a price control which is at first effective will sooner or later meet counteracting forces, and the more effective the price control the greater will be the forces to defeat it. For instance, if the Rice Control Act becomes effective in Japan proper, the production of rice in Chosen and Taiwan will immediately be increased, because the cost of production in these regions is much lower than in Japan.

With the increased complexity of production, price control can be exercised only if co-ordinated with the control of production, for a price control which is independent of the control of production can be effective only over a relatively short period of time. Thus, in the case of rice cultivation in Japan, a plan for increasing production cannot be immediately realized, since it takes several years [1] for a newly opened rice-

---

[1] Coffee, for example, does not yield a crop until six to seven years after. Therefore if a valorization policy raises its price to-day, and if there is no interference on its production, the production of coffee will have been enormously increased by 1940 or so. In that case, assuming that the demand for coffee remains the same as it is to-day, the valorization policy is bound to face much more serious difficulties then (see Wallace and Edminister, *International Control of Raw Materials*, Washington, 1930).

field to attain sufficient productivity, and during that gestation period it is possible that conditions will change so that the price control of several years back will no longer be adequate.

Another factor which tends to discourage the adoption of any far-reaching price-control policy is the shortness of tenure in political life and the lack of continuity in governmental policies. The aim of politicians is to put through measures which are efficacious only for a short time. No price-control policy which is carried out with only temporary aims in view can possibly be of any benefit.

So far, price control in Japan only has been considered. If, however, we consider the same problem in connection with some commodity which is produced in almost every country of the world, say wheat, is there any possibility of controlling the production of this foodstuff? The problem set before the world which is suffering from over-production is not a technical one concerned with increasing production, but a political one, which demands the regulating and distributing of production in many countries of the world. The wheat problem, for instance, is vital not to one country alone, but to the numerous wheat-consuming countries of the world, with the exception of Japan. Happily, however, Japan's central problem turns only upon the reconciling of the conflicting interests of producers in Chosen and Taiwan with those of producers in Japan proper.

The price control attempted to-day is apt to be over specified staple commodities. It would be difficult, however, to maintain for a long time the price of any given commodity at a level higher than that of other commodities, as, for instance, if the price of rice is raised there will also be a general rise in wages as well as in the price of other commodities, and the effect of the high price of rice would be nullified in the long run. To what extent the general price-level will rise is not a matter for discussion here.[1]

It is self-evident that, in present-day price economy, partial control by the raising of the prices of staple commodities would not be effective for long.[2] For this kind of control it would be necessary to raise prices artificially, and to keep on doing so for an indefinite period. This would

[1] According to the calculation of Professor M. Hijikata, of the Tokyo Imperial University, out of sixty-three cases of rise and fall in the general price-level recorded between 1887 and 1926, the movement of the price of rice preceded in twenty-two cases, and followed only in seven cases, the movement of the general price-level ; while in thirty-four cases the two prices moved simultaneously.

[2] We should not forget that the raising of the general price-level will serve to emancipate the producer from the burden of debts made in times of high price-level.

be not unlike the grain tariff in Italy, where the tariff rate has to be raised indefinitely in order to be effective. If this evil is to be avoided it would be necessary to exercise price control, not separately over particular commodities, but simultaneously and systematically over a group of certain staple commodities, and in such a way that a raising of the prices of these commodities would not cause a general rise in prices.

Will not price control remove a stimulus towards technical improvement in production? The question of combining price-raising with agricultural progress is a serious one to-day. Price control is apt to take into consideration the cost of production not for the most efficient producers, but for those who are less so, as has been the case in the Government monopolies in Japan in tobacco, salt and camphor. The Rice Control Act is intended for controlling the price of rice, taking into consideration the cost of production borne by the largest number of producers. This being the case, there is the possibility that these producers on receiving the costs for producing their rice will make little effort towards improving the method of production. It is in this sense that price control may discourage technical improvement.

So far we have been concerned only with a price control which would apply over a long period of time. The control of short-period fluctuations in price is most valuable because, first, the reduction of monthly fluctuations in the price of rice would greatly relieve farmers of the burdens involved in the low prices after harvest. Secondly, the price at which farmers sell rice does not vary at the same rate as the wholesale and retail prices of rice, and in a period of falling prices, especially, the price received by farmers for rice falls more sharply than the wholesale price. It is, therefore, most expedient that this inequality in the prices should be remedied.

CHAPTER V

SILK CONTROL IN JAPAN

by Taikichiro Mori

INTRODUCTORY

THE raw silk industry in Japan is now approaching a critical pass: whether it will get through the present depression and recover its old prosperity is one of the most important social as well as economic problems of the country.

Two million sericultural families and many thousands of small silk reelers have been severely hit by the prevailing depression; the contraction of their consuming power in turn has proved a blow to the greater part of the business sections of the country; the Government's relief work for the silk reelers and cocoon farmers has added to the country's financial difficulties, which were growing very serious. But this was not the whole story; the worst part is that the rise or fall of the industry is not merely an economic and financial problem, but rather a social and political one; the present social unrest in Japan, indeed, is substantially attributable to the bad state of the industry, in which millions of sericulturists, small silk reelers and merchants have been almost deprived of their means of livelihood. Furthermore, a national hardship of such magnitude is not unlikely to result in economic and political difficulties internationally; the Far Eastern situation especially seems to be particularly sensitive to the state of Japan's agricultural population. Viewed in this way, then, how to control Japan's raw silk industry is a problem not only for Japan alone, but also for quite a number of foreign countries.

The purpose of this paper is to trace the development of the raw silk industry in Japan from its birth as a modern enterprise to its present crisis. But, in so doing, we shall pay attention to how the industry has been assisted and controlled by both the Government and the industrialists themselves rather than to giving a detailed description of the development.

The début of Japanese raw silk in international trade took place in 1859—that is, seventy-five years ago—when three Japanese ports, Yokohama (which was substituted for Kanagawa), Hakodate and Nagasaki were opened to foreign trade; the occasion was unusually

198

favourable because of two events—the spread of the pebrine plague through the silk districts of France and Italy, and the depreciation in the value of silver. First, the spread of the cocoon disease in France and Italy presented a particularly lucky opportunity for the Japanese silk industry to expand abroad, because it had practically ruined the silk industry in the two countries, with the result that the producers there had to turn to Japan for a healthy stock of eggs to rebuild their industry; thus, to a semi-medieval industry, which constituted only a subsidiary occupation of the farmers in the mountainous villages of Middle and North Japan, the door was suddenly opened and demand poured in on such a scale as had never been dreamed of. The industry was now given a great stimulus and progressed rapidly, and by the time the exportation of the eggs to France and Italy was no longer required, Japan had acquired enough strength effectively to compete for the American market with these two senior countries.

Secondly, the fall in the value of silver was no less favourable to the export trade of Japan, then still a silver-standard country. But this advantage was by no means confined to Japan alone, but was shared by China. Not only that; when Japan adopted the gold standard in 1897, after the victorious war against China, she was at once to feel China's formidable rivalry in the silk trade.

The Russo-Japanese War (1904-1905) gave another turn to the Japanese silk industry, for after the war the industry began to expand at a great rate, and at the beginning of the Taisho Era (1912-1925) it finally beat the Chinese industry in the silk-trade competition, thereby establishing its supremacy in the world silk market. There were again two events which occasioned the expansion: a great increase in the American demand for silk after the Russo-Japanese War, and the rise in the price of silver bullion, which considerably impaired the competitive power of China.

The true explanation of this development, however, must not be sought so much in these lucky incidents as in the concerted efforts of the Government as well as the industrialists themselves in reorganizing the industry, which, old as it was, found its productivity altogether too inadequate to meet demand when brought into contact with the foreign markets. At the same time it must be admitted that the inherent weakness of the industry has by no means vanished, for the production of cocoons, the raw material of silk, has been entirely left in the hands of very small-scale farmers. Moreover, even the capitalistic reeler and exporter alike have not sufficiently endeavoured, as every enterprising capitalist should have done, to seek new markets, or cut down costs of production so as to put the industry as a whole on a sounder foundation. No wonder they now find themselves quite helpless facing the two crises which have simultaneously arisen—the collapse of the American market, and the remarkable growth of artificial silk.

We might divide the development of Japan's raw silk industry into four stages: first period—from the opening of the ports (1859) till the Russo-Japanese War (1904-1905), which roughly corresponded to the period of the French and Italian competition; second period—from the Russo-Japanese War till the end of the Meiji Era (1912), which was characterized by competition with China; third period—from the beginning of the Taisho Era (1912-1925) till that of the present depression (1929); fourth period—from 1929 till the present time.

FROM THE OPENING OF THE PORTS (1859) TO THE END OF THE RUSSO-JAPANESE WAR (1905)

As we have already mentioned, Japan's silk industry, though it has its origin far back in olden times, is to be regarded as commencing its modern career in 1859, when the first Japanese ports were opened. In those days the whole process of raw silk production was solely a household activity, constituting an important source of income to the farmers, and each one of them who earned his living in this way made it a rule to engage in every activity from mulberry-tree plantation to silk-reeling. Under such circumstances the raw silk put out by each producer was necessarily small in amount and varied in quality, which was a great obstacle to any extensive development of marketing. Although there were wholesale dealers and commission merchants to collect the raw silk from the numerous and scattered producers, and either to market it within the country or sell it to the silk exporters in fairly large amounts, it was quite impossible to meet the growing demand from the newly acquired foreign markets without large-scale production and standardization, the two essential conditions for modern commodity-trading. So it was most urgent for the development of the industry that the reeling of silk should be transformed from a household to a factory enterprise, and it was the Government who led the way by establishing in the first year of Meiji (1868) a model silk-reeling filature at Tomioka (with a capital of 280,000 yen and 300 basins) and by securing the services of a Frenchman to teach the modern technique of reeling. Guided and encouraged by the Government in this way, the rise of capitalistic

200

silk reelers and the mechanization of the reeling process steadily followed.

Of course the disappearance of hand-reeling is by no means universal; for, even at the end of 1929, out of the total 69,407 silk-reeling establishments in Japan, the numbers of motor-operated filatures, dupion mills and hand-reeling mills were respectively 3719 (5·4 per cent.), 9539 (13·7 per cent.) and 59,149 (80·9 per cent.). But mere comparison of such numbers is meaningless, for these filatures, which represented such a small percentage of the total reeling establishments, accounted for as much as 74·7 per cent. of the total number of basins and as much as 89 per cent. of the total output of raw silk. So we may assert that the reeling of silk is now essentially a factory enterprise and, distinct from sericulture, has established itself as one of the greatest capitalistic industries of the country.

Apart from the Government leadership in the mechanization of silk-reeling, it is necessary to mention some of the Government measures which played an important part in bringing up the raw silk industry. In those early days when silkworm eggs were being exported to France and Italy, the Government naturally found many problems in controlling the exportation and the production of the eggs; at first the Government rather wanted to limit the export trade, realizing that the export of the better eggs tended to do harm to the silk industry of the country, but later, in 1877, the restrictions were removed, in face of the opposition from both the foreign buyers and the Japanese producers.

After the demand for Japanese silkworm eggs subsided, due to the revival of the French and the Italian silk industry, the Government's efforts were mainly directed towards the improvement and standardization of the raw silk for export, the most important measure taken being the Raw Silk Conditioning Act of 1895. This law enabled anybody, whether a Japanese or a foreigner, who wanted to deal in home-reeled raw silk to ask for it to be examined free of charge at the raw silk conditioning house. However, throughout the period under consideration, as sericulture was still in a very backward state of development, we may say that the Government aimed above all at the prevention of pebrine, and the examination of silkworm eggs. Thus, in 1897, the Silkworm-Egg Examination Law was promulgated over the whole country; in 1906 Government supervisors to see to pebrine prevention were sent to each prefecture; and in 1906 the Central Government decided for the first time to give the local governments a subsidy, to the amount of 160,000 yen each year, for the purpose of controlling silkworm-egg production.

The raw silk producers, on their part, endeavoured to guide the development of the industry, for instance establishing among themselves the Dainihon Sanshi Kai (Sericultural Association of Japan) in 1892. Aside from these controlling measures, taken by the Government and the industrialists alike, there took place in 1892-1897 a great collapse in the price of silver bullion—it fell by 40 per cent. Under such circumstances, Japan, still on a silver standard, together with China, could easily hold her own in her silk competition with France and Italy.

THE PERIOD OF COMPETITION WITH CHINA

The situation entirely changed after 1897, when Japan adopted the gold standard, as she obtained the necessary supply of gold from the Chinese war indemnity; and China's raw silk, favoured by the exchange depreciation, began at once rapidly to compete in the markets with the Japanese silk. The following figures will show the extent to which Japan's export of raw silk increased after 1897:

TABLE I.—EXPORT OF RAW SILK, 1896-1920 *

Year	1000 kilograms			Percentage Share	
	Japan	China	Total	Japan	China
1896–1900 . .	3,459	6314	9,773	35	65
1901–1905 . .	4,865	5997	10,862	45	55
1906–1910 . .	6,368	7191	13,559	47	53
1911–1915 . .	10,771	7647	18,418	58	42
1916–1920 . .	14,118	7033	21,151	67	33

* Figures are five-year averages taken from the official statistics of exports and imports, at Yokohama and other places, of raw silk and manufactured silk.

But this was not to check for long the steadily growing Japanese silk trade — firstly because the industry had already acquired enough strength effectively to compete with foreign rivals, and secondly because the low price of silver bullion, which gave a special advantage to China, eventually showed an upward tendency. How decisive the Japanese victory was in the Sino-Japanese silk competition is eloquently told in the above figures.

SILK CONTROL IN JAPAN

In 1906-1907, immediately after the Russo-Japanese War, Japan witnessed the greatest business boom she had ever experienced, and the price of raw silk (1907) reached the unprecedented height of 1250 yen per 100 kin. This boom was short-lived, however, and soon to be followed by a depression just as great in extent: in 1908 the price of raw silk fell below 1000 yen and in 1910 it was 881 yen on the average. But we may assert that this depression has done good to the Japanese silk industry, for it was chiefly this crisis that induced the Government to enact the Raw Silk Industry Act of 1911, aiming at strict control of the industry—the law which contributed a great deal to that remarkable development of the industry during the Taisho Era.

The salient features of the Raw Silk Industry Act may be summarized as follows:

1. The production of silkworm eggs was prohibited to unlicensed persons.
2. Regulations for the prevention of pebrine were made stricter.
3. New regulations concerning the production and the conditioning of silkworm eggs were provided.
4. For the purpose of securing improvement in the quality of raw silk and the increase of exports, through the co-operative societies especially, a Central Organization for Sericulturists' and Raw Silk Producers' Associations.

This new Act of 1911 is fundamentally different from any former laws in that its scope has been extended from the prevention of cocoon diseases to the control of silkworm-egg production itself. It was also in 1911 that the Government organization of silkworm-egg production was first established, by which the Government was given power to produce and distribute original or standard silkworm eggs.

As another cause of the industry's remarkable development during the Taisho Era we must point out the enormous increase in the American demand for silk during that period, not to mention the industrial expansion of both America and Japan due to the World War. The quantity of Japan's raw silk export increased so much that the increase in its total value greatly outstripped the fall in the price of raw silk.

COMMODITY CONTROL IN THE PACIFIC AREA

TABLE II.—EXPORTS OF JAPANESE RAW SILK

(Quantities in 100 kin. Values in 1000 yen)

Year	Total Exports		Exports to U.S.A.	
	Quantity	Value	Quantity	Value
1908 . .	115,218	108,609	—	—
1912 . .	171,026	150,321	128,876	114,460
1916 . .	217,420	267,037	181,206	223,797
1919 . .	286,224	623,619	275,278	600,925
1922 . .	344,192	670,048	321,419	610,844
1925 . .	438,449	879,657	421,600	848,362
1929 . .	580,950	784,150	555,895	755,377
1930 . .	477,322	419,107	448,674	398,713
1931 . .	560,577	356,932	536,664	342,478
1932 . .	548,541	382,950	512,966	360,145
1933 . .	483,131	390,779	437,419	355,805

Source : *Manual of the Raw Silk Industry.*

In 1925 the total quantity and the total value of Japan's raw silk exports were respectively three times and eight times as much as those of 1908. Parallel with this development, the scale of production in the raw silk industry has also gradually grown bigger, as shown by the following figures:

TABLE III.—DEVELOPMENT OF THE SILK-REELING INDUSTRY

(Number and size of establishments)

Year	Less than 10 basins	10-50 basins	50-100 basins	100-300 basins	300-500 basins	500-1000 basins	Over 1000	Total
1908 .	386,995	3068	645	..	405	..	..	391,114
1912 .	342,164	2819	765	..	531	..	..	346,279
1916 .	280,641	2316	882	..	661	..	..	284,500
1919 .	254,992	2228	1002	..	901	..	..	239,123
1922 .	204,311	1696	854	683	114	71	9	207,738
1925 .	181,841	1683	804	623	108	82	8	185,149
1932 .	57,070	1674	846	687	120	64	..	60,461

Source: *Manual of the Raw Silk Industry*, published by the Department of Agriculture and Forestry.

The number of the small reeling households using less than 10 basins has decreased, while that of the bigger filatures employing 50 to 100 basins has rapidly increased; this tendency is particularly noticeable since 1917-1923, when even such big filatures as employed more than 1000 basins appeared for the first time.

It is characteristic of the silk-reeling industry that expenses for raw materials constitute the greatest item in its costs of production: as much as 70 per cent. of the total cost is paid for raw materials, only 30 per cent. being incurred in the manufacturing process. Therefore, the best way of improving the business condition of the silk-reeling industry is not found so much in economizing on the manufacturing process as in reducing the expenditure for cocoons, by rationalizing their production and marketing. This consideration naturally leads us to the question: how efficiently has sericulture been carried on in Japan?

TABLE IV.—THE DEVELOPMENT OF THE SERICULTURAL INDUSTRY

| Year | No. of Farm Households | Sericultural Household | | Area of Mulberry-Fields (cho *) | Approximate average Cocoon production per Sericultural Household (kan †) |
		No.	Percentage of Farm Households		
1908 .	5,408,363	1,436,805	27	412,445	24
1912 .	5,438,051	1,500,409	28	453,626	29
1916 .	5,457,793	1,765,937	32	465,520	32
1922 .	5,439,409	1,785,079	33	512,833	34
1925 .	5,548,599	1,948,706	35	549,307	43
1932 .	5,642,509	2,064,639	37	652,514	43
1933 .	..	2,092,196	..	640,086	48

Source: *Manual of the Raw Silk Industry* and *Statistics of Cocoons*, published by the Department of Agriculture and Forestry.
* *Cho* = 0·992 hectare or 2·45 acres.
† *Kan* = 3·75 kg. or 8·267 lb.

In tracing the development of sericulture during the period under discussion, we may say roughly that the number of sericultural families increased by 500,000, its percentage of the total farming families increased from 25 to 39, and the acreage of mulberry-fields was almost doubled. But the most important development is this: the average volume of cocoons produced by one sericultural family increased from 18 kan (1834 koku) in 1905 to 43·5 kan in 1926. We may not, perhaps, conclude from this fact alone that sericulture has been transformed to a large-scale enterprise, but we may safely conclude that productivity in sericulture has been increased through technical improvements.

The logical conclusion from the existing relationship between the silk reeler and the sericulturist, in which the latter is essentially

" exploited " by the former, might be that the silk reeler wanted to prevent sericulture from ever growing into a large-scale modern enterprise, for the purpose of securing the cheap supply of cocoons from the competing small sericulturists. On the other hand, it has become necessary for the now large-scale silk-reeling industry to secure the supply of cocoons of standardized quality, and this in large quantities. To meet the situation, the silk reeler has gradually come to organize the sericulturists' associations, with a special contract obligating it to sell him its whole output of cocoons.

Next, the scale of production of silkworm eggs has grown bigger since the enactment of the Raw Silk Industry Act in 1911, as shown by the following figures:

TABLE V.—PRODUCTION OF SILKWORM EGGS

Year	No. of Producers of Silkworm Eggs	Eggs produced *
		(Number of moths)
1910 . .	15,006	764,525,281
1916 . .	11,566	782,854,384
1922 . .	8,782	710,674,910
1925 . .	7,676	793,926,488
		(grams)
1932 . .	5,616	236,903,300
1933 . .	5,324	294,587,808

Source: *Manual of the Raw Silk Industry.*
* 28 moths produce 9·375 grams of eggs. Thus the corresponding figures for moths in 1932 and 1933 are approximately 705,669,400 and 877,495,600.

We see that during the Taisho Era the output of silkworm eggs increased by 50 per cent., whereas the number of producers decreased by 56 per cent. This tendency is accounted for largely by the fact that since the Great War the big silk-reeling industrialists have come to take up the production of silkworm eggs for themselves, thus organizing the whole process of raw silk production under their own management. In 1920, out of the total 9835 silkworm-egg producers, 447 were producing more than 10,000 egg sheets, and only 10 were producing more than 100,000 sheets; and in the 10 producers were included the three biggest raw silk industrialists, Katakura, Gunze and Sanryusha. When we come to as late as 1929, we find Gunze producing over 1,000,000 sheets and Katakura 750,000 sheets. In that year, among those who were producing more than 50,000 sheets were Sanryusha, Kansai

Seishi, Shinayabe Seishi, Nihon Seishi, Toa Seishi, Chosen Seishi, etc., all silk-reeling industrialists, and of course a considerable number of silkworm-egg producers as such. But none of them could possibly rival Gunze and Katakura in productive capacity.

Upon the whole, then, it has been an inevitable tendency that on the one hand the scale of silkworm-egg production should grow bigger and bigger, while on the other the position of the independent silkworm-egg producer was gradually weakened.

So far we have roughly described the fundamental forces behind the development of Japan's raw silk industry up to the World War. One cannot deny that the development as a whole has been great and rapid, but at the same time one must not overlook one serious weak point of the industry. Not only is the price of the product raw silk dictated, as it were, by outside influences which it is beyond the industry's power to control, but this price also fluctuates to a great extent. Fluctuations in the price of raw silk are clearly shown by the following figures:

TABLE VI.—PRICE OF RAW SILK

(per 100 kin)

Year		Price	Year		Price
		Yen			Yen
1905	.	989	1920	.	2191
1906	.	1063	1921	.	1592
1907	.	1250	1922	.	1947
1908	.	942	1923	.	2150
1909	.	902	1924	.	1840
1910	.	881	1925	.	2006
1911	.	892	1926	.	1657
1912	.	879	1927	.	1423
1913	.	934	1928	.	1335
1914	.	943	1929	.	1350
1915	.	853	1930	.	878
1916	.	1228	1931	.	629
1917	.	1375	1932	.	698
1918	.	1521	1933	.	809
1919	.	2175	1934 (June)		611

Source: *Manual of the Raw Silk Industry.* Figures for 1933 and 1934 from the *Monthly Report of the Silk Trade.* Prices shown are not market quotations, but represent the value of total raw silk exports divided by the quantity.

Still greater fluctuations than the above are certainly to be expected for the month-to-month figures. Especially the outbreak of the war and the American participation in the war brought the silk market into complete confusion; and the destruction of the market was completed (as it would seem) by the post-war depression. How have both the Government and the industrialists tried to cope with the problem?

Control of Production in 1914

With the outbreak of the war in August 1914 began the precipitous fall of raw silk prices: on the 4th, the quotation at the market for " futures " was 1078 yen—that is, 19 yen 50 sen below the average price of the previous month; on the 8th, a fall of 220 yen took place in a " spot " transaction, " Shinshu No. 1 " being quoted at 780 yen. On the 28th, the Yokohama Raw Silk Exporters' Association called an extraordinary meeting to discuss the question of controlling production, and on September 2 they invited all the silk reelers whose output of raw silk was over 500 bales a year to a national council of raw silk producers, and all of them agreed upon the following terms:

1. Overtime in the morning and at night should be prohibited.
2. Reeling operations should be stopped on November 30 and started again not before March 1, 1915, in the Sinshu Province, and February 1 in the other prefectures.
3. The above should not be applied to any previous contracts which were made before September 2; but all such contracts should be presented for approval by the Yokohama Raw Silk Exporters' Association.

The Government's relief measures were as follows:

1. The Bank of Japan granted loans with which to buy cocoons and re-discounted bills on the dried cocoons stored in authorized warehouses.
2. The Yokohama Specie Bank carried on its foreign exchange business at its own risk at the time when world exchange transactions were practically stopped.
3. The Government Railway reduced the freight charges of cocoons for August 15-October 31.
4. The Government facilitated the export of raw silk by enacting the Law for Guaranteeing Wartime Marine Insurance.
5. The Treasury Deposit Bureau granted loans to the exporters of raw silk, cocoons, etc., to the amount of 5 million yen through the Bank of Japan, and 3 million yen through the Industrial Bank of Japan.
6. The Bank of Japan changed its loan policy on the security of raw silk and granted about 350 yen on one bale.
7. The Government sent an agricultural technician (Mr Shido) to the United States of America to survey the situation there.

The silk-trade people's agreement of 1914 is very significant in the sense that it was the first of the kind to be applied to the whole country.[1]

[1] There had been a partial control of production in 1912 for Nagano Province, when a two-hour curtailment per day was practised.

Even more significant was the fact that the Government for the first time took upon itself the relief of the raw silk industry. For at the seven previous crises—of 1882, 1890, 1896, 1900, 1901, 1907 and 1908—all the measures taken by the Government were more or less long-term measures to control or encourage the development of the industry. But this time, in 1914, the depression was so severe, and the position of the industry had grown so important for the national life, that the Government was forced to take some drastic relief measures of immediate effect.

Beside those relief measures which we have roughly described above, one thing stands out as of special importance, that is the establishment of a relief syndicate in the form of the Teikoku Sanshi Kaisha (Teisan Kaisha)—Imperial Raw Silk Company Ltd.—with a capital of 6 million yen, of which 5 million yen was a Government loan out of the Treasury surplus, granted at the urgent request of the National Council of Raw Silk Producers, and 1 million yen was subscribed by the producers themselves. The purpose of this company was to buy up the accumulated stock of raw silk at Yokohama, thereby reinforcing the effect of the production control which had been agreed upon by the silk producers, so that the price should be maintained at a reasonable level, the desired figure at which they wanted to maintain it being 750 yen. They began buying the stock in April 1915, but they could buy no more than 12,000 bales, about 30 per cent. of the stock existing at the time, through lack of funds, and, as they did not succeed in getting their request for additional loans accepted by the Government, they finally decided to dissolve the company in May. In fact they dissolved the company with great success, for in August the price of raw silk began its sharp rise due to the war boom, reaching in November the height of 1300 yen, with a result that the company realized a profit of 1,700,000 yen by selling out the 12,000 bales at their disposal. Part of this profit was divided among the subscribers and the rest paid back to the Treasury. There is no doubt, however, that this success was almost entirely due to the fortuitous war boom.

Relief Measure of 1917-1918

In February 1917 the news of the American participation in the war came with a great shock to the raw silk traders in Japan, and prices at once began to fall. In September the United States resorted to the gold embargo; at one time it was even rumoured that she would prohibit the importation of raw silk. To save the situation, in October the Central

o

Organization for Sericulturists' and Raw Silk Producers' Associations drew up a draft resolution at a meeting, and in November had it presented and accepted before the combined meeting held at Yokohama of the silk reelers and the Yokohama Raw Silk Exporters' Association. Article I., the most important part of the resolution, stipulated that a " cartel " should be formed to stop sales of raw silk at a price lower than 1300 yen. Consequently part of the " spot " transactions was suspended until January 1918, when the American President's declaration of his Armistice principles rendered the continuation of the resolution no longer necessary.

But this was not the end of the war-time confusion. In July the American Government announced its war-time emergency policies—controlling railway transportation, the consumption of coal and, most important of all from the Japanese standpoint, the importation of raw silk (no unlicensed persons could import it) and the production of all kinds of silk fabrics (for six months, from December 1, production was to be reduced to 50 per cent. of the average amount of the preceding three years). The Central Organization for Sericulturists' and Raw Silk Producers' Associations, together with both the Sericultural Association of Japan and the Yokohama Raw Silk Exporters' Association, called a national meeting at Yokohama of all the silk reelers and merchants. In accordance with the resolution then passed, silk-reeling operations were stopped for thirty days, beginning on December 1, 1918; besides, a kind of labour control was sought after, the silk reelers agreeing not to compete for women workers. This agreement, with that of the previous year, should be remembered as marking a stage in the " cartel movement " in the Japanese silk industry.

Relief Measures of 1920

In Japan the raw silk industry was the first that fell a victim to the post-war depression which swept the whole world in 1920 and 1929. This was natural because the industry, being essentially a raw-material enterprise producing for foreign markets, is particularly susceptible to the general business condition of the world. The magnitude of the depression may be indicated by the fact that one of the representative kinds of raw silk, " Shinshu No. 1.," which was quoted at 4360 yen (per 100 kin) at a "spot" transaction in January 1920, fell to 1560 yen in September. No price fall of such magnitude could be easily redressed; as a matter of fact, the raw silk producers and merchants resorted to all possible measures, among which the more important were as follows:

in May the Yokohama Raw Silk Exporters' Association passed a resolution advocating stoppage of sale at prices lower than 1800 yen; in June the Yokohama Raw Silk Traders' Association agreed to reduce the amount of silk to be received for export by 30 per cent. every month from July 1 to the end of the year; in August the silk reelers and merchants decided at a national assembly not only to extend the percentage of the reduction to 50, but from October 22 to the end of the year to receive no raw silk at all; further they agreed to reduce the hours of labour in the reeling process to nine hours a day, as well as establishing the system of one holiday a month from September 1 to December 31.

TABLE VII.—PRICE OF RAW SILK IN 1920

(per 100 kin. Shinshu Grade A)

Year of 1920	Futures	Spot
	Yen	Yen
January . .	4440	4360
February . .	3849	..
March . . .	3625	3380
April . . .	3288	3080
May . . .	2431	1990
June . . .	1906	1620
July . . .	1590	1400
August . .	1040	1280
September . .	1697	1560
October . .	1649	Selling
November . .	1675	discon-
December . .	1550	tinued

The only possible relief for the raw silk producers and traders was to get a Government relief fund. They asked for, and succeeded in getting, a much larger sum than during the crisis of 1914-1915: the Government, through the Industrial Bank of Japan and the Hypothec Bank of Japan, lent 50 million yen out of the Treasury Deposits Bureau to the second Teisan Kaisha (relief syndicate), which was established with a capital of 13 million yen. One-half of the capital was subscribed by the raw silk producers and traders. Between January 1920 and February 1921 the company bought up 30,000 bales at 24 million yen, and later 40,000 bales more, the total amount thus bought up being 70,000 bales. This time, too, a change of fortune soon ensued: in September 1921 the American business world began to recover, and towards the end of 1922 the price of raw silk in Japan recovered the level of 2000 yen; then, the Teisan Company sold out all its stock of raw silk, realized 8,700,000 yen, paid all the costs incurred, and obtained a net profit of 3,600,000 yen, which they contributed to the Government on condition that the Raw Silk Conditioning House should be extended and that new silk warehouses should be built. This successful end of the second Teisan Company was again, like that of the first, mostly due to the improvement of the American market.

We may now turn to the fourth period, featured by the 1929-1934 depression. But, before doing so, we may find it worth while to describe the joint storing of raw silk in 1927-1928. From 1924 to 1929 the price of raw silk showed a fairly stable, if somewhat downward, tendency; so the Government, putting aside relief works for the raw silk reelers and merchants, concentrated on a relief policy for the sericultural farmers. But in 1927 a financial panic broke out and seriously depressed the silk price; thereupon the raw silk producers and merchants tried to prevent the price from falling below 1350 yen, by jointly storing 12,000 bales of raw silk with funds which they borrowed at the lowest rate of interest from the Bank of Japan.

The significant fact concerning this loan was that it was guaranteed by two bodies: the third Teisan Kaisha with a capital of 1 million yen and the Teikoku Senshi Soko Kaisha (Imperial Silk Warehouse Company Ltd.) newly established with a capital of 3 million yen (this company obtained the use of the warehouse which the Government built with the second Teisan Company's contribution, for storing silk). Side by side with the joint storing, the raw silk producers resorted to a 20 per cent. curtailment of production; but the measure failed and there was an increase of production. Fortunately, however, the joint storing movement created a very favourable impression on the American market and caused the demand from this source to be so increased as to absorb most of the surplus stock. The true significance of the joint silk storing of 1927 was that it essentially served the purpose of mitigating the seasonal fluctuation of the raw silk price by controlling the marketing of raw silk within the country over a year. By this means, therefore, it could hardly be expected to prevent the long-term price of raw silk from falling—that is, irrespective of seasonal fluctuations. We must now turn to the long-term measures taken against the extraordinary price fall caused by the present depression.

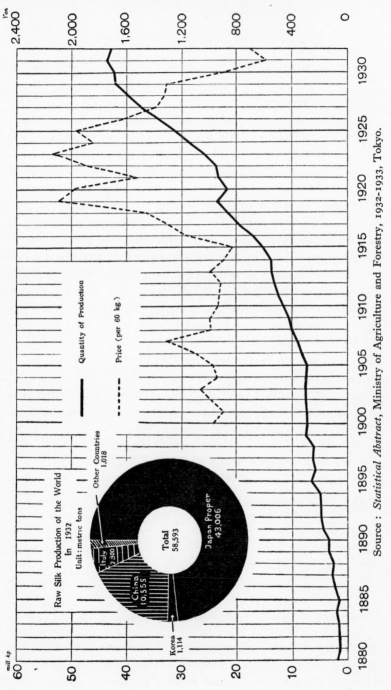

RAW SILK PRODUCTION IN JAPAN

Raw Silk Production of the World
in 1932
Unit: metric tons

Other Countries
1,018

Italy
2,300

China
10,555

Korea
1,114

Japan Proper
43,006

Total
58,593

Quantity of Production

Price (per 60 kg.)

Source : *Statistical Abstract*, Ministry of Agriculture and Forestry, 1932-1933, Tokyo.

The value of Japan's exports of silk to America in 1929 was 780 million yen, but in 1930 it fell to 420 million, in 1931 to 350 million; in 1932, notwithstanding the extreme depreciation of the yen, the total was only 380 million yen, and 390 million in 1933. As about 80 per cent. of Japan's total output of raw silk is exported abroad, these figures will amply indicate the severity of the world economic depression and its effects on the raw silk industry in Japan. Some idea of how severely the sericultural farmer has been hit may be seen from the price of cocoons, which before 1929 was 5 yen per kan, but fell even below 2 yen in 1931-1932, and though in 1933 it rose again to 5 yen, another serious decline followed in the first half of 1934. Estimating the amount of cocoons reared in a year at 100 million kan, this fall means that the total income of the farmers through sericulture has been reduced from 500 million to 200 million yen, and that the income per family has fallen from 250 to 100 yen. Wages of daily workers in sericulture were 1.80 yen (male) and 1.37 yen (female) in 1926, but fell to 0.86 yen and 0.67 in 1932 and 0.89 yen and 0.69 yen in 1933. In the silk-reeling industry the average daily wages fell by 20 per cent. in 1930 and by 40 per cent. in 1931, compared with rates of 1929; indeed, in many cases, small reelers could not pay wages at all. Under such circumstances the disappearance of small reeling enterprises and their concentration into bigger units went on steadily, as is shown by the following figures:

TABLE VIII.—NUMBER OF SILK-REELING ESTABLISHMENTS, CLASSIFIED BY
SCALE OF OPERATION

Year	Less than 10 basins	10-50 basins	50-100 basins	100-300 basins	300-500 basins	500-1000 basins	Over 1000	Total
1926 .	88,311	1747	838	649	113	85	8	91,751
1928 .	72,299	1909	930	730	132	82	8	76,090
1930 .	66,790	1977	972	769	138	77	5	70,728
1932 .	57,070	1674	846	687	120	64	0	60,461

Source : Statistics of the Department of Agriculture and Forestry.

According to these statistics, between 1926 and 1932 about 300,000 small reeling establishments disappeared; the smaller the establishments the greater the number of those which disappeared. At the same time it is interesting to notice that in 1932 some of the largest filatures, employing over 1000 basins, disappeared as well. It should be noticed, however, that though these establishments have " disappeared " in the statistics, they have not necessarily gone permanently out of operation. Disappearance, in the case of the small household establishments, simply means that a few basins are no longer used for the time being. Similarly one cannot assume that the large businesses which have disappeared will not later come back into operation if conditions improve.

A new factor exerting an important influence on the silk industry was the growth of the rayon industry. Although the first appearance of artificial silk to the consuming public dates back before the war, serious competition for use between raw silk and artificial silk did not really begin until 1929-1930; previously artificial silk had developed, if at all, at the expense of cotton and wool. Since 1929-1930, however, the competing nature of artificial silk against raw silk has become more and more evident, as appears from the Table below showing the output of four textile goods since 1913:

TABLE IX.—WORLD PRODUCTION OF PRINCIPAL FIBRES

(in 1000 metric tons)

Year		Cotton	Wool	Silk	Rayon
1909–1913	.	4527·9	1416·7	25·6	..
1923	. .	..	1284·6	39·9	49·9
1926	. .	6102·0	1632·9	50·4	102·4
1929	. .	5760·0	1724·9	61·4	208·5
1930	. .	5640·0	1664·6	59·6	199·6
1931	. .	5970·0	1664·0	58·1	224·1
1932	. .	5000·0	1505·9	50·5	232·5

Sources: *Statistical Yearbook of the League of Nations* and the United States *Commerce Yearbook, 1933.*

It is instructive to examine how the use of rayon has been extended. For instance, in the United States of America during the period of 1912-1932 the percentage of rayon in all the textile fabrics used for underwear increased from zero to 22 per cent., and in Japan between 1921 and 1928 the use of rayon for *obi* increased from 4 per cent. to 25 per cent.; moreover, in both countries the substitution of a mixed fabric of rayon and silk for pure silk has been carried on extensively. Of course the growth of rayon has tended to reduce the consumption of cotton as well, at least to the extent that cotton goods have been displaced by the mixed fabric of rayon and cotton. Nevertheless, the pressure of rayon on raw silk causes by far the greatest concern, at least to Japan. Unless and until the demand for raw silk revives through the recovery of the American business world, and unless the Japanese silk industry itself is reorganized on a much sounder and more economic basis, it is not unlikely that the consuming public will cease to demand raw silk, if not wholly at least to such an extent as to reduce to a negligible quantity the economic importance it possesses at present. What measures, then, have been put forward by both the Government and the industrialists to save the industry from its possible collapse?

MEASURES FOR THE RAW SILK INDUSTRY SINCE 1930

During the year March 1929 to February 1930 the price of raw silk fell by 39 per cent. while the general price-level dropped by 20 per cent. This disproportionately heavy fall in the silk price was a direct occasion for the enforcement, in March 1930, of the law for the Government's guarantee against any bank's loss incurred from loans for the purpose of stabilizing the price of raw silk, which had been inoperative for a year. As this is an important law, we give a summary below:

Article I. When it is considered necessary to stabilize the price of raw silk, the Government is authorized to make a contract guaranteeing a bank against any loss it may incur from granting loans to the raw silk producers by discounting bills on the security of raw silk in accordance with the terms prescribed by the Minister in charge.

Article II.—The Government may make such contracts for five years after the enforcement of the law.

Article III.—The total sum of such Government guarantee shall not exceed 30 million yen.

Article IX.—A bank, when guaranteed against its loss by the Government, shall endeavour to call in its loan as much as it can and pay it back to the Government.

Article X.—Should the bank which has made such contract with the Government act contrary to the stipulations of the said law, or any orders promulgated according to the said law, or the terms of the contract itself, the Government can cancel the contract, thereby refusing to guarantee all or part of the bank's loss, or ordering the bank to repay all or part of the Government guarantee, as the case may be.

Article XI.—Should it be considered necessary, the Minister in charge is authorized to order the raw silk producers to whom the guaranteed bank's loans have been made to report on the conditions of business management or property, or to take any other necessary steps to examine such state.

Article XII.—As far as the said law is concerned, the Central Bank of Co-operative Societies shall be regarded as a bank.

At the time when this law was put into practice the price of raw silk was barely over 1000 yen per 100 kin. The Government, by guaranteeing banks to the amount of 190 yen for every 100 kin of raw silk, enabled the raw silk producers to get loans of over 100 million yen from banks and to store 200,000 bales of raw silk at the price of 1250 yen per 100 kin. Notwithstanding this, the price of raw silk fell below 800 yen in June and dropped to 600 yen in September. Apparently, then, this particular law was effective only in facilitating the storing of raw silk by means of bank loans, but not in stabilizing the price. Facing such a violent price fall, the producers could not possibly have repaid their loans even if they had sold all the stored silk. The Raw Silk Association of Japan (the central organization for sericulturists', raw silk producers' and dealers' associations) realized the danger of forcing the silk reelers to sell the stored silk, and they thus requested the Government to put off the disposal of it until a more favourable time, when it might be done without depressing the price so heavily. The Government consented; the term of storage was extended from six to twenty-seven months, and the rate of the guarantee was increased from 1900 yen for every 1000 kin to 3516 yen, so that it should cover the interest on the loans, the storage charges, and the deterioration of the raw silk, resulting from the extended storing. The detailed account of the Government's guarantee, as it was published by the Department of Agriculture and Forestry, is as follows:

(1) Sum of Guarantee (per 1000 kin) . . . . . . 3516 yen
    (a) Original sum . . . . 1900 „
    (b) Increased sum . . . . . . 1616 „
        For interest on loans and storage charge, 816 yen
        For deterioration of silk . . 800 „
(2) Total Sum of Guarantee (8,394,000 kin) . . . 29,513,304 „

The law, when put into practice, was to involve an expenditure of 30 million yen for five years (the duration of the law), but, as is clearly shown by the above, almost all of the sum had gone before barely half-a-year had passed. To dispose of the 200,000 bales of raw silk, it was decided that half was to be put on the market within the country for home consumption and half to be exported at the rate of 5000 bales a year, from March 1931 onward. However, the price of raw silk never improved; and certainly the existence of the 200,000 bales was one of the reasons.

After the change of Cabinet in 1931 there first appeared the raw silk producers' movement asking the Government to extend the guarantee by another 50 million yen. Although this did not materialize, the situation appeared to be saved, in April 1932, because of the contract by the Asahi Silk Company (which was closely connected with E. Gerlie & Co. in the United States) to take over all of the stored raw silk. The conditions of the contract were that the raw silk should be taken over within three months at a price of 450 yen per 100 kin and that 150 yen per bale be paid in as a guarantee in case the Asahi Silk Company should fail to keep the standard price of 516 yen. But before one month had elapsed the price of raw silk fell below 400 yen; the contract was abandoned, never to be fulfilled.

With the time of marketing the spring cocoons drawing near, prospects looked black. On July 4 the Government again came to the rescue; in spite of its already big financial burden, it decided to buy up all the stored raw silk. A sum of 50 million yen, the net loss over the Government's purchase, was to be shared by the bankers and the raw silk producers in the proportion of 15 and 35 respectively.

In addition to these measures, relief for sericulturists was furnished during 1930-1931 by a sum of 120 million yen loaned by the Industrial Bank of Japan, the Hypothec Bank of Japan, and the Central Bank of Co-operative Societies.

Next the limitation of the output of cocoons and raw silk was taken up. Although in 1930 resolutions were passed by various meetings of sericulturists, deciding to limit the output of the summer-autumn cocoons by 50 per cent. or buy up and destroy some part of the silkworm eggs produced, few were actually put into practice. It was only in 1931 that some of these schemes were realized. The necessity of limiting the cocoon production was strongly advocated by many people, including the Minister of Agriculture and Forestry himself. Compared with that of the previous year, the output of the spring cocoons (52,667,000 kan) decreased by 60 per cent. and that of the summer-autumn cocoons (40,225,000 kan) by 20 per cent. As for the reeling industry, all the filatures were closed for the month of March; the commission merchants in Yokohama and Kobe stopped receiving any consignments of raw silk for the same period; and bankers' loans were restricted. The results were not, however, as satisfactory as in the case of cocoons.

The law for sericulturists' and raw silk producers' associations was enacted on March 30, 1931, for the purpose of bringing about an effective control of the industry as a whole. We have already mentioned the Raw Silk Industry Act (March 1911), which primarily attempted to control the production of silkworm eggs or prevent cocoon diseases, and which only secondarily laid down regulations about a central organization for sericulturists' and raw silk producers' associations. This central body was to be reorganized in 1931, and this led directly to the enactment of an independent law specifically for the sericulturists' and raw silk producers' associations.

The Raw Silk Association of Japan is the central organization for sericulturists', raw silk producers' and dealers' associations. As defined by the law, these associations are of six kinds: Sericulture Association, Raw Silk Merchants' Guild, and Raw Silk Exporters' Association; these are all to form their own federations and the six federations are to come under one central body, *Nippon Chuo Sanshi Kai*, the Central Raw Silk Association of Japan. The function of each of these bodies is that while each federation is to be responsible for the study, investigation, rationalization and control of the industrial activities in its own sphere, the new Central Raw Silk Association is to take up the work of rationalizing and controlling the raw silk industry as a whole.

It is not time yet, of course, to evaluate the result of this reorganization; but one important question presents itself—namely, how effectively the new central organization, whose controlling power is rather weaker than that of the former body, will be able to control the divergent interests or demands of the different sections of the industry as these are represented by the six independent federations.

Since August 1932 a licence system has been applied to the silk-reeling industry; this is the first time that a licence system has been extended to a purely private enterprise other than public utilities in Japan, for such system had previously been applied only to such enterprises as railways, gas, electricity, water, finance, or such professions as law, medicine, or nursing. This is important in itself, but still more significant is the fact that the raw silk industry in Japan has fallen into such a plight that it needs control of the first order, no measure short of a licence system being sufficient. Of the 60,461 silk-reeling establishments in 1932, 94·4 per cent. employed less than 10 basins and were essentially household enterprises, and 2·7 per cent. employed 10 to 49 basins. Thus as much as 97 per cent. of the total was represented by those small units which employed less than 50 basins. Of course the tendency to concentration has been noticeable lately, yet the present state of affairs is that an overwhelmingly large part of the silk reelers consists of extremely small producers. On the other hand, so far as the amount of output is concerned, these small reelers all together can produce only 11 per cent. of the total output of raw silk. Yet this small amount can exert an influence which is far from welcome, as it is an element in hindering the standardization of quality which is all important in the export trade, and it is apt to undersell the market whenever depression sets in.

This state of affairs must be described as very peculiar and, more than that, very precarious; naturally, it has come to be realized that a wholesale reconstruction is necessary if the industry is to prosper. On this vital point the bigger silk reelers, the bankers and the Government all agreed, and a law, after being modified to some extent in order to meet the opposition on the side of small reelers and co-operative reelers, was enacted on August 26, 1932, prohibiting the establishment of any new filatures employing less than 150 basins, if it is a capitalistic enterprise, or less than 100 basins if it is on the co-operative basis, and further requiring a Government licence for any new filature to be built.

CONCLUSION

Since 1914, measures for maintaining the price of silk have been repeatedly carried out. In times of crisis the aim of these schemes has been to maintain the price of silk at a certain level until the return of better times. Success in pursuing this policy, however, depended upon economic conditions in the United States, for, as has been said, 80 per cent. of the total amount of silk produced in Japan is destined for markets abroad, nine-tenths of it for the American market. As long as prosperity in the United States continued, such temporary measures were effective to a certain extent, and even succeeded in improving the conditions in the silk industry in some instances. With the changed economic conditions in America, however, the relief policy hitherto adopted has no longer been effective. Meanwhile silk interests which had waited for the return of American prosperity could no longer depend on the relief which the Government measures promised, and from looking to improved conditions in America, they were obliged to consider a fundamental change in Japanese silk policy itself.

In the past the policy for maintaining the price of silk was usually carried out by means of loans from the Government or banks, by the limiting of the sale of silk, curtailing production, and similar measures. This policy was first initiated to meet the immediate need following the slump of the silk market, and as such was to serve as a temporary measure until the silk market revived. As long as this measure brought relief in times of emergency, the real defects of the silk industry itself remained unnoticed, though they grew more and more serious under the surface. But with the recurrence since 1914 of repeated crises in the silk market, the same measures have been applied, until a few years ago when the Government by law put the scheme on a permanent basis. Even more recently the Government has bought up the surplus silk on the market in order to maintain the price at a certain level, when it found that it was no longer possible to maintain the price by means of the old measures. In the changed situation, no matter how far the Government goes in its effort to relieve the situation by following the same old methods, the chances of achieving the desired effect are very remote, especially if one considers the fact that there is little hope of an immediate recovery of the American market, and that the rapid superseding of real silk by artificial silk is going on. The silk industry is beset with difficulties on all sides, so that no temporary measure can set the industry free. Some fundamental policy which considers the silk industry as a whole is of vital importance. This new situation has arisen since about 1930, when the depression in the silk industry was so acute that the very basis of the industry was shaken.

After the crisis of 1930 not only did the price of silk fall sharply, but the structure of the industry itself underwent a great change. Those to suffer most were the sericulturists. Sericulture had begun as a subsidiary source of income for the farmers, but it developed rapidly with the abandonment of the cultivation of cotton (which had been one of the main sources of income to the farmers), when cotton-spinning became an important industry and the duty on imported cotton was abolished. Sericulture had been termed an enterprise for middle-class farmers, since it required some capital to begin with. For instance, the mulberry-tree which is necessary in the feeding of silkworms requires several years before it can produce sufficient leaves, and other expenditures for breeding-houses for silkworms, miscellaneous tools and so forth, must also be incurred.

Sericulture thus began as subsidiary work, but as the demand for silk increased, especially during the war boom, the number of farmers who made sericulture their main work increased. These were mainly middle-class farmers, so that when they were stricken by the silk depression the result was disastrous to the agricultural districts. So long as they had been able to maintain themselves through a temporary crisis there was no fundamental change in their economy; but since about 1930, when the depression showed no sign of lifting, the farmers have begun to realize that they could no longer depend upon sericulture for their main source of living. To meet this situation, and especially to lower the cost of production of cocoons, the farmers reduced the scale of their cocoon production, and from a main occupation, sericulture became, as in former times, a subsidiary business of the farmers. Consequently, it became something in the nature of household enterprise, and, in order to cut down the cost of labour, the first to be thrown out of work were the poorer class of farmers who had worked as seasonal helpers. Another significant change was the reduction in the acreage of mulberry farms.

One method for sericulturists to cope with the situation was to establish co-operative filatures, and thus if possible to secure for themselves whatever profit was to be had from silk-reeling. This meant the encroachment of the raw material producer into the field of the manufacturer. In this manner some branches of the silk industry could be simplified and scattered sericulturists organized. The Government, too, gave its encouragement to this new development, and in so doing facilitated the better co-ordination of the silk industry, which until now had met its greatest obstacle in the unorganized condition of the sericulturists.

At the same time there took place a similar merging of the two industries, cocoon production and silk-reeling, proceeding, however, from an opposite direction—that is, from the silk reelers, who by means of a system of special contracts for purchasing cocoons were able to effect this combination. This special contract had been originally invented with a view to monopolizing the supply of the best cocoons of uniform quality, a most important factor in production of raw silk. Reelers even gave financial assistance to sericulturists in order to get cocoons of the desired quality. With the continued depression, however, their relations have undergone a change, and their position has become more like that of the factory workers who are paid piece-work wages. In this way the silk-reeling industry has partially absorbed sericulture. Figures show that 35 per cent. of the total production of cocoons has been contracted for in this manner, and 17 per cent. consumed by the co-operative filatures; the rest, less than half of the total production, is disposed of in the open market.

As has been said previously, those to suffer most from the silk depression were the sericulturists. In the past, all the relief measures taken by the Government were usually favourable to the silk merchants and the big silk reelers, but seldom advantageous to the sericulturists. Since about 1923 the sericulturists, realizing their plight, began to organize themselves in an effort to protect their own interests. With the forming of these organizations much progress was made in improving the methods of production and marketing, for, generally speaking, the sericulturists are the more progressive of the farmers. Nevertheless, many small sericulturists have been left unorganized, as is still the case with many small silk reelers.

To effect any important control over the silk industry it is necessary that these small units be organized. Of late this need has come to be felt more and more acutely as the depression has deepened. It is true that the Government has already done much toward the organizing of the industry. Laws prohibiting the establishment of small filatures and sericultural units have been enacted. Yet these measures constitute only a small and minor part of the fundamental plan necessary for the reconstruction of the silk industry. If the relief schemes organized by the Government and the trade associations for the various branches of the industry are studied, one is surprised at the number and details of the various programs. But these unrelated measures are not enough. It is urgent that a basic reorganization policy be formulated to co-ordinate all these separate programs.

The production of silkworm eggs, sericulture, silk-reeling, marketing the raw silk, exporting—these are the main links of the silk industry, and the industry is paralysed when any one of these links shows weakness. Now, at a time when all the links of the silk industry have given way, a fundamental policy for the industry has been considered seriously for the first time. The time is not far off when it will be necessary to go still further and re-examine the ultimate position of the silk industry in its relation to the whole economic structure of Japan.

CHAPTER VI

CONTROL IN THE AUSTRALIAN SUGAR INDUSTRY [1]

by J. B. Brigden

INTRODUCTION, BOOM AND SLUMP

The World's Sugar

SINCE its development as an industrial commodity not more than a hundred years ago, sugar has been a subject for political regulation and control in all countries. The " dumping " of a surplus over local consumption at rates below cost of production dates back to early European practice. A series of international conferences commenced in 1887, the chief problems of which were the rivalries for the British market between bounty-fed European beet and the tropical cane produced in the British West Indies. The other main feature was the rapid growth in consumption as prices fell, and the extension of production in tropical countries. But by the end of the century Cuba was producing but little more than the present Australian output. By 1914 Cuban production had reached 2½ million tons, and European about 8 million tons. Then came the war, and its entire disorganization of the world's sugar. The output of beet sugar fell in Europe to 2·6 million tons in 1919-1920, and prices soared to preposterous heights. In May 1920 raw sugar in New York was sold for 22·5 cents per lb; the equivalent of about £100 per ton, or 11d. per lb.

During those years the Australian price was increased by steps to £21 per ton, and export was prohibited by Federal embargo. In the middle of 1920 world prices collapsed, and by the end of the year the price fell to one-quarter of what it had been six months before. This was due to the maturing of planted crops supervening upon the immediate post-war depression, and the price fell to its lowest a year later. There was a recovery in 1923 and 1924, but by 1929 prices had fallen again lower than ever, and have continued to fall, until in May 1932 the price of Java sugar was £6 per ton (freight included), while for Australian exports in 1931 the value of British " preference " and exchange on sterling together comprised about 62 per cent. of net receipts.

[1] Based on a report originally prepared for Section G of the Australian and New Zealand Association for the Advancement of Science, Sydney, August 1932; and published, as *The Story of Sugar*, in November 1932, by the Queensland Bureau of Economics and Statistics. Subsequently amended and revised.

The story of the war and its effects on sugar is much the same as the story of metals, rubber, coffee, wheat, and of much industrial equipment. And, when the influence of tariffs is added, it explains many of the causes of the world crisis.

The consumption of sugar has increased much faster than the consuming populations, especially in the United States, which in 1929 consumed about 22 per cent. of the whole. Nevertheless, and despite drastic crop reductions in Cuba, stocks carried over in 1929-1930 exceeded 4 million tons, and 9 million tons in 1931. A contributory cause of this condition was that, after the sugar famine, many sugar-producing countries (to quote Mr J. W. F. Rowe) " determined to develop supplies under their own control, no matter what the cost." Australia was one of these countries.

TABLE I.—WORLD SUGAR PRODUCTION

(millions of tons)

Year (at five-year intervals)	Europe	Cuba	Java	Under U.S.A. protection		All Others	Total
				Internal	Hawaii, etc.		
1909–1910 .	6·0	1·7	1·2	0·7	0·9	6·8	17·3
1914–1915 .	7·6	2·6	1·4	0·7	1·0	5·2	18·5
1919–1920 .	2·6	3·7	1·3	0·8	1·1	6·0	15·5
1924–1925 .	7·1	5·1	2·0	1·1	1·8	6·6	23·7
1929–1930 .	8·4	4·7	2·9	1·1	2·3	7·4	26·8
Depression years							
1930–1931 .	10·5	3·1	2·8	1·2	1·6	9·3	28·5
1931–1932 .	7·5	2·6	2·6	1·2	1·8	10·7	26·4
1932–1933 .	6·4	2·0	1·4	1·4	1·7	11·2	24·1
Estimated for							
1933–1934 .	7·0	2·3	0·6	1·7	1·8	12·0	25·4

Early years from a memorandum by Mr J. W. F. Rowe, published by the London and Cambridge Economic Service and the Royal Economic Society, October 1930.

NOTE.—" All Others " include all British Empire sugar. British India has recently increased production very rapidly and now exceeds 5 million tons a year.

Queensland Sugar before the War

The industry in Queensland has always been worked under unusual and " unnatural " conditions. It was established with imported Kanaka labour, which was subsequently repatriated. The " black labour " phase was itself " unnatural " in that it was unlike the utilization of native labour elsewhere. By 1880 the abuses of recruitment in the islands had stimulated the ambition to avoid it. This, together with the growth of the " White Australia " ideal, caused the establishment of mills in the Mackay district to crush sugar grown by white labour. These were at first ineffective, and later legislation providing for conditional advances to such mills had the prospect of Federation in view. When the Commonwealth was established about 86 per cent. of the sugar grown was grown by black labour. For many years the question of whether white men could in fact do the work was a matter of controversy. At first the white labour available was poor and untrained, but all such doubts now belong to the past.

The years 1901 to 1915 mark the second stage of the industry. The Federal Government imposed a customs tariff of £6 per ton on imported cane sugar and of £10 a ton on beet sugar, the difference being a countervailing duty to offset the bounty-fed beet sugar from Europe. An excise duty of £3 per ton was imposed, increased later to £4. It was only £1 per ton net for sugar grown entirely by white labour. This gave what was called a bounty to the growers of sugar employing white labour. The protection given to sugar grown by white labour had been £6 customs duty less £1 excise, or £5 per ton net. The transition to white labour was virtually completed by 1909, and both excise and " bounty " were formally abolished in 1913. The abolition of the excise was a substantial advantage to the industry, for it left the duty as before, and the price of sugar rose. Until 1910 it had averaged £11, 8s. 6d. per ton. From 1911 to 1914 it averaged £14, 4s. 8d. and production increased, reaching 265,000 tons in the good season of 1913.

The War Period

The world sugar shortage had its effects in Australia. In 1913 and 1914 production was such as to give prospects of a small surplus for export, and world prices had then not risen as they were about to rise. In July 1915 the Federal Government took the drastic step of imposing an embargo on both imports and exports, and assumed complete control in the interests of consumers. The 1915 crop was poor, and no exports were allowed, but the price was raised to £18 per ton. Meanwhile the Federal Government had already contracted for sugar which cost more than that to land duty-free. In the ensuing twelve months the large volume of 123,133 tons of raw sugar was imported, at an average duty-free landed cost of £20, 2s. 3d. per ton.

This large proportion of imported sugar, bought at increasing prices, made it necessary for the Government to raise the retail price of refined sugar by ½d. per lb, to 3½d., in January 1916. The next season produced a better crop, and only 73,981 tons were imported, at an average duty-free landed cost of £21, 1s. 3d. The larger volume of local sugar and its lower price enabled the retail price to be maintained. In 1917 the unprecedented volume of 328,349 tons of Australian sugar was produced and purchased, and no sugar had to be imported. In consequence the Government made substantial profits.

In 1918 the production fell again, and heavy loss was incurred by the Government through a cyclone, but only 57,038 tons were imported, the average duty-free landed cost being £22, 2s. 5d. In 1919 the Australian production fell again to 173,354 tons, and the large importation of 116,855 tons was made, the average duty-free landed cost being £44, 6s. 2d. The volume and the price of the imports involved the Government in a loss of £863,723 on the season. Obviously it was high time that the retail price of sugar was increased. Two shipments of mill whites contracted for in February 1920 had cost £95, 10s. 2d. and £98, 12s. 5d. to land duty-free. In the following year 104,940 tons had to be imported at an average duty-free landed cost of £60, 19s. 6d. The Government's loss for that year was £951,492 on both local and imported sugar. The losses on imported sugar only, threatened to reach £4,000,000 a year.

The Boom and its Causes

This brings the story to the post-war period and to a remarkable act of policy sponsored by the then Prime Minister, the Right Hon. W. M. Hughes. In fairness to everybody concerned, the situation as it then was needs to be clearly stated. Sugar prices abroad were still soaring and local costs had increased with rising prices. The retail price for refined sugar in England was 1s. 2d. per lb, and consumers were severely rationed. In European countries and in America it was still higher. In Australia the price was still 3½d. per lb, and manufacturers using sugar were undercutting the world with their exports. In February 1920 Mr Justice Piddington, as a Royal Commissioner, advised an increase of £1 per ton. Prices were rising rapidly and wages were following them. The recommendation seemed to be obsolete immediately it was made. In May the world's price of raw sugar reached its peak. There were no signs of a break.

The price the Federal Government was paying for imported raw sugar was £80 or more per ton at about this time. A retail price of 6d. per lb for refined sugar would be much less than the world price, and it would both cover the costs of the locally produced sugar and the imported sugar, and gradually recoup the loss already incurred on imports. The price was so fixed as from March 1920, and it remained at 6d. per lb until November 1922, when it was reduced to 5d. per lb.

The position in 1920 was that 6d. per lb was wanted for the Federal Government. Fivepence might have been enough but for the desire to recoup previous losses. The 6d. influenced the price payable for local sugar, and in July of that year the price per ton for raw sugar was increased to £30, 6s. 8d. An agreement at this price was entered into for a period of three years from 1st July 1920. This increase of £9, 6s. 8d. a ton was intended to avoid further dependence on expensive imports, to compensate the growers for past denial, and to rehabilitate the mills. The price was unnecessarily high. Two years later the Commonwealth Joint Committee of Public Accounts estimated that £26 would have been sufficient. But behind the price was the policy of promoting enough production to avoid further imports, and the buoyant optimism of the time. The ten years of care-free borrowing had commenced, and " a vigorous policy of development " was in progress elsewhere. Why not in sugar also? The settlement of the tropical north could not have been pushed ahead under more auspicious circumstances. Had we not won the war? Was not a garrison a necessity? And the guaranteed price on which the sugar-growing " garrison " was to subsist was less than half of the then world price for its product.

No sooner was the agreement signed than the slump began. Sugar prices overseas fell away, and other prices also. The trifling amount of sugar that was imported in the year following cost about £26 per ton. But Queensland production achieved three record years. It had fallen after 1915, but the sudden increase of £9, 6s. 8d. per ton was in the aggregate almost comparable with " the dance of the millions " in Cuba between 1916 and 1920. Acreage increased, land values duly absorbed their increment, and some former growers collected these values and retired. All of these consequences were the delayed consequences of the world sugar famine. Had there been free trade in sugar these things would have happened before, and with much more disturbance at the time.

In the period 1915 to 1921, a total of 475,947 tons of sugar was imported, and 1,540,655 tons were produced in Australia. In the first three years profits were made by the Federal Government amounting to £573,181. Between 1917 and 1921, losses totalled £1,990,195. In 1921 the higher price charged for sugar, and the large Australian crop of 300,004 tons, reduced the net loss to £302,138. Meanwhile the consumers had been protected, and the manufacturing consumers had been subsidized in effect by the sugar industry.

In this period of control the Federal Government paid a duty-free landed cost (less receipts from sacks) of £16,790,800 for its imported sugar. Had the same prices been paid for the Australian sugar actually produced, the growers would have received about £11,000,000 more than they did receive. Consumption would no doubt have fallen, and the actual production plus the actual imports consumed would not have been sold at the world's price. But with complete free trade and no regulation import parity would have determined the local price for all the sugar that could have been produced. How much would have been produced? The average for the two years 1913 and 1914 was 255,000 tons. The average for the six years of controlled imports was 206,000 tons. Had only the average for 1913 and 1914 been maintained during the years of booming world prices the growers would have received a further £10,000,000 at least. All things considered the restriction imposed on the industry for the sake of Australia deprived the growers of about £15,000,000 net. While the consumers have since paid much more than this sum in prices in excess of world parity, the growers have not received it because of losses on exports.

A famous Irishman remarked of Irish history that it was a thing which Englishmen should remember and Irishmen should forget. The famine period is one that southerners should remember—and Queenslanders should forget.

It is easy to be wise after the event. It should have been easy when the boom agreement was made to foresee that trouble would arise later. Those in the industry who saw the dangers were either silenced or feared to speak. And it should be reiterated that the Government boom price was less (and much less) than the free-trade boom price would have been at the time. The essential difference is that, while under free-trade conditions the slump would have brought new growers and new mills to ruin and have had them clamouring for assistance, under the regulated conditions the effects of both boom and slump were smoothed out, and the future of the industry became a national obligation.

The disturbing effects of the war have not been escaped in any country. Governments have had to step in at some stage. Under the influence of modern large-scale marketing the comparatively small-scale reactions and adjustments of former days are no longer possible. The economic " machine " works less evenly than it used to work, simply because it is larger. Its adjustments are perhaps just as numerous, but they are bigger, and they affect more people. The intervention of governments in these times is due not only to the increased expectations from governments everywhere, but to the fact that it is more inevitable.

It is by no means certain that the mistake made by the Federal Government made things worse than they would have been without any control. The lesson is not a lesson to avoid intervention at such a time, but to use more " economic sense " in doing so. There is no excuse for the £3 per ton given to all producers for three years, beyond what was necessary to expand production, and as an expedient to compensate former growers and the mills it was clumsy in the extreme. It enriched landowners and sowed the seeds of our present troubles. But it was a Federal act, and merely one of the consequences of a Prime Minister with strong dramatic instincts.

Over-Production and Later Agreements

Before the first three years of the agreement had expired, the future had to be determined. There was no going back on the objective of a sufficient production to supply home needs. The famine period had seemed to point a moral, and after the immediate post-war slump sugar prices were again rising. World consumption had increased greatly. The objective was still valid, and indeed it had been virtually attained.

Adjustments were made. The embargo was renewed as necessary to secure the market. The " compensating " £3 per ton was abolished, and the price was reduced to £27. The retail price was reduced to 4½d. per lb as from October 1923, and the Queensland Government assumed control. At the time the agreement was renewed the world price was again higher than the reduced Australian price.

When the agreement was again to be renewed, in 1925, world prices had fallen to about £12 per ton. The local price should then have been reduced also. But by that time the boom period had produced an excess of sugar. New lands with matured crops and a good season threw the large volume of 227,001 tons on to the depressed export market, and the average return to the mills was only £19, 10s. 7d. per ton. In these circumstances the agreement was renewed at the same price of £27 per ton for local consumption; the Federal Government requiring a rebate of £6, 5s. 1d. per ton on all refined sugar used by fruit processors and a guarantee that losses on exports would be borne by the industry (whatever that might mean).

The average price recovered in the following year to £24, 10s. 10d., because smaller crops required smaller exports. It fell to £22, 0s. 4d. in 1927 for the opposite reason, and further in 1928, to £20, 17s. 11d., when the agreement was renewed for a further three years. Over-production had come to stay. Indeed the industry, although adapted to costs based on a higher price, had to face the problem of a still increasing production from the momentum of the boom years, and from areas where costs were lower or people were too hopeful, as they commonly are in agriculture. A reduction of the local price seemed to be too great a hardship to impose in the circumstances, and on people receiving a lower average price each year. Australia was prosperous, " migration and development " were still being carried on elsewhere regardless of cost, and the price was continued, with rebates on import parity to industrial consumers who exported the product.

This agreement continued until August 1931—the second year of the depression. In August 1930 the Federal (Scullin) Government appointed a Committee of Enquiry. The majority — comprising Queensland representatives, a Commonwealth Government representative, and a fruit-growers' representative—recommended the continuance of the price for three years and of the embargo for five years, subject to a definite contribution of £315,000 a year to fruit growers in lieu of the two former rebates to fruit processors. The minority of three—comprising the chairman (the Hon. J. Gunn, Commonwealth Director of Development) and the representatives of manufacturers and consumers —also recommended a further five years of embargo on imports, but proposed a reduction of £2, 6s. 8d. per ton for two years and action to reduce over-production. The Federal Government accepted the majority report and the agreement was renewed virtually as recommended. Provisions were inserted for the variation of the price in abnormal circumstances, but substantially the former price was guaranteed for a further three years.

The Scullin Government was succeeded by the Lyons Government in December. In 1932 indignant propaganda against the agreement became very active in the southern states, provoked by the continuance of the depression and by what seemed to be the maintenance of the same income to a favoured section by prohibiting competition and fixing prices. After a series of conferences, a reduction of ½d. per lb in the retail price was agreed to, and an extension of the embargo on imports until 1936, with a reduction of the payments to the fruit industry (in abatement of the price of sugar paid for processing) to £200,000 a year. A new Agreement embodying these principles was signed on behalf of the Commonwealth and Queensland governments at the end of October 1932, to operate from January 1933 until 1935-1936.[1]

Summary of Recent Events

During the last three years production has averaged just over 600,000 tons per year owing to a succession of good seasons. In consequence the aggregate value received has fallen very little. The Australian price fell gradually to £23, 18s. 6d. per ton but consumption recovered. By 1933 the local price had fallen 10 per cent. but the local receipts only 9 per cent. from the pre-depression level, while they were above the figures for 1931. The increased output (of about 73,000 tons average) went overseas. In all 45 per cent. of production was exported during the three years, and realized an average price of only £8, 11s. 6d. per ton net in Australia. Throughout the period, 62 per cent. of this price was due to exchange premiums on sterling, and to lower duties imposed in England. These lower duties have been worth £3, 11s. 10d. per ton and the amount forgone by the British Government in revenue on this account has been about £1,000,000 sterling a year. These two items—" British preference " and exchange premiums—have saved the industry from serious depression.

The consequence of the fall in the price of sugar both at home and overseas has been a fall by 1933 of 23 per cent. in the average price per ton for all sugar. But some of the production is not " pooled," and the average for most producers has fallen 18 per cent. Meanwhile the good seasons have increased the tonnage yields, and the industry has reduced its unit costs, and almost maintained its total income. More work had to be done and to be paid for, but in 1932 the total sugar income was 90 per cent. of the pre-depression average, and in 1933, with a record crop of 667,000 tons, 97½ per cent.

RATIONALIZATION

In all countries where the violent dislocations to industry caused by the war led to over-equipment, consequential adjustments have been forced on the particular industries. This has been called rationalization.

[1] For the new Agreement, see Appendix.

The word has been debased to mean nothing in particular and rational methods in general, but here the original German meaning is intended— namely, an organized system of rationing production. In some primary industries (*e.g.* wheat) this method was impracticable, and efforts to stabilize prices failed because rationing did not accompany them. In some others (*e.g.* metals, rubber, coffee), where the product required some years to mature, control failed also because rationing was not effective. There was either insufficient agreement or no process stage in which the flow could be controlled. With sugar, the process stage of crushing the cane provides an opportunity, but for the world as a whole attempts to reach agreement have failed. In Australia as in other individual countries agreement has been reached, and increasing degrees of rationalization have been effective for some years. The sugar industry has been compelled to govern itself, and its methods are of some interest to other industries.

Agencies of Control

The conditions for control are favourable. The cane must be purchased by some mill and the raw sugar by some refinery. The industry was well organized before the war. Indeed its organization was a favourite subject of attack. But when the Federal Government imposed control in 1915, it was able to do so very simply. The Colonial Sugar Refining and Millaquin Companies already were buying all the raw sugar on a standardized agreement with the mills. They were taking delivery at the nearest port, making cash advances at an agreed rate, and final payments at the end of the seasons. All of this was simply continued, and is still continued. The growers were organized at the same time for purposes of determining cane prices, and all machinery was in action. In 1915 the Queensland Government legally acquired all the sugar as it was milled, and sold it to the Federal Government. The refiners became the agents and administrators. This simple method continued until in 1923 the Federal Government withdrew from legal control and the Queensland Government took its place under a series of agreements with the Federal Government. It appointed a Sugar Board of three members to administer control, and there has been a series of agreements with the two refining companies (covering the New South Wales mills also) and of proclamations prescribing the conditions under which the raw sugar is acquired in Queensland. The Board now has four members. The legal power remains in the background. The Sugar Board in effect represents the industry and, subject to the Federal agreement in force, the whole arrangements are self-governing.

Since 1923 the output of raw sugar has been pooled and an average price paid to the mills. A further development occurred in 1930 as the result of the " peak year " scheme under which the Sugar Board determines both the price paid and the quantities purchased from each mill. A different and older legal authority, the Central Cane Prices Board, determines the relations between the mills and the growers.

In addition to these State-constituted boards, there is the Bureau of Central Sugar Mills (administering the advances made to co-operative mills, the total of which has been £2,500,000), a State Bureau of Sugar Experiment Stations, and Cane Pests Boards, while the State Industrial Court regulates labour conditions. A " Queensland Cane Growers' Association " is constituted under the authority of the Primary Producers' Organization Act, applicable to all such producers. Under this Act the Association is empowered to levy on all growers for its expenses, and it does so. The Association is conducted by a Council and an annual Conference. It is purely a growers' organization. Finally there is the older and more comprehensive voluntary association of growers and millers known as the Australian Sugar Producers' Association, which speaks for the industry as a whole. These organizations may not all be necessary, but many growers consider they need a separate representation. The State as such is conspicuous throughout, but it holds the reins loosely.

Districts and Mills

The sugar districts proper are all north of the 26th parallel of latitude —*i.e.* about 2 degrees south of the Tropic of Capricorn. The Queensland production south of that parallel is only about 2 per cent. of the whole. It is old-established production with small mills, the largest being the Moreton Mill at Nambour, with a peak output of 11,586 tons. The New South Wales production across the border on the Tweed, Richmond and Clarence rivers is a good deal larger than in the most southern districts of Queensland, the average of recent years being 22,000 tons—4·2 per cent. of the whole. The sugar districts are spread along the coast for 1200 miles. The 5000 tons of beet-sugar production in Victoria is incidental to the price of cane sugar and might increase. The cane is grown chiefly on river flats and rich chocolate or red volcanic soils where rainfall and temperatures are adequate. The central and northern districts are separated by stretches of relatively barren country.

Northern.—The northern district comprises the newest areas north of Townsville from Ingham to Mossman. Here the soil is still rich in its native humus, rainfall is ample, and mills are large and most efficient. It is this district, with probably the lowest necessary costs, that has developed the over-production and where " excess " sugar is produced. The smallest mill is the most northern at Mossman, and the other nine mills have an average and fairly uniform peak output of 30,125 tons of 94 net titre. This district has a peak allocation of 47 per cent. of the total for Queensland. This peak is never reached by all mills in the same season.

Central.—The central (Mackay) district is older. It comprises the Mackay delta country with extensions north to Ayr (where irrigation is practised). Here the rainfall is less reliable, and the more exhausted soil requires more careful farming. This district has a peak allocation of 34 per cent. of the Queensland total, but can reach that proportion only in good seasons. The mills in this district are older and smaller than in the north. There are twelve with an average peak output of 17,518 tons, ranging from two at about 9000 tons to two at about 25,000 tons.

Bundaberg.—This old district has patches of very rich red soil, and it is intensely cultivated. The Fairymead and the Bingera (Gibson and Howes) Mills (with their cane production) are survivals of family plantations. This district has the Millaquin Mills and Refinery, and a peak output of about 15 per cent. of the total raw sugar for Queensland. It has two small mills and five others averaging 15,240 tons each at their peak. Climatic conditions vary the output.

Southern.—From Maryborough southwards there is a peak output of about 4 per cent., the cane supplies being divided amongst many mixed farmers. The largest mill is the Moreton at Nambour, with a peak of 11,586 tons. There are five others, ranging from 6231 to two tiny survivals of about 260 tons each. The New South Wales district has three small mills (one on each river) conducted by the Colonial Sugar Refining Company.

The history of the mills cannot even be sketched here, but the beginnings of the present system of control are in that history. The Colonial Sugar Refining Company (which owns four of the large northern mills and one in the Bundaberg district) fostered the system of cane farmers, and the policy of the State has been to encourage this further. This has been the general Australian practice with agriculture, and the " White Australia " policy seemed to demand it. This policy dates back in Queensland to 1880, when Griffith became Premier. " Central " mills were promoted in the Mackay district in 1885 (Racecourse and North Eton) but without success until in 1893 the Sugar Works Guarantee Act provided for advances for such mills. Eleven were established by 1897. The most recent mill was a State mill, but it has now been handed over to the customary co-operative association of growers. The financial results of these enterprises are satisfactory.

There are now fifteen " central " mills controlled co-operatively by the growers, one other co-operative mill, two large plantation proprietary mills (which crush cane for other growers), five owned by the Colonial Sugar Refining Company, eight other proprietary mills of substantial size, and four small proprietories; in all thirty-five mills. Originally small " juice " mills were very numerous. By 1901 sugar mills had dwindled to sixty-two (twenty-two being in the Bundaberg district). The growth of production in the north and south and the progress towards centralization are both shown by the following summary Tables:

TABLE II.—SUGAR PRODUCTION IN QUEENSLAND

Year	North of Townsville		South of Townsville		Total	
	Mills	Production per Mill	Mills	Production per Mill	Mills	Production per Mill
		(tons)		(tons)		(tons)
1910 . .	7	8,162	42	3657	49	4,301
1922 . .	9	13,402	31	5407	40	7,206
1929 . .	10	27,382	25	9788	35	14,815

The years are chosen to give typical seasons. The averages have increased since 1929 with more production. The average for all mills and for those south of Townsville is depressed by the inclusion of several very small mills, the effects of which are negligible on the whole. The peak average, excluding the mills south of the Bundaberg district, is 20,263 tons per mill.

TABLE III.—TONNAGES AND PROPORTIONS PRODUCED

Years	North of Townsville		South of Townsville	
	Tons	Percentage	Tons	Percentage
1910 . .	57,135	27	153,621	75
1922 . .	120,617	42	167,618	58
1929 . .	273,820	53	244,696	47

NOTE.—Late in 1932 the small Alberton Mill in the south was closed and the C.S.R. Mill at Childers, in the Bundaberg district, was dismantled, reducing the total number of mills to thirty-three.

Technique and Efficiency

The milling of sugar offers an example of the economy of regulation as compared with *laissez-faire*. Some degree of centralization is essential to reduce unit costs to their minimum, and this degree is not achieved without regulation, or the cataclysmic destruction of small mills by economic pressure, which is itself not economic. In Queensland the regulation now has a legal form. It may not have been carried far enough if there are still too many mills. The same applies to the regulation governing the " assignment " of lands for cane; a subject to be dealt with presently.

There is no doubt that the greatly increased production of cane, and of raw sugar, has been accompanied by greatly increased efficiency. Queensland seems to have marched with the best of the world's producers in its rapid progress in technique both in field and factory. There has been ample incentive in the falling average price received and in the system of paying both the mills and the growers on the sugar content produced, and not on mere volume—*e.g.* of cane. The increased output has been largely responsible for reduced milling cost per ton. The minority of the 1931 Committee of Enquiry, which reported at length on costs, assessed the milling costs at £6, 12s. 2d. per ton of raw sugar for the years 1925-1928 and £6, 4s. 2d. for the year 1928 only. For 1929 the average cost was estimated to have been £5, 16s. 8d. per ton.

Progress in the fields and in the mills have together increased the yield of sugar from cane. In 1900 the cane required to yield one ton of raw sugar was 10·09 tons; in 1910 it had been reduced to 8·73 tons; in 1920 to 8 tons, and in 1929 to 6·91 tons. The yield per acre also improved. In 1900, 11·68 tons of cane were crushed per acre, yielding 1·20 tons of raw sugar per acre. In 1929 the crushing was of 16·67 tons per acre, and the sugar yield 2·41 tons per acre: double the former quantity. The pre-war average was around 2 tons of sugar to the acre. The yield varies with the season. Between 1919 and 1925 it averaged about the same. Between 1924 and 1930 it averaged 2·37 tons, an improvement of 18 per cent. These improved yields have partly compensated the growers and the mills for the reduced price per ton. Indeed the present position seems to be that the more efficient growers and mills have, on balance, merely lost a margin of profit, due to the advantage of situation, soil, or management. Other producers are less fortunately situated. It is very doubtful whether in recent years many Australian industries in farm or factory have improved their efficiency as much as has the Queensland sugar industry.

The Origins of Assignments

It has already been hinted that the regulation of the industry has its roots in the history of " central " mills. The history goes back over fifty years. The first principle of this policy is that all growers supplying cane to any mill shall be paid the standard price for the sugar content at the farm. The second principle is that the mill shall have as certain a supply as the season and the growers can guarantee. In default of these principles neither the growers nor the mills can rely on any price, quantity, or magnitude of operations.

These principles violate all the canons of free competition, and they were not adopted suddenly or without lessons of experience. The policy of paying a standard price for all cane was a purely commercial policy, designed to get enough cane for economic crushing, and to avoid the irritating anomalies of a zoning system of competitive purchase, under which the mills might pay more for more distant cane than for cane close at hand (despite cost of haulage), in their endeavours each to get a maximum tonnage for crushing. It should be explained also that the " central " mills were not promoted easily, or without the taking of risks by the growers. Capital had to be provided, and land had to be mortgaged by co-operative shareholders. There was often no particular inducement to grow cane at all on the lands nearer to the mills. The system, therefore, developed as best it could, with less regard to the inherent qualities of land and location than to the enterprise of the owners of land in each district. Such is the common experience with private enterprise, and parallels are to be found in the dairying industry.

The principle of a standard payment, irrespective of distance from the mill, has smoothed out the differences in land values. It may have promoted some waste in haulage, such as accompanies the normal operation of free competition. It must have militated against a more intensive use of land closer to the mills. If so, these have been merely the customary consequences of purely commercial enterprise. State regulation may not have been commenced soon enough, and it may not have been carried far enough. Such as it is, it has merely continued, rather rigidly, the situation it inherited. The faults are not faults of State regulation but of industry regulation which has had to recognize " vested interests," and to adapt itself as best it might.

Prior to the war there had been agitation among growers for protective legislation, and a Bill had been introduced in Parliament to give

238

effect to this objective. Nothing was done until the Ryan Government introduced the Regulation of Sugar Cane Prices Act and established a Central Board in 1915. This Board has a Judge as chairman, two members representing the growers and the millers, and two technical members appointed by the Government. Local Boards could be established by petition, in respect of each mill and of the growers associated with each mill. The principles followed are that all cane-growers are in effect licensed to supply a particular mill, that they have a voice in the price paid by that mill, and that they all receive the same price for the same product.

This definite association of particular growers with particular mills was a new idea, and it was originally made for no other purpose than to establish an electoral roll. The original Act allowed a grower full liberty to supply any mill he wished, and, in fact, cane was sometimes carried past the doors of three or four mills for distances of thirty or forty miles from the farm. The first Act required the grower to notify any change of mill, and merely prevented such change during the season. Once definitely tied for the season to the mills of their own choosing, the growers and the mills were to make a binding agreement for the sale and purchase of cane. The principles of self-regulation were thus imposed, and the mills gained from the guarantee of whatever crop was produced by a certain group of growers.

In the first year regulations were issued for the compilation of a roll of growers, and a general form of assignment to mills was used, to the effect that the lands of the cane growers who supplied cane in the previous season were assigned to the same mill for 1916. The mills supplied the lists, and the names shown thereon were accepted as the names of the growers on assigned lands, and the assignments were made by Order in Council. The original lists were incomplete, but at that stage accuracy and changes of ownership were unimportant. No questions arose of the right to supply cane from any land. The only question was the right to vote, and to change from one mill to another. These were not serious problems.

In 1917 the Act was amended, and the grower's personal right to change to another mill was deleted. The Central Board was given power ("notwithstanding any Order in Council") to assign land at its own discretion. The lands were described as best they could be in their respective parishes. In the years immediately following, numerous assignments were made of new lands. There was then no question of limiting the total areas, but only of allotting them to the mills. Large areas were assigned irrespective of their suitability for cane, and indeed without any real consideration of the capacity of mills. The Colonial Sugar Refining Company did decline to assist in developing new lands in the Herbert river district while existing assignments exceeded mill capacity. The Board was urged to limit the assignments made, but by a majority declined to do so.

During this period of assignments (from 1917) the price of sugar was increased by £3 per ton, and world prices were reaching famine levels. Production increased temporarily, and there were prospects of further increase. There was never any question at that time of limiting production, and apparently there was only one occasion when a mill found itself embarrassed by over-supplies. This was the (southern) Moreton Mill at Nambour. It was then found that many of its suppliers had no assignments, despite the provisions for control. It was not until 1923, when over-production was almost in sight, and the three years of the £30, 6s. 8d. agreement were at an end, that the Central Board made an attempt to compile a complete list of assignments.

The Limitation of Assignment

In 1924 production overtook Australian consumption, and in 1925 a record crop resulted in an export of 227,001 tons. The average price fell suddenly and there was consternation in the industry. The Central Cane Prices Board had been occupied with its price-fixing duties, and in the determination of numerous and lengthy " awards " similar to those of an Arbitration Court. Now it had thrust upon it the imperative and unanticipated duty of regulating production as well as prices. After 1923 it had tightened its procedure, and required the assent of the mill to a particular assignment. As time went on, it even refused to grant some applications approved by the mills. Eventually the industry requested the Board to use such discretion. In March 1925 the Board resolved that assignments for new land would be refused when a mill was adverse, and would otherwise be limited (in general) to land already ploughed, or which had grown cane. The Board stated in 1926 that " the effect of assignment is that any mill to which land is assigned is bound to take delivery of and pay for cane grown thereon." And it added, with equal significance, " refusal of assignment does not prevent suppliers from growing cane, nor a mill from accepting cane from unassigned lands." [1]

At that time the (northern) Tully Mill had not been completed, and

[1] *Government Gazette*, No. 52, 1926.

in 1926 the Board did " not think it advisable to refuse to assign lands to the Tully Mill " on the grounds of its 1925 resolution, stating that " if the Board did refuse, its decision would not affect the right of the mill to crush nor the growers' right to supply the cane required by the mill." The Tully Mill was a State mill. The Board referred the general question to the Government for decision. In July 1927, more than two years after its resolution to restrict assignments, the Board arrived at a decision to take definite action. It declared its opinion to be " that the assignment of lands . . . should be rescinded and a new defined area assigned in lieu thereof." It proposed to eliminate land still in its virgin state, or which had not been cultivated since 1923, and to assign only such land as had been systematically used for cane-growing. An officer was deputed to determine the areas, and on his report certain applications were refused. The position nevertheless continued to be ambiguous, and the determination of areas took a considerable time.

The whole position of the Cane Prices Board was anomalous. Obviously the liability on a mill to accept cane from certain land determines the value of that land. The Prices Board was never intended to be an authority for determining the value of land. It was and is an arbitration authority between the growers and the mills. But incidentally to this function it became much more, and at no time was it directed to use any judgment in selecting the land to be assigned, according to its suitability for economic production. The Board itself accepted the *status quo* without question and gave legal authority to what it found. In consequence the problem was neglected, and the neglect has had serious consequences. Land once assigned to grow cane has, in general, continued to be so assigned, irrespective of its relative suitability. Other land cannot be used, and, despite the intention of rescinding old assignments, there appears to have been no discrimination other than whether the land was being used. The legal position is obscure, and the Cane Prices Board appears to have no authority for rescinding or reducing the assignments on its own volition.

It is characteristic of the drift that the acts under which the Cane Prices Board is constituted made no direct reference to assignments until 1931, except as an obligation on the mills. The Amending Act of 1931 declared a certificate of the Board is to be conclusive evidence for the identification of any assigned land, and limited the millowners' obligation to a " percentage of any assigned area " which the Board may declare. The Board has powers, but both their adequacy and their interpretation are ambiguous. The Board has, in fact, taken no action which has been effective in limiting production. All that it has done is to stop increasing the already excessive areas formerly assigned.

The Peak Year Scheme

In April 1930 the Cane Prices Board, through an Order in Council, issued a schedule of growers, of their lands, and of their mills, with figures giving " gross area " and " area for annual harvest," which in all cases where the gross area is over 20 acres was 75 per cent. of the gross area. Amplifications were made later. At September 1931 the aggregate gross assignment was 462,174, and for annual harvest for the five years ending 1930 was 209,131 acres. The assignments are greatly in excess of the excessive area now harvested; they take no account of differences in productivity, and the solution of the problem has yet to be found.

The peak year scheme as evolved by the industry represents the first definite practical step towards limitation of production. Before the opening of the 1929 season a conference was held, representative of all sections and of the two Government boards. At a cost of £21 per ton the industry had then lost some £6,000,000 on exports, and increasing losses were in prospect. Indeed the loss to date is about £12,500,000, despite cost reductions. This conference was called at the instance of the New South Wales growers, who objected to the average price being depressed by excessive production in Queensland. They succeeded in obtaining a provision that 80 per cent. of their production should be paid for at the Australian price.

The conference was unable to do more than to arrive at a limit much in excess of any production hitherto achieved. The limit set was, for each mill, the highest output since 1915, inclusive of the year then commencing. This was in practically all cases the maximum ever reached. It protected the older districts and mills, and did not reduce the output of the newer areas in the north, although it limited their growth. It was agreed that any sugar produced by a mill (even from cane grown on assigned land) in excess of its limit should not be admitted to the pool in which both Australian and export receipts are combined and from which the average price is paid. It was also agreed that sugar from unassigned land should not be admitted. Excluded sugar was to receive the export price only, as " excess " sugar. There were 21,660 tons of this sugar in 1931, and the newest northern area, which produced much of it, has been rebellious. But the scheme was reaffirmed in 1931.

The Sugar Board undertook the administration of this scheme and the Government gave the necessary authority by proclamation. The aggregate of the individual mill " peaks " under the scheme is 611,428 tons. In 1931 the output for Queensland was actually 581,556 tons, inclusive of " excess " sugar.

In 1933 the total output for Queensland was 637,944 tons—owing to a record crop in a generally good season. This was 26,516 tons, or 4 per cent., more than the aggregate of the " peaks " allowed. The incidence of excess tonnage gave a quantity of 72,097 tons of " excess " sugar, not pooled. This caused further controversy, but after much conference the original scheme was again reaffirmed in 1934, and efforts are to be made to ensure the gradual reduction of " excess " sugar (by a system of " farm peaks," if possible), and its complete elimination by the 1937 season.

LABOUR—COSTS AND EARNINGS

The industry is inevitably seasonal, as so much of its work is in the harvesting and crushing of the cane. The crushing season lasts from nineteen to twenty-two weeks, and the more it is concentrated in time the higher is the yield of sugar. The rationing of the cutting and the distribution of each grower's supply over the crushing season is one of the minor accomplishments of rationalization. It has to be reconciled with payments according to sugar content, which varies according to the maturity of each individual field each season. The costs and earnings of the labour employed are higher than usual because the employment is seasonal.

The total number of men employed in 1930 in the Queensland raw sugar industry was given in evidence before the 1931 Committee of Enquiry by the Cane Growers Council as 21,053. This would be at the peak of the season. In addition, there were said to be 7684 cane farmers, some of whom were mixed farmers. The total of men occupied was 28,737. Perhaps a round figure of 25,000 would represent the total number regularly dependent on the industry for their main source of livelihood. Of the 21,053 employees, 6823 were field workers, more or less regularly employed, who with the cane farmers proper would total about 14,500 men. There were in addition 8142 cane cutters employed for some twenty weeks in the year, or less, and 6088 mill workers employed for a longer average period. For New South Wales the total of employees was given as 1946.

The wages costs submitted for the Cane Prices Board to the 1931 Committee, exclusive of the value of the farmer's own labour, averaged 15s. per ton of cane for cultivation and harvesting. An additional 10s. per ton was claimed to be the value of the farmer's own labour. The wage cost ranged from 17s. 2d. per ton of cane in the north, where wage rates are higher, to 12s. 1d. per ton in the south. About half of the wage cost is for cane-cutting (on contract). With an average yield of 1 ton of raw sugar to $7\frac{1}{2}$ tons of cane, the average wage cost for the cane was about £5, 12s. Including the value of the farmer's own labour, and allowing a sufficient range of conditions, the cane labour cost per ton of sugar was from £7 to £10. These figures are the average for the years 1925 to 1928 inclusive. The State factory statistics indicate a mill labour cost averaging £2, 5s. per ton of raw sugar in 1930. For both field and mill the total labour cost in 1930 probably exceeded £10 per ton of raw sugar.

Since the average price has fallen, the farmers are doing more of their own cutting. Even the small cane farmer has been inclined to leave this to the specialists, either because he could afford to do so, or under the influence of custom and trade union opinion.

The earnings of the employees vary in the three districts, and have been determined by the State Industrial Court or by other regulation or agreement since 1911. In 1912 the Tudor regulations were promulgated by the then Federal Government as a condition of the abolition of the excise duty. Wage rates increased with other wage rates during and after the war, reaching their peaks in 1926, after the phase of over-production had begun. They have fallen with the general fall in Queensland rates, and are now at levels comparable to those for waterside workers in southern ports. Efficiency has no doubt greatly improved, but the contract price per ton for cane-cutting is high.

The scale of minimum wages in the central district is fairly representative—the rates being lower in the south and higher in the north. It has varied as shown in Table opposite.

By custom of the Industrial Court a " northern parity " of 10s. per week is added to the basic wage ruling in Brisbane, and is applicable to all occupations in the northern district. It applies to all sugar workers in that district. The rates shown in Table IV. are intermediate, and include a " central parity " of 5s. 6d. per week. The weekly rate for field workers in the north is £4, 7s.

The rates per ton for cutting cane are based on an average cut per man per day of $3\frac{1}{2}$ tons, estimated in 1920. Since then the average has increased, partly because softer varieties of cane are now planted, and in 1930 the cutters in one northern mill area averaged 4·6 tons, and £204 each for the season of twenty weeks. The men work in gangs; they often train for the task, and their output is astonishingly good. At the reduced rates now ruling the earnings of the most skilled and

TABLE IV.—MINIMUM WAGE RATES

Central District	Field and Mill Workers	Cane Cutters	
	s. d. Per day	s. d. Per day	s. d. Per ton
1914	9 2	12 0	5 3
	Per hour	Per hour	Per ton
1917	1 6	2 0	6 6
1920	2 0	2 5	7 9
Temporarily increased 1d. an hour in 1921 ¾			
1923	2 0	2 5	7 9
1926	2 $3\frac{2}{11}$	2 $8\frac{7}{11}$	7 9
Increases due to introduction of 44-hour week			
1929	2 $3\frac{2}{11}$	2 $8\frac{7}{11}$	7 9
1932 *	1 10½	2 3½	7 5

* £4, 1s. per week for field workers engaged by the week. Decreases are due to forty-eight hours and reduced basic wage. The reduction in labour cost for time workers is about 17 per cent.

physically fit gangs probably average up to 30s. per man per day, but for 40 per cent. of the year only.

The Australian Workers' Union fully organizes the employees in the industry, and it is in close association with the organizations of the employers. A comprehensive State Award regulates the conditions of employment, but subordinate agreements are made—e.g. with the intention of limiting the employment of foreigners. The so-called " alien influx " has been a troublesome question in the northern district, and some 43 per cent. of the cutters and 34 per cent. of the field workers are of foreign birth and unnaturalized. Indeed in that district the British and Australian employees comprise only 42 per cent. of the cane cutters and 36 per cent. of the field workers. Very few mill workers are of foreign birth, but naturalized foreign farmers are 36 per cent. of the whole. Innisfail is a cosmopolitan town. There can be no objection to this unless it is that the foreign element forces up the price of land, or is less amenable to trade union policy, or that " White Australia" means " British Australia," for the people concerned are good citizens. In the other districts the question scarcely arises.

The labour conditions imposed by the Industrial Court and the Union are liberal to the workers, particularly with regard to accommodation and such-like conditions, but wages and conditions generally have conformed to Australian standards. There are high seasonal wages rates and high piece-work earnings. The cane cutter's average of 4 tons per day is comparable to the Java native cutter's output of about half-a-ton per day. There is no complementary seasonal work for other times of the year (the summer period). Doubtless the industry is largely responsible for the level of money wages in Queensland (the climate and easy housing is responsible for the high real wages). But the money wages have been normal for prosperous times and the wage-earner is scarcely responsible for over-production.

The general sentiment governing these conditions can be illustrated by an episode that occurred when an investigator visited the fields in the north where the population is mixed. There had been complaints that some Italians were cutting cane as early as three o'clock in the morning. The field was visited at the time, and sure enough the men were there. The chauffeur was a local native, and also a full-blooded Chinese. He remarked on arrival: " There you are, sir; that's no good to us Australians."

REFINING AND MARKETING

This survey does not purport to cover the industry outside Queensland. But the degree of rationalization ruling in the industry is most notable in the refining and marketing arrangements in the other states. The production of cane depends not only on what the consumer pays for refined sugar, but perhaps as much on the intermediate costs. In this industry the wastes of competitive milling, refining and selling have been eliminated. The absence of competitive selling costs is notable; the more so in these days when increased costs of selling manufactured goods tend to absorb the economies of production.

In the early days the refining companies were objects of suspicion on all sides, and especially the Colonial Sugar Refining Company. Its operations are still somewhat mysterious. Its profits are said to come from abroad, and no doubt the fact that it sells its Fiji sugar in protected Empire markets accounts for some of them. But everything that this company makes out of the Australian consumer is made out of economies. Its agreements with the Queensland Government are made with representatives of the raw sugar producers, and any further economies they can bargain for are gained by their constituents.

The convenience and economy of the Colonial Sugar Refining Company's management, financing and selling are well recognized in Queensland. The shipping arrangements are highly rationalized, both interstate and overseas. The marketing of overseas exports is done simply on the physical content of the sugar, with one (the largest) English importer, and on the basis of the market price at the time of landing, and the " polarization " of the sugar upon analysis.

The following paragraphs summarize the general principles of control, and the prices now ruling and to be reduced.

The retail price of best refined sugar is 4d. per lb in state capital cities. Virtually no stocks are required; the article is a standardized staple; there is no waste, and its costs of handling and selling are about the minimum for retail trade. The fixed prices for sugar are wholesale prices for refined sugar; neither the retail price nor the price paid for raw sugar is fixed in the Federal agreement, but wholesale prices are the same in all capital cities. Manufacturers for export pay the Australian-in-bond equivalent of the world's price, and for local consumption at a reduction of £2, 4s. a ton on the standard price. These concessions are given as rebates. Standard prices are given in an Appendix hereto summarizing the present agreement. These rebates totalled £80,272 in 1929-1930 and £94,783 in 1930-1931. Manufacturers of fruit products for home consumption receive a rebate of £6, 5s. 1d. per ton of the sugar used in such manufacture. (This gives them an advantage over home-made jams.) These two rebates are not now given directly but through a committee, which receives a fixed sum of £315,000 a year for distribution in the interests of the fruit industry. The two rebates totalled £277,328 in 1929-1930 and £237,738 in 1930-1931.

The Colonial Sugar Refining Company (in terms of the annual agreement with the Queensland Government) receives definite credits per ton for refining, managing, financing and selling; also for the costs of transport from the points of delivery by the mills, and other costs as set out in the agreement made for each season. The agreement also covers the management and financing of the export of sugar overseas, for which no extra managing or financing charges are required. The operations of the Millaquin Company are similarly determined.

The agreements further determine the price to be paid for raw sugar. Two prices are declared by proclamation, one for a definite proportion declared to be for Australian consumption, and the other for export.

The agreements provide for one price to be paid to the mills immediately on delivery at the nearest port. This price leaves a sufficient balance to cover the costs of the refining companies and something in hand for a final allocation at the end of the season.

The sugar is made the property of the Queensland Government from the time of delivery in its raw state by the mills to the time of its sale as refined sugar by the refining companies. The companies are agents. The mills are required to deliver the raw sugar as directed by the Sugar Board's authority. The deliveries and the shipping are both managed to avoid congestion, to give the mills prompt payments, and to avoid the accumulation of stocks at the mills and the ports. An even flow is very important, both to secure the lowest transport costs and for the sake of the sugar itself. Interstate sea-transport is contracted for by one company specializing in the business, and overseas transport by arrangements with the overseas companies as a whole. Overseas freights are low because sugar is good ballast.

At the end of each season the total of the home-consumption fixed charges and the various rebates, discounts, trade allowances (*e.g.* for syrup) and freights (on both raw and refined sugar) are determined, and settlements are made with the refining companies. The Sugar Board's administrative costs are deducted, and the net receipts for the season are arrived at. The same is done for exports. The average net receipts for both are then declared and the balance of the payments is made to the mills. Each mill is entitled to receive the average price for its quota under the " peak year " scheme, and the net export receipts only for any sugar supplied in excess. The prospective consumption in Australia has to be estimated from time to time and stocks vary with the actual consumption and the time of year.

The District Cane Prices Board attached to a mill determines the price to be paid for cane to the growers supplying to that mill. At present the proportion made available to the growers is about 70 per cent. of the receipts. This award is made prior to the commencement of the season. There is a right of appeal to the Central Board from a decision of a District Board. The expenses of the Central Board are met by a levy of 1d. per ton of cane supplied to the mills. The mills, if they are to cover their costs (including the price to be paid for cane), require to achieve what is called a coefficient of efficiency of 90 per cent.—that is, a standard of sugar recovery is set, and upon their ability to equal or exceed this standard depends their ability to cover or show a surplus on their costs.

The general economic principles running throughout are payments by results and pressure from below at each stage. The export price reduces the average receipts by the growers, and the growers have also the pressure of the cost of labour and materials. These two influences are powerful inducements to secure the maximum of sugar content in the cane (on which the growers are paid) as well as high tonnages. The growers are continually exerting pressure on the mills, which must abstract the maximum of sugar from the juice, and their technicians are judged by their results. The mills in turn watch every item of expense in transport and handling, and the charges of the refining companies. Their agreements are renewed each year after negotiation.

The fact that the pressure from Australian influences is all from the primary and producing end probably makes that pressure more effective than if it were from the consuming end also, for if the benefits of efficiency were to be shared with the consumer the incentive would be reduced. This notion may be a heresy. It does not depend for its validity entirely on the prior conclusion that rationalization is a less wasteful method of economic control than competition. There are numerous examples known in business where an economy is not achieved because its benefit to the business would be lost by a successful demand for lower prices. With the growth of trade associations these examples increase. In any event there is the very powerful pressure of the overseas price.

Summary—The Weak Spot

It is not possible here to deal with technique and such subjects as " ratoons " (second and subsequent crops), mechanization, the use of molasses, and the like. Many of the omitted facts are accessible in the reports of the 1931 committee. Some will be dealt with below, including questions of necessary cost.

The general problem is one that faces many industries throughout the world. It is in part due to the similar promotion of the sugar industry in other countries, and to the similar " dumping " of exports on a world market, itself a confusion of tariffs and regulations, and with an absorbing capacity not unlimited. Queensland over-production has synchronized with world over-production, and the problem is one of the legacies of the war.

The industry has been too slow to face the situation as it developed, and its rationalization has not gone far enough. It has stopped short of grappling with its own vested interests, and the weak spot of land assignments remains. The industry may be compelled to pool its land values as it pools its sugar receipts, to compensate certain owners, and to start afresh, reassigning land according to its suitability. For this next stage the existing machinery is inadequate, and opinion is far from ripe. Critics in the southern states would be more effective if they were to recognize the degrees of efficiency and of rationalization that have been accomplished in this industry. Its failure to go far enough is common experience, but its success in going so far is something which might be studied with advantage by, and for, some other protected industries in the south. These have no stones to throw at sugar. Their advantage is that the glass houses in which they live are less transparent to the public eye.

READJUSTMENT

The sugar industry has halted the march of over-production. This was a pre-depression policy, and the halt has been reached only when the production has doubled the volume of Australian consumption.[1] The depression has created fresh problems—namely, a further fall in export prices, a reduction in Australian consumption, and now a reduced local price. The first two are temporary; the third has come to stay. The wild vagaries of the world's price for sugar since the war offer a very precarious foundation on which to base any estimates for the future, and the only use there can be in making any is to assist in getting these questions down to something tangible.

The Balance of Costs to Date

Since the world famine period ended, the average cost per ton of comparable raw sugar landed c.i.f. duty-free at United Kingdom ports has been as follows:

	£	s.	d.		£	s.	d.
1921	24	17	6	1928	11	12	6
1922	15	10	5	1929	9	0	10
1923	25	15	0	1930	6	11	8
1924	21	15	0	1931	7	2	0
1925	12	15	0	1932	6	5	0
1926	12	5	0	1933	5	16	6
1927	13	15	0	1934 (6 months) . .	5	7	0

These figures can be taken to represent about the same cost landed at Australian refinery ports in those years. There might be some deterioration in transit.

[1] The example of embargo or tariff-induced over-production of sugar is a good international specimen. There is more than the world wants even if normal consumption were restored. There is real over-production of a particular commodity, and no producers willing to give way, or to distribute the surplus to the hungry at their own expense.

Since 1930-1931 the price in sterling has been increased because of depreciation, and the Australian rate of exchange would require a still higher price in Australia for imported sugar. Indeed the rate of exchange itself would probably be higher than it is at present if, instead of export credits being established abroad, some £2,500,000 to £3,000,000 had to be found in sterling or other currencies to pay for the sugar we consume in Australia. Under free trade conditions, imported raw sugar would cost us at least £10 per ton to land in Australia at present.

From 1921 to 1926 the average cost (c.i.f. duty-free United Kingdom ports) was £18, 16s. 4d. per ton. The excess cost to Australia at the prices paid in those years for Australian consumption was about £19,000,000. By 1925 nearly the whole of the £15,000,000 of which the industry had been deprived in the boom years was restored by the Australian consumers. But substantial losses on exports had already commenced.

Since 1926 the excess cost to the Australian consumers has been increasing as world prices have fallen. In the five years to 1931 inclusive the excess cost over free import prices totalled some £30,000,000. About £10,000,000 of this was due to the absurdly low prices ruling in the world's markets, and not to differences in costs of production. Most of the cost imposed on consumers has been due to the losses on exports.

When all is considered, therefore, the net cost to date of this white labour industry in the tropical regions has been about £20,000,000 to £25,000,000, and this large total has been due to an over-production stimulated by national policy, which has had to be sold on a world market already over-supplied. The total cost for the whole period and to date is about equal to the cost of protected manufactures—situated chiefly in Sydney and Melbourne—for one year (1926-1927), according to the estimates of the Tariff Committee which reported in 1929.

The Future Cost to Australia

The price to Australian consumers was, in 1932, to be reduced from 4½d. to 4d. per pound of refined sugar. Costs of production in Australia are in process of reduction. Costs of production in other countries have fallen, and the future economic price, c.i.f. duty-free Australian ports, will be less than in the years prior to the depression. No reliable figure can be estimated; it may be anywhere between £12 and £16 per ton. If £14 is used for estimation, and the Australian consumer's cost for raw sugar delivered at the refineries is reduced from the former cost of about £29 to £26 or thereabouts, the excess cost to Australian consumers will be about £12 per ton, or about £4,000,000 a year, on

251

normal consumption. This sum covers the necessary extra cost of producing sugar for Australian consumption, and a contribution towards losses on exports. At present the costs of production are still too high, the proportion of sugar exported is too large, and the price received for it is too low, for the prospective average price to cover costs. It will require the maintenance of the protection now given in the British market and a very substantial recovery in the world price of sugar, as well as further reductions in costs, to enable the industry to maintain itself in the future.

Until Australian consumption recovers, the exports are likely to be at least 40 per cent. of production. While export prices remain at no more than £10 per ton at the ports, the export receipts may be £2,000,000 or so less than the costs. This sum would not be covered by the contribution made in the Australian price, and a considerable proportion will be borne by the growers.

Present Costs

The 1931 Committee of Enquiry made efforts to determine the costs of production in the industry. The majority arrived at a figure for raw sugar of £18, 12s. 9d. per ton as the average cost, exclusive of any return on capital invested, and a " fair sale value " of £22, 7s. 9d. per ton. But as the average price received in the six years ending 1930 was only £21, 3s. 1d., and production continued to increase during those years while the price decreased, it is difficult to accept the figures as representing typical cost. The minority estimated the cost to have been £18, 7s. in 1931, inclusive of sufficient return on capital invested. Since then labour costs have been reduced further.

An average price of £18 per ton would probably eliminate many small growers, as soon as they could produce something else. The average price received last year, including " excess " sugar, did not reach £18; nevertheless the " excess " sugar was produced. Probably the particular growers had no option. Certainly the growers generally are badly off compared with their customary standards. It is claimed, and to all appearances justly claimed, that no hardship is involved by living and working in the sugar districts. If the standards of comfort which Australians generally have to look forward to are to be applied to sugar workers and farmers, the figure of £18 per ton at the ship's side and £20 at the refinery ports is not too low an assessment of the necessary cost. It may have to be reduced to £19 delivered at refineries. It may be objected that the low costs here given could not be achieved unless the mills were able to handle their present output, including the exports manufactured. The unpleasant answer is that fewer mills would be required, especially in the central and southern districts.

The following gives a rough distribution of the above costs. It is based on a large output and on the estimates of the minority of the 1931 Commonwealth Committee. (The majority placed the costs higher, but these members were more concerned with " fair sale value.") Interest is allowed on capital invested in cane land at the rate of £30 per acre. The interest allowed for capital invested in land and farm equipment is about 36s. per ton of sugar; 7½ tons of cane are reckoned per ton of sugar.

TABLE V.—DISTRIBUTION OF PRODUCTION COSTS

Distribution	Cane Costs			Mill Costs			All Costs		
	£	s.	d.	£	s.	d.	£	s.	d.
Labour (including growers') . .	7	0	0	2	0	0	9	0	0
Materials, plants, rates and repairs .	2	15	0	2	5	0	5	0	0
Interest and depreciation . . .	2	15	0	1	5	0	4	0	0
	£12	10	0	£5	10	0	£18	0	0
Add c.i.f. mill ports to refinery ports (now reduced to 32s. or less) and a margin for bad seasons or labour costs in excess of those given above							2	0	0
Cost at refinery ports (say)							£20	0	0

As in all primary production the range of necessary costs is very great. As in all production the costs actually incurred depend to a considerable extent on the price received. The above figures are about as near to a standard as can be achieved, and no purpose would be served by setting them out here in greater detail. In practice the total cost on farms and at the mills range around the above figures, and on both sides there may be a large number of producers with substantial margins of profit or of loss. Growers who have contracted to pay high prices for land are necessarily getting less than the average income for their own labour, and at the price given above they will continue to do so, unless their land or their efficiency is better than standard. Other growers are now receiving, and must continue to receive, less than formerly as a return on their investment.

The above costs are the average costs over a large output. Sugar production varies with the seasons. In common with other primary industries, sugar has experienced good seasons and an increasing quantity of product, reaching a purchased total of 605,000 tons net titre in 1931. The average output is nearer 500,000 tons. The cost of production varies with the yield of cane and of sugar content. The above average of £18 per ton at the mill ports is certainly low for an output of 500,000 tons, and probably a figure of £19 would be the lowest cost reasonably attainable for this output, or for the quantity required for Australian consumption only. Additional output derived solely from higher yields would cost less. On the output for 1931 the present or prospective cost may be as follows:

500,000 tons at an average cost of £19	£ 9,500,000
100,000 tons extra, costing £13	1,300,000
600,000 tons, averaging £18	£10,800,000

From Refinery Ports to Consumer

The story of raw sugar ends with its arrival at the refineries in the other states. Any excess costs that may exist in refining (or in distribution) are not costs of the Queensland industry. But it is desirable to trace the distribution of the costs until they reach the householder. The following summary states the position approximately as it is at present.

Under the Colonial Sugar Refining Company's agreement separate charges are made for refining expenses, for overhead costs, and for charges in selling and financing stocks, as agents. Refining charges have been reduced 3s. 6d. per ton, and now total 50s. per ton, inclusive of 1s. 6d. incidental to exports. " Managing " charges for interest, selling and overhead expenses total 34s. 5d. This gives a total of £4, 4s. 5d. per ton of raw sugar exclusive of transport costs.

It is impossible to express both summarily and accurately the various costs incurred in transport, and to convert costs per ton of raw sugar into costs per ton of refined sugar in the processes of transport and refining. Some transport costs are properly chargeable to the refining process—e.g. landing and wharfage—but they are not separated in the accounts, and transport costs on refined sugar sent to Tasmania and Western Australia are charged to the raw sugar industry.

There is a loss of weight and strength, and some waste, in the process of refining—the whole not exceeding 1 per cent. On about 6 to 7 per cent. of the material there are lower receipts than for refined sugar of standard grade, and there are charges for syrup packages and other incidentals. The simplest way to express these costs is to estimate them in terms of raw sugar converted into refined sugar. The cost per ton is increased by these various items from the £4, 4s. 5d. given in a preceding paragraph to about £6 per ton of refined sugar. Transport costs on raw sugar from the mill ports is not included in that figure, except such proportion as is chargeable to the receipt of the sugar, and would be payable on imported sugar c.i.f. from overseas.

There are other charges, including concessions to manufacturers for export, and to fruit processors, which add to the costs of refined sugar sold for domestic consumption. There are also the costs of distribution included in the retail selling price, and a further allowance in that price which is received by the mills which is in effect a contribution towards losses on exports. Some of these items are small in themselves and vary from time to time, their variations determining the net receipts for raw sugar. The general position is set out in the Table given below.

The following is merely an approximate summary of the distribution of the payments made by the ordinary consumers of refined sugar per ton of sugar purchased at retail. The concessions are charged to such consumers, because a higher retail price is required on their account. For the sake of simplicity the figures are stated approximately, to illustrate the position, rather than to attempt any precise estimates.

TABLE VI.—DISTRIBUTION OF RETAIL PRICE

Distribution	Per ton of Refined Sugar	
	Former	Future
	£ s. d.	£ s. d.
Retailers' profit	4 13 4	4 2 8
Trade discount and lower price to manufacturers	0 14 6	0 12 10
Concessions to fruit processors and all exporters on sugar content . .	1 2 0	0 13 6
Refining and incidental costs (say) .	6 0 0	5 15 0
Transport, handling, insurance, etc. .	2 10 2	2 2 8
Cost at mill ports (for 500,000 tons output) .	19 0 0	19 0 0
Balance as a contribution to losses on exports	8 0 0	5 0 0
	£42 0 0	£37 6 8
Per lb of refined sugar	4½d.	4d.

NOTE.—The former costs on a 500,000-ton output would not leave as much as £8 per ton for losses on exports, but cost reductions are in progress. Some further reductions in labour costs may be necessary to reduce them to the figures given. Concessions to manufacturers are less in magnitude under the new Agreement because the price of sugar will be less. The above figures are in terms of raw sugar. About 30s. per ton should be added in terms of refined. This is charged above in " incidental costs."

Effects of the Price Reduction

The effect of the reduction of ½d. per lb will save a total of about £1,300,000 to Australian consumers, or an average per head per year of about 4s., at the present rate of consumption. Traders are to forgo some £180,000, and reductions in concessions account for about £130,000; the two totalling £310,000, and leaving £990,000 to be borne elsewhere. After reductions in costs *ex* mills (at present uncertain in amount), the growers, the millers and their employees will lose upwards of £900,000. The benefits are diffused; the sacrifices are concentrated. While the sugar producers are still sheltered absolutely for their local market, the general effect is to reduce the payments made by the community generally in aid of export production.

The Australian consumption of sugar has fallen from around 340,000 tons a year to some 300,000 tons. This difference of 40,000 tons has meant a reduction in the income of the raw sugar producers of about £700,000 a year, because the difference in the price received for it overseas, as compared with the Australian price, has been about £17, 10s. a ton.

The following Tables illustrate the effects of differing proportions of an output of 500,000 tons sold in Australia at the prospective net price received at the mills—namely, £24 per ton—and the net return of £9, 10s. a ton for exports. (The net return last year was £9, 7s.) The cost used is the £19 per ton for an output of 500,000 tons, which is double the price received for exports.

A.—*With Normal Australian Consumption*

500,000 tons costing £19 per ton at mill ports: £9,500,000

340,000 tons sold in Australia at £24	£8,160,000
160,000 tons sold abroad, netting £9, 10s.	1,520,000
Total receipts at mills	£9,680,000
Margin over bare cost (£19)	180,000
	£9,500,000
Margin of £5 per ton on Australian sales	£1,700,000
Loss of £9, 10s. per ton on exports	1,520,000
Net margin (7s. 2d. per ton)	£180,000

Additional tonnage derived from seasonal conditions and exported for £9, 10s. net may reduce the margin, or cover its own extra cost.

B.—*With Present Australian Consumption*

500,000 tons costing £19 per ton at mill ports: £9,500,000

300,000 tons sold in Australia at £24	£7,200,000
200,000 tons sold abroad, netting £9, 10s.	1,900,000
Total receipts at mills	£9,100,000
Loss on output (at £19 cost)	400,000
	£9,500,000
Margin of £5 per ton on Australian sales	£1,500,000
Loss of £9, 10s. per ton on exports	1,900,000
Net loss (16s. per ton)	£400,000

Additional tonnage derived from seasonal conditions and exported for £9, 10s. net may increase the loss, or cover its extra cost.

C.—*With Australian Consumption at 360,000 tons*

500,000 tons costing £19 per ton at mill ports: £9,500,000

360,000 tons sold in Australia at £24	£8,640,000
140,000 tons exported, netting £9, 10s.	1,330,000
Total receipts at mills	£9,970,000
Margin over bare cost (£19)	470,000
	£9,500,000
Margin of £5 per ton on Australian sales	£1,800,000
Loss of £9, 10s. per ton on exports	1,330,000
Net margin (18s. 9d. per ton)	£470,000

An Australian consumption of 360,000 tons per year is a reasonable anticipation for normal world conditions. £12 per ton might be realized for exports when the world recovers. In that event the loss on 140,000 tons exported would be reduced to £7 per ton—a total of £980,000—allowing of a net margin over bare costs of 32s. 9d. per ton. There should then be no loss on extra sugar exported—and derived from yields of cane or sugar content in excess of a normal acreage production of 500,000 tons.[1]

Such are the prospects before the industry. It is most unfortunate

[1] Such substantial reductions have been made in the production of sugar in Cuba and Java that world stocks are being reduced. World prices are likely to recover next year, and the realized net price for Queensland exports may reach £12 per ton before Australian consumption recovers. No forecasts can be made with any confidence, but with Australian consumption increased to 330,000 tons, and with only 170,000 tons sold abroad, the bare cost of £19 per ton would be met by local sales and the amount now being realized per ton for exports. Every 1s. per ton in addition from exports would give a margin of 4d. on all production up to 500,000 tons. Every additional 1000 tons consumed in Australia (over 330,000) would increase the margin by about 7d.

R

that the substantial reduction in the Australian price should synchronize with a reduced local consumption and with ruinous overseas prices. Production costs cannot be reduced as quickly as the fall in the price, and the industry is faced with difficult conditions until Australian consumption and world prices both recover. It has become more than ever dependent on the protection given in the British market (by the forgoing of tax revenue on our sugar), on sterling depreciation, and on Australian exchange premiums, which alone amounted to £676,000 in 1931. There is at present a loss of about £2,000,000 a year on exports despite these supports. The contribution towards this loss by the Australian consumers is being reduced to about £1,500,000.

When costs are reduced to £19 per ton for an output of 500,000 tons, the producers will be losing about 16s. per ton so long as present conditions continue. Meanwhile, and until costs are reduced to those levels, they will be losing more. With a reduced output confined to production from the better lands, a peak output of 500,000 tons may be produced at a cost of £18 per ton, and even a smaller output at that figure. When the normal *per capita* consumption in Australia is restored, and world prices recover to reasonable levels (*e.g.* to world costs), the industry should be once more profitable, provided that its reduced costs remain reduced. It seems that the reduction in price now to be made is a reasonable one for the future, but that the lesser reduction (of a farthing retail) proposed by the 1931 Commonwealth Committee minority would have been more judicious for the present. However, the industry rejected this compromise.

The Problem of Exports

The industry will be provided by local consumers with a subsidy in excess of necessary costs equal to about £1,750,000 a year. Without export losses, the local prices could be reduced by about ½d. per lb, to 3½d. Is it worth while to maintain export production at a cost to consumers of ½d. per lb of the sugar they use? Would Australia be better off with no exports and £1,750,000 to spend on something else? These questions are postponed by the new Agreement until 1936. Until then there is an incentive to reduce exports, for every £1 saved by reducing them will be saved by the producers through a higher average price. After 1936, however, the benefit may be transferred to the consumers. Smaller losses on exports would provide a reason for demanding a further reduction in the price of sugar. The outlook is unsatisfactory.

At the moment there is no alternative production for sugar producers to pursue, and the pooling system gives no incentive to anybody to reduce exports. This is the weakness of the system. It could be amended. The tendency is to protect old producers, districts and assigned lands, irrespective of their costs of production. The problems are exceedingly complex and "humanly" difficult, because of the vested interests involved. Such interests are even less amenable when individually small than when individually large, because numbers of such people are concerned. The interests are not "small" to the individuals.

Two general principles can be stated as covering the direction of sound policy:

(a) The producers should stand to gain something substantial by further economies, rather than that the prospect of all benefits going to consumers should defeat the incentive altogether.

(b) The pooling system should not perpetuate the more costly production nor control prevent the use of more appropriate lands. Vested interests in less productive lands might be given time or compensation to relieve their difficulties in transferring to other production.

The industry did not deliberately enter upon the bad business of selling sugar at less than cost; its export business is a by-product of national policy. But it cannot continue indefinitely. It cannot be altered quickly, but we are not so poor in resource that the surplus sugar lands cannot be used more profitably for the community. To get into this dilemma was all too easy, as it has been with other of our troubles, and to get out of it will take time and some ingenuity. The industry should get ready for the expiration of the Agreement.

Meanwhile the prosperity of the industry will depend on its success in reducing "excess" sugar and its consequential losses on exports in excess of the subsidy provided by Australian consumers. It will depend also on any increase in that subsidy from increased local consumption. At present (1934) the local price is three times the price received for exports, despite the protection received in the English market.

It should be possible to reduce the proportion of exports to one-third of production and to realize £10 a ton for it when the world depression lifts. Given an Australian consumption of 360,000 tons by the time the present Agreement comes to an end, the total average production would then be 540,000 tons, and the average price nearly £20 a ton. This would be quite profitable, and when Australian consumption increased to more than 400,000 tons a year the retail price in Australia could be reduced to 3½d. per lb of refined sugar.

The Embargo and the Controlled Price

The embargo on imports is continued and is likely to be continued. It is more straightforward than a prohibitive duty. There appears to be no case at all for the admission of imported sugar. The industry is one to which the following observations of the 1929 report, *The Australian Tariff* (page 126), apply with special force:

If only sufficient protection is given to place the manufacturers on an equality with importers, the trade will be divided between them, and the possibilities of lower costs through mass production will be defeated. " Effective " protection may therefore be necessary to secure the lowest costs.

With sugar the case is very clear because no questions arise of shutting out, or penalizing by prohibitive duties, varied grades or varieties of a product which cannot be produced economically at home. Raw sugar is one standardized product. The economy of a standardized price is important also. A variable price gives more scope to speculation and less stability to manufacturers using the product. The extra risk has to be paid for, and the consumers pay for it. This industry appears to offer one of those examples (becoming less rare) when the regulation that exists is clearly more economic than competition.

Conclusion

The necessary costs of producing raw sugar for Australian consumption only, and of refining and selling it to consumers, are now less than $3\frac{1}{2}$d. per lb for refined sugar retail. It is not an insignificant feat to be able to do this under Australian conditions. In the process the raw sugar industry supports a farm and central mill population extending for over a thousand miles along the tropical and subtropical coastline of the Australian continent, and supports it under conditions unexampled elsewhere.

Moreover, the costs of production are swollen probably by 10 per cent. through the general costs of tariff protection for all Australian industries. Without these costs, " white labour " sugar could be produced, refined and sold in Australia for 3d. per lb retail. This could not be done under competitive conditions.

The value of the industry as an " outpost " can be exaggerated and the sentiment associated with it can be exploited. Nevertheless the value exists. The widely spread areas of cultivation and the mills which serve them are no " backyard " aberrations of intoxicated protectionism, and the stalwart men who earn high piece-work wages in the fields are worth something in the assets of a nation. The industry should no doubt decrease its production, and confine itself generally to local requirements, and this it can do in time. Its costs need continued scrutiny, and its incentives need to be maintained. As a specimen of control it is now particularly interesting because of the thoroughness of that control and of its peculiar character, and it is likely to become still more interesting in the future.

APPENDIX

The New Agreement.—Former agreements between the Federal and the Queensland Governments had no specific legislative sanctions, and their legal validity was ambiguous. The embargo on imports was dependent on the validity of Federal proclamations. The original embargo—on exports— derived its authority from emergency defence powers, and a continuance of dependence on Federal proclamations was constitutionally irregular and potentially without any legal basis. The embargo might have been challenged successfully before the High Court.

The new Agreement is incorporated as a schedule to a Commonwealth statute —The Sugar Agreement Act 1932. The Act has two clauses, one approving the Agreement, and the other prohibiting the import of sugar except with the consent of the Minister. This Act was passed by the Commonwealth Parliament in November 1932, with three dissentients to the embargo in the House of Representatives and eleven in the Senate.

The Federal Minister, in introducing the measure, stated that " when the last agreement was made, the Government of the day was attempting to maintain the old levels of wages, prices, and living standards," and that " the subsequent adoption of the Premiers' Plan completely altered the situation." He explained that " two serious menaces " threatened the existence of the old agreement, as a legal protection to the industry. The High Court had ruled in the " wool tops " case that the Commonwealth could not bind itself effectively by an agreement without specific parliamentary sanction (which had never been attached to any sugar agreement). The High Court had declined to declare the agreement *ultra vires* on the application of an individual, but pointed out that a state could approach it if it thought fit. Further, the method of prohibiting imports by proclamation was authorized only by a section of the Customs Act dealing with noxious drugs and the like, and the Parliament was against the principle of allowing the power of prohibition to a Government, except under regulations that could be disallowed by either House of Parliament.

For both of these reasons parliamentary sanction was required, and the conditions of the Agreement, including the prices fixed, had to be approved by the Federal Parliament. A majority in the Senate was hostile to the former agreement.

The 1931 Agreement was due for revision as to prices in August 1933, in any event. It was therefore voluntarily abandoned; and a reduction of ½d. per lb was accepted as from January 1933, with security for the domestic price and for the embargo on imports for four years.

The new Agreement dates from January 5, 1933, and is to continue until the end of the sugar season 1935-1936. The prohibition of imports dates until August 1936.

Prices.—The price for refined sugar of IA grade is £33, 4s. per ton in ½-ton lots or more (reduced from £37, 6s. 8d.), and £32, 10s. 9d. for IXD grade to manufacturers (reduced from £36, 11s. 9d.)—both prices being for net cash; and consequential reduced prices for other grades and products. The price to manufacturers is the same as the net price to merchants.

Merchants are allowed a discount of 2 per cent., subject to their terms of sale being approved by the Queensland Sugar Board (as agent for the Queensland Government, which acquires all cane sugar manufactured). The Agreement does not specify the retail price of 4d. per lb.

Concessions.—£200,000 per annum is to be provided from the proceeds for the benefit of the fruit industry, through a representative committee, on conditions as to use of Australian products, prices paid for fruit, and the determination by arbitration of wages, etc. From this sum a rebate of £2, 4s. per ton of sugar used by fruit processors is to be given to them. Such processors exporting their manufactured products from Australia are also to receive a rebate of the amount of the excess (if any) of the Australian net home-consumption price (£30, 6s. 9d.—*i.e.* £32, 10s. 9d. less £2, 4s.) of the sugar contents of such products over the world's parity price (as prescribed). The balance of the fund is to be applied to assist the use and sale of manufactured fruit products.

Exporters of other manufactured goods are to receive a rebate of the amount of the excess (if any) of the Australian net home-consumption price (£32, 10s. 9d.) of the sugar contents of such goods over the world's parity price (as prescribed).

Other Matters.—Employees in the sugar industry are to have access to arbitration on wages, etc. The Queensland Government is to take such action as it thinks fit to control production. The prescribed prices of refined sugar apply to delivery in Sydney, Melbourne, Brisbane, Adelaide, Perth, Fremantle, Hobart and Launceston, inclusive of bags, and, if required, a depot at Hobart is to be established. Sugar imports are to be allowed only after consultation with the Queensland Government, and to meet a shortage, or of kinds of sugar not available in Australia.

TABLE I.—

			Season				Season	
	1926	1927	1928	1929	Average of Seasons 1927, 1928 and 1929	1930	1931 (provisional)	1931 compared with average of 1927-1929 (percentage)
A. Thousands of tons purchased—								
Total	416	509	537	538	528	535	605	14·6
For Australian consumption	338	350	345	335	343	325	303	11·6
For export	78	159	192	203	185	210	301	62·7
B. Value (£1000)—								
Total	10,205	11,200	11,223	10,956	11,126	10,476	10,975	1·3
Australian quota	9,045	9,277	9,209	8,957	9,148	8,745	8,157	10·8
Export quota	1,160	1,923	2,014	1,999	1,978	1,731	2,818	42·4
C. Price per ton (see note below)—	£ s. d.	£ s. d.	£ s. d.	£ s. d.	£ s. d.	£ s. d.	£ s. d.	
Average	£24 10 10	£22 0 4	£20 17 11	£20 5 10	£21 1 4	£19 13 1	£18 6 6	13·0
Australian quota	£26 15 0	£26 10 0	£26 13 6	£26 16 0	£26 13 2	£27 0 0	£26 19 0	1·0
Export quota	£14 18 10	£12 2 6	£10 10 0	£9 17 0	£10 16 6	£8 5 0	£9 7 0	13·6
D. Percentage exported	18·7	31·2	35·7	37·7	34·9	39·2	49·8	14·9
E. Losses on exports at per ton cost	£21 0 0	£21 0 0	£20 0 0	£19 0 0	..	£19 0 0	£18 0 0	
Per ton exported	£6 1 2	£8 17 6	£9 10 0	£9 3 0	..	£10 15 0	£8 13 0	
On total exported (£1000)	470	1407	1822	1857	..	2256	2607	
F. Excess over cost in Australian price—								
Per ton	£5 15 0	£5 10 0	£6 13 6	£7 16 0	..	£8 0 0	£8 19 0	
Total loss borne by consumers (£1000)	1944	1925	2304	2146	..	3602	2716	

NOTES.—*Price per ton.*—The price for the Australian quota and the export quota is the final "declared price" for the season concerned. It applies to both the Queensland and the New South Wales output, but since the 1928 season the latter state has been allowed a higher home-consumption quota. The average price quoted is the average for the Queensland output (which over this period was about 96 per cent. of the total output) and excludes "excess" sugar. "Excess" sugar is sugar made from cane grown on "unassigned" lands, and sugar produced by mills in excess of their allotments under the "peak" year scheme adopted in 1929. "Excess" sugar was produced in the 1930 and 1931 seasons, the tonnages being 6728 and 21,660 respectively. This sugar is paid for at the export quota price, and, if included, the average price for the Queensland output in these two seasons is £19, 10s. 1d. and £17, 19s. 10d. respectively.

Exchange on the 1931 season's sugar exported amounted to about £2, 4s. 10d. per ton. The value of the preference accorded Australian sugar in Great Britain is £3, 11s. 10d. per ton, so that with exchange the total benefit is £5, 16s. 8d.

An absolute reconciliation between all the figures shown in sections "A," "C," and "B" is not possible, as the average price quoted in "C" is not the Australian average price, and adjustments have been made by the Sugar Board to certain of the figures in "B." All figures are on the basis of 94 net titre sugar.

Calculations of losses on exports are made on rough estimates of cost. For 1925 the loss was £2,205,000.

COMMODITY CONTROL IN THE PACIFIC AREA

TABLE II.—PURCHASES AND PAYMENTS—LAST THREE SEASONS

(A summary of the position during the last three seasons in terms of sugar of 94 net titre, the standard by which payments are made to the mills.)

	Season 1929	Season 1930	Season 1931 (provisional)
Total tons purchased . .	538,300	535,101	604,844
For home consumption . .	335,386	325,248	303,414
Exported	202,914	209,853	301,430
	£	£	£
Total amount paid . . .	10,955,968	10,476,367	10,975,541
For home consumption . .	8,957,265	8,745,077	8,157,171
For exports (net receipts) .	1,998,703	1,731,290	2,818,370
The Queensland Output *			
Tons purchased . . .	518,114	515,579	581,556
For home consumption . .	319,275	309,537	285,549
Exported	198,839	206,042	296,007
	£	£	£
Amount paid	10,513,637	10,057,255	10,463,210
For home consumption . .	8,555,073	8,357,406	7,695,545
For exports (net receipts) .	1,958,564	1,699,849	2,767,665
Amount paid per ton—	£ s. d.	£ s. d.	£ s. d.
For home consumption † .	26 16 0	27 0 0	26 19 0
For exports	9 17 0	8 5 0	9 7 0
Average †	20 5 0	19 13 1	18 6 6
Percentage exported ‡ . .	38·4	39·2	49·0

* Exclusive of New South Wales output, 20,186 tons in 1929, 19,522 tons in 1930 and 23,288 tons in 1931.

† The increase in the amount paid in 1930 was due to reductions in refining charges and for sacks, and to a reduction in assets, the latter being equivalent to 2s. 4d. per ton.

‡ Excluding 6728 tons of " excess " sugar in 1930 and 21,660 tons in 1931. This sugar was in excess of allotments to mills under the " peak " year scheme adopted in 1929, and sugar manufactured from cane grown on " unassigned " lands.

AUSTRALIAN SUGAR CONTROL

TABLE III.—QUEENSLAND SUGAR PRODUCTION

Average three Seasons ended with Season	Area cultivated (acres)	Area crushed (acres)	Proportion crushed to cultivated (percentage)	Tons of Sugar of 94 net titre	Tons of Sugar per acre cultivated	Tons of Sugar per acre crushed	Tons of Cane to each ton of Sugar
1921 .	165,199	98,992	59·9	203,912	1·23	2·03	7·96
1922 .	183,145	117,649	64·2	245,795	1·34	2·07	7·88
1923 .	202,260	134,183	66·3	279,719	1·38	2·09	7·75
1924 .	225,262	149,080	66·2	322,032	1·43	2·14	7·63
1925 .	247,664	165,286	66·7	387,965	1·57	2·31	7·63
1926 .	263,182	182,142	69·2	427,998	1·63	2·35	7·61
1927 .	270,289	194,175	71·8	453,534	1·68	2·33	7·46
1928 .	274,944	202,911	73·8	465,212	1·69	2·28	7·34
1929 .	283,325	211,434	74·6	508,294	1·79	2·40	7·14
1930 .	290,402	217,533	74·9	518,640	1·79	2·38	6·89
1931 .	299,183	223,409	74·7	538,858	1·80	2·41	6·89

CHAPTER VII

CO-OPERATION IN THE HAWAIIAN PINEAPPLE BUSINESS

by Royal N. Chapman

INTRODUCTION: THE PINEAPPLE INDUSTRY

THE pineapple industry in Hawaii furnishes an interesting example for study of co-operation in that it is less than forty years old and is controlled and operated by a small group who are at once growers and canners, and who produce roughly 85 per cent. of the world's supply of canned pineapple. The general course of the industry's growth is best illustrated by Figure 1, which represents the pack of pineapples from 1895 to 1933. The relative position of the Hawaiian pineapple industry, with respect to the pack of canned pineapple produced by the more important pineapple countries of the world, is shown in Table I. Its commanding position in world production is well illustrated, and it will be seen that its next competitor is considerably behind it.

During its brief history the Hawaiian pineapple industry has passed through many of the stages characteristic of the development of industries in general. It began with relatively small plantings of pine-apples. When it was found that a suitable variety could be grown, canning was undertaken; and then followed a stage in which a number of small canning companies came into existence and passed out. Large-scale operations were introduced on the plantations and then in the canneries. Next there came a great expansion in which each individual company proceeded to increase its output without regard for the others or the total production of the industry.

While this Hawaiian industry stands almost alone in the world, it is in every way a characteristic capitalistic industry. It has had a rapid growth; there have been mergers; there has been keen competition; and there has been over-production followed by a strained financial situation coinciding with the world-wide depression. In the face of this crisis the industry evolved a co-operative plan for its own protection which resulted in the control of production from within the industry. However, it cannot be said that this control arose entirely because of the industry's own foresight. It was largely forced by the financial plight—a situation in which the creditors had a great deal to say.

266

HAWAIIAN PINEAPPLE CONTROL

The fact that the Hawaiian pineapple industry is confined to a relatively small area and to a few individuals does not mean that co-operation has been either general or easily brought about. On the contrary, the generalization may be made that the various members of

PACK IS GIVEN IN CASES OF 24 CANS OF ABOUT 2 LBS. EACH

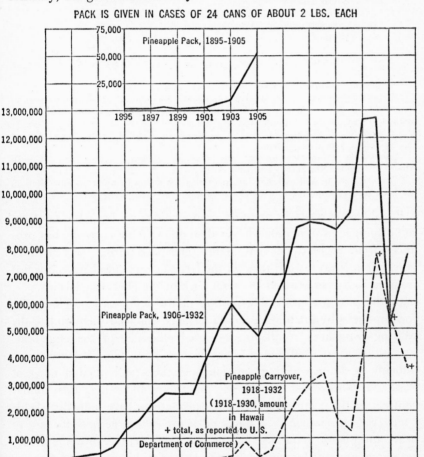

FIGURE 1.

the industry have co-operated only when the alternative has seemed to be serious financial loss. The opinion often expressed, that much commercial conflict and misunderstanding could be avoided if individual producing interests knew and understood each other, does not seem to be substantiated by the history of the pineapple industry in Hawaii. Many of the same individuals have been dominant and closely associated during some thirty years of competition.

COMMODITY CONTROL IN THE PACIFIC AREA

TABLE I.—WORLD PINEAPPLE PRODUCTION

Cases of Canned Pineapple produced by principal countries, 1930

Malaya *	1,600,000
South Africa †	277,088
Formosa (1929) ‡	450,082
Queensland (1930 estimate) ‖	280,000
Hawaii ¶	12,672,296
Total	14,299,466

* *Malayan Agricultural Journal*, vol. xix., pp. 420-445, 1931.

† Report submitted by Dr Wayne G. Clark, Assistant Trade Commissioner at Johannesburg, South Africa, dated April 13, 1932, No. 150938. (Converted from pounds to cases of 24 two-pound cans.)

‡ *Canned Foods Industry in Japan*, published by Canned Foods Association of Japan, Tokyo, Japan, p. 7, 1930.

‖ *Queensland Pineapple Growing and Canning Industry*, report from Consul Albert M. Doyle, No. 21163, Brisbane, April 1931.

¶ This figure, as well as other information given below without specific citation, has been secured from the records of the various Hawaiian pineapple associations.

Possibly one obstacle to ready co-operation has been the fact that some companies were much larger than others. One company has produced from 30 to 50 per cent. of the total pack during the last thirty years. From 1903 to 1933 three of the largest companies have controlled from 70 to 85 per cent. of the total pack of the Hawaiian Islands.

In the past a considerable portion of the total pack of pineapples was produced by small independent farmers who sold their fruit to the packing companies. With the increased efficiency of the large-scale agriculture these small independent farmers have found it increasingly difficult to compete with plantation operations. A limited number of them are, however, still producing pineapples and selling them under contract to the companies. The large plantations have individual fields which vary in size up to a thousand acres, which permits the use of heavy machinery, some of which is operated twenty-two hours a day, stopping one hour for service at noon and at midnight, thus decreasing the overhead cost. This has resulted in efficiency in agricultural operation which is probably not surpassed in any other part of the world.

The company " agencies " manage the buying, shipping, insurance, and other business transactions for the plantations. The cans are manufactured and delivered on belts direct to the three largest canneries, while small can factories are located on the outlying islands to accommodate the smaller canneries. Thus it is possible for the pineapple companies to take advantage of large-scale operations in the purchasing of supplies, the growing of the pineapples, the making of cans, the canning of their fruit, and the shipping of their product to the mainland where their sales departments handle the distribution.

The activities in which the various companies have co-operated as an industry from time to time have included advertising, the support of research work in connection with the growing, improvement and protection of pineapples, the allotment of space on boats, and, in co-operation with the Hawaiian Sugar Planters Association, the importation of labour.

The Emmeluth Plan

At various times in the brief history of the Hawaiian pineapple industry, co-operation of various companies in all phases of pineapple production and canning has been proposed. However, these plans have failed to mature except in cases where the alternative was severe financial loss. In 1904 Mr Bentley of the California Fruit Packers Association spoke before the Agricultural Society of Hilo, calling attention to the benefits to be derived from co-operation in the canning of pineapples—that more efficient machinery could be installed in the canneries, and that the canning process could be much more economically done.[1] In 1905 Mr John Emmeluth outlined in the *Hawaiian Forester and Agriculturist* a plan for an Hawaiian pineapple co-operative association which would provide for the co-operative canning, warehousing and shipping of pineapples, but permit the various companies to maintain the identity of their brands.[2] Emmeluth's plan was partly based upon the fear of competition from the Federated Malay States, who then had a pack ten times that of Hawaii.[3] His plan provided for as few canneries as necessary on the different islands to put up the pack of pineapples. This plan outlined in 1905 has essentially all the advantages which are being sought at present and, in addition, would have prevented the excessive cannery capacity which now exists in the Territory. It undoubtedly would have meant a great saving in capital and in the standardization of the product. However, he failed to receive the backing of the industry. At that time one company was controlling

[1] Report of the Annual Meeting, Agricultural Society of Hilo, *Hawaiian Forester and Agriculturist*, vol. i., p. 45, 1904.
[2] Emmeluth, " Co-operation in the Pineapple Industry," *op. cit.*, vol. ii., pp. 251-254, 1905.
[3] Editorial, *The Malayan Agricultural Journal*, vol. xix., pp. 420-445, 1931.

over 47 per cent. of the pack, and had he been able to interest this company, undoubtedly the plan would have succeeded. How much the industry would have lost in individual initiative in the development of new methods and machinery, which competition is commonly supposed to foster, will never be known.

Advertising

In 1907 the United States passed through a financial panic. At the same time, the Hawaiian pineapple industry doubled its pack from 1906 to 1907, and again from 1907 to 1908. In February 1909 it found itself with about 70 per cent. of the entire pack of the previous year still on hand.[1] The Hawaiian Pineapple Growers Association, which had been organized in May 1908, now became active, and a co-operative advertising campaign was organized with 50,000 dollars appropriated for the purpose. Faced with this large carry-over and the low price of pineapples the industry united and was able to dispose of its pack by the middle of June of the same year. When the large crop of pineapples on hand had been disposed of, the industry returned to individual competition. In 1912 the industry was again faced with a large carry-over of pineapples and another advertising campaign seemed the only alternative to a heavy loss. A new organization was formed—the Association of Hawaiian Pineapple Packers. An appropriation of five cents a case on the year's pack was voted and the advertising campaign was carried out. Assessments have been made more or less continuously from this time on for the purpose of advertising.

Notwithstanding the co-operative advertising, the individual companies have continued to advertise their individual brands, emphasizing any characteristic that might be used to make their brand appear superior to that of the other members of the co-operative association.

Agricultural Research

In 1914 the necessity for control of the various pests and diseases of the pineapple became so evident that the Association arranged with the Experiment Station of the Hawaiian Sugar Planters Association for a certain amount of work to be done by various members of their staff. In the same year, a first appropriation of 4000 dollars was made for one year. The next year this was increased to 7000 dollars. Profiting by

---

[1] Dole, "Some Recollections of Twenty-five Years of Pineapple Industry," *Proceedings of the Pineapple Men's Conference*, Association of Hawaiian Pineapple Canners, pp. 10-14, Honolulu, 1927.

the example of the Hawaiian sugar planters, a representative of the Experiment Station was sent to Central America in search of new varieties in 1919. By the early twenties the pineapple wilt was becoming more and more serious. The question was raised as to whether it would be possible to continue raising pineapples in the Hawaiian Islands indefinitely. The reduced pack of 1921 and 1922 was ascribed to various causes, mainly wilt, but with a suspicion that dry weather was a contributing factor. However, the records of the United States Weather Bureau in Hawaii do not bear out the contention that dry weather was a major factor at this time (see Table II.). In 1922, in co-operation with the Territorial Board of Agriculture and Forestry, an explorer was sent to Central America in search of parasites of various pests of the pineapple plant. At about this time one of the companies had to withdraw from a large area of land on windward Oahu because the production of pineapples there was no longer possible. Being afraid that this was the beginning of a withdrawal from various areas, the companies began to explore in Fiji, Haiti, the Philippines and South Africa.

TABLE II.—ANNUAL PRECIPITATION IN INCHES

Year			Honolulu	Wahiawa
1916	.	.	44·96	74·33
1917	.	.	41·64	60·17
1918	.	.	37·46	61·38
1919	.	.	14·59	19·99
1920	.	.	25·49	50·41
1921	.	.	26·58	41·21
1922	.	.	20·11	38·54
1923	.	.	37·34	No record
1924	.	.	26·31	57·82
1925	.	.	16·82	52·29
1926	.	.	11·27	24·55
1927	.	.	43·52	63·06
1928	.	.	15·34	26·02
1929	.	.	26·97	43·45
1930	.	.	31·04	48·69
1931	.	.	16·35	23·49
1932	.	.	24·77	56·11
1933	.	.	19·96	39·64

In some of these areas the activities of the companies progressed to the point of the erection of canneries and the actual production of canned pineapple. These foreign lands proved to be subject to various pests, diseases and soil difficulties, and one by one they have been abandoned. Whatever their difficulties, whether political, financial, labour or agricultural, they have concluded that Hawaii is the place for the most efficient production and canning of pineapple.

In 1922 a new association was formed and 100 acres of land were leased at Wahiawa for experimental purposes. Two years later the research work was withdrawn from the Experiment Station of the Hawaiian Sugar Planters Association and organized under the direction of the University of Hawaii, but supported by an assessment on the pack of pineapples, with a budget of 69,537 dollars. This amounted to a little over one cent a case on the pack. From that time on the budget has increased as shown in Table III. In 1925 a new disease, pineapple yellow spot, appeared in the Territory and for a time appeared to be a real threat to the permanence of the industry.

TABLE III.—PINEAPPLE EXPERIMENT STATION BUDGET

(The budget is assessed on the basis of the pack of the previous year.)

Year	Amount	Pack (Previous year)
1924 . .	$69,537·00	5,895,747
1925 . .	67,720·00	6,825,904
1926 . .	82,825·00	8,728,580
1927 . .	148,550·00	8,939,590
1928 . .	150,000·00	8,879,252
1929 . .	175,000·00	8,663,056
1930 . .	215,000·00 *	9,211,376
1931 . .	263,665·00 *	12,672,296
1932 . .	202,930·50	12,726,291
1933 . .	161,188·58	5,063,793

* In each of these years, a capital investment for land and buildings amounted to over 50,000 dollars.

In 1926 Dr A. L. Dean was induced to resign his position as President of the University of Hawaii and become Director of the Experiment Station of the Association. It is interesting that the initiation of the work with the Hawaiian Sugar Planters Association in 1914, the leasing of 100 acres at Wahiawa for experimental work at the end of 1922, and the setting up of the independent research work at the University of Hawaii from 1924 to 1926, coincided with the three reductions in pack increase in the history of the industry (see Figure 1). It was economic necessity rather than any logical plan or forethought that brought about these three important steps in the history of the industry's co-operative activities.

The individual companies were quick to take advantage of the results of the Experiment Station. With qualified agriculturists in charge of their fields they were able to put new methods into operation almost overnight. Soon the method of mass planting was introduced and the number of plants per acre was increased from a range of 8000 to 10,000 to one of 14,000 to 20,000, with a corresponding increase in the yield of fruit. Expansion into the drier areas followed rapidly upon the demonstration of the pineapple's ability to grow under conditions of low rainfall. Each company relied upon its ability to compete with its competitors and the expansion of fields went on without restriction. With more plants to the acre and more acres available, the potential production of the Territory was greatly increased.

Shipping

The history of co-operation in shipping is an incident in the history of the World War. In 1916 the industry was faced with the difficulty of getting sufficient shook and other materials into the islands for putting up the pack of pineapples. In 1917 an arrangement was made with the shipping company to guarantee space for shipping all of the materials to Hawaii and for shipping the pineapples to the coast. The space was allotted on the basis of the reports of the various members, and it was agreed to pay the steamship company one dollar per ton over the regular shipping rate. Some difficulty continued in obtaining space up to 1921 and even in 1922. There can be little doubt that the expansion of the pineapple industry in Hawaii has had a great influence in inducing shipping companies to enlarge their facilities for shipping on the Pacific between the mainland United States and Hawaii.

Maintaining a Labour Supply

The pineapple plantations were dependent from the start upon the labour supply of the Territory, which in turn was maintained by the co-operative activity of the Hawaiian Sugar Planters Association. The sugar planters had reason to feel that their labourers were deserting the sugar plantations for the pineapple-fields, and that the pineapple plantations should either get their own labourers or co-operate in a common enterprise. Accordingly, a gentlemen's agreement was entered into, without any actual contract, whereby the Association of Hawaiian Pineapple Canners has contributed with the sugar planters to the cost of labour importation on the basis of the number of labour days used each year in the two industries.

S

In the wide-open competition which obtained in the pineapple industry through the twenties and up to 1931, a large part was played by competition for land in Hawaii. The islands of Lanai and Molokai were explored and opened up for pineapple production. The competition for leases on the island of Oahu was very keen, and the obtaining of the lease for a large portion of the best pineapple land in central Oahu was a factor in forcing one of the companies to look to other areas for pineapple land. The acreage devoted to pineapples mounted rapidly from 1928 to 1930. With the announcement by the Experiment Station that the mealy bug was responsible for the transmission of wilt and that a carefully planned campaign for controlling the mealy bug would protect the fields from this disease, there was a greater possibility of increasing the pineapple pack.

It became evident in 1930 that there would be more pineapples than the world could consume. Certain of the companies became concerned with regard to the size of the pack, and in September most of them agreed to stop short of the end of the season. Consequently, the pack was less than the 13 million cases for which there was fruit in the field. The fields for 1931 were already planted and the estimated pack was about 16 million cases. With a world depression in full force, and the carry-over at the beginning of 1931 equal to 61 per cent. of the pack of the year before, the Hawaiian pineapple industry was again faced with conditions similar to those experienced in 1907 to 1909.

Advertising failed to maintain sales in measure with the increased pack, in face of the widespread economic depression. The price of pineapples was cut to below the cost of production, but conditions became worse rather than better. There was keen competition and bitter feeling between the companies with regard to methods of marketing; and the smaller companies blamed the larger concerns for the over-production. Two of the smallest companies found the financial situation too serious and they ceased operation. As each of these packed approximately 1 per cent. of the total Hawaiian pack, their elimination from the industry was more significant in reducing the number of companies to be involved in co-operation than from the standpoint of the quantity of pineapple that they actually produced. Again it became evident that the industry must unite to save itself, and that the particular interests of individual companies would have to be subordinated to the interests of the industry in general. An important factor in forcing

274

the companies to come together was the realization that if one of the large companies were to pass through bankruptcy and the creditors were to throw its stock of pineapple on the market, the rest of the companies would face financial ruin.

Consequently, a series of conferences ensued. There were but seven pineapple companies involved. Inasmuch as two of these were under one agency, the number of principals involved in the negotiations was essentially reduced to six. Many of the principals of the companies had been involved in the industry almost from its beginning. However, in this seeming simplification of the situation were prejudices and feelings which had been built up during thirty years of bitter competition. The industry seemed to be faced with the alternatives of wide-open competition for the survival of the fittest, and a co-operative effort involving both a reduction in the pack of pineapples, leaving uncanned fruit in the field, and a national advertising campaign.

Reduction of the Pack

Negotiations were begun for an agreement on the reduction of the pack. It was generally agreed that the pack of pineapples in Hawaii should not be more than 10 million cases, at least for a period of several years. The first step was the organization of a new association, which was the Pineapple Producers Co-operative Association, having all the advantages of agricultural co-operatives in the United States. An advertising campaign was outlined to spend a million dollars in advertising pineapples, to be assessed on a case basis.

It is interesting to notice the similarities between the aims and objects as outlined at the present time and those outlined by John Emmeluth in 1905. At the present time there are nine pineapple canneries in the Territory, with a total annual capacity of something over 20 million cases of pineapple. Had the original suggestion of co-operative canning been carried out, there certainly would not be over five canneries. It is evident that, since these canneries are all in existence and equipped, the saving to be made by closing a part of them must inevitably be smaller than the economy which could have been made if only the proper number had been built in the first place.

Co-operation among the members of the Pineapple Producers Co-operative Association has been far from complete. The sales agencies have maintained their separate identities, and competition between them has been just as keen as before. In fact, co-operation has gone little beyond the agreement as to the total pack to be put up each year and the allocation of the percentages of the pack to the individual companies. Technically, the canned pineapple has become the property of the Pineapple Producers Co-operative Association as soon as it has been put into the can. It has been warehoused in warehouses which actually belong to the individual companies but which have been leased to a warehouse concern under contract with the Co-operative Association. Withdrawals have been made by the individual companies, and these have sold their products under their own brands in competition with the other members of the Association. As the general economic conditions of the United States have improved there has been a tendency on the part of the members of the Co-operative to wish to pull apart, rather than to continue or to increase the co-operative activities.

During the period of the depression, when large quantities of pineapples were left in the field, various companies began the packing of a superior pineapple juice preserved by a new process giving it a flavour essentially like that of fresh pineapple juice. These companies, however, have not permitted the canning of pineapple juice to be controlled by the Co-operative Association. Here again is evidence that the companies feel fundamentally that greater progress can be made and greater profits realized by independent competition than with co-operative endeavour. So long as this feeling exists it is difficult for one to be too optimistic as to the future of the co-operative activities of the pineapple industry in Hawaii.

Situation in Malaya

At the same time the second largest group of pineapple canners is experiencing a similar situation in Malaya.[1] In a prospectus of a plan for co-operative canning, buying and selling, the following statements are made:

At the present period, all commodities are undergoing an unprecedented economic decline; this especially applies to pineapples. Every endeavour is being made, the world over, to reduce costs and stabilize prices by co-operation. Therefore, the present is a very opportune time to reorganize and establish the pineapple industry on a co-operative basis.

In order to combat this downward tendency, the hatchet of internal dissension (competitive spirit) must be buried, and in its place the building up of all factories on a united basis must be undertaken. Unity being strength, it is only by this means that overseas competition can be met successfully.

This can be done by closer co-operation among all canners. It is ludicrous

---

[1] United States Department of Commerce, *Economic and Trade Notes*, No. 201, submitted by Darwin DeGolia, Assistant Trade Commissioner, February 2, 1933.

that the industry, being in the hands of only eleven men, is yet in such a deplorable condition, when by sympathetic co-operation this can be revolutionized and stopped, thereby putting the industry on the highroad to success.

It would seem that the next logical step would be the formation of an international trade agreement whereby the potential sales areas of the world would be allocated, as has been done with certain other industries, thus eliminating competition between co-operatives.

SUMMARY

The Hawaiian pineapple industry furnishes over 80 per cent. of the world's canned pineapple. The eight individual companies involved are each trying to derive all the profit possible from the production of canned pineapple. In the case of the newly developed pineapple juice the companies concerned have refused to let it be handled under the co-operative agreement, feeling that their chance for the greatest profit and aggressive sales campaign might be impaired. Whenever the carry-over of pineapple has exceeded 50 per cent. of the pack of the previous year, it has been necessary to put on an intensive advertising campaign. Since it is impossible for one company to advertise its own goods without helping its competitor, co-operative advertising has been resorted to.

When agricultural difficulties have arisen, such as pests, diseases, and questions of soil depletion, the pineapple companies have co-operated in agricultural research, and have done individual exploring for new territory. At each break in the curve of rising production, attention has turned to co-operative research.

Co-operation in advertising, agricultural research, shipping, and labour importation, with all its attendant benefits to the industry, has in each case had its origin in adversity. The present period of the world depression has visited upon the industry the greatest adversity of its history, and has also resulted in the outlining of the greatest co-operative program in the history of the industry. The greatest aid to the organization of co-operative activities is at present, as in the past, the imminence of financial disaster. The greatest hindrance is the lack of mutual trust. The latter is not due to a lack of understanding, for the same individuals have been associated almost throughout the history of the industry. There have been far-sighted individuals who have, in the past, outlined sound co-operative programs, but they could not be heard in times of prosperity. The benefits of co-operation could not be enjoyed until the disaster of destructive competition had been experienced.

At a time when control of industry, either by the Government or from within industries themselves, seems inevitable, the pineapple industry is serving as an interesting case. When times are sufficiently prosperous the individual members prefer to take a chance on independent competition, but when threatened by diseases, pests, or creditors, they will co-operate for mutual protection. If these generalizations are applicable to industry in general, the present world situation may prove to be one of the most promising epochs that society has ever experienced.

CHAPTER VIII

COMMODITY CONTROL IN NETHERLANDS INDIA

by Cecile G. H. Rothe

INTRODUCTION

IN Netherlands India the regulation of production and trade has always been left as much as possible to private initiative. The Government has traditionally been averse to intervention in private business. The present economic world depression, however, has obliged it to abandon this policy. Netherlands India thus became involved in international agreements concerning control of production, and the various restriction measures with regard to export products are based upon these agreements. Such measures are: the restriction of the sugar export based upon the Chadbourne Agreement; the tin restriction; the restriction of tea-planting and tea export. The recent rubber restriction must be mentioned too, although it is international in scope, and thus extends outside Netherlands India.[1] The cinchona restriction has not an international character, because Netherlands India has practically a world monopoly of cinchona production. In addition, the regulations concerning export products have a considerable influence on the general economic situation of Netherlands India, a country which depends for the greater part of its prosperity on the export of a comparatively small number of products.

In Netherlands India the need for crisis import regulations was not felt so early as in European countries; this is due to the fact that in general the articles imported into Netherlands India are not in competition with articles made in the country, with the important exception of rice. Therefore an open-door policy could be followed by the Netherlands Indian Government; only lately have special measures of a politico-economic character become inevitable, because in some cases the local market had to be protected against a fatal foreign competition. Such measures have been the temporary prohibition of rice imports; the Crisis Import Ordinance; the Cement Quota and the Beer Quota. Moreover, the Crisis Export Ordinance and the Crisis Culture Ordinance must be mentioned, the last one concerning the financing of the experiment stations.

[1] See Chapter XII. below.

The above-mentioned regulations will be dealt with in turn. Only those Government measures concerning agricultural and mineral production taken in connection with the crisis will be considered, and the Government monopolies of salt and opium and the Government-operated industries will be left out of the discussion.

SUGAR RESTRICTION

The first of all the crisis measures taken in Netherlands India has been the regulation of the production and export of sugar. After the war the position of the sugar market became more and more critical. In the year 1923-1924 for the first time world production exceeded consumption. After that year sugar prices declined gradually, as appears from the following Table showing the price of Java sugar at Amsterdam in guilders per 100 kg:

January 31, 1928	.	.	.	.	.	$17\frac{1}{2}$
„ „ 1929	.	.	.	.	.	$13\frac{3}{8}$
„ „ 1930	.	.	.	.	.	$11\frac{1}{4}$
„ „ 1931	.	.	.	.	.	$8\frac{1}{4}$
„ „ 1932	.	.	.	.	.	$7\frac{1}{4}$
„ „ 1933	.	.	.	.	.	$5\frac{1}{4}$
„ „ 1934	.	.	.	.	.	$4\frac{3}{4}$

As a natural adjustment of production to consumption appeared to be out of question, the countries which were feeling the burden of this crisis most severely—namely, Cuba, Java, Germany, Czechoslovakia, Poland, Hungary and Belgium—considered it necessary to take measures to reorganize the market, and after extended negotiations they entered into the so-called Chadbourne Agreement. According to this agreement the annual export of each country should not exceed a fixed quantity; above this quantity one-fifth of the existing surplus stock was allowed to be exported yearly. In the meantime production was also to be restricted so that the stocks, increasing at first, would find an outlet within a few years.

The Chadbourne scheme, which did not prove as effective as had been expected, had one very weak side: it concerned only those countries which produce cane and beet sugar wholly or partly for export, and not those countries which produce for home consumption and import sugar as well. Though conditions for sugar cultivation are less favourable in these countries the restriction agreement tended to increase their production, whereas in countries with favourable conditions production was curtailed.

In order to carry out the Chadbourne scheme in Netherlands India the Sugar Export Ordinance (1931) and the Sugar Export Decree have been enacted.[1] The Sugar Export Ordinance prohibited for five years the export of sugar from Netherlands India without a written licence from the Governor-General. The total yearly quantity of sugar to be exported on licence, according to the Sugar Export Decree, must not surpass 23 million quintals for the year April 1, 1931, to March 31, 1932, and 24 million quintals for the following years. The export quantity for each factory was fixed for the first restriction year, 1931-1932, by multiplying the quantity of its production of 1931 with the fraction: 22 million quintals divided by the total production in 1931. Besides this each factory received a separate licence for the export of the assigned part of its stock.

Instead of the production of 1931 the " normal sugar production " of the factories is taken as a basis of the calculation for the year 1932-1933 and the following years; the normal yield per hectare, the normal planted area and the normal total production of each factory is fixed by the Directors of Agriculture, Industry and Commerce after consultation with an Advisory Committee. The export quantity allowed each factory is calculated by multiplying the normal production figures by a fraction which is the total quota of that year (reduced by the quantity of special licences) divided by the sum of the normal productions. All figures are calculated in crystal equivalent. Factories about to stop milling need the approval of the Directors of Agriculture, Industry and Commerce. In calculating the export quotas a yearly increase of world consumption of 3 per cent. had been estimated; but in fact this has been too high.

For the production year 1931-1932 a restriction of 15 per cent. of the planted area was considered to be necessary in order to reach a yield not surpassing the fixed export quantity of 2,300,000 tons, so that the existing stocks would not be increased. However, the curtailment of production proved to have been too small, because owing to the decrease in consumption the export of Netherlands India amounted to no more than 1,543,000 tons on April 1, 1932.

Of all sugar-exporting countries Java was in the most critical position, as it had a comparatively unimportant home consumption and depended largely on the East Asiatic countries for its market. This market has shrunk considerably; of the four most important buying countries

[1] Netherlands India Statute Book, 1931, No. 114; and 1931, No. 175, revised by 1932, No. 198, and 1933.

British India is now developing a home sugar industry, and has imposed high duties on foreign sugars; China is unreliable as an outlet on account of internal disturbances; Japan protects Formosa sugar and Australia has imposed high import duties on foreign sugars. At the same time other sugar-producing countries enjoy advantages which Java lacks: thus Cuba profits by a preference in the United States of America, and the other countries have proportionally a larger home consumption.

During the first restriction year world sugar production decreased from 29·3 to 26·3 million tons. This, for the greater part, was at the expense of the best producers, Java and Cuba. The production of the United States and the Philippines showed an increase. Java was, notwithstanding its low cost of production, unable to place its sugar on the world market, and saw its stocks increase at an alarming rate. In 1932 the export was again disappointing, 1,502,000 tons; the stocks rose to 2,534,000 tons on April 1, 1933.

In these circumstances Java has been very much interested in bringing down still further its cost of production. This has meant that, instead of applying restriction indiscriminately and proportionally over all existing factories, those companies which own several factories aim at cultivating only the best lands, closing down some mills to enable others to work at full production. Skilful organization and scientific management have made Java rightly proud of its achievements in sugar cultivation. The yield obtained per hectare grew steadily from 75·60 quintals in 1895 to 98·99 in 1920, 151·39 in 1928 and 152·30 in 1932. But with the improvement of the cane and the higher yield obtained per hectare the selling price dropped. The economic results thus obtained by scientific work have been destroyed in comparatively few years, and sugar, which for many years was by far the most important export product of Netherlands India, has now been pushed into the background. The planted area has been reduced as follows:

Harvest Year						Hectares
1931	.	.	.	.	.	199,577
1932	.	.	.	.	.	170,715
1933	.	.	.	.	.	84,022
1934	.	.	.	.	.	34,978

For the harvest year 1930, 179 estates planted sugar cane; for 1931, 178; for 1932, 171; for 1933, 113, and for 1934 only 45.

Since 1918 the sugar market has been managed by the Association of Java Sugar Producers, the so-called V.I.S.P. The need for co-operation in the selling of sugar was first felt by the Java sugar planters in 1917, when shortage of cargo space hindered the shipment and the stocks accumulated in an alarming way. It was feared that as soon as the war ended, and ocean shipping was free again, the producers would throw their stocks on the market and prices would fall. This consideration induced the sugar planters in Java to form a co-operative sales association, and so the Java Sugar Association (*Java Suikervereeniging*) was instituted, to be replaced a year later by the Association of the Java Sugar Producers. The majority of the sugar estates were associated with this organization and the selling of about 90 per cent. of the sugar produced in Java was entrusted to it. The satisfactory results obtained by V.I.S.P. as a selling organization for the combined sugar estates induced the sugar planters to continue it, although the emergency conditions which had given rise to the Association were no longer present.

The sales policy of V.I.S.P. had always aimed at selling the sugar without delay for the best prices obtainable. But when in the last few years the prices declined more and more, the Association did not realize sufficiently that the depression would be of long duration and held back the sugar, trying to raise the prices to a higher level than the circumstances permitted. This mistake resulted in a very alarming increase of stocks. Dissatisfaction with the action of V.I.S.P. induced a number of sugar companies to leave the Association, and with that the apprehension arose that in 1933 an unlimited sale of the stocks of these free sugar planters would cause a still greater fall in prices.

The holding of large stocks was especially ruinous to the estates which did not possess large capital resources and to whose interest it was to sell their sugar at any price they could get. But for the Java sugar industry as a whole it was of the greatest importance that a further slump in the price should be prevented. This view induced a number of sugar planters, in September 1932, to apply to the Government for intervention, because they were of the opinion that, if the Government could not bring about an arrangement, a calamity would be inevitable. The majority of the producers and almost all the exporters advocated the formation of a selling organization which would dispose of all the sugar to be exported, thus supporting the principle of the " single seller," because such a single seller would ensure the strongest position on the market; besides, it would be able to organize the sale to markets which are for the present not profitable, but which presumably will give profits in the future, and to divide equally over all the producers the loss which such a sale entails.

These discussions resulted on December 31, 1932, in the establishment of the Netherlands Indian Association for the Sale of Sugar, the N.I.V.A.S., in which the Government has a right to intervene. At the same time the Sugar Single Seller Ordinance and the Sugar Single Seller Decree [1] were promulgated. The Sugar Single Seller Ordinance prescribes that unsold sugar from previous crops and all sugar from future crops must be sold only through the Netherlands Indian Association for the Sale of Sugar.

Only owners of sugar factories are admitted as members of the N.I.V.A.S. At least fifteen from among them are elected annually to form the Managing Board, together with a Chairman (appointed by the Governor-General and not necessarily a member of the Association) and a representative of the Java Bank. An Executive Committee is annually elected, consisting of six members of the Managing Board, the Chairman, the representative of the Java Bank and two members appointed by the Governor-General. The direction is entrusted to the Chairman and—if the Board considers it advisable—to two co-Directors, nominated by the Executive Committee and subject to the approval of the Governor-General. Besides this, the Governor-General appoints a Government Committee having an advisory vote at the meetings, and he has the right of veto against decisions of the Association. According to the Sugar Single Seller Ordinance all transfer of sugar is prohibited except by a " proclamation " of the N.I.V.A.S., or by a contract sanctioned by it. This prohibition does not apply to the case of transfer of sugar between members of the N.I.V.A.S.—an important exception because it means that sugar cane cultivated by one factory may be milled by another, so that the most productive fields can be held in cultivation, independent of the question of ownership. The sales regulation also includes a prohibition against transporting sugar except with a licence from the N.I.V.A.S.

The Sugar Single Seller Decree prescribes that the share of each member in the sale is represented by the fraction of his export *quantum* divided by the total export *quanta*. The Director of the N.I.V.A.S. takes care to give to each member as far as possible his share in the sale. Refined sugar, made by a very few factories in Java, is excluded from the Single Seller's regulation. Any infringements of the regulations are punished with severe penalties.

[1] Netherlands India Statute Book, 1932, Nos. 643 and 644.

In the statutes of the N.I.V.A.S. an article has been included which stipulates the formation of a crisis fund, which will be used for supplying assistance to the personnel of the associated factories who have been unemployed since January 1, 1931. The proposal of the sugar planters that, instead of a contribution per quintal of sugar delivered, they pay a lump sum, and that this sum be fixed at 500,000 guilders per year for the first three years, was gratefully accepted by the Government. This means that the sugar industry pays more for the relief of the unemployed than all the other agricultural industries in Java put together.

It cannot be said that the various regulations have resulted in a marked improvement in the sugar situation, but the greater part of this is due to the extraordinarily unfavourable conditions existing in the countries of destination.

The development of the stocks was anything but satisfactory, as may be seen from the following Table:

	May 1, 1932	May 1, 1933
Cuba	3,250,000	2,925,500
Java	1,526,800	2,411,100
U.S.A.	671,400	471,500
Europe	4,018,700	3,820,900
	9,466,900	9,629,000

The situation is still critical, especially for Java; in March 1933 the harvest of 1931 was sold, and practically the entire crop of 1932 was stored.

The stocks may be calculated as follows:

	1000 tons	
Original stocks as of April 1, 1933	2533	
Production	1370	
Total available		3903
Export	1200	
Consumption [1]	418	
Delivered		1618
Final stocks on March 31, 1934		2285

In the course of 1933 an area of 34,178 hectares was planted with sugar cane, which, on an estimated yield of 160 quintals per hectare, will produce about 550,000 tons of sugar. The following

[1] Including a loss of 50,000 tons through storage and reclaiming.

calculation has been made on the basis of an estimated export of
1,200,000 tons:

		1000 tons
Original stocks as of April 1, 1934 . . .	2285	
Production	550	
Total available		2835
Export	1200	
Consumption [1]	375	
Delivered		1575
Final stocks on March 31, 1935		1260

The N.I.V.A.S. suggested that in 1934 no sugar should be planted,
with a view to clearing off the present stocks.

The decline of the Java exports during the last few years may be
demonstrated by the following figures:

	1930	*1931*	*1932*
Total (in tons)	2,217,501	1,553,997	1,502,057
To Europe	14,008	49,288	416,949
,, British-India . . .	1,070,060	601,777	481,320
,, Japan	271,732	173,669	42,867
,, China	286,493	154,155	114,357
,, Hong Kong	370,404	351,688	228,884
,, Singapore and Penang . .	107,843	90,952	82,326
,, Siam	40,547	36,601	30,326
,, Australia and New Zealand .	19,212	62,274	54,502

It is of the greatest interest to Java to keep a watchful eye upon the
development of its natural markets, and moreover to try to increase its
sales to Europe. But it may be expected that many factories which at
present have been temporarily closed will never be reopened and that
the Java sugar industry will have to resign itself to a permanent and
considerable restriction.

TIN RESTRICTION

The story of tin restriction in Netherlands India is simply a part of
the international tin control scheme considered in more detail in a later
chapter of this book.[2] The Netherlands Indian Government is one of
the important tin producers in the world, since it operates the
Government Tin Industry of Banka. It has, therefore, been vitally interested in the international restriction plan and is keenly interested
in seeing that the present agreement is continued.

[1] Including a loss of 25,000 tons through storage and reclaiming.
[2] See below, Chapter XII., " The International Tin Restriction Plan."

COMMODITY CONTROL IN NETHERLANDS INDIA

The condition of the Netherlands Indian tin industry has been rather unfavourable in the past two years. In consequence of the devaluation of the pound sterling the restriction measures have not had the financial results expected for the Netherlands Indian industry, because tin prices did not increase in proportion to the fall of the pound sterling. Netherlands India is the only country joined to the Tin Association which has held to the gold standard.

The sharp restriction of production makes a reduction of the cost price of tin very difficult to achieve. In 1932 the cost price was calculated by the three tin industries in Netherlands India as follows:

Banka	1133 guilders per ton
Billiton	1670 ,, ,,
Singkep	1570 ,, ,,

During 1932 the Billiton Company succeeded in lowering the cost price from 1670 to 1480 guilders per ton.

In spite of drastic economy measures the situation of the Netherlands Indian tin industry cannot yet be considered favourable. In the last few years the quantity of Banka tin sold on the American market had considerably decreased, having been replaced by Straits tin, which is somewhat cheaper. In 1932 the selling Bureau of Government Mining Products of Netherlands India itself took in hand the sales in America, with the result that the export to America rose from 177 tons in 1931 to 548 tons in 1932.

It may be expected that a regular market will thus be created again in America.

TEA RESTRICTION

In the last few years world tea production has more and more exceeded consumption, resulting in accumulated stocks and declining prices. In 1930 the Netherlands Indian, British Indian and Ceylon producers decided to restrict the output of their estates to a total of 57.5 million lb below that of the 1929 crop, the restriction for Netherlands India being 10 million lb. This attempt at voluntary restriction was not sufficient; and in 1931 it was abandoned by the British Tea Producers Associations. The gradual decline of the prices continued; the price of medium quality tea (Pecco Souchon) per one-half kg. at Amsterdam was:

January 1929	74 Dutch cents
,, 1930	61 ,, ,,
,, 1931	55 ,, ,,
,, 1932	26 ,, ,,

The serious financial condition of a large number of tea estates, both Dutch and British, made it manifest to producers that some restriction scheme had to be drawn up. The export restriction of British India and Ceylon was no more than 38 million lb in 1931; that of Netherlands India was only 3 million lb, in consequence of the increased export of native tea bought up by Chinese. Owing to the previous failure of uncontrolled limitation, the feeling was strong that without Government sanction and without proper control a restriction scheme could not have any success.

In December 1932 a scheme for international restriction of tea production was drawn up by the Netherlands Indian, British Indian and Ceylon producers associations. China, Japan and Formosa, Indo-China, Nyasaland and Georgia (S. Russia) remained outside the restriction. These countries produce, with the exception of Georgia, a quantity of 60,000 to 70,000 tons annually. That this important bloc of outsiders has not hindered the restriction scheme is mainly due to the fact that 30,000 tons of their production consist of green China tea, which has its own market and which is not competitive with black tea. The scheme contained the following proposals:

1. The export of tea from the producing countries should be regulated in order to restore equilibrium between supply and demand.
2. The governments of the respective producing countries have to make regulations to prohibit exports in excess of the quotas agreed upon.
3. The standard on which regulation is based shall be determined by the maximum exports of each of the countries reached in any of the years 1929, 1930 or 1931.
4. The percentage of the first restriction year will be 85 per cent. of the standard export; the figures for the following year will be fixed before expiration of each year.
5. The agreement shall be for a period of five years.
6. The existing tea areas shall not be extended during the period of the scheme, except in special cases. Under no circumstances shall such extensions exceed $\frac{1}{2}$ per cent. of the present total planted tea area of each country.

In February 1933 the representatives of the joint associations signed the agreement. The respective governments promised their co-operation for carrying out the scheme. The year with the highest export figure after 1928 had to be chosen as the base year. For Netherlands India the year 1931 has been indicated, for both the other countries 1929. The base exports were in lb:

Netherlands India	.	1931 .	173,597,000
British India	.	1929 .	382,594,800
Ceylon	.	1929 .	251,522,600

As a consequence of the international scheme the Tea-plant Ordinance, the Tea Export Ordinance and the Tea Export Decree have been promulgated in Netherlands India.[1] Owing to the prolonged negotiations the regulations became effective only on June 12, 1933, with retro-active force to April 1. By virtue of these laws it is prohibited to plant tea without having a written licence of the Director of Agriculture, Industry and Commerce. The licences for extending the tea area may be given only for a maximum total of 880 hectares. (The area planted with tea amounted in 1931 to 131,440 hectares and in 1932 to 135,704 for European estates; in 1931 to 41,801 and in 1932 to 39,375 for native plantations.) During a period of at most five years, export of tea from Netherlands India is allowed only with a written licence, to be given by the Director of Agriculture, Industry and Commerce.

These licences are delivered for a total amount to be fixed yearly, the proportion between estate tea and tea bought up from the native being 9:2. The export amount for the first restriction year has been fixed at 66,931 tons. The Director of Agriculture, Industry and Commerce fixes the standard production for each factory by multiplying its average production per hectare during the years 1929, 1931 and 1932 by the number of hectares of the area planted in the restriction year. The standard production of bought-up tea is the production of the year 1931. For young plantations special calculations have been made in adopting certain percentage scales in connection with the production of the fully grown plantations. Each factory received a licence for export up to an amount fixed by multiplying its standard production of estate and bought-up tea by a fraction equal to the total export quota divided by the sum of the various standard productions of estate and bought-up tea. The tea production for home consumption has been left out of the restriction scheme; not the quantity produced by the natives but only the quantity bought up by the factories has been regulated. In each regency where tea is cultivated by the natives a Committee of Consultation is appointed to give advice on the buying up of the native tea.

Towards the end of 1933 an extraordinarily large quantity of native leaf was offered to the factories as a consequence of the raised prices. The Director of Agriculture, Industry and Commerce, who expected such a course of things, had expressly advised the managers of tea factories to apportion the buying of leaf regularly over the remaining months of the first restriction year, this being considered essential in

---

[1] Netherlands India Statute Book, 1933, Nos. 221, 220 and 222.

T

the interests of the native holders. Some time afterwards it appeared that in some districts the prices paid by the factories for native leaf had decreased after the restriction had come into force, the factories having taken double advantage of a large offer of native leaf on one side and of the increased market prices on the other side. The Director of Agriculture, Industry and Commerce felt obliged to issue a circular in which the price for bought-up wet leaf was fixed at 5 Dutch cents per kilogram (22½ cents per kilogram dry leaf), leaving in this price a margin for reasonable profits to the factory. The licences of tea manufacturers buying leaf at a lower price were to be withdrawn.

It is not yet possible to express an opinion about the results of the tea restriction in the few months since it came into force, for a favourable influence on the market position can be attained only gradually. Just prior to the restriction large quantites of tea were exported from the various countries, which caused a further increase of the stocks in London and Amsterdam. The production of 1932 has not been exceptionally high—430,000 tons against 421,600 tons in 1931—but the consumption remained far behind, and stocks in London rose from 173 million lb on May 1, 1932, to 287 million lb on May 1, 1933. Stocks in Amsterdam rose from 73,635 chests of 45 kg. on May 1, 1932, to 114,156 chests on May 1, 1933. Towards the end of 1933 the stocks showed a reduction. In spite of these unfavourable factors the Java tea market has shown a fairly regular price improvement in the past few months. The tea prices had already risen somewhat in prospect of the restriction scheme and after its coming into force the gradual rise continued.

The following Table shows prices of Java tea in Amsterdam in Dutch cents per ½ kg. Prices in Java show a still greater rise.

End of Month		Pecco Souchon	Orange Pecco
June	1933	31	40
July	,,	32	41
August	,,	35	43
September	,,	35	43
October	,,	41	48
November	,,	37	43
December	,,	41	46

[The

The statistics below indicate the planted area, production and exports of tea in Netherlands India:

Area in Tea (in hectares)

	Java		Sumatra	Total
	Estates	Smallholders	Estates	
1929 . .	95,987	37,686	24,455	158,128
1930 . .	98,589	42,128	28,407	169,124
1931 . .	99,593	42,907	31,847	174,347
1932 . .	102,311	40,550	33,393	176,254

Production (in metric tons)

	Java		Sumatra	Total
	Estate Leaf	Bought-up Leaf	Estate Leaf	
1929 . .	48,467	16,001	11,116	75,634
1930 . .	46,227	14,689	11,075	72,034
1931 . .	52,280	15,329	13,700	81,358
1932 . .	53,728	12,715	15,493	81,971

Export (in metric tons)

	Java	Sumatra	Total
1929 . .	62,025	10,424	72,449
1930 . .	61,417	10,602	72,019
1931 . .	65,920	12,822	78,742
1932 . .	65,188	14,579	78,767

The principal countries of destination are Great Britain, Holland, Australia and the United States of America. The tea exports from Java and Sumatra considerably decreased during the first restriction months; the following figures for the period April to October show a reduction of more than 15 per cent. in comparison with the same period in 1931:

	Java (metric tons)	Sumatra (metric tons)
April 1–October 1, 1933 . .	24,409	5961
,, ,, 1931 . .	31,147	6821

The quantity of 16,275 tons exported from April 1 to June 11, 1933, has to be deducted from the export amount fixed for the first restriction year, thus leaving 50,656 tons for 1933-1934. It is clear that in the period June 12, 1933, to March 31, 1934, a far greater percentage than 15 per cent. must be restricted if this quantity is not to be exceeded.

British India and Ceylon have also diminished their exports, but the exports of Japan and Formosa, neither belonging to the restriction countries, show an increase. It will depend partly on the development of consumption whether the improvement of the market situation will continue. Various symptoms point, however, to the fact that world tea consumption is certainly diminishing.

Early in December 1933 the restriction percentage proposed by the International Tea Committee for the second restriction year was published as $12\frac{1}{2}$ per cent. It is self-evident that the restriction of the individual producing countries must be greater in consequence of young plantations coming into production. When the export quotas are somewhat enlarged, the consumption may possibly diminish in consequence of the raised prices. The rise of tea prices has already stimulated the export of countries outside the restriction scheme, especially China; a further restriction would have stimulated these exports still more. A sudden increase of tea prices would thus cause damage to the Netherlands Indian and British Indian cultivation.

It may be expected that the restriction as it is proposed at present will lead to a gradual restriction of the tea market. There is no great home consumption of Java tea; the natives drink almost exclusively the cheap Formosa tea. In the last few years the Tea Export Bureau has started a vigorous campaign to increase the consumption of Java tea among the natives. This campaign, which also serves a hygienic purpose, has already had considerable success, as is shown by the following Table of imports of Formosa tea:

Year				Tons	1000 guilders
1929	.	.	.	3599	8817
1931	.	.	.	2750	6737
1932	.	.	.	1720	2921

Beginning in 1934 the Tea Export Bureau has started a large campaign to stimulate tea consumption, this being a result of the enactment of the Crisis Tea Culture Ordinance, to be dealt with at the end of this chapter. In August 1933 the Tea-seed Export Ordinance [1] came into force, as a consequence of which the export of tea-seed, tea-plants, and all plant material with which a vegetative propagation of the tea-plant may be possible, has been prohibited. The regulation, which will be in

[1] Netherlands India Statute Book, 1933, No. 326.

force during the same period as the Tea Export Ordinance, is an outcome of the Provisional Tea Export Regulating Agreement into which the tea producers of Netherlands India, British India and Ceylon entered in February 1933. In the Memorandum of Recommendations published on that occasion, the prohibition of tea-seed export was recommended in connection with the tea-export restrictions.

CINCHONA RESTRICTION

In spite of the various measures taken by the Association of Cinchona Producers in Netherlands India, in order to limit production, the consequences of an over-production of cinchona have become more and more evident. The production of cinchona bark is twice as large as the consumption. The production of sulphate of quinine from bark increased from 600,000 kg. in 1913 to 1,100,000 in 1932; meanwhile the yearly consumption remained steady at some 500,000 kg. The Netherlands Indian Government has thus felt obliged to interfere because it was to be expected that those producers not members of the Association of Cinchona Producers, and unwilling to limit the sale of their product, would seriously aggravate the over-production, and thus cause a dislocation of the world cinchona market. The maintenance of a regular cinchona production is of importance not only to Netherlands India, but, for obvious hygienic reasons, to the whole world. Therefore in December, 1933, two bills for regulating cinchona production were presented to the People's Council of Netherlands India, one proposing a restriction of the cinchona export, the other a restriction of the cinchona area.

A few remarks on the development of the cinchona industry in Netherlands India and on the history of the Cinchona Producers' Association may be useful as an introduction to the recent regulation. During the years 1884-1913 the cinchona market had suffered from heavy price fluctuations, which made cultivation very risky. Especially because cinchona cultivation requires the yearly investment of considerable capital, which yields no full return until after fifteen years, the uncertainties of the market often caused serious losses to the producers.

The Government encouraged cinchona cultivation in those years. In a few years the price per kilogram of sulphate of quinine fell from 51·50 to 18 guilders; in 1896 the price was as low as one-tenth of the price in 1884. In spite of the sharp fall in the price of bark, the manufacturers of quinine in Europe nevertheless realized a high price for their product. In order to restore the relation between the market price of bark and that of quinine, a quinine factory where the producers could sell their bark was established in Bandoeng in 1900. The reaction of the European factories was a lowering of the quinine price even below the cost price. In consequence of the low market price the area of the cinchona plantations was reduced; this resulted after some time in a shortage of quinine, which made the price rise. Again the plantations were extended, with the result that the market price decreased sharply once more. There can be little wonder that, in consequence of the repeated disappointments, private initiative was discouraged from cinchona cultivation in spite of the stimulation of the Government.

The Director of Agriculture considered a stabilization of quinine prices to be the only method to keep up a sound cinchona industry able to meet the increasing need of quinine. He convinced the planters of the benefits of an agreement with the manufacturers according to which the planters would obtain the security of realizing a price for their bark corresponding to the world consumption, and the manufacturers on the other hand could depend on a regular supply of bark at a price in a reasonable proportion to quinine prices. In 1913 the first Cinchona Agreement came into effect. An Association of Cinchona Producers was established with the purpose of regulating the sale of the cinchona bark in accordance with the market demand and of improving the market price in this way. This free Association, of which almost all the cinchona producers were members, has had favourable results in that it caused an improvement of the market price; it has, however, not resulted in a diminution of the cinchona production.

The danger of such a producers' agreement is the risk of a disproportionate inflation of the price. The Netherlands Indian Government, which produces 10 per cent. of the total production in its own plantation, foreseeing the danger of price inflation, consented to enter as a producer into the agreement, only on condition that every producer would co-operate to deliver the quinine at a low price in malaria territories, and with the proviso that the Government would terminate the partnership when it considered the agreement to be an impediment to a cheap quinine supply.

After difficulties, the cinchona producers in co-operation with their buyers stabilized the price in 1927 at 35.50 guilders per kilogram sulphate of quinine. This price is often considered to be too high in relation to the cost price. During the period 1928-1930 the area in Java planted with cinchona decreased from 17,260 to 16,140 hectares, that in Sumatra increased from 2490 to 2950 hectares; the decrease of the total area does not point to an extraordinarily remunerative industry.

In 1931 the Association of Cinchona Producers applied to the Health Organization of the League of Nations with the proposal to deliver a yearly quantity of 500,000 kg. of quinine at a price of 20 guilders instead of 35'50 guilders, on condition that this quinine would not be sold, but would serve only to supply the natives in malaria countries. This quantity would be sufficient for 25 million malaria patients; however, hardly any use has been made of this offer up to the present.

When the results of the present Cinchona Agreement are considered, the advantages may be summarized as follows. The intermediate trade, which in former years kept large stocks of quinine in order to inflate the market price, has been eliminated from the market. The industry no longer suffers from heavy price fluctuations. The contract opens the possibility to supply the malaria territories with cheap quinine. The agreement has tried to regulate cinchona production in accordance with consumption; in this point, however, it has not succeeded. In fact, production has increased considerably, while the consumption has remained stationary, so that there is at present a considerable over-production.

In a case of over-production a restriction measure can only have any success when at the same time the planted area is not extended and when the cultivation methods do not lead to a higher production per hectare. But the potential production per unit has considerably grown in the course of years, and may be calculated at least at 50 per cent. above the 1913 figure. Thus the disproportion between production and consumption has gradually increased since 1913, mainly as a result of this increase of the potential production; in 1914, of 580 tons of sulphate of quinine tendered, 450 tons were sold; in 1930, while 1020 tons were tendered, only 510 tons were sold.

The rather high cinchona price has stimulated outsiders to start cultivation, and thus the price regulation has had a reverse effect. The outsiders took advantage of the steady market price without having the drawbacks of the production restriction. When in 1932 the Cinchona Agreement was extended to 1938, this fact again caused an increase of the outsiders' plantations. This extension is considered too dangerous to the Netherlands Indian cinchona industry, though at present the Producers' Association controls 98 per cent. of the cinchona plantation. In fact the quantity of cinchona bark tendered on the free market by outsiders, and consisting partly of native bark, partly of bark from an unknown origin, is larger than 2 per cent. of the production. When this quantity is calculated at 3 per cent. of the total potential production, and it is considered that the associated producers have sold in 1932 30 per cent. of their potential production, it is clear that the outside production means at present almost 10 per cent. of the production of the Cinchona Association. It is to be feared that, without a legal limitation, this percentage of the outsiders will quickly increase.

In order to prevent such an increase the Government felt obliged to draw up a scheme of regulation of the cinchona production which was laid down in the Cinchona Export Ordinance and the Cinchona Plantation Ordinance, coming into force in February 1934. These legal regulations covering all the producers, and thus equally dividing the disadvantages of restriction, may be supposed to avoid the serious failings of the free producers' association and, therefore, to be able to redress the balance between production and consumption.

The Cinchona Export Ordinance prescribes that for a number of years the export of cinchona bark will be allowed only with a licence to be given by the Director of Agriculture, Industries and Commerce. It has been determined provisionally that the regulation will remain in force till March 1937; it will be continued or suspended by Government decree according to circumstances. The total quantity to be exported will be determined every year by Government decree; this quantity may, however, be raised in the course of a year whenever this seems desirable in view of the needs of consumers. The latter prescription in particular has been inserted with a view to the supply of cheap quinine to malaria territories. Moreover, the Governor-General may prematurely terminate a licence year whenever the promise of the producers and manufacturers to deliver a yearly quantity of cheap quinine to the Health Organization of the League of Nations is not being observed. An Advisory Committee will be appointed to inform the Government as to the normal production of bark of each estate and the quantity to be allowed for sale.

The present quinine stock will be included in the total export quantity of the first restriction year. As regards contracts already concluded, a quantity amounting to 75 per cent., 50 per cent. and 25 per cent. respectively will be allowed in excess of the export quotas to be prescribed during the first three restriction years. The total export quantity to be fixed by Government decree for each restriction year will be divided among the cinchona estates according to their normal production, to be determined by the Director of Agriculture, Industry and Commerce. The production regulation includes all the cinchona producers—namely, the members of the Cinchona Association, the producers who are not members, and the native producers.

The division of the export quantity differs as between the members of the Cinchona Association and the other producers; the quantity to be exported by the former is fixed as a whole by the Director of Agriculture and divided among the members by the Association; as to the other producers, the Director of Agriculture stipulates the quantity of the export licence of each producer separately. It may be considered an advantage that the restriction will include the native producers, as otherwise wild native cultivation might partly frustrate the effect of the restriction. In the last few months of 1933 native cinchona plantations were strongly encouraged by Japanese. It still remains to be seen how far a control of the native cultivation will be practicable.

The export of cinchona seed and plant material will also be prohibited during the same period. The Cinchona Plantation Ordinance, passed at the same time, prohibits all extension of cinchona plantations; it is permitted to sow or to plant cinchona only when the new plantation replaces a previous cinchona area and does not exceed the area of that which has been pulled up. This prohibition will also apply to the native plantations. No decrees executing both the ordinances have yet been published (February 10, 1934), but it may be expected that in course of time the restriction measures will restore some degree of stability to the cinchona market.

RUBBER RESTRICTION [1]

In the past few years many different schemes for rubber restriction have been drawn up. Several of these schemes have been laid before the Netherlands Indian Government. The attitude of the Government has long been unfavourable, not because it was averse to restriction in general, but because it was of the opinion that none of the restriction schemes in question could be carried out. Some eleven years ago, when the Stevenson scheme was drawn up for Malaya, the question was first taken into consideration. The Netherlands Indian Government considered the application of this system to the native rubber cultivation to be difficult, because it would deprive the native population of an important source of income, and lead to other injustices.

The rise of rubber prices, a consequence of the restriction, had induced the native rubber planters as well as the estates in Netherlands

[1] For a more extended description of international rubber control see Chapter XIII. below.

India to extend their area and to increase the production. When at the end of 1928 the Stevenson scheme was abolished, the production exceeded consumption considerably and a disastrous fall of prices (from 20d. in January 1928 to 8½d. in December) set in, so that the position of the rubber producers grew more and more critical. In 1929 the Dutch Committee for promoting the interests of rubber producers applied to the Minister of the Colonies who promised that, if the English rubber producers would promise their co-operation, the Netherlands Indian Government would study measures for regulating rubber prices. The Government was willing to support restriction measures based on free co-operation of the producers and of a purely private character, but it would not actively interfere since it wished to avoid the risk that the problem would take on a political colour.

In May 1930 rubber-tapping on the estates was stopped for one month on the proposal of the Joint Committee, consisting of representatives of the Dutch and the English rubber growers. The Netherlands Indian Government showed its sympathy with this action by stopping the tapping on the Government Rubber Plantations. The Dutch producers, recognizing that a restriction could not be effective without the participation of the native planters, and seeing that this participation was not to be attained voluntarily, applied in July 1930 to the Government in order to obtain a compulsory restriction of the native rubber export. The Government, however, once more refused a direct intervention, since it was opposed to coercing the native producers against their will to adopt restriction measures, and, morever, considered that control would be very difficult and costly to enforce.

A definite scheme of the Rubber Committee was laid before the Government at the end of 1930. After discussion in Holland by the Director of Agriculture, Industry and Commerce with the Minister of the Colonies, and after a thorough study by a Working Committee in Holland, the Netherlands Indian Government, in November 1931, expressed its positive opinion that any forced restriction measures were to be considered undesirable. After that, various schemes were again laid before the Government; at the beginning of 1932 a new scheme, the so-called Quota Scheme, was proposed by the supporters of restriction, but the Government considered the proposed fixation of the export of native rubber at 90,000 tons a year to be unjust.

After many negotiations both the Dutch and the English governments declared in a communiqué that the prevailing conditions made it impossible to draw up an international restriction scheme. The

Netherlands Indian Government considered any interference in the matter to be unjustified unless a great majority of producers, both European and native, should desire it, and such a majority did not exist.

The Government considered any scheme to be impracticable unless it would answer the following requirements:

1. All rubber-producing countries would have to co-operate.
2. Not only would all rubber-planting have to be prohibited, but also an increase of the potential production of existing plantations would need to be prevented.
3. The price should not be raised to an excessively high level which might lead to a failure of any regulation as a consequence of the decrease of consumption.
4. The production capacity of young plantations would have to be taken into account in calculating the quota of each country.
5. Restricting measures should not be more onerous for the native cultivation than for the European estates.
6. The scheme must be workable, especially as regards native cultivation.

It will be apparent to readers that the native rubber cultivation was not the only impediment preventing the Netherlands Indian Government from co-operating in a restriction scheme, but it was, nevertheless, one of the most serious difficulties. If a restriction scheme had proved to be not enforceable among the native producers, it would bring all the disadvantages inherent in a limitation of production to the European producers without any of the advantages. Native rubber cultivation is quite important in Netherlands India, especially in Sumatra and Borneo. The production has varied in the last few years between 76 and 55 per cent. of the estate production, and the *potential* production of the native holdings is far greater than that of the estates. The area planted by natives cannot be stated, since the trees are not planted in regular plantations.

The following figures demonstrate the position of the rubber industry in Netherlands India in the last few years:

| | Planted Area in hectares | | Production in tons of dry Rubber | | |
	Estate	Native	Estate	Native	Total
1928 . .	525,646	Unknown	140,928	91,353	232,281
1929 . .	547,556	,,	150,620	107,557	258,177
1930 . .	573,014	,,	154,736	88,920	243,656
1931 . .	582,161	,,	172,559	87,987	260,546
1932 . .	582,196	,,	152,973	61,281	214,254

During the years 1932 and 1933 a great number of rubber estates stopped planting, the total tappable area of the 1060 rubber estates being 396,747 hectares in 1932. At the end of October 1933, 335 estates with an area in production of 51,413 hectares had stopped tapping; 133 estates with an area of 22,672 hectares had stopped partly. Altogether 74,085 hectares or 18·7 per cent. of the area in production at the end of 1932 was out of tapping.

The development of rubber prices in London and Amsterdam may be demonstrated by the following figures in Dutch cents per ½ kg. and pence per lb.

	1929		1930		1931		1932		1933	
	c.	d.	c.	d.	c.	d.	c.	d.	c.	d.
January . . .	61½	11	42	8	21½	4	12	3	8½	2
May . . .	61	11	39	7	19	3	7½	2	11½	3
September . . .	58	10	22½	4	13	3	11	3	14½	4

In the second half-year of 1933 negotiations for rubber restriction were renewed in Holland and Netherlands India as well as in other countries. The attitude of the Netherlands Indian Government with regard to restriction measures had somewhat altered in view of the urgent circumstances, which seemed to make a restriction almost inevitable. In April 1933 the Minister for the Colonies stated that compulsory limitation was desirable as soon as it proved possible to draft a practical scheme applicable to native producers and acceptable to the British Government. Several Netherlands Indian producers, who until then had been opposed to restriction, now changed their opinion. Negotiations between the International Association of Rubber Producers in Netherlands India and the British Rubber Growers Association seem to have led to an agreement on matters of principle. In Holland as in Netherlands India a number of meetings were held after consultation with the Government, though hardly anything was published concerning the discussions. But in August 1933 a scheme was laid before the Netherlands Indian Government and the British Government, both of which agreed in principle to restriction, though certain points of disagreement still remained. Negotiations with French as well as Dutch and British producers were therefore continued.

France has refused to co-operate in restriction with regard to Indo-China, because the country as a whole cannot be considered a rubber-producing country, its production being insufficient for the consumption of the industries in the mother-country. Siam and Sarawak also refused their co-operation for the time being. At the end of September 1933 rubber restriction was discussed at a meeting held between Government officials and native rubber planters of south-east Borneo and various districts in Sumatra. In general the native producers were convinced of the necessity of rubber restriction. The majority preferred a system of individual production restriction according to which each holder was allowed to tap a limited quantity which might only be exported under licence. On the other hand it was admitted that the great number of small native holdings, the production of which is quite unknown, would no doubt cause great difficulties. The native rubber production varies in relation to the price of rubber. In an unfavourable period, rubber cultivation is considered more or less as a secondary industry, and a great many of the trees are left untapped. A restriction would bring profit to the native rubber industry only if prices should rise considerably. The opinion was expressed by native producers that levying an export duty would have the result that the planters would not profit directly by a rise in prices.

In December 1933 a so-called Working Committee was appointed, consisting of the president of the General Agricultural Syndicate, the president of the General Association of Rubber Producers on the East Coast of Sumatra, and two representatives of each of these associations. This committee was to work out a restriction scheme in detail. At the beginning of 1934 the negotiations in Holland were resumed.

Throughout the year 1933 a revival of the rubber trade had been taking place. World consumption increased from 670,000 tons in 1932 to 810,000 tons in 1933. Unfortunately production also showed a substantial increase, totalling 844,500 tons in 1933 against 704,000 tons in 1932. Consequently the world rubber stocks rose to 650,000 tons at the end of 1933 (the estimated required stock being 304,000 tons). Rubber prices gradually rose during 1933 from $8\frac{1}{2}$ cents per $\frac{1}{2}$ kg. (Amsterdam) at the beginning of the year to 16 cents in December.

The preparation of the restriction plan took much more time than was expected. Meanwhile the prospect of a restriction caused prices to rise to a level out of relation with the true market position, for monthly production still far exceeded consumption.

Estate production was not immediately influenced, but the rise of prices caused a quick increase of native production, a fact that gave rise to new difficulties.

RUBBER PRICES IN AMSTERDAM AND LONDON

				Cents per ½ kg.	Pence per lb
January	.	.	.	17	5
February	.	.	.	17½	5⅛
March	.	.	.	18¼	5½
April	.	.	.	22½	6¾
May	.	.	.	23	7
June	.	.	.	22½	6¾
July	.	.	.	24	7¼

On April 28, 1934, the international agreement concerning restriction of rubber production was accepted by the British Rubber Growers' Association, the *International Vereeniging voor de Rubber en andère Cultures in Nederlandsh-Indië*, the *Union des Planteurs de Caoutchouc en Indochine*, the delegate of the Government of Sarawak and the delegate of the Government of Siam. On May 7 the Governments of France, Great Britain, India, the Netherlands and Siam entered into an agreement which was in general of the same tenor as the planters' Agreement.[1]

The functions to be conferred on the International Rubber Regulation Committee, which has to decide upon the export percentages, are scheduled in the scheme.

In May the Netherlands Indian Government prepared legislation for enforcing the restriction measures. The restriction of the estate rubber will be brought about as an individual restriction by means of a licence system. Moreover, there are in Java about 9900 small native rubber holdings with an average yearly production of more than 240 kg. To these holdings an individual restriction will likewise be applied, though in a somewhat different way; their share in the export will be accounted for in the quota allowed to the estate rubber.

Another system, however, had to be followed with regard to the extensive native rubber cultivation in Sumatra and Borneo. An individual restriction system was considered likely to give rise to serious difficulties. Moreover it was kept in mind that the export quantity of the native has a different significance from that of the estates, because the natives tap only when it is profitable. Therefore a system of limiting the export by means of an export duty was decided on. This measure means an artificial lowering of the price received by the native producer. It is expected that this will lead to a restriction of the export to about the amount fixed for the native share; it will have to be modified in accordance with the results obtained. The drawback of the system of an export duty is, that the producers have the disadvantage not only of

[1] For the provisions see Chapter XII.

a reduced production, but also of a lower price. The proceeds of the export duty will be spent to defray the cost of restriction measures and rubber research work, and also for works of public interest in the native rubber-producing districts.

The laws enforced in Netherlands India as a consequence of the rubber restriction agreement are the following:

1. An ordinance modifying the Tariff Law, by which it will be made possible to introduce special export duties on rubber by Government decree (Netherlands India Statute Book, 1934, No. 341).
2. The Estate Rubber Export Ordinance (No. 342) and the executive decree, the Estate Rubber Export Decree (No. 348), applicable to all estates (first group) and to the small native holdings in Java (second group). The large native rubber plantations in the Outer Districts are taken as the third group. No estate rubber may be exported as native rubber and vice versa.
3. The Native Rubber Export Ordinance (No. 343) and the executive decree, the Native Rubber Export Decree (No. 348), applicable to native rubber in the Outer Districts (Sumatra and Borneo).

According to the Estate Rubber Export Ordinance the export of estate rubber without a licence and without a certificate of origin is prohibited.

The proportion between the quantities of estate and native rubber to be exported will be 100: 71½, this being the proportion existing in 1929, the most favourable year for the native rubber export. Thus the basic export quotas for the coming years are fixed (in tons) as follows:

	Total Quota	Estate	Native
1934 . . .	357,632	208,532	147,100
1935 . . .	406,400	236,968	169,432
1936 . . .	450,088	262,442	187,646
1937 . . .	474,472	276,660	197,812
1938 . . .	492,760	287,324	205,436

The Director of Economic Affairs determines each period for which a certain export percentage will be in force; this period will always be of a short duration.

It has been fixed for the first period of four months (June 1 to September 30) at 95 per cent.; the percentages fixed by the International Committee are 100 for the first two months and 90 for the third and fourth months. The quota of estate rubber to be exported in the same period has been fixed at 66,035 tons. The export quota of native rubber for the same period has been fixed by the Director of Civil Service at 47,183 tons of dry rubber. With regard to the export of estate rubber, licences will be delivered to an amount equalling the standard production of each estate, multiplied by the export quota of estate rubber for a licence period, and divided by the sum of all standard productions. The standard production of estates of the first group is determined annually by taking the average production of the years 1929-1932 of an estate plus an increment for the young plantations, this being different for seedling and budded plantations. When during the basic years 1929-1934 a part of the plantations has been pulled up, the average production of those years is reduced by a certain amount of rubber.

The standard production of estates which have not yet been tapped during the base years is merely an estimate. This calculation is rather superficial; but it will be worked out and improved for 1935 and following years. An amount of $\frac{1}{2}$ Dutch cent per kg. of rubber has to be paid for the licences.

The small rubber holdings of the second group have been registered according to the number of tappable and not-tappable trees per hectare. In connection with this, their standard production has been fixed at $1\frac{1}{4}$ kg. of dry rubber per tappable tree; holders may protest against this if they can prove the area of their holding, in which case the standard production will be determined at 400 kg. per hectare. As it would be too complicated to deliver individual export licences to all these small holders, the Assistant-Residents or other Government officials receive licences for exporting a certain amount of rubber during a licence period and allocate monthly harvest licences to the rubber holders. Export licences for estates of the first group can be transferred with the approval of the Director of Economic Affairs. Export licences of the second group cannot be transferred, but monthly harvest licences of this group can always be transferred.

In accordance with the requirements of the international agreement, the rubber stocks of the estates may not exceed a production quantity of two months, the total rubber stock not exceeding one-eighth of the total export quota. In order to carry out this prescription it will be necessary to control the stock of each rubber trader. As for native rubber, in which trade is very dispersed, such a control is difficult. Therefore no one, except exporters and dealers who have been licensed, is permitted to keep a stock of dry rubber exceeding 200 kg. Larger native producers who have a tappable area of more than two hectares will be allowed to have a stock of 100 kg. of rubber per hectare of tappable area; licensed exporters and dealers in native rubber may have a maximum stock of three times their average monthly sale. All these rules concerning stocks will be enforced at a later period, after some time of preparation.

4. The Rubber Planting Material Export Ordinance (No. 344) prohibits all export of rubber seeds and planting material.
5. The Rubber Import Ordinance (No. 345) prohibits all import of crude rubber into Netherlands India, except by special permission of the Director of Economic Affairs in certain cases. The international agreement only prohibits import without a certificate of origin.
6. The Rubber Planting Ordinance (No. 346) gives the same prescriptions as have been laid down in the international agreement. Rubber planting is prohibited except for a replacing of seventy-five trees per hectare. It is possible only with the permission of the Director of Economic Affairs to extend the area for scientific purposes to one-quarter of the total area at most, and to replant existing areas, provided that the area replanted in any control year shall not exceed 10 per cent. of this area or 20 per cent. during the total restriction period.
7. A decree fixes a special export duty to be levied on native rubber, commencing July 1, 1934 (No. 349). This duty will be levied in addition to the export duty of 5 per cent. of the value of native rubber exported, which was introduced some years ago. The special export duty was fixed at 10 guilders per 100 kg.

By decree of the Director of Civil Service the percentage of dry rubber was fixed for scraps (Group II.) at 50 per cent., so that the export duty amounts to 5 guilders per 100 kg.; that for wet rubber (Group III.) in Acheen, West coast of Sumatra, Riouw and Banka at $82\frac{1}{2}$ per cent., so that the duty amounts to 8·25 guilders per 100 kg.; in all other ports at 70 per cent., so that the duty amounts to 7 guilders per 100 kg. This difference is explained by the fact that the rubber from the first-mentioned districts is of a drier quality than that from elsewhere. Due to the fact that dry rubber requires a longer time for preparation, and consequently remains for a longer period in the district before being exported than the wet rubber, the special export duty on dry rubber came into operation on July 16, 1934, that on scraps and wet rubber on June 1, 1934.

By a later decree (No. 360), the export duty per 100 kg. was revised as follows: dry rubber, 16 guilders; scrap, etc., 8 guilders; wet rubber in Acheen, West coast of Sumatra, Riouw and Banka, 13·20 guilders; in all other ports, 11·20 guilders. A still later decree in July again brought a modification, so that the export duty has become: dry rubber, 20 guilders per 100 kg.; scraps, etc., 10 guilders; wet rubber in Acheen, West coast of Sumatra, Riouw and Banka, 16·50 guilders; in all other ports, 14 guilders. This revision came into operation for scraps and wet rubber on August 1, 1934, for dry rubber on September 16. It is expected that with the present market prices the levying of the duty will be sufficient to bring the exports of native rubber down to the desired level.

The Native Rubber Export Ordinance makes it possible to abandon the system of an export duty in certain districts and gradually to introduce another system of restriction. In Palembang preparations have been made to introduce a system of individual restriction. It may be remarked that if such a system were to be enforced only in one district, while other neighbouring districts have an export duty, this might give rise to difficulties and evasions.

The general significance of the rubber restriction for Netherlands India may be demonstrated by the following figures:

EXPORT OF DRY RUBBER FROM NETHERLANDS INDIA IN TONS

	Estates		Natives		Total	Monthly Average
	Total	Monthly Average	Total	Monthly Average		
1929 .	150,620	12,552	107,557	8963	258,177	21,515
1930 .	154,736	12,895	88,920	7410	243,656	20,305
1931 .	172,559	14,380	87,987	7332	260,546	21,712
1932 .	152,973	12,748	61,281	5107	214,254	17,855
1933 .	170,523	14,210	114,658	9555	285,181	23,765
1934 .	208,532		149,100	..	367,632	29,803
1935 .	236,968		169,432	..	406,400	33,867
1936 .	262,442	basic quotas	187,646	..	450,088	37,507
1937 .	276,660		197,812	..	474,472	39,539
1938 .	287,324		205,436	..	492,760	41,063

For the years 1934-1938 the basic quotas of the restriction scheme have been divided for estates and natives in a proportion of $100 : 71\frac{1}{2}$, as determined for the first period. These figures show merely a regular continuation of the exports of the last few years. When however the monthly exports of the estates and those of the natives during the years 1933 and 1934 are compared with the monthly exports allowed from June 1934 it will be apparent that, particularly for the native exports, which have enormously increased during the last few months, the regulation will mean a serious limitation. It has to be seen whether this level will be reached under the export duty now fixed.

For the months after September the proportion between estates and native exports has not yet been published, because the People's Council did not agree with the decision.

MONTHLY EXPORTS FROM NETHERLANDS INDIA OF DRY RUBBER IN TONS

Month	Percentage of the basic quotas	Estates	Natives	Total
1933—				
January . .	..	10,983	4,864	15,847
February . .	..	10,755	4,102	14,857
March . .	..	12,731	4,454	17,185
April . . .	..	12,105	5,508	17,613
May . . .	..	15,117	9,205	24,322
June . . .	..	14,218	10,884	25,102
July . . .	..	15,499	12,731	28,230
August . .	..	13,888	11,854	25,742
September .	..	14,035	12,102	26,137
October .	..	14,168	12,164	26,332
November .	..	15,134	12,779	27,913
December .	..	16,791	14,011	30,802
1934—				
January .	..	13,570	15,285	28,855
February .	..	15,408	14,675	30,083
March .	..	17,711	20,744	38,455
April . .	..	15,830	21,098	36,920
May . .	..	25,643	27,140	52,783
June . .	95	16,508	11,796	28,304
July . .	95	16,508	11,796	28,304
August .	95	16,508	11,796	28,304
September .	95	16,508	11,796	28,304
October .	80	..	..	23,842
November .	80	..	..	23,842
December .	70	..	..	20,862

The situation of the rubber estates in Netherlands India has improved in that during the first months of 1934 a larger area was taken into tapping. On June 1, 210 estates with an area in production of 24,814 hectares had stopped tapping, while 160 estates with an area of 30,566 hectares had stopped partly; in all 14 per cent. were out of tapping (against 17.9 per cent. on June 1, 1933). For the year 1934 a considerable decrease of the rubber stocks cannot yet be expected; with the percentages allowed, the world export for June to December 1934 will amount to 506,544 tons, whereas the consumption during that period, calculated in accordance with the level of the first half of 1934, may be estimated at some 525,000 tons.

COMMODITY CONTROL IN THE PACIFIC AREA

RESTRICTION OF RICE IMPORTS

The production of rice in Netherlands India, though considerable, is not sufficient for the needs of the native population; an important quantity is yearly imported, into Java as well as into the other islands. In the last few years the imports have been decreasing: in 1931 the import into Java amounted to 287,000 tons, and in 1933 to 149,800 tons; the import into the other islands amounted to 321,835 tons in 1931 and to 273,124 tons in 1932. The import of foreign rice has had an adverse influence on the production of the Netherlands Indian rice. Since 1930 the market price of rice has been declining. As it is the most important food product of the native society, large groups of the native population are dependent on the market price.

A country which exports a considerable quantity of rice normally profits as a whole by high rice prices. In Netherlands India, however, a sharp divergence of interests exists, which makes it difficult to judge the rice problem for the country as a whole. In Java a great part of the population find their livelihood in rice-growing; an area of $3\frac{1}{2}$ million hectares is annually planted with rice, yielding about $3\frac{1}{4}$ million tons of husked rice. The greater part serves for home consumption; but 40 per cent. is sold on the local market and a high market price is thus profitable to the rice growers; on the other hand, groups of natives such as those living in the towns have an interest in a low consumption price.

In the Outer Provinces the clash of interests is sharper because there are districts where the cultivation of commercial crops prevails and where conditions are less favourable for food crops, so that the population has to use rice imported from elsewhere. Such districts are Djambi (Sumatra) and Borneo, both important native rubber-producing territories, Banka (tin production and pepper cultivation), and Northern Celebes, where the population lives on coconut cultivation. On the other hand there are districts, such as Southern Celebes and Lombok, which are very suited to rice cultivation and which export a considerable excess quantity.

In view of these divergent interests of the population in the market price of rice it is not to be wondered at that the Government has hesitated to interfere in order to control the rice situation. But the market position grew gradually worse. The local market for Java rice is closely related to the price of imported rice. In 1931 the price of Saigon rice was 50 per cent. of the average price in the years 1922-1929, and in 1932 it dropped to 45 per cent. During 1931 the Government had not yet found occasion to take measures for regulating the price of rice, because the general level of prices had declined and because rice distribution had not yet met difficulties. In 1932, however, the position of the rice growers grew serious, as a consequence of factors in the export countries as well as in Netherlands India. At the end of 1931 the currency of Burma was depreciated. In the first half-year of 1932 Indo-China lowered the export duties on rice; at the same time Siam abandoned the gold standard, thus stimulating her rice exports. The crop of 1932 was abundant in both the last-mentioned countries, and a sharp fall on the rice market followed at the end of 1932.

The home rice production in Netherlands India had been increasing considerably in the last few years, mainly as a result of the reduction of the sugar-cane area; in 1932 the increase amounted to 127,000 tons of husked rice, and for the crop of 1933 it was estimated at 312,000 tons. The greater part of this rice found an outlet in the inland market, but in the coast towns a relatively greater quantity of imported rice was consumed than in former years because it was cheaper. A part of the excess of the 1932 crops could not be sold to districts with a rice shortage because of the competition of very cheap rice from Siam, Burma and Indo-China.

The Government therefore considered a regulation of imports indispensable in order to prevent a dislocation of the home rice market. In March 1933 a preliminary ordinance was promulgated to prohibit rice imports for a period of four months.[1] This temporary measure had to be passed at short notice in order to prevent a sudden rise of the price when negotiations about an import regulation became generally known; in the meantime a more definite regulation for limiting the import was prepared. The preliminary ordinance authorized the Director of Agriculture, Industry and Commerce to grant exceptions to the prohibition by means of an import licence; this measure made it possible for the Government to consider the rice situation in each province or district individually. In the rice-importing part of Sumatra, and other islands, licences were allowed on a large scale during the first months. In Java the rice sales depend to a great extent on the question of transport, so in March 1932 the Government railways agreed to a reduction of freight for rice amounting to 20 per cent., and for paddy, 30 per cent. The Royal Packet Navigation Company also lowered its freight for rice transport in order to stimulate the sale of excess rice.

The publication of the temporary import prohibition caused much

[1] Netherlands India Statute Book, 1933, No. 116.

speculation and a sudden rise of rice prices. The Government served warning that rice distribution would be taken into its own hands in territories where speculators sold rice at abnormally high prices. This warning was sufficient to bring about a prompt readjustment of prices. By means of the system of licences the market can now be kept in balance. That the market price of rice was not at first visibly raised by the prohibitive measure—except for the short speculative boom— may be explained by the fact that from the beginning licences were allowed on a large scale. The inland rice price can of course be influenced only very gradually.

As mentioned above the Rice Import Ordinance was no more than an emergency provision; at the same time a bill containing more definite measures to prevent a dislocation of the home rice situation had been presented to the People's Council. It was expected that the area planted with rice and maize would be still further extended in the following year as a consequence of the further reduction of the sugar-cane area, so it may be possible that in 1934 Java will be self-supporting as to rice. If a large quantity of cheap imported rice should be offered, the transport of home rice to various consuming territories will no longer be remunerative, and thus local stocks of unsaleable rice will accumulate. Some territories of Netherlands India will for the time being, however, remain dependent on rice imports because the quantity of the total home production is insufficient for consumption.

Of the three systems of limiting the rice import—namely, a licensing system, a quota system and the levying of a high import duty—the first-mentioned seemed to be the most appropriate. The levying of a high import duty would cause serious trouble in the territories which depend on imports of rice; and the Government considered it undesirable to introduce a system of differential duties for the various territories of Netherlands India.

In July 1933 the Rice Import Ordinance and the Rice Import Decree were promulgated,[1] prescribing that the import of rice is allowed only with a special licence. The executive decree regulates the way in which the licences have to be applied for; the total import quantity has not been limited.

A system of quotas for imports from the various countries on the basis of a certain percentage of their imports of previous years was considered likely to cause difficulties in connection with the special needs of various territories. In the system of licences the total quantity to be

[1] Netherlands India Statute Book, 1933, Nos. 299 and 300.

imported is not determined beforehand, but is regulated for each territory in relation to its needs. It cannot be denied that a system of import licences has the defect of a possible unfair division between the importers, but the disadvantage can be largely removed when the licences are distributed in accordance with the advice of the Governmental officials who have a thorough knowledge of the local conditions. A so-called Rice Import Commission has, therefore, been instituted. The Government aims at stabilizing the inland price of rice; but the level of the price could not be determined beforehand by decree, because it is for the greater part dependent on the general state of business; at all events an undesirable inflation of the price must be prevented.

The Government's intention to prohibit as far as possible the import of foreign rice is demonstrated by a recent regulation regarding the import into Atchin (North Sumatra), a territory which, in spite of a rice excess, imports yearly a quantity of rice of a higher quality than the Atchin rice, which has a very small grain. In the first quarter of 1934 this import may not exceed 40 per cent. of the normal quantity imported. The East coast of Sumatra had to import in January 1934 a quantity of 1000 tons of rice from Java and Lombok instead of from foreign countries. The Government will give compensation for freight, which will be higher than that from British India and Siam, even though the Royal Packet Navigation Company has already lowered its rice freight.

In 1932 several attempts were made to sell a part of the yearly rice surplus of Atchin, calculated at 30,000 tons of paddy, to the East coast of Sumatra, which imports every year a quantity of more than 100,000 tons of foreign rice for the estate labourers. It proved, however, to be impossible to compete with the cheap Rangoon rice, mainly because of the high carriage from Atchin to Medan.

One defect of the rice import regulation was that sometimes, immediately after the harvest, the rice dealers sold too great a quantity of rice to a territory where the price was higher. In such a case the Crisis Export Ordinance makes it possible to prohibit the transport of rice in order to prevent a local shortage arising after some months. At the end of December 1933 the shipment of rice from the East coast of Sumatra, Western Borneo, South Sumatra, S.E. Sumatra and Banka to districts situated on other islands had been thus prohibited by Government decree.

Now that the import regulation has been in force for some time the opinion may be expressed that it generally fulfils its intended purpose. The rice surpluses of various territories are regularly sold to districts which up to the present have imported exclusively foreign rice. The stabilization of the inland market is thus promoted, because it is less influenced by the prices of the foreign rice. A few examples of the improved rice distribution may be mentioned. The import from Macassar and Pare Pare (South and Central Celebes) into Menado (North Celebes), amounting in 1932 to no more than 4500 tons, increased to 6750 tons during the first nine months of 1933, while the foreign import to Menado, amounting in 1932 to 27,347 tons, was during the first nine months of 1933 only 20,000 tons, and was stopped on November 1. The rice export from Macassar to other territories has also increased. Palembang has been closed for foreign rice import from November 1, 1933; the foreign import of the district decreased from 12,000 tons in 1932 to 5000 tons in the first nine months of 1933; a quantity of about 4000 tons of Palembang rice was even exported to other parts of Sumatra. The import of foreign rice into Banka decreased from 27,400 tons in 1932 to 18,000 tons during January-September 1933; that into Billiton from 7100 tons in 1932 to 4500 tons during January-September 1933; a considerable quantity of Java rice is being imported at present.

Though various difficulties are still to be overcome, such as the problem of transporting Java rice, the general opinion of the new distribution system is rather favourable.

THE CRISIS IMPORT ORDINANCE

Since 1931 the Netherlands Indian market has been flooded with foreign articles sold at exceptionally low prices. This must be considered as one of the causes of the depressed condition of several local Netherlands Indian industries. Their position grew so critical in 1933 that the Netherlands Indian Government considered it necessary to take protective measures. The Government has been of opinion that a temporary system of quotas would be the right method to protect the Netherlands Indian industries and to prevent them from having to compete unduly with foreign products on an unprotected market in which their very existence is threatened. A system of quotas has been chosen as being most in the line of free trade policy and apparently the most appropriate system in the prevailing circumstances. It is to be expected that quota regulations will keep an exceedingly large quantity of foreign goods out of the country.

COMMODITY CONTROL IN NETHERLANDS INDIA

A protectionist system of high import duties is not always effective for the protection of home industries, as has been proved in several countries. Moreover, the Government definitely desires to keep the price-level for inland consumption as low as possible. The levying of high import duties causes an immediate rise of the prices of the imported articles, while a system of quotas usually does not result in a rise of the prices, especially when a free quota system is applied. The system of import duties in Netherlands India is not protectionist, but almost purely fiscal. In January 1934 a new tariff of import duties came into force. The modification consists in a considerable raising of the duties and in a revised arrangement of the groups of imports according to the international tariff scheme, but not in a fundamental change of the tariff system. The tariff has been raised in general but without any concealed intention of limiting competition from foreign countries or supporting home production. A distinction between raw materials and consumption goods has been made; the destination of the goods has been taken as a criterion for the tariff; raw materials for luxury goods and goods having a character of luxury are taxed with a higher duty. The fact that some article is manufactured also in Netherlands India has not been taken as a criterion for levying an import duty. The raised import duties bear equally upon the whole population. Only a very few goods, consumed chiefly by the poorest of the natives, such as salt fish, are exempt from the increase of duty.

In January 1933 cotton yarns for the weaving industry were exempted from import duty by virtue of a special law in order to stimulate the Netherlands Indian textile industry. This exemption has been continued in the new tariff law. This is the only tariff regulation especially drawn up for protecting the home industry. The fact that no preferential tariff exists for imports from Holland makes the competition of the mother-country in the Netherlands market particularly difficult at a time when other importing countries have a depreciated exchange whilst Holland and Netherlands India have kept on the gold standard.

A change of the fiscal tariff system of Netherlands India to a preferential system would have little effect on the existing international treaties. Most treaties concluded by the Netherlands include the territories outside Europe: that is to say that Holland and Netherlands India are considered to be a unit and that in applying the most-favoured-nation clause the relation of Holland towards Netherlands India remains out of consideration. But Holland has entered into two treaties with England especially regarding Netherlands India: first, the

London Treaty, according to which the tariff for British goods imported into Netherlands India may not exceed twice the tariff levied on similar Dutch goods, or may be at the most 6 per cent. when the Dutch goods have been exempted from import duty; second, the Sumatra Treaty, according to which the tariff levied on British goods imported into certain self-governing territories of Sumatra may not be higher than the import duty on similar Dutch goods.

In regard to the London Treaty a preferential tariff is indeed possible; but for those parts of Sumatra mentioned in the Sumatra Treaty no preferential system can be introduced, as a consequence of the most-favoured-nation clause. As to the Sumatra Treaty, the introduction of a preferential system would make it necessary to divide the customs territory into two parts, which would give rise to difficulties. Between Netherlands India and Poland a treaty has also been concluded, which mutually prohibits the levying of surtaxes on the import duties in case of depreciation of the rate of exchange in one of the two countries. Even without a special prohibition, the levying of any additional duty for depreciation of exchange seems to be inadmissible from the standpoint of the most-favoured-nation clause.

So in connection with the existing treaties a system of quotas will be more effective than a modification of the tariff system. The Netherlands Indian Government has expressed its opinion that no fundamental changes should be made in commercial policy. The necessary measures will be taken within the limits of the existing commercial treaties. Any quota measure will, therefore, not be applied exclusively to one particular country, but to all countries with which Netherlands India maintains regular trade relations.

In September 1933 the Crisis Import Ordinance [1] came into force, which has made it possible to prohibit temporarily the import into Netherlands India of certain goods or groups of goods in so far as the total value, the total quantity or the total weight of that import would exceed an amount to be fixed separately for each case. The prohibition has to be issued by Government decree; such a decree can remain in force during ten months at most; after the expiration of that period an ordinance concerning the subject has to be enacted if necessary. The regulation has no protectionist character, and it does not aim at a rise of prices, but only at a limitation of an extraordinarily large import of foreign goods which has driven the home goods from the market. The Memorandum on the Bill says that as a rule it will be

[1] Netherlands India Statute Book, 1933, No. 349.

considered sufficient for Netherlands India to pursue a system of free quotas, according to which the total quantity to be imported is stipulated, whilst the trader is free to obtain the goods from the country with the lowest prices; free competition will thus be left untouched. In a system of quotas by countries the various importing countries have no encouragement at all to offer their products at a lower price, because they have no opportunity to get a greater share of the market; on the contrary they will try to obtain the highest possible prices.

The terms of the Explanatory Memorandum, however, do not exclude the introduction of a system of so-called " quotas by countries," whereby the share of each import country in the total quota may be determined on the basis of the imports of a past year. The fact that a system of quotas by countries is not excluded thus creates a possibility of passing on within the limits of the international treaties to a certain change in commercial policy.

A system of quotas by countries would provide a means to arrive at an international exchange of advantages. The Government has expressed the opinion that such a system could be accepted only when the possibility of interchange of advantage with a country in question was assured—e.g. a country will obtain a higher percentage of the Netherlands Indian import quota when it promises in return advantages for the sale of Netherlands Indian products on its own market. A clause has been inserted in the ordinance stating that the Director of Agriculture, Industry and Commerce may lay down regulations concerning a certificate of origin of the goods imported; this prescription points to a possible quota by countries.

It has been pointed out that a system of free quotas is more in the line of the Netherlands Indian trade policy; but in the last few years great changes have taken place with regard to the *share* of the various countries of origin in the Netherlands Indian imports. Thus by choosing the *period* which would have to serve as a base year for the import quantity, it would be possible to favour any country or group of countries even in a system of free quotas.

With a free quota system the international treaties can remain out of discussion. When such a system is applied, the import from the mother-country is internationally included. If necessary a quota measure can of course be drawn up with an eye to the interests of the mother-country. The quotas for bleached textiles mentioned below is an example of this kind.

The possibility of limiting the imports to certain ports has also been suggested as a means to facilitate control. The Government is not bound to a certain base year in fixing the quotas; this will be determined for each case separately.

The quota regulations have to be applied at short notice, for it is quite undesirable that the measures to be taken should become known beforehand, causing a sudden extraordinary import, and rendering the measure ineffective at the beginning. The technical execution of the quotas will consist of a licensing system. Much will depend on the way in which this is handled in actual practice. Grave difficulties for trade may arise if the measures are not applied with great tact and caution.

Serious foreign competition has affected several local industries which supply the inland market: the efforts to establish a textile industry in Netherlands India are greatly hindered by foreign competition; the existence of the young weaving industry, which was in a fair way to develop, is severely threatened. The cement industry and the breweries can hardly keep going in consequence of the sale of cheaper foreign products; for the same reason the soap industry and the paint industry have had a hard time. The measures now to be taken in virtue of the Crisis Import Ordinance will offer an opportunity of securing existing industries, and may be expected to result in a stimulation of industrial production for home consumption.

The first quota decree based upon the Crisis Import Ordinance has been that concerning cement imports, the second one the Crisis Beer Import Decree. At the beginning of 1934 quota decrees concerning various textiles also were enforced, while restrictions have likewise been imposed on the import of maize and soya beans.

THE CRISIS EXPORT ORDINANCE

In October 1933 the Crisis Export Ordinance came into force,[1] prescribing that in urgent cases affecting the provision of necessities of life for the native population, or in order to prevent an undesirable export of plant material obtained in Netherlands India, temporary export prohibitions or restrictive measures may be issued; the measures may concern the export of certain goods from the whole of Netherlands India, or from certain parts only, and the transport of certain goods from one part of Netherlands India to other enumerated parts of the country. The export of certain goods can be limited to some ports, or even to one port. Such a temporary regulation must be proclaimed by

[1] Netherlands India Statute Book, 1933, No. 353.

Government decree, which may cover a period of no more than six months; after that term an ordinance has to be enacted to regulate matters.

The possibility of a limitation of inland transport at short notice has been allowed for with a view to preventing a shortage which might result from the selling of a product, necessary for the living of the population, to other parts of the Archipelago where the prices are higher. An example of this kind may be found in the rice trade, as described above. The Rice Import Ordinance keeps in view mainly the interests of the rice producers. Difficulties for the rice consumers may arise when the trader profits by selling so great a quantity of rice that shortage may arise in the producing district. So, at the end of December 1933, the shipment of rice from the east coast of Sumatra, Djambi, Riouw (South Sumatra), Western Borneo and Banka to districts situated on other islands was prohibited by Government decree.

The Crisis Export Ordinance does not aim at entrusting the Government with the power to introduce important restriction measures, such as a cinchona restriction or a rubber restriction, or measures to stimulate the compensation trade, by virtue of a decree, or without the co-operation of the People's Council. Such far-reaching measures will be taken only in consultation with the People's Council. The purpose of the Ordinance is simply to make it possible to effect a temporary limitation of the export of less important products without enacting a separate ordinance for each of them.

THE CRISIS CULTURE ORDINANCES

Another Government measure important for the agricultural industries has been the enactment of the Crisis Culture Ordinances—namely, the Crisis Rubber Ordinance, the Crisis Tea Ordinance, the Crisis Cinchona Ordinance and the Crisis Coffee and Cacao Ordinance.[1] Up to 1933 the organization and the financing of the private experiment stations had been left entirely to private initiative; the system of a free membership was followed, which means that the planters who were not members also profited by the experimental work. In 1932, however, the financial position of the experiment stations for rubber, tea, cinchona, coffee and cacao had become so unfavourable that an intervention of

[1] Netherlands India Statute Book, 1933, Nos. 202-205, and the respective executive decrees, Netherlands India Statute Book, Nos. 206-209.

the Government was considered necessary in order to assure their existence.

This interference has resulted in the enactment of four Crisis Culture Ordinances, which aim to make all proprietors of European estates share in the costs of the experiment station work. By virtue of the ordinances mentioned it is forbidden to transport rubber, latex, tea, cinchona, coffee and cacao from the estates without a licence to be given by the newly instituted Crisis Culture Centrals. Rubber, Tea, Cinchona, and Coffee and Cacao Centrals have been established to handle the financial administration of the experiment stations in question. The amount to be paid for a licence is annually fixed by the central in accordance with the quantity produced in the previous year, and calculated on a unit-amount per 100 kg. of the product, which unit-amount is annually fixed by the Governor-General on the recommendation of the Crisis Culture Central. The unit-amount for the years 1933 and 1934 have been fixed: for tea at 32 Dutch cents per 100 kg. (1934: 59) for Java and Southern and Western Sumatra; 16 cents (1934: 29) for native tea in the territories just mentioned, and 9 cents (1934: 39) in the other parts of Sumatra; for rubber and latex at 29 cents (1934: $27\frac{1}{2}$) per 100 kg. for Java and Southern and Western Sumatra; 15 cents (1934: $24\frac{1}{2}$) for the other part of Sumatra; for coffee and cacao at 26 cents (1934: 21) per 100 kg. (estates in Acheen, East Coast of Sumatra and Tapacelie have been exempted from paying for the time being); for cinchona at 34 cents (1934: 51) per 100 kg. of bark. The unit-amounts for East and North Sumatra could be fixed lower, because the Experiment Station of the Avros (General) Society of Rubber Planters at the East Coast of Sumatra is not in such a bad financial condition.

The funds collected in this way by the Crisis Culture Centrals have to be used: (*a*) to conduct the scientific work of the experiment stations; (*b*) to start research on new uses of rubber and latex; (*c*) to promote the consumption of tea.

In the first budget of the Crisis Rubber Central the amount to be paid for research work is calculated at 6 Dutch cents for each 100 kg. of export rubber; the total amount thus available for rubber research is estimated at 70,000 guilders, of which 50,000 guilders will be spent on research in new uses for rubber, to be performed by the Technical Section of the International Rubber Society in Holland. This institution has already done valuable work of the kind, but on a smaller scale. 5000 guilders will be placed at the disposal of the Experiment Station of the General Society of Rubber Planters on the East Coast of Sumatra (Avros) to carry out special experiments, and 15,000 will be reserved for the Committee for the Extension of Rubber Sales, working in Java. The amount to be received for tea promotion is estimated at 80,000 guilders for the first year, calculated at 10 Dutch cents per 100 kg. of export tea; 40,000 has been allocated for the work of the Tea Propaganda Bureau in Holland, 30,000 for propaganda work in Netherlands India. A large-scale campaign to stimulate tea consumption in various countries has also been started.

CHAPTER IX

EXPORT CONTROL BOARDS IN NEW ZEALAND

by R. G. Hampton

INTRODUCTION

IN conformity with a national tendency to turn to a paternal Government for assistance in all endeavours, primary producers in New Zealand have asked the Government to assist in gaining ends that producers in other countries have sought by purely co-operative means. The Government has indulgently given the necessary backing, and New Zealand is now provided with a series of co-operative producers' associations reinforced by State compulsion. Pools, associations and combines generally suffer from one or two disruptive weaknesses. Probably the most important is the small outside element which, while benefiting with other producers from the operations of the organization, stands aloof, and too often provides a focus of disruption. In New Zealand we find an attempt to make this impossible. With Government sanction compulsory membership is enforced in every case but that of the fruit trade, where a more elastic system is being tried out. Thus not only is there a system of State-sanctioned control in the export of primary produce but, to make the experiment more interesting, several variations of the main scheme are working side by side. Economic planning is here to be seen in one of its most interesting forms. It is for economic advisers to determine which is best adapted to the needs of the industries concerned.

THE MEAT EXPORT CONTROL BOARD

War Commandeer

New Zealand's attitude towards marketing control has for many years been shadowed by the establishment during the war of what was known as the " War Commandeer." Under the control of the British Ministry of Food, foodstuffs were purchased by the Governments in the Dominions, at definite controlled prices, for dispatch to the Homeland. At the conclusion of the war the commandeer was relaxed, but in the case of meat Government purchases were continued (at the request of the Dominions Governments) until 1920. On the realization of Government stocks, which was completed in 1921, the control of prices was finally removed. The immediate result was a slump in meat prices on the English market. The New Zealand producers then, through their very efficient organizations, agitated for some sort of control of meat export. In view of the satisfactory results which had accrued under the war commandeer, they naturally gravitated towards Government action.

A further factor influencing the direction of the agitation was the experience of the British Australian Wool Realization Association (B.A.W.R.A.). Under the British Government's war purchases of wool in Australia the wool was not bought outright. As the Australian producers retained a share in its ownership they were consulted, and the British Australian Wool Realization Association (representative of both the British Government and the Australian producers) was set up to manage the realization of the considerable stocks on hand. The final winding-up of the B.A.W.R.A. took place as late as 1933. The operations of this Association in regularizing the supply of wool upon overseas markets set a useful precedent, which was helpful in determining the choice by New Zealand meat producers of their control scheme.

New Zealand experience along similar lines had been obtained also by the New Zealand Wool Committees, which carried out somewhat the same functions as the B.A.W.R.A. on a very much smaller scale.

The Meat Export Control Act, 1921

The position in 1921 is thus summarized in the preamble of the Meat Export Control Act, 1921:

Whereas the economic welfare of New Zealand has lately been adversely affected by reason of a reduction in the net returns receivable by persons engaged in the business of the production of meat for export, such reduction being due in part to falling prices and in part to the charges payable in respect of freight and other services: And whereas conferences have lately been held of representatives of the Government and of persons whose business is the production of meat for export, and it has been resolved that the public economic welfare will be promoted by the establishment of a Board of Control, with power to act as the agent of the producers in respect of the preparation, storage and shipment of meat, and in respect of the disposal of such meat beyond New Zealand: And whereas it is desired to give effect to the resolution aforesaid, and to provide by law accordingly: And whereas it is further deemed necessary and desirable that the expenditure of the Board of Control should be subject to audit as if it were public expenditure, and that the expenditure of the Board should be guaranteed by the Government of New Zealand, be it therefore enacted, etc.

x

By this Act the New Zealand Meat Producers Board was set up, consisting of eight members, of whom five are elected by vote of the meat producers, one appointed by the stock and station interests, and two by the Government. It will be noted, although this Board was constituted under the Meat Export Control Act, 1921, it is known as " The New Zealand Meat Producers Board," and " control " in its true sense is not exercised. The Board has full authority in respect of the following matters:

(a) The grading, handling, pooling and storage of meat;

(b) The shipment of meat on such terms and in such quantities as it thinks fit;

(c) The sale and disposal of meat on such terms as it thinks advisable;

(d) The insurance of meat until disposed of;

(e) Generally all such matters as are necessary for the handling, distributing and disposing of New Zealand meat;

(f) The securing of any advances that may be made to the Board, or to the owners of any meat at the request of the Board, with full power on behalf of the owners to give security and to execute all mortgages, etc., as if the Board were the legal owners.

All moneys received by the Board are paid into a separate account and applied as follows:

(a) In payment of the expenses, commission and other charges incurred.

(b) In payment of salaries, wages, travelling allowances, fees, or other remuneration to members of the Board and the London Agency (not being persons permanently in the service of the Government) and other servants.

(c) In advances to owners of meat on account of the price of that meat.

(d) In interest and other charges and repayment of principal, in respect of moneys advanced to the Board by the Minister of Finance.

(e) In payment into a Reserve Fund at the Board's discretion.

(f) In payment of the balance to the owners of meat controlled by the Board in proportions to be fixed by the Board, by reference to quantity and grade of the meat handled.

The Working of the Board

The expenses of the Board are paid by means of a levy which the Board itself fixed later at 1d. on every carcase, and at a relative figure on other meat exports. The amount was reduced to ¾d. from January 1, 1931. The most important functions of the Board include:

(a) The regulation of shipments whereby supplies on the British market are spread as required over the whole year, having due regard to the months of highest consumption of each class of meat, thus avoiding gluts or storages.

(b) Supervision of grading, and inspection of loading and unloading of vessels.

(c) Negotiations for shipping contracts, and reduction of costs in any direction possible.

(d) Research and experimental work.

(e) Advertising New Zealand meat products on the British markets.

(f) The exploitation of potential new markets.

(g) Watching the interests of producers in every respect.

Results claimed

The following results claimed from the operations of the Board are drawn from the Board's Annual Report for 1932. The figures for lamb are taken as an illustration, as these are the lowest quoted. The others range from the next highest, 44 per cent. over 1922 rates (in the case of mutton) to 64 per cent. (in the case of frozen sundries). In 1922, when the Board was constituted, the shipping freight rate for lamb was $1\frac{3}{4}$d. per lb plus $2\frac{1}{2}$ per cent. The improvements effected since that date are best seen in the following Table:

1922	1922-1923	1923-1924	1924-1925
$1\frac{3}{4}$d. + $2\frac{1}{2}$ per cent.	$1\frac{1}{2}$d. net.	$1\frac{3}{8}$d. net.	$1\frac{9}{32}$d. net.

1926-1927	1927-1929	1929-1930	1930-1933
1·19d. net.	1·18d. net.	1·121d. net.	1·089d. net.

The rates in the three-year contract 1930-1933 show reductions over the 1922 rates of—

Per lb	Per head	Per cent.
0·704d.	2s. 0·64d. on 35 lb lamb.	39·24

The total savings for the seasons in question are estimated at—

Season	Accumulated Savings since 1922	Seasonal Savings	Total Seasonal Savings
1922–1923 . .	. .	575,000	575,000
1923–1924 . .	575,000	164,000	739,000
1924–1925 . .	739,000	40,000	779,000
1925–1926 . .	779,000	40,000	819,000
1926–1927 . .	819,000	40,000	859,000
1927–1928 . .	859,000	50,000	909,000
1928–1929 . .	909,000	50,000	959,000
1929–1930 . .	959,000	50,000	1,009,000
1930–1931 . .	1,009,000	$16,666\frac{2}{3}$	$1,025,666\frac{2}{3}$
1931–1932 . .	1,025,666	$16,666\frac{2}{3}$	$1,042,333\frac{1}{3}$
1932–1933 . .	1,042,333	$16,666\frac{2}{3}$	1,059,000
	£8,716,000	£1,059,000	£9,775,000

These figures show since 1922 an estimated total savings in freight charges to the New Zealand meat producers of £9,775,000, a figure probably in excess of that which would have resulted from the general world-wide decline in freights over the period. They cover only a small section of the costs incurred between producer and consumer. Savings have also been made in insurance rates, handling charges, cold storage rates, etc.

The question has been raised as to whether, with falling world prices and costs, these reductions would not have accrued in the ordinary way. While it is safe to say that some reductions would have taken place, there seems little doubt that the Board has obtained savings above what would otherwise have been made. In the Board's 1928 balance sheet is the sum of £29,125, representing the cost of a site purchased for a cold store in London. This purchase was followed by a reduction in cold-storage rates, which was estimated to be worth £50,000 per annum to the Dominion. Consequent upon this reduction the Board agreed not to build within a period of three years. That period has now expired, and negotiations are afoot for further reductions. On the whole it appears that the operations of the Meat Producers Board have brought about definite reductions in many costs.

Expense to the Industry

The expense at which these reductions have been made is another factor to be reckoned with. The amount collected by way of levy in 1932 was £36,435, less the cost of collection, £364. The expenses incurred by the Board were £38,860. The apparent deficiency is offset by two further sources of revenue—interest on investments, £3106, and net income from cold-storage site, £279—leaving an excess of income over expenditure of £596. The corresponding excess for 1931 was £1606. While the cost to the industry seems relatively high an examination of the accounts shows a number of directions in which the expenditure is reasonably likely to bring the industry a considerable return which it is difficult to assess. Such items are:

Advertising	£17,397
Research grants and experiments	£616
Prize moneys, etc.	£225
" Eat More Beef " campaign	£205

Further information as to savings of this type with which the various New Zealand boards may be credited will be found in Appendix A, which reproduces the accounts and balance sheet of the Dairy Export Control Board, the operations of which cover ground very similar to that of all the New Zealand boards. It is worthy of consideration that the savings shown in the Board's annual reports far outweigh the cost of $\frac{3}{4}$d. per carcase represented in the levy.

THE DAIRY EXPORT CONTROL BOARD

A little over a year after the establishment of the New Zealand Meat Export Control Board, the dairy producers of the Dominion found themselves confronted with a similar pressing problem. Prices of dairy produce had fallen steadily since the revocation of the war commandeer in 1919—two years earlier than the date when support was withdrawn from the meat producers. To dairy farmers who had been carrying on under adverse conditions which showed no sign of improvement the inauguration and apparently successful operation of the Meat Board suggested a similar organization.

The first campaign resulted in the setting up of a Parliamentary Committee in 1922 to hear evidence from producers and exporting firms. A parliamentary General Election being close at hand the matter was shelved, but next session a bill was introduced which, after searching investigation, was passed as the Dairy Export Control Act of 1923. Under this Act a Board was set up, consisting of twelve members— nine (of whom three retire annually) nominated by the producers; two nominated by the Minister of Agriculture, and one by the proprietary and mercantile interests.

A London agency of the Board was set up, consisting of such number of members as the Board might prescribe, one being appointed by the Minister of Agriculture. The duties of this agency are similar to those of the Meat Board's London agency.

Finances for the Board's operations may be obtained by a maximum levy of $\frac{1}{8}$d. per lb on butter and $\frac{1}{16}$d. per lb on cheese. Actually, however, the Board since 1927 has levied at the rate of $\frac{1}{32}$d. per lb on butter and $\frac{1}{60}$d. per lb on cheese. To finance the producers over the long period of waiting until sales are effected overseas, advances are made to them through the dairy factories upon the security of the produce supplied.

Limited or Absolute Control

Provision is made for assuming either limited or complete control. Under limited control produce would be exported under licence of the Board, the control of the method of selling at the London end being left to the factories and dairy companies concerned. This system would give the Board control over quality, regularity of supply and continuity of shipping arrangements. Complete or absolute control requires, in addition to the licensing of export, that all produce must be placed unconditionally in the hands of the Board. Shipment, insurance, freight, storage, port of destination, dealers and sale price are entirely at the discretion of the Board, which, after deducting the necessary charges, returns to the producer the balance of the price obtained. All produce is in this way pooled, and each factory receives its returns according to the grade and quantity accredited before export.

As required by the Act, notice of intention to institute absolute control was given by the Board, and on September 1, 1926, the Board assumed absolute control of the dairy produce exported. This measure was continued for less than a year. On July 1, 1927, the Board reverted to limited control. The story of that momentous year is worth detailed study.

With unusually heavy stocks on its hands, following a record reason, and with a curtailed demand in Britain following the short General Strike and more protracted coal strike, the Board commenced its policy of absolute control. For a period prices rose steadily, merchants taking advantage of the low prices to purchase stocks for an increase in demand, which it was anticipated would follow the coal strike. An increase in price was noted in a few weeks from 144s. to 174s. per cwt. In the months of December, January and February the Board announced weekly minimum prices below which New Zealand butter was not to be sold. At the price fixed the demand proved inactive, and reductions which were made in two weeks, and which brought the figure to 160s. per cwt., had little result. A struggle had developed. The trade was obviously strongly organized in opposition to what it classed as " price fixation " in the interests of the New Zealand producer. After some four months of this experiment the London Agency of the Board advised its abandonment, and in March the Board decided as recommended. Great quantities of produce were in hand, however, and, to prevent speculation in buying up at the ruling low prices, arrangements were made to release them by degrees.

Policy under Limited Control

Finally, in July 1927, the Board reverted to a policy of limited control. It would now occupy itself simply with the following operations:

1. Regulation of shipments by adjustment of quantities throughout the season.
2. Supervision of loading, unloading and handling at both ends.

3. Collective and comprehensive insurance to cover all products.
4. Auditing of accounts and supplying particulars of sales and consignments by factories, if required by them.
5. Continuance of the use of the national brand and the term " finest " in the grading of produce.
6. An aggressive advertising policy.
7. Making of freight contracts.
8. Provision of suitable cold-storage accommodation at British ports.
9. Control of sales of whey and second-grade butter.

As the reserve fund, amounting to £50,000, was considered ample, the Board also decided to halve the levy on produce. Thus ended one of the most interesting phases of State planning in a section of New Zealand's distributive machinery. We may trace several factors contributing to the collapse of absolute control. First, there was the unfortunate choice of season for the commencement of operations, due to (a) considerable surplus of old season's stocks in store, with new season's stocks coming on, and (b) shortened demand owing to industrial unrest and contributing factors. Moreover, there was organized opposition by merchants in the trade in London, due partly to jealousy of the Board's activities and to the self-interest of merchants, and partly to an honest antagonism to price fixation as being likely to exploit consumers. Finally, there was the difficulty of maintaining contact with the London position. Exaggerated reports no doubt affected the producers and assisted in bringing about a decision by the Board which might not have been made in a calmer and more reasoning atmosphere. Of these three causes the last is probably the one which would offer the greatest obstacle under any circumstances. While it is conceivable that the other two could be overcome by means of forethought and tact, it would appear that the third must always remain a great difficulty.

The system of limited control is now functioning with considerable success, and very little opposition is now shown in New Zealand to the operations of the Board. An important recent development is the demand which sprang up in the early part of 1933 for a restriction upon the quantities of dairy produce, both foreign and Dominion, which were entering the British markets.

The Ottawa Conference (1932), which was attended in an advisory capacity by members of both the Meat and Dairy Control Boards, gave a decided indication that the Dominions would not favour quantitative restrictions upon their produce. In view of this the British Government was slow to press for restrictions upon Dominion dairy produce even when the problem of over-supply had become acute. When, however, Dominion representatives approached the British Government with suggestions for a 25 per cent. restriction upon foreign dairy produce, to ease the position, the Government replied with a proposal for a 12 per cent. restriction upon foreign and a 6 per cent. restriction upon Dominion produce.

The Sydney Conference

This did not find favour with the Dominions, and in April 1933 a conference of members of the New Zealand and Australian Dairy Export Control Boards was held in Sydney. There considerable unanimity was shown. Though at the opening there was a minority of the Australian Dairy Board which favoured restriction, as a result of the discussions a very large majority voted against it. Thus both Boards —as representing the industry in the two Dominions—are now committed to oppose restriction. Judging by recent cablegrams, however, the British Minister of Agriculture is anxious to renew with the Dominions the debate on this issue.

At the conclusion of the Sydney Conference great satisfaction was expressed with the results obtained. On the question of regularization of supplies from both Dominions it was generally agreed that some co-operation would be of value. Co-operation in freight and insurance contracts was also favourably entertained, although the New Zealand members did not anticipate any great advantage. The extension of control by the closer working of the New Zealand and Australian Boards, affecting, as it does, a large proportion of the supply to the British market, embodies an important advance in the rationalization of marketing. It was brought about by the supply exceeding the quantity that could be profitably marketed. It is possible that the Sydney Conference foreshadows some degree of centralized marketing control of the Empire's primary products, thus forging another link in that chain around the British Empire whose first links are discernible in such organizations as the Empire Marketing Board and in such Empire consultations as the Ottawa Conference.

THE FRUIT EXPORT CONTROL BOARD

The Voluntary Principle

In the year 1924 the fruit growers of the Dominion, no doubt encouraged by the example of the Meat and Dairy Export Control

Boards, made representations to Parliament which resulted in the setting up of the Fruit Export Control Board.

For purposes of representation, the Dominion is divided into provinces, and the growers in each province decide by personal vote whether they will put themselves under the control of the Board. A favourable vote of 70 per cent. is required to bring a province under the Act, and at any time a province may petition itself out of control by obtaining the requisite percentage (70) of exporters, such petition not taking effect until the conclusion of the season current. Herein lies a most important distinction between this and the other Control Board Acts. A much greater freedom is given to growers, and dissatisfaction with the policy of the Board can be put to the test by the use of the power granted to contract out. No other Act makes this provision. Until recently the fruit growers of Otago, representing some 5 to 10 per cent. of the Dominion growers, have been the only section which has remained outside the control of the Board. Otago has been operating separately through the ordinary channels.

Provinces accepting the control are each entitled to members on the Board, selected by the vote of the growers. Representation on the Board is more or less proportional to the quantity exported from the provinces concerned. The Government is represented by two nominated members. Growers' representatives retire for re-election every three years.

The finances of the Board are derived from a levy per case arranged each year according to need. Individual growers may secure advances upon the security of their produce pending the sale of the fruit overseas, this being made possible through bank credit consequent upon Government guarantee. Thus the Board has removed one of the great difficulties of the fruit trade—the endless competition of agents in offering " advances " to growers in order to obtain their fruit.

Early this year (1933) arrangements were set afoot to enable the marketing of the whole Dominion supply of fruit through the Board to be undertaken by a single firm of wholesale merchants on the British markets. The province of Otago, however, is not wholly under the scheme. In return for concessions on the part of the firm, all supplies will be put into their hands for disposal. It was the opinion of the Board that employing a number of agents tended to cause overlapping in distribution and consequent competition in selling. Limitation of the number of agents employed had previously been practised, and the policy is now carried to its logical conclusion—that is, limitation to one firm with numerous sub-agencies.

Otago exporters representing the major portion of fruit exported from that province have now agreed to join with the Board under the new distribution scheme, and it is anticipated that some 120,000 cases of Otago fruit, out of a total of 140,000 cases, will be exported through the Board. This brings practically the whole of the export fruit under its selling policy.

Government Guarantee and Pooling

An important development in the fruit industry has been the provision of a guaranteed price by the New Zealand Government. In the first year of the Board's operations the guarantee was set at 1d. per lb net. In the next season the basis was changed to 11s. 6d. per case gross, to simplify accountancy calculations. The guarantee has varied about that level, and is at present established for 1933 at 10s. 6d. on the two highest grades, and 7s. on other grades. There is no doubt that the Government guarantee has been of inestimable value to the industry. The security provided has greatly encouraged production. It has facilitated the financing of shipments and the making of advances to growers.

An indication of the degree to which the Government has been called upon to redeem its guarantee is given in the following figures, which show the claims made under the guarantee for the last six years:

1927 .	.	.	.	.	No claims
1928 .	.	.	.	.	·089d. per case
1929 .	.	.	.	.	·0017d. „
1930 .	.	.	.	.	·88d. „
1931 .	.	.	.	.	3·28d. „
1932 .	.	.	.	.	·2d. „

Upon a basis of guarantee involving an average of 11s. per case the claims appear almost negligible. In order to protect the Government, and show appreciation of the guarantee, growers were obliged to pay in 1932 the sum of 1½d. per case extra levy to establish a protective fund upon which first calls would be made in the payment of guarantee claims. This levy was a prior condition of the Government guarantee.

Another important feature of the fruit industry is the development of a pooling system. In 1928 a vote was taken throughout the industry to ascertain whether there was a definite wish for pooling. The Auckland district was the only one to carry the proposal; its fruit was therefore pooled through the 1928 season. The results proved satisfactory. At the end of 1929, after two seasons of pooling, another vote taken in Auckland showed an overwhelming majority of 102 to 11 to retain pooling. Auckland's lead was followed by several other districts, until in the 1931 season all provinces had organized their own pools. The principle is still being extended, with certain districts dividing into subdistricts for pooling purposes. With its equalization of returns in accord with grade, variety and size, and the sharing of risk, the pooling system thus seems to be firmly established.

THE HONEY EXPORT CONTROL BOARD

In 1924 the honey producers requested the setting up of the Honey Export Control Board, on similar lines to the earlier boards. From 1914 the honey export business had been developed and almost wholly controlled by the New Zealand Co-operative Honey Producers Association Ltd., whose export marketing policy was to standardize and sell in retail packages. Under this system New Zealand honey attained a very favourable reputation overseas. This reputation was threatened by honeys inferior to the standard being offered to the British public. The Board was set up to control distribution, to eliminate the mixing of New Zealand with other honeys, and other practices detrimental to its reputation.

The Board consists of three members (two producers' representatives elected biennially and retiring alternately, and one appointed by the Government). The Government representative must always be present at the meetings. The Board does not exercise any control over prices and has no responsibility for the sale of honey. It simply controls export in the usual way, and sees that no honey is exported unless consigned to the Board's European agents, who distribute to the trade. The Honey Producers Association continued to act as exporters under the supervision of the Board until early in 1933. It has now gone out of business, and the Board (in accordance with a request made by the National Beekeepers Association) proposes to take full control of exports. The actual position will probably be little changed. The office work previously undertaken by the Association simply falls upon the shoulders of the Board. The exact manner and scope of control is still under consideration, but no revolutionary changes are expected.

THE KAURI GUM EXPORT CONTROL BOARD

Representations by those concerned in the industry led to the passing in 1925 of the Kauri Gum Control Act, and the appointment in 1927 of the Export Control Board. It consisted of five members: two appointed by the Government, one by the exporters, and two elected by vote of the licensed gum diggers (one representing the northern and one the southern district).

The objects of the Board, as outlined in the first annual report, 1928, are to encourage production; to prohibit adulteration; to eliminate unnecessary costs between producer and manufacturing user of kauri gum; to prevent abuses and encourage new and better methods of production, cleaning, drying and grading; and to ensure regular and consistent supplies to the world markets.

Although very full powers were given it was decided to use only a limited number of them. The Board (under regulations gazetted in 1927) was empowered to make advances to producers up to 50 per cent. of the value of gum delivered to the Board. To meet expenses a levy of $\frac{3}{4}$ per cent. is made upon the value of the gum exported, and a brokerage charge of 5 per cent. is made upon gum bought and resold by the Board. In the hope of bringing into production areas of land previously worked over for bigger sizes, or not considered worth working owing to the broken and dirty state of the gum, the Board in 1929 set up a gum-cleaning plant for the treatment of poorer grades of gum. The plant was provided under a loan of £3150 from the Government. In 1929 reductions in freight rates, averaging about 5s. per ton, were obtained. These were expected to save the industry £1250 in one year, which was, roughly, the amount realized by the Board's annual levy.

During the last two years the industry has been affected by the prevailing depression and the competition of tung oil, copal and dammar. The result is reflected in the Board's finances. Its revenue both from the levy and from commission obtained as broker between the producers and the buyers fell off considerably, while the expenditure for storage of accumulated stocks increased. Requests were made to the Government for financial assistance, but it was finally decided, in July 1932, that the Board be disbanded. Although not legally abolished, it has practically ceased to function. Its affairs are being wound up, and there is little likelihood of its revival in the future. The present position is, however, very little changed from that under the Board. As full control was never exercised the cessation of the Board's functions makes very little difference to exporters.

THE WHEAT PURCHASE BOARD

In January 1933 an Order in Council established a body to be known as the Wheat Purchase Board. This Board consists of nine members: four appointed by the Minister of Industries and Commerce on the recommendation of the Wheat Marketing Agency Company, Ltd., as representatives of the wheat growers; four appointed on the same recommendation as representatives of the flour millers; and one appointed by the Minister to act as chairman.

The functions of the Board are to control the purchase and marketing, both internally and externally, of all except " free " wheat in New Zealand. Free wheat is that which has been rejected by the Board as not up to f.a.q. (fair average quality) milling wheat standard; wheat which has been resold by the Board for gristing into wheat products for human consumption only; and wheat resold to an intending grower, broker, or seed merchant for seed purposes only. Thus the Board controls the purchase and resale of all f.a.q. milling wheat in New Zealand. All purchases and sales of wheat by the Board are made through the agency of brokers appointed by the Board, each broker being authorized to act in a particular district only, and to operate upon prices set from time to time by the Board for various varieties and qualities of wheat. The brokers receive $\frac{1}{2}$d. per bushel from the Board as commission upon either purchase or sale.

Although not primarily designed to control export or import, the Board has already taken steps to maintain internal supply and price-levels by importing f.a.q. milling wheat from Australia before the commencement of the New Zealand milling season, and by controlling the export of a part of the unusually bounteous crop of wheat harvested during the early months of 1933. There appears every evidence that the rational planning which is the objective of this newest of the New Zealand Boards will provide a definite improvement from the point of view of growers, flour millers, consuming public and all concerned in the industry.

CONCLUSION

It may now be advisable to sum up the operations of the various boards and the extent of their success. Their aims have been much the same as those of every organization, co-operative or otherwise, which has set out to organize and rationalize a great primary industry. These may be summed up as:

(1) Organized marketing of all produce under one control.
(2) Regulation of shipment to prevent gluts or shortages on overseas markets.
(3) Bargaining in bulk to reduce unit expenses in freight, insurance, etc.

333

(4) Supervision of handling at both ends, to minimize loss through deterioration, etc.
(5) Establishment of overseas agencies to keep touch with the market.
(6) Supervision of production to maintain quality.
(7) Encouragement of improvement in quality, by means of premiums, competitions, etc.
(8) Research to improve quality, check deterioration in transit, storage, etc.
(9) Extension of advertising, selection of national brand and similar selling measures.

There seems little doubt that these aims have, in the main, been achieved, with advantage not only to the producer but also to the consumer.

The methods by which the various boards have sought to attain their objects may be set out as follows:

At producer's end:

(a) Limited control of export with power to districts to contract out from control of the Board.
(b) Control of all export by means of licence from the Board.

At consumer's end:

(c) Limited control, to arrange for regularization of shipments, bulk bargaining, etc., and to provide licences, but to do no more than disembark the produce overseas into the agents' hands.
(d) Absolute control, including complete ownership, marketing, pooling and sale of the produce.

Advantages and Disadvantages

The advantages and disadvantages of each type of organization may be shortly summarized:

In (a) we find the theoretical advantage that the element of compulsion is absent. Thus opposition is reduced and the influence of malcontents is removed from the Board's activities. Opposed to this is the argument that outsiders are thus enabled to profit by the operations of the Board without cost to themselves. This constitutes a serious weakness, conditioned, however, in the case of the Fruit Board, by the fact that the outsiders are almost negligible in number, and that it has been definitely found profitable to contract in for the numerous advantages accruing. Freedom of choice has, however, operated in assisting to gain the good will of the producers, and from this angle has proved of considerable value.

In (b) we find the analogous argument that by compulsory control of the whole supply the possibility of outsiders reaping the benefit of the operations of the Board is eliminated. Greater control is effected also over the supply on overseas markets, as unregulated shipment from any large body of outside producers might easily cause small gluts or shortages, with an adverse effect upon the prices obtained by the whole industry. On the whole, it appears that for most industries complete control of the supply is definitely a valuable asset.

From the overseas side it appears that (c) is the safer and wiser policy. While we can by no means conclude that the policy outlined in (d) is bound to fail under any circumstances, there can be little doubt that the experience of the Dairy Control Board while venturing upon absolute control has demonstrated that few, if any, industries are prepared at present for such a policy.

A new departure which may point the way to a method which will embody the essential features of both (c) and (d) is now being considered by the Fruit Board. The delegation of the functions of control over the marketing end into the hands of a private concern, while it may appear to be a distinct departure from the ideals of the Board, will provide new information and experience which may be of service in the ultimate solution of the major problem.

It is apparent that New Zealand has organized a system of rationalized marketing for its primary producers which has achieved a measure of success. Would it be too much to hope for the institution in Britain and other countries of elementary measures in marketing control by consumers to enable them to share the benefits between producer and actual consumer? The vision of a series of consumers' co-operative control boards, operating to extend the benefits of the Producers' Board, is foreshadowed by the development in the fruit industry, where a private concern is being offered the chance of undertaking just those functions which a consumers' control board might reasonably be expected to deal with.

An indication of the confidence with which the control schemes are viewed in New Zealand was the introduction of a bill in the 1933 session of Parliament to create yet another Board. This was to be the Poultry Producers' Board, to provide subsidies to producers on the basis of their egg export. A technical detail held the bill up in committee, and it was shelved when Parliament rose a few days later. This action of poultry producers indicates that rationalized planning is likely to extend still further in New Zealand's affairs, where considerable scope still remains.

335

CHAPTER X

CONTROL OF PRIMARY COMMODITIES IN AUSTRALIA

by G. L. Wood

THE CLASH OF DEVELOPMENTAL POLICIES

BOTH in effect and in intention it is true to say that Australia has been implementing an N.R.A. policy for close on thirty years. Having regard to the essentials of reconstruction, reform and recovery which N.R.A. implies, and allowing also for both differences in scale and in urgency of operation, the facts are that planned national development in Australia is generically similar to the reorientation now taking place in the economic life of the United States. Two cautions are necessary, however, before accepting any sweeping generalization. In the first place, the problems of development in the two countries differ widely in character; and, in the second, dependence upon world conditions is much greater in Australia. Nevertheless, in the attempts to secure a balanced development of primary and secondary industries, and in the general consideration given to the interests of industrial employees, there is to be discerned a broad similarity in the two plans.

The general principles which have been responsible for the partly voluntary, partly compulsory, regulation of the production and export of primary commodities in Australia are, as yet, largely unformulated. Many times during nearly four decades of planned industrial development, either lack of co-ordination or positive inconsistency has been noticeable. This situation has led to attempts to buttress weak positions, or to reconcile the interests of one section of producers who have been harshly treated with those of other sections who have been specially privileged. In its economic aspects, and those are all we are now considering, this situation has resulted in a continuous contest between protected and unsheltered industries, which has tended to dominate the political life of the Commonwealth.

Contrasted with this internal pressure of forces towards a balanced economy is the external pressure exerted upon national production by an overseas debt of approximately £600,000,000, or measured in Australian currency 2400 million dollars. The service of this debt specializes export industries, for the greater part, in the production of goods suited for world markets. Restricted by this dependence upon world trade, Australian statesmanship has attempted to steer a middle course between a free-trade policy consistent with a thoroughgoing specialization in primary industry, on the one hand, and a " whole-hog " policy of protection necessary to secure the maximum of diversity and self-sufficiency on the other.

The report of the Commonwealth Grants Commission presented in July 1934 emphasizes the contradictory nature of Australian developmental policies, and calls attention to the problems of the primary as opposed to the secondary industries of the Commonwealth.[1] In particular, the burden of a tariff system designed to expand manufacturing is felt as a deterrent to rural expansion, and the reconciliation of these policies has become Australia's supreme political problem.

The Grants Commission declared in plain blunt language that a tariff which extracts from export industry a substantial subsidy must add seriously to the disabilities of both rural producers and rural

[1] Extracts from *Report of Grants Commission*, pp. 57-58:

" It follows that, if Australia were devoted solely to primary production, the total population it would carry would be small. The committee of economists which inquired into the tariff in 1929 suggested that, with all ancillary industries, the population might not have amounted to more than 2 millions. Moreover, the consuming power of such a population would be small, and an extremely large proportion of its production would have to be exported. The result would have been a badly balanced community, almost entirely dependent on the chances of the export market determined by conditions on the other side of the world. Such a population might be an optimum population so far as production per head is concerned, but it could hardly call itself independent from the economic point of view, and it is doubtful whether the conditions would exist for the normal political and social life of a British community.

" These facts led to the policy which the states contend *is the main cause of their disabilities—the policy of protection*. . . .

" The policy of protection was, therefore, in every sense a development policy. This method of development involved increased costs for other production, and the main burden settled upon export industry. The chief export industries, wheat and wool, had been able to bear this burden, but there was evidence at the time of the report that the burden of excess costs of the tariff was becoming oppressive.

" It will thus be seen that the policy of protection has been adopted by the people as a means of developing the full potentialities of the continent. . . .

" It follows that, in so far as the *establishment of secondary industry involves a subsidy from the community, which falls with especial severity on export industry*, there is a clash of interests between secondary industry and the interests which depend upon primary industry. Moreover, the secondary industries tend to be developed in the Eastern States. These are nearer the great coal-fields, and have the larger populations, and, as they had an early start, the modern tendency to concentration tends to make these industries even larger. The more sparsely settled outer states could never establish these industries except at great cost to themselves. As a result the clash between the interests of primary and secondary industries tends to grow into a clash between the more largely populated eastern states of Victoria and New South Wales and the sparsely settled marginal states of South Australia, Western Australia and Tasmania."

Y

producing states. " Moreover," it asserted, " as one developmental activity, that connected with land settlement, is in the hands of the States, while the other developmental instrument, the tariff, is controlled by the Commonwealth, there is a lack of consistency and co-ordination in the two policies. There is almost a competition between the two factors of development; each frustrates the effect of the other; *the burdens created by the one make the protection required by the other the greater, so that the clash becomes more intense as each protective effort grows.*" It is in this situation that the explanation of most of the control exercised over the production and export of primary commodities in Australia has to be sought.

FUNDAMENTAL SOCIAL AND POLITICAL FACTORS

The clash of policies outlined above originates, however, from causes more deeply seated in national thought than was there indicated. Beneath the purely economic framework, the basic structure of social objectives must be discerned. It is these national aspirations that are working themselves out largely through economic policies, and they are responsible for much of the inconsistency in the economic organization of the Commonwealth. Looked at in this light, the " White Australia " policy, the system of wages fixation and the tariff are merely instruments being used to promote nationally desirable, but often uneconomic, ends. Unless these underlying causes are understood it is difficult to appreciate the strength of the forces to which Australian governments are subjected, or to interpret properly the growing number and range of expedients deliberately designed to preserve national standards.

The three main policies which have been mentioned must, therefore, be examined in their relation to the control of primary commodities. The " White Australia " policy, in the first place, is the expression of a plan for racial homogeneity. Australia has, however, constantly to face the criticism that the tropical north is being kept undeveloped. The facts are quite otherwise. In order to induce white labour to undertake the tasks of tropical settlement, the people of Australia have, in effect, chosen to subsidize the state of Queensland, and to pay the workers employed higher wages for the climatic discomfort involved. Such tropical industries as the production of sugar, cotton, bananas and pineapples are affected by the specific protection extended to them. As a result the coastal area of Northern Queensland carries a white population of 110,000, and this represents the greatest experiment in white-man development of the tropics to be found in the world.[1]

The second influence is the system of wage fixation which has developed from the national resolve that the standard of living of the ordinary working man shall be kept as high as possible. This general objective has many effects upon the relations between primary and secondary industries and, in particular, upon the prices obtained in the home market for their respective outputs. The widespread notion that the farmer suffers under this policy because of higher labour costs entirely overlooks compensatory advantages due to the higher purchasing power of workers in factory industries. As a matter of fact, and regarding these factors only, the Australian farmer probably enjoys a net balance of advantage.

The third and, economically considered, the most difficult factor is the tariff policy of the country. Regarded merely as the instrument for securing diversity of occupations and national self-sufficiency, the costs of the tariff have been the cause of serious political controversy for many years. In Australia, as in the United States, the tariff has been responsible for the emergence of a third political force—the Country Party—in both State and Federal politics. Owing to the disabilities of farmers, especially during depressed world conditions, the Country Party has become more self-assertive and less inclined to co-operate with the other two major parties. Thus, the " White Australia " policy, the fixation of wages and tariff policy have constantly to be borne in mind if the expedients aimed at control of production or export of primary products are to be properly estimated and understood.

THE PRESSURE OF EXTERNAL INDEBTEDNESS

In the light of this clash of domestic policies, something more must be said concerning the control exercised over economic conditions by the overseas debt. Fluctuations in world prices exercise a supremely important effect upon Australian national income. The urge to compensate for a fall in the *value* by an expansion of the *volume* of exports is explained by national emergency; and, in turn, the resistance to the restriction of either production or export, on the one hand, and the desire to extend special assistance to export producers, on the other, can be easily understood. In this way general assistance to export producers by way of exchange depreciation is justified and endorsed

[1] See R. W. Cilento, *The White Man in the Tropics*, Commonwealth Department of Health Service Publication.

339

by all parties; and depreciation of currencies inevitably promotes price-cutting in certain foreign markets. The competitive aspects of exchange manipulation, and the retaliatory measures which it provokes, need only be mentioned in passing in order to draw attention to a fresh crop of difficulties which spring up as defensive measures against unemployment and depression are devised and adopted.

Thus, especially after the onset of depression in 1930, the policy of reserving home markets for home producers was strengthened. The principle of compensating the unsheltered export producers, by extending to them subsidies collected from home consumers by raising the home price of export goods above world parity, had been put into operation long before the onset of the economic crisis. As industry after industry got into difficulties after 1930, the temptation to apply this palliative was irresistible. At the present moment wool, metals and a few minor products are the only Australian export commodities to which the extension of a so-called " bounty " is neither in operation nor in contemplation.

SUBSIDIZATION OF RURAL PRODUCTION

Assisting home producers by means of subsidies of any kind is merely taxing consumers by making them pay higher prices for that part of the output of unsheltered industry which is produced at home. The attempt to secure higher returns for farmers than those warranted by world prices is, in essence, an attempt to bring their costs and prices into something like equilibrium. The objective is, therefore, to maintain the stability of home produce not by lowering the tariff—*i.e.* lowering costs—but by raising returns to the farmer by some direct method which will relieve acute political situations caused by the disabilities of rural producers. These disabilities are admitted by all sections, but the chief difficulty is to discover the correct compromise—*i.e.* that which will afford relief without unduly penalizing the home consumer, on the one hand, and without saddling secondary industry with higher wages due to rising costs of living, on the other. In the end too the added costs come back in part to rural industry, and the vicious circle is complete.

The disadvantages—part real, part apparent—under which rural producers labour have, under the conditions outlined, been responsible for the growth of an unco-ordinated series of direct and indirect subsidies somewhat sardonically entitled " bounties." The general objective, as was shown earlier, is to compensate the farmer for being forced to produce under a rigid system of fixed tariff and wage costs and to sell a great proportion of his output in unsheltered world markets. To implement the policy of paying bounties to specific industries three types of control have grown up, all operated by keeping domestic prices above world parity. These types are: (1) Controlled Production—*e.g.* sugar and rice; (2) Controlled Export—*e.g.* dried fruits; (3) Controlled Import—*i.e.* through the tariff; and each needs some further examination for our purposes.

THE FACTS OF CONTROL

The first report of the Royal Commission on Wheat [1] states clearly the reasons for the intensification of interest in plans for subsidizing or controlling rural production in Australia: " Throughout the world and particularly throughout those portions of the world where industrialism is an important factor, the maladjustment of internal economic conditions and international relations has forced the governments to extreme measures to keep their people employed and to reduce to a minimum the flow of credits to other countries in payment for primary products. . . . Import restrictions and/or quotas, summarily applied, combined with price fixation within each country have reduced markets for wheat from the main wheat-exporting countries seriously. . . . Any forecast as to the possibility of abandonment or modification of the policy of maintaining high home-consumption prices in European countries is impossible. . . . The price of wheat in certain European countries, calculated in Australian currency has been maintained at figures varying from 7s. to as high as 15s. per bushel."

The key to control of primary commodities in most exporting countries to-day is to be found in situations like this; and the arguments advanced in favour of some control scheme for wheat, such as a compulsory pool and a fixed home price, may be applied to most other primary products. " Pending an improvement in the general level of wheat prices . . . considerable aid to the industry is essential. . . . In the past three years Australia has endeavoured to hold the position by financial contributions from the Commonwealth and State governments, which have been in the form of annual grants based upon no particular policy or guarantee to the industry. Future assistance should be placed upon a systematic basis in justice to the industry and to the peace of mind of the community." Thus do expedients develop into

[1] Presented August 1934 to the Federal Government Chairman, Sir Herbert Gepp.

permanent policies, and there is little doubt that the growing extent of organized interference with the flow of trade commodities in almost every country is merely exacerbating a condition which it sets out in the first place to cure.

The Australian community is to-day paying subsidies to the producers of sugar, dried fruits, butter, cheese, bananas, rice, butter, tobacco, maize, pineapples, and several other commodities. The Royal Commission on Wheat declared that, " Without doubt wheat must be added to this list so long as the principle applies generally to so many other primary products, which principle after all is only the application of the policy of protection to the primary industries." They, therefore, recommended, " That the policy applied to most other rural industries of ensuring better returns by means of the principle of a home-consumption price for that part of the product consumed within the Commonwealth should be applied to the wheat industry," and that a subsidy amounting to £4,000,000 should be paid to growers in the 1934-1935 season.

Typical control schemes now in operation may be noted:

1. *The Sugar Agreement* [1]

The Commonwealth and Queensland Governments agreed in 1925 that the embargo on the importation of foreign sugar, which was first introduced in September 1915, should be extended for three years from September 1, 1925. The home-consumption price for the raw sugar was fixed at £27 per ton, less £1 per ton to defray administrative and general expenses of the Sugar Board, and to provide special concessions to certain consumers of sugar. For the portion exported the price was fixed at a much lower figure. The embargo was later extended until August 1, 1931, on practically the same terms as before. In response to representations that the " sugar bounty " was too expensive for the benefits received, the Commonwealth Government appointed a Committee of Inquiry in 1930, to report on the industry. The Committee represented the various interests concerned, and its reports were made available in 1931. The renewal of the sugar agreement with certain modifications was recommended, and the terms of the present agreement differ little from those previously in force, particularly as regards the embargo on imports and fixation of prices. The assistance to the fruit industry has, however, been increased from £205,000 per annum to £315,000 by way of grant from the sugar industry. The agreement was signed on June 1, 1931, and remains in force for a period of five years from September 1, 1931. In 1932, however, conferences were arranged between the Commonwealth Government and representatives of the industry, and it was decided to provide for a reduction in the retail price of sugar by ½d. per lb from January 1, 1933, and that the reduced retail price of 4d. per lb should continue until the end of the period of the agreement (August 31, 1936). It was recom-

---

[1] As set out in the *Commonwealth Yearbook* No. 26.

mended also that the amount of assistance to the fruit industry should be reduced by £115,000 to £200,000. It should be noted that the acreage planted to sugar is controlled by a policy of " assignment," which means that growers have practically to take out a permit to plant.

2. *Dried Fruits* [1]

The Dried Fruits Export Control Act, 1924, was passed by the Commonwealth Parliament, at the instance of the dried fruit industry, to organize the overseas marketing of Australian dried fruit. The Dried Fruits Control Board consists of seven members, including four growers' representatives, and controls the export, and the sale and distribution after export, of Australian sultanas, currants and lexias. " In conjunction with its London agency the Board has improved the overseas marketing and increased the demand for Australian dried fruits. Its system of appraisement has resulted in more satisfactory realizations, and its methods of ensuring continuity of supply, regulating shipments, advertising and securing reductions in freight and insurance have benefited the industry considerably. Regulations were framed providing for the issue, under certain conditions, of licences to exporters to enable Australian sultanas, currants and lexias to be shipped overseas.

" The regulation of sales and fixation of home-consumption prices for dried fruits is in the hands of the Australian Dried Fruits Association, which has, in addition, power to regulate interstate transfers. The prices fixed for home consumption are somewhat higher than those realized on exports overseas."

3. *Dairy Produce* [2]

The control in the case of dairy produce is rather complex. Mention must be made of three aspects of regulation:

(i.) The Dairy Produce Export Control Act, 1924, introduced at the request of the dairying industry, was passed by the Commonwealth Parliament with the object of organizing the marketing overseas of Australian dairy produce. Regulations were approved providing for a poll of producers to enable the Act to operate and for the election of members to the Dairy Produce Control Board as in the case of dried fruits. " This Board, consisting of thirteen members, of whom nine are producers' representatives, was appointed under the Act to supervise the export, and the sale and distribution after export, of Australian dairy produce. In conjunction with its London agency the Board has improved organization on overseas markets, ensured continuity of supply, regulated shipments, stabilized overseas prices, obtained reductions in overseas freight and insurance, and participated in an advertising campaign in the United Kingdom. Provision was made for the issue, under certain conditions, of licences to exporters to permit of butter and cheese being exported from Australia."

(ii.) The Dairy Produce Export Charges Acts, 1924 and 1929, provide for the imposition of a levy on all butter and cheese exported from the Commonwealth to cover administrative expenses of the Board, and for advertising and other purposes.

[1] The situation for dried fruits is outlined in *Yearbook* No. 22.
[2] The situation for this commodity also is outlined in *Yearbook* No. 22.

(iii.) A scheme for stabilizing the prices of butter and cheese, or perhaps more accurately a valorization scheme, known as the Paterson Plan, was introduced in January 1926. The working of the scheme, which is purely voluntary, is controlled by a body known as the Australian Stabilization Committee. Provision is made for levies on all butter and cheese produced in Australia sufficient to pay a bounty of not less than 3d. per lb on butter. The levy has been as high as 4¼d. and as low as 2½d.

THE COSTS AND LIMITS OF CONTROL

The essentials of the situation may now be summarized.

Australian export production is dominated by price fluctuations in overseas markets, whereas costs of production are influenced by wages and tariff policy. The attempt by unsheltered export industries to counteract rising costs due to tariff revision, in particular, has been responsible for schemes resulting in bounties and subsidies on the one hand, and in monopoly of the home market with regulation of domestic prices on the other. These schemes represent a more or less successful attempt to secure the benefit of a protective tariff for export industries. Prices for primary products in Australia would, in the absence of regulation, tend towards world price parity less shipping expenses to the overseas market. The resistance to natural price control of this sort by primary producers has been strengthened, especially in the post-war period, by the desire on the part of the Federal and State governments to placate rural interests, which were becoming increasingly exasperated by rising costs due to high protection for secondary industries. The emergency tariff measures of 1930-1931, formulated by the Scullin Government, intensified the pressure for relief to primary producers, and in this situation is to be found the cause of the dissatisfaction exhibited in recent months by country parties with the terms of the Ottawa agreement. The reactions to tariff policy from this angle form a rather confused picture because of independent action taken by Federal and State governments and by marketing organizations of various types in each state.

As far back as 1928, Professor L. F. Giblin [1] indicated an important difference between the usual objectives and devices of a protective tariff and this extension of the benefits of protection to export industries: " The object of protection is to raise the price received by the Australian producer for his goods so as to make it possible for those engaged in the industry to earn a decent living at the Australian standard. In the

---

[1] *Economic Record* (Marketing Supplement), 1928: " The Costs of Control."

ordinary protected industry there is no question of exports, and the raising of the price of the product for the Australian consumer to the required 'profitable price' is all that is required. But that is not enough in the case of an exporting industry. The price received for exports must also be raised, and this can be done only indirectly and at the expense of the Australian consumer, who, in consequence, must be called upon to pay a price higher than the 'profitable price,' in order that the return received for the total output of the industry, both home consumption and exports, may average out at the profitable price. Where exports are small in comparison with home consumption, the additional price required will be negligible, and it is in these circumstances that schemes of export and price control may be accepted with a light heart. As exports increase, this cost of protecting them increases, and it is at this stage that the cost of control schemes becomes an economic deterrent and a political irritant."

The methods of control adopted in Australia range, as we have seen, from restriction of actual production to organization of marketing, although both objectives are sometimes found within the scheme affecting one particular commodity. Actual restriction of acreage, by " assigning " land to be planted, may be supplemented by fixing the price for domestic consumption, as is done in the case of sugar. Purely marketing schemes range from voluntary or compulsory " pools " to organize the trade from the producer's end, as in the case of wheat, to schemes for controlling standards and distribution, as in the case of dried fruits. The control of some commodities—e.g. sugar, butter, dried fruits, meat—is organized on a Commonwealth basis; for some other products—e.g. wheat—each state has evolved its own scheme of handling. In some cases control is exerted in order to limit production to a volume approximating home consumption—e.g. rice, sugar; in others regulation has been established with the aim of stimulating and standardizing exports. Lastly, some production is closely linked with national developmental policy—e.g. wheat and dairying; in others racial and political factors influence the policy—e.g. sugar.

In so far as control represents a real cost totalling many millions a year to Australian consumers it is more or less willingly regarded as a sacrifice necessary to maintain social and racial objectives, rather than as tending to depress Australian living standards. Indeed, the special committee which conducted an exhaustive inquiry into the Tariff in 1929 [1] stated that Australian resources in relation to population were sufficient,

---

[1] *The Australian Tariff—An Economic Enquiry* (Melbourne University Press).

under the circumstances then prevailing, to carry the net burden without distress, and that " the same average income for the same population could not have been maintained without protection." The impact of depression has greatly complicated the situation, however, and another Tariff Inquiry is really overdue.

It is difficult to measure the order of the cost of control to the Australian consumer. Taking butter first, production for five years, 1927-1928 to 1931-1932, averaged 322 million and exports 156 million lb a year. Butter consumers in Australia are, therefore, paying about £2,750,000 a year to offset the costs of the tariff. The average production for dried fruits is about 57,000 tons a year, of which about 30,500 tons of raisins and 11,000 tons of currants, or 31,500 tons, a year were exported. Since the Australian price for raisins averaged 1½d. and for currants 2¼d. per lb above the export price the cost of control to the Australian consumer averages about £275,000 a year. In the case of sugar, production was stabilized at about 335,000 tons in 1930-1931, of which about 200,000 were exported, leaving 335,000 tons for home consumption. Until 1936 the wholesale price is fixed at £37, 6s. 8d. per ton. The average price for five years received by mills for raw sugar is £21, 10s., and as the overseas price may be taken at £11, 10s., Australian consumers paid about £3,500,000 a year to offset the costs of protection and to sustain an experiment in tropical settlement.[1] Wheat growers have been subsidized by the Federal Government by means of a bounty of 4½d. a bushel. Organizations for marketing wheat have been established in each state. Co-operative voluntary pools exist in New South Wales, Victoria, South Australia and Western Australia. The single compulsory wheat pool is established in Queensland, where the small crop is marketed by the State Wheat Board. The average production for ten years, 1921-1930, was 135,400,000 bushels per year, of which flour and wheat to the equivalent of 97,500,000 bushels a year were exported. Costs of subsidizing wheat probably total £4,000,000 a year; but unless the world price recovers this will be largely increased. In addition to these aids, privileges that are, in effect, monopolies of the home market are granted to rice, tobacco and wine by the devices of import restriction or subsidy, or both. Rice production is limited to home consumption, along the lines of the control in the case of sugar, while the tendency for tobacco is in the same direction by arrangement with the principal manufacturers

[1] *Vide* J. B. Brigden, *The Story of Sugar* (Queensland Bureau of Economics and Statistics).

and the Federal Government. The total costs of control to the consumers in Australia for the commodities examined are thus of the order of £11,000,000 a year.

Some limit to these methods of encouraging home production and protecting exports of primary commodities must of course exist. The home price cannot be raised for long above the costs of imported goods without producing an outcry from producers for higher protection. Although the device is one capable of wide application the question ultimately arises as to the point at which the assistance breaks down under its own weight. The answer to the problem is well stated by Professor Giblin.[1]

" The tendency is, as pointed out above, for such schemes to begin with general assent, when the exportable surplus is accidental and small, and the cost to the community negligible. The scheme, however, once adopted removes the proper economic check to the growth of the industry, and expansion takes place at the general expense up to the limits imposed by the tariff. When exports are much greater than home consumption, a very large increase must be put on home prices to give any substantial help to the industry."

What then will decide the issue in the final analysis? That raises a spectre of ultimate disaster. " The cost to the consumer must be paid for out of production, and in the last resort out of production for exports. The sheltered industries and occupations (including, of course, the professions), as well as the protected industries, are all supported by the exporting industries, and as these one by one themselves demand and receive protection, it looks as if the day were not far off when the whole burden would fall on wool. The vision that comes is of Australia as one enormous sheep bestriding a bottomless pit, with statesman, lawyer, miner, landlord, farmer and factory hand all hanging on desperately to the locks of its abundant fleece."

As we began this essay by drawing an analogy between the United States and Australia, we may conclude in the same manner. If world trade continues to contract, it would seem that Australia, like America, must choose between a general loosening of trade restrictions in order to stimulate the demand overseas for her primary commodities, and a general redistribution of population. If, for example, 70,000 wheat farmers produce 150 million bushels of wheat annually, and the export falls from 120 million to, say, 60 million bushels, the real economic problem would turn on the actual number of wheat growers that could

[1] *Economic Record* : " Costs of Control."

be continually employed in the industry, and the problem would not be confined to wheat-growing. All this simply means that the situation can be saved only by the concerted action of countries importing primary products, on the one hand, and the producers of those products on the other—the sort of co-operation, in short, that the World Economic Conference of 1933 was unable to agree upon. With the passing of another year, the urgency of the need for that action has not in any sense diminished.

CHAPTER XI

PETROLEUM CONTROL IN THE UNITED STATES

by Barnabas Bryan, jun.

INTRODUCTION

R ECENT discoveries of oil-fields and modern methods of extracting and refining petroleum have immensely increased the world supply of petroleum products.[1] At present the supply exceeds the demand to such an extent that it does not net what the producers consider a fair return on the capital invested. At the same time that it is an essential to the industrial system as the chief source of lubricants, petroleum is also an irreplaceable natural resource. Therefore, the control of oil production is of international importance from at least two points of view. For a nation that needs oil as a fuel essential for national defence, the main question may be the strategic location of reserves. The automotive and other industries which depend on gasolene are interested in an abundant supply at a relatively constant price. The investor has learned that uncontrolled individual exploitation of the supply of oil may mean the loss of a large part, or even all, of his investment; while to the oil producer himself an inequitable control may be as great a hazard as a speculative drilling of new wells.

The International Scope of the Oil Industry

Whatever means is attempted to secure the social control of oil production must, of necessity, be international in scope. The day is past when a nation or group of nations can control the oil trade of any region. With the opening of the Panama Canal, the oil resources of the whole world have become interdependent in a new way. To-day it is tanker rates, in the main, that govern the price differentials, and with the more recent improvement and enlargement of the Diesel-driven tank ships, differentials have lessened in greater degree than relative distances. Thus the oil-fields of the Caribbean and Gulf Ports have become almost as accessible to the Far East as are the fields of California. Owing to these advances in transportation, the pressure on prices of an excessive oil production anywhere has an immediate effect

---

[1] In thousand barrels, the average production of petroleum and its products was 541,733 in 1916-1920, as against 1,096,823 in 1926 and 1,418,723 in 1930. See also the United States figures in Appendix III.

on distant producing fields and on all deep-water markets. Thus the effort of Russia to improve its export balance by enlarged sales of kerosene and gasolene has a bearing on prices in India, and increases the difficulties of the independent producer in Oklahoma. In the importing countries of the Pacific area, available supply must be measured by the pressure of exports from any country which, because of new discoveries, or unbridled competition in crude-oil production, seeks to force its oil or oil products upon foreign markets. Such forces as these, because of their unsettling effect upon the industry as a whole, make the control of production imperative for the oil-producing countries and companies. The uncontrolled development of new high-pressure oil pools at any accessible point may destroy the profits of the oil industry throughout the world.

At the same time it must be recognized that the new facility of movement from field to market in itself gives added incentive to the development of production in many regions far in excess of the needs of their domestic markets and the known requirements of their steady foreign customers, leading to increased export and, eventually, to exhaustion of the oil supplies. An example of this acceleration and its consequences may be seen in Mexico. Here a too-rapid rise in production led to the early exhaustion of the gusher pools, and the sudden replacement in world markets of Mexican production by that of Venezuela.

It is thus apparent that the condition of the oil industry in any one area, such as the Pacific, is not dependent simply on the supplies of the neighbouring countries, of California, Peru, the Netherland East Indies, India, Japan and Sakhalin, but on all that which is accessible to the oil tanker. For example, oil products are being moved from the Baku fields of Russia to the consuming territory of India through the Black Sea and the Suez Canal, while at the same time the excess production of Rumania has invaded Russian provinces. While these movements are taking place in the crude-oil trade, refined products are being moved from the Netherland East Indies to Europe, from Persia to Australia, and from the Eastern United States to the Far East.

Unit Operation—a Prerequisite of Controlled Oil Production

In that the control of oil production must be on an international basis, it offers problems similar to those faced in the control of other essential raw materials. But the possibilities of control within each producing nation, upon which international action is predicated, are unusual, because of the peculiar nature of the occurrence of oil in the earth. Oil and gas are found together, in most cases, and are the only important natural resources which must be extracted in the liquid or gaseous form. This distinguishes the oil industry from mining and from the production of other raw materials. Hence, also, there cannot be applied to it the same laws of ownership, or the same procedure for control.

" As regards the geological character of oil production, it will be remembered that oil is found in subterranean porous rock formations in intimate association with gas and water. These substances have distributed themselves in their underground reservoir on a basis of their specific gravity, and remain in a delicate condition of equilibrium, frequently under great pressure. In a typical oil pool, gas is found in the uppermost part of the underground formation, oil beneath the gas, and water under the oil. Such a distribution represents a geological unit. Scientific development of such an oil pool, designed to secure a maximum of oil at a minimum of cost, would take as its point of departure the geological unit—the oil pool. It would endeavour to utilize in the most efficient manner possible the expansions of the gas and the movement of the water as expulsive agents in oil recovery." [1]

There is, to-day, general agreement among authorities on the importance of taking as the unit for economic exploitation the oil pool confined within a single geological structure, and on the impossibility of voluntary economic control of production on the basis of lesser units. The following official statement expresses this widely held belief:

" The data show conclusively that the conservation and efficient utilization of gas are of paramount importance in the conservation and economic production of oil. Gas dissolved in oil makes the oil more fluid, and more capable of movement through the pore spaces of the reservoir rock to the well. The energy stored in the same gas is the chief motive power behind the movement. The more gas, the easier the oil moves and the greater the force available to move it. To dissipate gas from an oil sand is to lessen the propulsive force and increase the need for it. The energy and solution values of an oil-field gas are of tremendous importance. The proper utilization of gas results in greater and more orderly recovery at lower cost. The data show that the way to use gas to the best advantage is to use it in its original state, and that the condition in a sand, once destroyed, can never be completely restored.

[1] G. W. Stocking, " Stabilization of the Oil Industry; its Economic and Legal Aspects," *American Economic Review*, vol. xxiii., No. 1, Supplement, March 1933, p. 55.

" The data show that many, probably most, of the best methods for gas utilization can be practised advantageously only when they can be applied systematically to a whole field; that competitive drilling in individual fields almost inevitably leads to gas waste and lessened ultimate oil production; and that either complete co-operation or unit operation is the ideal operating condition for the conservation of both gas and oil." [1]

Basis of Control in Principal Foreign Producing Countries

Outside the United States and Mexico, more than 300 million barrels of oil were in 1932 produced under unit operation—that is, with a system of operation controlling units no less than entire oil-fields comprised in a single geological formation. This was over 66 per cent. of the total produced by those countries, or 24·4 per cent. of the entire world production. In 1924 this percentage was 85 per cent., or 13·3 per cent. of the world production. During this interval, therefore, the total percentage of foreign production under unit control has decreased, while the proportion of unit production to total world production has increased.

A brief account of the conditions in the principal exporting countries will make this significant fact more concrete.

Venezuela, thus far, has only one field not under unit control, the La Rosa-Lagunilla region of Lake Maracaibu, where, fortunately for world reserves, the oil is stored in a fine sand which flows with the oil and chokes the wells if they are produced at full capacity. The other proven fields are in the hands of single companies in each case. Such drilling and other geological study as has been done so far suggest that this condition will continue.

In both Colombia and Peru, all present production is by unit operation, through ownership; and this is likely to apply also in the future to new fields that may be developed. In the Argentine, about one-half of the present oil production and of remaining oil reserves are in the hands of the Government.

In Sumatra, where all the oil of the Netherland East Indies is produced, there was an absolute monopoly until ten years ago, when an American company opened a new field by drilling deeper than usual. While this step hastened production, each field, as a unit, is in the hands of either the original company or the American concern.

[1] Federal Oil Conservation Board, *Report to the President*, Report III., February 23, 1929, p. 11.

In Sakhalin, the island off the coast of Siberia which is owned by Japan and Russia, the oil reserves have not yet been greatly developed, but may prove to be considerable. Here a problem of control definitely does exist. The division of the oil rights in North Sakhalin between Japan and Russia is by checker-boarding. If it happens that fields cross boundary lines of the subdivisions, the policy of one Power in regard to immediate production may cause irritation to the other. However, since on both sides the fields are Government-owned, so that but two parties are involved, this difficulty should be capable of friendly adjustment.

The U.S.S.R., which possesses immensely rich deposits in the Caspian region and elsewhere, is, of course, entirely under unit control through Government ownership of all natural resources.

Persia is the best example of scientific development and technical control of production through unit operation. Likewise the Irak concession will be handled by one company responsible to the Government, which, however, is in turn owned by several others of different nationality.

In Rumania and Poland there is peasant ownership of the land in very small tracts throughout the oil-fields, approximating the condition in the United States. But the small proprietors have sold their oil rights, and the operation of the fields is in the hands of larger companies, most of which are of foreign ownership.

This brief survey of the conditions in the principal nations involved in the international problem of petroleum production indicates that most of them are already so organized domestically that it would be possible to enforce within their borders an international agreement concerning production. However, in 1931, 62 per cent. of world production was in the United States, and 38·6 per cent. of world exports came from this country.[1] Therefore, " while stabilization of oil production in the United States is complicated by conditions in the world market, world-wide rationalization waits upon the United States." [2]

DEVELOPMENT OF THE OIL INDUSTRY IN THE UNITED STATES

Growth of the Industry

The history of the oil industry in the United States is a necessary background to any understanding of the origin of the movement toward

[1] Federal Oil Conservation Board, *Report to the President*, Report V., October 1932.
[2] J. H. Marshall and N. L. Meyers, " Legal Planning of Petroleum Production," *Yale Law Review*, vol. xxxi., No. 1, November 1931, p. 33.

z

control. Some of the difficulties confronting this movement, such as widespread ownership, are thrown into clear relief by the history of the industry.

With the initial opening of the Pennsylvania fields in 1859 the flood of oil might have foretold to a discerning observer the principal problems of to-day. The glut of oil and the inadequacy of the railroads as a means of moving crude oil indicated even then the need for some new means of handling an industry so different from any other known to mankind. The first result of the search for new methods of distribution was the invention of the pipeline for long-distance transportation. Then followed the discovery of oil seepages in many places and, very shortly after, the completion of the Standard Oil refining and marketing monopoly. The concentration of invention and organization that marked the rapid growth of this company proved sufficient to carry the industry through the period in which kerosene was its principal product. There was local movement of oil by canals, barges, and small ocean ships adapted to this use, but the largest quantity of oil was moved by pipeline, while foreign trade in petroleum products was chiefly through packaged goods.

The growing demand for gasolene in the years following 1910 put a strain on the old methods of organization and transportation. This culminated in the dissolution of the monopoly and the beginning of a period of destructive competition in refining, transportation and marketing.

The profits of the kerosene business facilitated the financing of new capital equipment, while the tremendous acceleration of the demand for gasolene obscured for nearly a generation the glaring defects of the industry's organization. The creation of new techniques was hastened in each branch of gasolene supply. The finding of oil changed from chance to semi-science; drilling methods and drilling materials advanced beyond expectations, both as to the speed of drilling and the depth attainable at low cost; refining methods doubled the amount of gasolene recovered from a barrel of oil; and transportation accelerated the supply through the building of competitive pipelines and improvements in tanker design.

The diversion of national effort to the World War accentuated the demand for both gasolene and fuel oil, decreased the energy previously available for development, and made possible scarcity prices through the fear of waning supply. This led the companies formerly associated in the Standard Oil Company to enter the business of crude-oil production, to ensure a supply for their refineries. At this time the American companies also invaded the foreign field in earnest. As a result, to-day, almost all the large oil companies are " complete " in the sense that they perform all four functions of supply: production, transportation, refining and marketing.[1] Only about one-quarter of the oil produced in the United States is not subject to the control of the refineries.[2]

The decline from the war-time pressure of demand was gradual until 1923, when the mechanism for continuous over-production was completed. The final developments were these: new discoveries of oil deposits were made in many foreign fields; production reached new depths—10,927 feet in California; a successful " cracking " process was developed, making commercially possible the synthesis of gasolene from practically any low-sulphur oil or refining residue, thus doubling the potential gasolene in the stocks of oil aboveground; transportation in bulk by pipeline and tank steamer was co-ordinated.

The Legal Basis of the Ownership of Oil

The rapidity with which this industry has exploited a natural resource about which relatively little was known has led to uneconomic forms of operation which have been supported and perpetuated by court decisions. Oil, from the start, has been a speculative industry. The risks of prospecting and drilling for new pools were borne at first by individuals. Even to this day there is no infallible method of locating oil without drilling for it. The adventurers in the early days did not have enough capital to buy all the land surrounding their drills. Therefore they were followed by land speculators, who sold small lots surrounding the " discovery " well. In many cases the purchasers of these lots were also making a gamble, and did not have the means to exploit their land. Therefore they in turn leased the land to an operator, on a royalty basis. This practice has led to the operation of oil lands in small plots by individual producers subject to a lease contract. These lease contracts almost always call for immediate drilling and constant production at the highest level possible. These requirements, which are the basic cause for the present over-production in the Amerian oil industry, are largely due to the legal interpretation of oil rights.

As the cumulative law of court decisions stands to-day, " if an

[1] See L. M. Logan, *Stabilization of the Petroleum Industry*, Norman, Okla., 1930, p. 22.
[2] See *Ibid.*, p. 98.

adjoining owner drills his own lands and taps a deposit of oil or gas extending under his neighbor's fields so that it comes into his well, it becomes his property." [1] The conception, " oil *or* gas," which is common to all decisions, shows a misconception of the facts of " oil *and* gas." The first statement of its kind by the United States Supreme Court was in a minor dispute concerning ten acres of land, with no indication that full technical knowledge of oil production was developed before the court. In this case, as in all later ones, court decisions have led back to the case of Brown *v.* Vandergrift, decided by the Pennsylvania Supreme Court in 1875.[2]

As Professor Summers states the case in his recent book, *Oil and Gas*, " some of the courts have in effect said that, because of the fluidity of oil and gas and their occurrence below the surface, they are like subterranean waters; others that, because oil and gas are minerals and are a part of the total physical aggregate land, they are like and cannot be differentiated from solid minerals; and still others say that, because of their ' fugitive and wandering existence,' oil and gas are like animals, *Feræ Naturæ*; and each group has drawn the conclusion that the legal status of oil and gas should be the same as those (of) substances with which it has compared them—and the reasons assigned are neither his ownership, qualified ownership, or non-ownership of the oil and gas *in situ*. When reasons so diverse result in the same conclusion, two situations become apparent: one, that there is error in some of the assigned reasons, and the other, *that the real reasons for the decisions were not disclosed*. The conception of oil and gas as fugitive wild animals is that which survives in present-day law." [3]

This law, known as " The Law of Capture," which amounts to " letters of marque," granted by the courts to landowners to take oil underground by force of capture, was highly desirable for a refining monopoly in that it assured an ample supply of raw material, while the monopoly could prevent that supply from having too drastic an effect on the price of refined products. When the monopoly was dissolved, and the component companies entered the production business, their lawyers failed or neglected to point out that, in developing oil, the companies were spending money for something that they could not own as reserves; and that, before doing so, they should in some way establish the ability to own oil *in situ*.

---

[1] B. Bryan, jun., " Oil Conservation by Court Decision," *Oil and Gas Journal*, December 1927.
[2] *Ibid.*   [3] *Ibid.*

PETROLEUM CONTROL IN THE U.S.A.

The Situation on Government Oil Lands

The Federal Government and the State Governments both are owners of vast amounts of oil land—the States in the land set aside for educational purposes, and the United States in Federal reserves and on Indian reservations. In the early years of the oil industry the Government was far from thoughtful in the conservation of the country's oil. Early Federal statutes in regard to the oil rights on Indian lands embodied all the possible evils of competitive production. They required that a certain amount of land be offered for oil lease each year. They limited the size of the tracts that might be leased by one operator; they required immediate exploitation to validate the lease; and they did not provide for a sliding scale of royalties, which alone makes possible the continued operation of wells after the first flush production is past. Not until 1909 was any action taken toward conservation. In that year, with the increasing fear of declining supplies, President Taft withdrew from lease the Government lands containing known reserves of oil. But not until much later was action taken to protect new discoveries on other land. In 1920 an Act allowed the reduction of royalties paid by lease-holders on low-production wells. In 1929 the Secretary of the Interior was authorized to refrain from issuing exploration permits if the demand for oil was not sufficient to justify it. This right was upheld in court.[1] Finally, in 1929, all further leases of Government lands were stopped.[2]

CONTROL OF OIL PRODUCTION IN THE UNITED STATES

As is perhaps evident from the preceding sections, there are two major aspects of the control problem. These may be differentiated by the terms " stabilization " and " conservation." Stabilization is the prevention of economic waste due to production in excess of demand. Conservation is the prevention of actual physical waste through the utilization of the most efficient means of recovery of oil and the temperate use of its products. Conservation is the goal of the Government in the interests of the public. Stabilization is the aim of the industry, and may or may not be in the interest of public welfare, depending on whether or not it is used to support an unnecessarily high

[1] U.S. *ex rel*. McLennan *v*. Wilbur, 283 U.S. 414.

[2] Order by President Hoover, March 12, 1929. " There will be no leases or disposals of Government oil lands, no matter what category they be in, of Government holding or Government controls, except those which may be mandatory by Congress " (Logan, p. 67).

357

price-level. Yet these two ends have in common their means of achievement. For both, proration is the palliative and unit operation the cure. Moreover, they are further closely linked in that " under our present system of property rights and individual initiative it is very difficult to enforce any kind of conservation program unless it can be proved that money can be made by it." [1]

The Movement toward Control in the United States

Since the earliest beginnings of the industry there have been periods of over-production which have led producers to try to regulate production to ensure a stable price.[2] There was the secret Producers' Protective Union to curtail production; later came the Producers' Associated Oil Company, which bought up land in order to standardize the " boundary-line contracts " and to prevent the drilling of more than one well in each twenty acres. However, " after 1900, drilling activities spread to other parts of the United States (from Pennsylvania). Industry was so scattered that little community action was obtained as far as curtailment of production is concerned until after the World War."[3] The only pre-war effort at joint control of any consequence, that in Oklahoma in 1914, was defeated by court action. Government efforts toward conservation were for long very limited. Some states had laws preventing waste of natural gas and regulating the distance between wells, but no effective measures of control were tried.

The modern movement toward control started shortly after the war. The American Petroleum Institute, an outgrowth of the National War Service Petroleum Committee, was formed in 1919. Through it, producers worked in co-operation with Government officials toward efficiency and eradication of waste. At the same time, due to the unprecedentedly high prices of crude oil, various Government agencies were led to investigate the industry.[4] In answer to their reports, some of which were favourable to the industry and some unfavourable, the so-called Doherty Plan was presented to the American Petroleum Institute. This constitutes the first proposal originating in the industry itself for extensive action toward control. The plan was in two parts: the first called for co-operative activity by the entire industry to expand the uses of petroleum—e.g. through advertising; and the second called for the operation of oil pools as units. It is this part of the plan that is of

[1] Logan, op. cit., p. 81.
[2] See Logan, op. cit., pp. 126 ff.
[3] Logan, op. cit., p. 127.
[4] E.g., Federal Trade Commission Investigation, 1920; Senate Investigation, 1922.

interest here. " He [Doherty] regarded any fundamental improvement in the situation impossible so long as the owner or lessor of each separate piece of property was compelled to protect his property from drainage by offset drilling with its attendant consequences of haste and waste." [1] His plan for unit control was to conserve resources by allowing exploration and discovery without the necessity of immediate exploitation. This would have provided large underground reserves, and have prevented the waste in volume and specific gravity which occurs in storing oil aboveground. Unit operation would have removed the necessity of offset drilling and, in minimizing the number of wells, would have conserved the natural gas. He felt that such a voluntary plan would result in stabilization and avert Government regulation. The American Petroleum Institute as a whole was not ready to accept such a plan; and this was formally disapproved in 1925. A large minority of the Institute went to the extreme in the other direction by endorsing a report which stated that the oil reserves of the country were almost inexhaustible, and that there was no waste in the present methods of production.

In 1924 the Government took a further step in co-operating with the industry by creating the Federal Oil Conservation Board, consisting of the Secretaries of War, Navy, Interior, and Commerce.[2] Co-operation between the Government and the leaders of the industry grew more and more friendly as the price of oil fell steadily. " Many of the leaders in the industry by 1928 were convinced of the need of some kind of legislation relating to the conservation of petroleum." [3] Mr Teagle, of the Standard Oil Company of New Jersey, and Mr Farish, of the American Petroleum Institute, both favoured Federal assistance to such an extent that in April 1929 the American Petroleum Institute asked the Federal Oil Conservation Board to help limit production to the 1928 level in the United States, Mexico, and northern South America. While this request was rejected on the advice of the Attorney-General, a committee of the Federal Oil Conservation Board, made up of representatives of the Government, of the American Bar Association, and of the American Petroleum Institute, published a report recommending a legislative program in regard to oil production. This provided for Federal and State legislation, exempting " unitization " and limitation of production from the anti-trust laws, allowing lease-holders of

---

[1] Logan, *op. cit.*, p. 140.
[2] This Board has recently been eliminated, as an economy measure.
[3] Logan, *op. cit.*, p. 151.

Government land to enter co-operative agreements, and preventing the further leasing of Government land.

This trend among the leaders of the industry toward Federal intervention is explained by the obvious fact that limitation of production in any one field or in any one state is not only inequitable but useless, since oil is produced in nineteen states and refined in twenty-nine. While some individual producers are still opposed to Government action, the majority favour it. The reason why this sort of planning and control has not progressed further is the difficulty of working out the details of a plan, and the legal and constitutional difficulties involved in any form of control.

Private Control Agreements

Control of petroleum production by private agreement without monopoly ownership is of very limited nature, due to the anti-trust laws of the Federal Government and of most of the states. The Federal laws prevent any widespread co-operation to control production which might affect the oil carried in interstate commerce. Since there is no motive to try to control production unless such action will affect the price-level of the whole domestic market, it is more than unlikely that it would be practised within the scope of legality. Many states have rectified this situation by exempting production agreements from their anti-trust laws.[1] The National Industrial Recovery Act recently passed by Congress may do the same in the national field by licensing trade associations.[2]

State Control

State control, while it is more effective than local private control, has still not been enough, in most cases, to affect the domestic price. Moreover, oil production is a large source of revenue in many states; and it is improbable that any one state will sacrifice its production to any great extent without similar sacrifices in revenue by other states. Nevertheless, a certain amount of control has been exercised in various states. This has been done on two different constitutional grounds under the police power of the State Governments. In most of them it is done with the aim of conserving the natural resources of the State for the public welfare.

Legislation based on a state's power to protect its resources has

[1] California Laws, 1929, Ch. 535, Sec. 8c; New Mexico Laws, 1929, Ch. 132, Sec. 1; Wyoming Laws, 1931, Ch. 95, Sec. 2; Mississippi Laws, Act, May 18, 1932, Sec. 40.
[2] See below.

been along the line of indirectly limiting oil production by enforcing a low oil-gas ratio, to prevent the waste of natural gas. Such conservation has ranged all the way from regulating the distance between wells to endorsing the shut-down of the fields by the State Militia. The other basis for use of the police power is to protect the rights of all the owners of land in one field. This is used only in those states which do not accept the non-ownership theory of the Law of Capture. They treat the control of oil on the same legal basis as the control of irrigation and drainage. " It is an old principle of property law that it is a just and constitutional exercise of the power of the Legislature to establish regulations by which adjoining lands, held by various owners in severalty, and in the improvement of which all have a common interest, but which, by reason of the peculiar natural conditions of the whole tract, cannot be improved or enjoyed by any of them without the concurrence of all, may be reclaimed and made useful to all at their joint expense." [1]

The immediate ground for interference in either case is physical waste. This police power cannot be used for the sole purpose of stabilizing prices. All these various types of legislation have been upheld in the courts.[2] Under them, although the State cannot force the merger of land titles, it would be possible for a State to enforce the unit operation of pools. As yet this has been tried in no instance.

A new power for State regulation has been suggested recently in Texas, in a proposal whereby taxes would be graded upward in proportion to the volume of production.[3] This has not been tried out or tested in court. " The State has proven its constitutional power to effectively regulate the production of oil and gas within its own borders. . . . The vital third phase, proration among separate States, remains relatively untouched." [4]

Federal Control

" Assuming that each State has enacted statutes to co-ordinate production with demand, there is no agency, corresponding to the single

---

[1] J. H. Marshall and N. L. Meyers, *op. cit.*, p. 63.

[2] Ohio Oil Co. *v.* Indiana, No. 1, 177 U.S. 190; Walls *v.* Midland Carbon Co., 254 U.S. 300; Bandini Petroleum Co., *et al.*, *v.* U.S. Superior Court, 284 U.S. 8; Champlin Refining Co. *v.* Corporate Commission, 286 U.S. 210 (1932).

[3] *The New York Herald Tribune*, April 4, 1933.

[4] Federal Oil Conservation Board, *Report to the President*, Report V., October 1932, p. 21. Case cited: Wurts *v.* Hoagland, 114 U.S. 606, 5 Sup. Ct. 1086 (1885).

Government of a foreign nation, which can negotiate with foreign producers to correlate world demand and production, or determine what domestic production should be, or allocate that production among producing areas." [1] Yet the Federal Government can co-operate in the task of control in several ways. In the first place, " The United States Government is the largest single owner of oil and gas lands. If a policy of conservation is to be carried out which will be beneficial to both the industry and to society in general, the Government must take the initiative and lead the way." [2] In regard to these lands it can and does exercise complete supervision and control in bringing its production in line with demand. That it has already made some progress in this direction is shown by the fact that only 3 per cent. of United States production comes from Government lands at present. Secondly, it is within the power of the Federal Government so to modify its anti-trust laws as to facilitate private co-operation among the producers in various states. Such action has not been taken to date, but it is envisaged in several bills now under consideration in Congress. [3]

The power of the Federal Government to supervise control and to require unit operation and proration is open to question. It seems unlikely that it would have such a right under the interstate commerce power, if a parallel may be drawn with the attempts to regulate child labour under the same power. On the other hand, there are those who feel that such regulation would come within the scope of Article I., Section 8, of the United States Constitution, providing for the common defence, since oil is at present essential for the survival of the nation and the operation of the army and the navy. That this point is debatable is shown clearly in the testimony given by C. E. Hughes, when he was counsel for the American Petroleum Institute in 1926: " The Government of the United States . . . is not at liberty to control the internal affairs of the states, respectively, such as production within the states, through assertion by Congress of a desire either to provide for the common defense or to promote the general welfare." [4] On the other hand, the Federal Government could authorize interstate agreements to control production, and could aid in enforcing such contracts through its ability to keep a check on interstate commerce, by pipelines as well as by other forms of transportation.

[1] Federal Oil Conservation Board, *Report to the President*, Report V., October 1932, p. 21.
[2] Logan, *op. cit.*, p. 68.
[3] See below.
[4] *The New York Times*, May 21, 1933.

Recent Legislation

The *National Industrial Recovery Act*, passed in June of this year, as an emergency measure to run for two years, gives the President special powers over the oil industry. The section covering this reads as follows:

Section 9 (*a*). OIL REGULATION

The President is further authorized to initiate before the Interstate Commerce Commission proceedings necessary to prescribe regulations to control the operation of oil pipelines and to fix reasonable, compensatory rates for the transportation of petroleum and its products by pipelines, and the Interstate Commerce Commission shall grant preference to the hearings and determination of such cases.

(*b*) The President is authorized to institute proceedings to divorce from any holding company any pipeline company controlled by such holding company which pipeline company by unfair practices or exorbitant rates in the transportation of petroleum or its products tends to create a monopoly.

(*c*) The President is authorized to prohibit the transportation in interstate and foreign commerce of petroleum and the products thereof produced or withdrawn from storage in excess of the amount permitted to be produced or withdrawn from storage by any state law or valid regulation or order prescribed thereunder, by any board, commission, officer, or other duly authorized agency of a state. Any violation of any order by the President issued under the provisions of this subsection shall be punishable by a fine of not to exceed $1000 or imprisonment for not to exceed six months, or both.

In addition to this special provision, the Act provides for licensing trade associations. Under such an arrangement the petroleum industry would be given further opportunity to co-operate on private initiative. The constitutional basis for these provisions is given in the first section of the Act, which states the purpose of the Act as follows: " To provide for the general welfare by promoting the organization of industry for the purpose of co-operative action among trade groups—and to conserve natural resources."

Along with this Act, there have been several other bills under consideration by Congress which deal specifically with the oil industry.[1] The most important of these is an Administration proposal forwarded by the Secretary of the Interior, Ickes.[2] This, again, is based on the welfare power and is to be enforced by the interstate commerce power. It provides, further, for fixing state quotas and, if necessary, fixing maximum and minimum prices for crude petroleum and its products

[1] H.R. 10862, S. 4231; H.R. 10863, S. 4232; H.R. 12076, S. 4624—72nd Congress, 1st Session.

[2] See A. E. Mackler, " Sweeping Provisions of Proposed Legislation for Federal Control of the Petroleum Industry," *Oil and Gas Journal*, May 11, 1933, p. 8.

under the direction of the Secretary of the Interior or an Administrator of Petroleum Conservation. It only affects the State in recommending definite action for their consideration.

Such action is supported by the Governors of the oil states, as is shown in the resolution passed at the close of their conference with Secretary Ickes: " We believe strongly in the policy of continuous co-operation between the Federal and State Governments in conservation of the petroleum resources of the nation and states, with the purpose that neither the Federal Government nor the States shall surrender or lose any of their power, but that each shall so exercise its power as to further the common policy of conservation." [1] The only strong opposition to these plans comes from small independent producers, who claim that the consuming public and the small operators are being disregarded.

METHODS OF CONTROL

Proration

Proration is of two general types, the allotment of production as between the producers in a single field, and as between entire pools or areas. It is somewhat easier to determine an equitable distribution as regards the second than as regards the first, since it is possible to determine more accurately the total oil contained in a pool than it is to determine the amount of oil beneath a single plot of land not covering an entire oil-field. It is the first type of proration that is of importance in controlling production in flush fields. This type of control was first practised in connection with the " Common Purchasers' Act " in Oklahoma. According to this law, pipelines were required to take all the oil that was offered to them. This was to prevent discrimination in favour of certain wells which would enable them to drain off the whole field, while the other wells might be glutted without an outlet to the market. In certain cases the pipeline facilities were not sufficient to carry the entire production of a field, and the pipeline outlets had to be allotted equitably among the wells. Hence proration was adopted. The control of pipeline outlets is still the method in use in enforcing proration agreements.

Proration in a Single Field.—The earliest proration plans divided the production among producers in proportion to their " potential production." This policy put a premium on drilling, as a producer's

---

[1] *The New York Times*, March 31, 1933.

potential production was immediately increased by each new well. This obviously led to further waste of gas pressure and to the unnecessary expenditure of capital in drilling wells which would subsequently not be operated to full capacity.

The alternative plan for rationing production according to the area of the land-holdings of each producer went to the other extreme, and was held to be unfair in that it gave no advantage to better locations on the oil-field. The owner near the non-producing areas on the margins of the field often received as large a quota as the owner in the best location. As a result, the method now in use is a compromise between the two.

The Yates Plan.—An example of such a compromise is the proration agreement of the Yates Pool.[1] This field is drilled to the extent of one well to about fifty acres. In 1927 the operators agreed to prorate the production according to the total potential production. This, as indicated above, stimulated drilling. In 1928 they started on an acreage basis, but finally, in July of that year, a new plan, based on the conclusions reached from their past experience, was put into operation. Two general principles for proration were determined: first, " That the potential (production) must be the governing factor and considered on an acreage basis," and second, " in order that acreage drilled should reflect the condition of the parcel, each type of acreage must produce its own oil." [2]

The field is divided into units of 100 acres. Lots less than 100 acres are considered units unless they are contiguous to a 100-acre unit owned by the same producer, in which case they are considered as fractions of a unit. 25 per cent. of the pipeline outlets are distributed equally among the units, and 75 per cent. according to the average potential production of each unit. The average unit potential is obtained by adding the daily potential of all the wells on the unit and dividing the sum by the number of wells. This plan was put into effect on the request of the operators by the Texas Railroad Commission. It is administered by an umpire appointed by the Commission, who is assisted by an advisory committee consisting of one representative of each company operating on the field.

Similar plans, varying in the size of the units and the percentage distribution between acreage and potential production, are in use elsewhere. A still better method of determining the quotas is being developed at present, using a most important new technical development

---

[1] H. C. Hardison, " Proration at Yates Pool," *A.I.M.E. Transactions*, 1931, p. 74.
[2] *Ibid.*, p. 75.

as a determinant—namely, bottom-hole pressures. This, according to ·one specialist, may be made to have the effect of removing some of the stimulus to drill.[1]

Intra-State Proration.—Proration as between fields within a state has been developed in many states, usually at the request of producers. A State Commission usually is in charge of this. The history of the attempts to prorate in Oklahoma is a good case in point. In 1921 the producers on the Hewitt field tried proration in addition to curbing drilling activities. This experiment was short-lived, as it became apparent that action on one field was futile. In 1927, following the failure of a voluntary curtailment plan in the Seminole field, operators there signed a compact and set up an umpire. This plan, too, proved unenforceable, and in 1927 the operators filed a contract and an agreement with the State Corporate Commission for the curtailment of production and for proration. Since then, the Commission has not acted until appealed to by representatives of the industry affected. In this state, voluntary control is most effective, but it is costly to the state as a whole, as long as it does not co-operate with other states.

In Texas the situation is controlled by the State Railroad Commission. By a constitutional amendment after the war, the Legislature was required to provide for the conservation of the natural resources. Before the end of 1932, when a new law was passed,[2] the Commission could concern itself only with physical waste, not with economic waste. By an Act signed in November 1932 the Commission is now empowered to consider " market demand " in determining the total production of the state. To strengthen the enforcement of these measures, Texas passed a bill, in May 1933, making it a felony to fail to comply with the proration orders and all the conservation regulations of the Railroad Commission.[3] The working of this method is shown in the present situation in Texas. Here the amount of oil to be produced is determined by the refining and pipeline companies. Each of these companies reports to the umpire the amount of oil in barrels per day which it is willing to buy from each field in the state. The umpire sums up the desires of the market for crude oil, as shown by the amounts which the oil companies are willing to buy, and decides whether or not their applications are reasonable. Normally, the umpire accepts the figures of demand as determined by the refiners, but he is not forced to do so.

[1] J. Pogue, " Economics of Proration," *A.I.M.E. Transactions,* 1932. Note, p. 70.
[2] *The New York Times,* November 14, 1932.
[3] *The Oil Weekly,* May 15, 1933.

Recently the Railroad Commission of Texas, which is the umpire in this case, decided that justice was not being done to the great East Texas field. A test of the potential production of the field suggested the enormous total of 125 million barrels per day if all the wells were allowed to produce at full capacity. This test did not show for how many days or hours the field could produce at anything approaching this rate, but it did convince the Commission that the production of 400,000 barrels per day allowed the field was too small. It therefore doubled the allowable production of the field, without giving any consideration to what the extra production would do to oil prices.

When the field was reopened after being shut in for the test of potential, and with the allowable production doubled, it was met by a production with no market and therefore a reduction of from 50 to 80 per cent. of the former price of fifty cents per barrel at the well. Thus the matter stood in the first week of May 1933. The production of this extra 400,000 barrels per day, or an extra 20 per cent. of the oil needed, will require a complete adjustment of production in other fields in the state and of those of other states, or will result in a breakdown of the price of oil generally, as well as of refined products.

Interstate Proration

The first attempt to prorate between states was made in 1929 by a meeting of Governors. This effort was fruitless, because the delegates had no real power to form an agreement. In 1930 the Federal Oil Conservation Board fixed tentative quotas for each state, giving California 610,000 barrels; Oklahoma, 655,000; Texas, 750,000; all others, 480,000; storage, 78,000. Again, in 1931, the Governors of Oklahoma, Kansas and Texas met, and this time reached an agreement curtailing production. Also, an Oil States Advisory Committee was established, made up of representatives of ten states. This Committee is to further co-operation through furnishing necessary information and advice.

The various steps in proration outlined above may now be summarized: first, co-operative agreements within a field, as at Seminole, with the appointment of an umpire of production; second, establishment of a State authority as a legally supported umpire; third, the use of executive authority through martial law in closing specified pools; and fourth, co-operation among producing states through the mediation of the National Government. The second step is still in practice the major method of control.

Advantages and Disadvantages of Proration

The advantages of proration alone are at best temporary as an expedient in slowing down production. To a certain extent it prevents waste through prohibiting flush flow. It is also a valuable precedent toward unitization, in that it has tested various methods of determining equitable division of production. The efforts at proration so far have two grave defects for which there is at present no method of correction. The first of these is that there seems to be no legal way to prevent the drilling of new wells which are not needed and which, if successful in producing oil, complicate the major problem. The second is that the enforcement of proration allowances is somewhat akin to the enforcement of prohibition. That this is no exaggeration is shown by a quotation from an oil journal of March 1933:

Conditions with regard to the production of crude oil in violation of the curtailment orders of the state commissions are worse than in the summer of 1931, when State troops took control in East Texas and in Oklahoma fields.

The cause, in both states, has been court decisions which have, bit by bit, stripped the state commissions of their authority to enforce their curtailment orders.[1]

In addition to these defects and the frequently voiced objection that proration introduces politics into the oil business, there are certain definite economic disadvantages in using proration as the sole method of controlling production. As Pogue points out, " The high-cost producer has apparently benefited from proration, for proration tends to give to the marginal operator a share of the market which he cannot command unaided." [2] This, of course, raises the average cost of production and prevents the essential readjustments within the industry to eliminate inefficient production. Likewise it tends to change overproduction into excess capacity for production, in failing to prevent wasteful drilling, as noted above. In short, " No mere scheme of proration will curtail excess drilling and eliminate the costs of unnecessary offset wells. Nor will proration ensure the proper location of wells on the geologic structure to secure the maximum recovery. These shortcomings of proration can only be obviated by unit operation." [3]

[1] *National Petroleum News*, March 22, 1933, p. 7.
[2] Pogue, *op. cit.*, p. 74.
[3] J. H. Marshall and N. L. Meyers, *op. cit.*, p. 59.

UNITIZATION

Unitization is essentially a problem of operation, not of ownership. It requires control of drilling, through the organization of a whole field by one agency. There are all degrees of this control, some classed as near-unit pools and some as complete units. In general, there are four methods of achieving this unity of operation.

1. One company may own the entire field. This type of unit operation involves no difficulties, but it requires a large outlay of capital and is almost impossible of achievement after oil has been discovered on a field.

2. One company may lease all the land in a field from the various royalty owners. This process does not solve the problem entirely, because the usual lease contract requires immediate drilling and production on the lease. Therefore, special arrangements have to be made with the owners to pay them according to their share of the total production of the field.

3. Royalty owners, or lease owners with special arrangements with the royalty owners as in (2) above, may pool their holdings in an unincorporated trust and have the trustee operate the field as a unit. The difficulty with this plan is greater even than that in (2), since all the leaseholds and all the royalty owners must come into the agreement.

4. Royalty owners and lease owners, as above, may incorporate and receive, in return for assigning their rights to the corporation, shares of stock in proportion to the oil value of their land. In this case the largest owner will control the corporation and hence the operation of the field.

The principal difficulty in the last three of the methods enumerated is to determine the amount to be paid to the individual owners. In a new field it is almost impossible to determine without drilling even what section of the land is productive, and much more difficult to determine the relative value of the different locations on the field. Since one of the objectives of unitization is to avoid drilling, it is necessary to come to an agreement on estimations, and to allow for adjustments as the estimates are corrected from time to time. On fields already open to production it is easier to allot these shares, but part of the value of unit operation is already lost. Moreover, on known fields the marginal producers hesitate to give up their rights to draining the oil beneath their neighbours' land, and to receive instead the share of oil that is actually beneath their own land.

In the United States the unit control of reserves by ownership is

2 A

greater than the control of present production. Many large tracts known or supposed to contain oil pools are under lease to individual companies. The reserves which they contain would be difficult to estimate.

The Kettleman Hills Plan.—In 1930 there were eleven unit fields and twenty near-unit fields in operation in the United States. The majority of these are in the Rocky Mountains area, where most of the Government Indian lands are located.

One of the most interesting of these is the North Dome of Kettleman Hills, California.[1] This is interesting not only because it is one of the largest reserves in the country, and contains the deepest well in the world, but because it is an example of co-operation between the Government and private enterprise.

When this huge field, which had been withdrawn from exploitation by President Taft in 1909, was reopened for drilling in 1928, it was thought that the California gas-oil ratio law might be sufficient to prevent flush production. But when it became apparent that the oil in the field was heavy, and would not be checked by this regulation, it was clear that, unless some consolidated action were taken, the flow from the field would entirely demoralize the industry. Therefore the Government took steps to prevent such an occurrence. In July 1929 the Government took action to prevent wasteful drilling, by altering the requirements for validating the Government leases. Ordinarily, discovery of oil is necessary; but on this field the wells are considered completed when a certain stratum is reached indicating the probability of oil. To compensate the lessors for not operating their wells, an agreement was made that the four producing wells would contribute 10 to 25 per cent. of their production to these shut-down wells, of which there were about twenty-five. All other drilling was prohibited for two years. These agreements between the operators maintained the *status quo* until arrangements for the future operation of the field could be reached.

The control of the land was divided between the Standard Oil Company of California, with 9460 acres, and a large number of lessees, collectively controlling 11,740 acres. These holdings were checkerboarded in units of one section. In February 1930 the Kettleman North Dome Committee was formed by the lessees, and it decided on unit operation instead of co-operative development. This action necessitated certain legislative changes which were easily obtained. The

[1] See J. Jensen, "Unit Operation in California with Discussion of Kettleman Hills North Dome Association," *A.I.M.E. Transactions*, 1931, p. 80.

limits of the land controlled by one operator were extended; royalty agreements and drilling requirements were modified, and Government leases were extended from twenty years to the life of the Association. All the landholders, except the Standard Oil Company and the holders of leases covering 530 acres, gave over their rights to the Association. The Standard Oil Company was hesitant to enter the Association, because, as the largest single owner, it would have had to operate the field, which it feared might lead to its prosecution under the anti-trust laws. Therefore an arrangement was made that the Oil Company would operate its land as a single unit and the Association operate as another unit, while the relations between the two units would be regulated by an agreement. This plan went into operation in April 1931.

" The Association does not take over the lands under lease in the Kettleman Hills but is merely granted exclusive possession and operating rights thereon. It will buy from the various members the wells that have already been drilled by them." [1]

The agreement calls for a minimum output of 50,000 barrels a day, to be increased in proportion to California's total production, provided it nets a fair return. The Government, in increasing the royalties on larger production, has placed an additional curb on excessive draining. During the first five years the income from the field is to be divided equally on an area basis. Then, as further drilling indicates the potential value of the land, non-productive sections will be removed, and the other land graduated in proportion to its potential productive value. In the short period in which the plan has been in operation it has been most successful, both in controlling production and in eliminating waste. "Considering the fact that the limits of the field are still unknown while its central portion is definitely proven productive oil land on a well-defined structure . . . the formation of the Kettleman North Dome Association represents an important development in unit operation as well as evidence of a willingness to co-operate upon the part of the operating oil companies, the Federal Government and the oil companies owning fee land." [2]

Advantages and Difficulties of Unitization

The advantages of unit production are obvious for both conservation and stabilization, for the first in ensuring the most economical production, and for the second in assuring absolute control of a producing

[1] See J. Jensen, " Unit Operation in California with Discussion of Kettleman Hills North Dome Association," *A.I.M.E. Transactions*, 1931, p. 91.

[2] *Ibid.*, p. 83.

unit. Furthermore, " in order to carry out any one of these (secondary recovery) methods, the pools must be organized into engineering units."[1] These advantages are overshadowed only by the difficulties in attaining them. Voluntary co-operation is very difficult to achieve for the reasons listed above. As yet, no state has tried to compel unit operation either on the ground of conservation or that of the protection of the common property rights of the various owners of a pool. It is through this action alone that real stabilization of the oil industry can be achieved, because only by this method can drilling be regulated. Drilling is necessary in order to find new reserves and to prevent fear of immediate exhaustion of supply; but it must be controlled to prevent immediate exploitation of these reserves. This can be done only through unit operation which would render obsolete the " law of capture." Such operation could be ensured on new fields if, instead of selling lots on oil-fields, promoters were obliged to sell proportionate shares in the future production of the field.

CONCLUSION

The picture of the oil situation in the United States at present has recently been described as follows. In spite of the fact that there is an abundance of petroleum, " it is timely to realize the significance which should be attached to well-founded figures showing that, at the current rates of production, the equivalent of our present known oil reserves will have been withdrawn from their underground reservoirs in ten to twelve years "[2] and that " the day of exhaustion is merely postponed a few months or a few years by each new discovery."[3]

The domestic industry is protected from outside competition by a tariff; and, while internal control is far from complete, it is much better than it was a few years ago. The problem of stabilization, as far is it is affected by the production of petroleum, lies in the fields with flush production. According to the American Petroleum Institute, less than 2 per cent. of the total number of producing wells of the United States are producing 50 per cent. of the oil.[4] With the exception of the East Texas field, almost all of these are under control. The Government lands are completely withdrawn from further exploitation until demand improves. " Thus far proration has been more effective than unit

---

[1] Logan, *op. cit.*, p. 179.
[2] Federal Oil Conservation Board, *Report to the President*, Report V., October 1932, p. 42.
[3] *Ibid.*, p. 7.
[4] Logan, *op. cit.*, p. 90.

operation, because it involves greater areas and greater potential production." [1] At the present time, a statement made in 1930 by Logan still holds true: " In the movement toward control on the one side are the big integrated companies, both ' Standard ' and ' independent,' who are more in favour of some kind of Government regulation and legislation controlling the production of petroleum. This group is closely co-operating with the Federal Oil Conservation Board in its efforts to bring about some form of conservation and stabilization. The second group (opposing it) does not represent as large an investment in the industry, but from the point of numbers is considerably larger than the first. This group includes the independent producers, royalty owners, independent refiners, intra-state pipeline operators, supply men, oil-field workers, owners of permits to operate on Government land, and lease and royalty brokers." [2] The fate of the legislative proposals now before Congress will be determined by the relative power of these two groups. In the past, " attempts to make world oil agreements or cartels have failed because of the inability of the American petroleum industry to co-operate." [3] This situation is likely to continue unless some integrated action can be taken under the new legislation. The fact that this is still a world problem is evident from an Associated Press dispatch of April 13, 1933: " The International Oil Conference, it was reported to-day, has agreed in principle to permit Rumanian production to remain at 18,500 tons a day pending effective control of the output of independent producers in the United States. The Rumanian delegates said that if the Americans were unable to curb production they would withdraw from the international combination." [4]

[1] Logan, *op. cit.*, p. 170.
[2] *Ibid.*, p. 154.
[3] J. H. Marshall and N. L. Meyers, *op. cit.*, p. 34.
[4] *The New York Times*, April 14, 1933.
On June 2, 1933, the Rumanians took advantage of this conditional clause and withdrew from the international agreement, on the basis that the required limitation had not been obtained in the United States.

TABLE I.—WORLD CRUDE-OIL PRODUCTION, 1930-1932

(in thousands of barrels)

Country	1932		1931		1930	
	Quantity	Per cent. of Total	Quantity	Per cent. of Total	Quantity	Per cent. of Total
United States .	781,845	59·9	851,081	62·0	898,011	63·6
Soviet Union .	155,250	11·9	162,842	11·9	125,555	8·9
Venezuela . .	116,300	8·9	116,316	8·5	136,669	9·7
Rumania . .	54,160	4·1	49,127	3·6	42,759	3·0
Persia . . .	49,470	3·8	44,376	3·2	45,833	3·3
Netherlands East Indies . .	39,000	3·0	35,539	2·6	41,729	3·0
Mexico . .	32,805	2·5	33,039	2·4	39,530	2·8
Colombia . .	16,417	1·3	18,237	1·3	20,346	1·4
Argentina . .	13,000	1·0	11,709	·9	9,002	·6
Trinidad . .	10,100	·8	9,744	·7	9,419	·7
Peru . . .	9,900	·8	10,089	·7	12,449	·9
India (British) .	8,370	·7	8,200	·6	8,887	·6
Poland . .	4,115	·3	4,662	·3	4,904	·3
Sakhalin (Russian)	2,800	·2	2,734	·2	1,805	·1
British Borneo .	2,400	·2	3,854	·3	4,907	·4
Egypt . .	1,790	·1	2,238	·1	1,996	·1
Japan (inc. Taiwan)	1,630	·1	2,050	·2	2,047	·2
Germany . .	1,617	·1	1,606	·1	1,222	·1
Equador . .	1,595	·1	1,762	·1	1,553	·1
Canada . .	1,057		1,543		1,522	
Irak . . .	910		830		909	
France . .	528		520		523	
Italy . . .	210	·2	124	·3	59	·2
Czechoslovakia .	190		134		157	
Bolivia . .	44		25		56	
Other Countries .	60		54		56	
Total . .	1,305,563	100·0	1,372,435	100·0	1,411,905	100·0

Based upon figures supplied by the American Petroleum Institute, April 5, 1933.

PETROLEUM CONTROL IN THE U.S.A.

TABLE II.—ESTIMATED RESERVES OF CRUDE OIL IN PROVEN FIELDS [1]

barrels

United States	12,000,000,000
Russia	3,000,000,000
Irak	2,500,000,000
Persia	2,200,000,000
Venezuela	2,000,000,000
Dutch East Indies	1,000,000,000
Rumania	500,000,000
Colombia	400,000,000
Mexico	300,000,000
India	100,000,000
Peru	100,000,000
Argentina	100,000,000
Trinidad	90,000,000
Poland	50,000,000
Japan	40,000,000
Sarawak (British Borneo)	30,000,000
Canada	10,000,000
Egypt	10,000,000
Germany	10,000,000
Equador	10,000,000
France	5,000,000
All Others	10,000,000
	24,465,000,000

[1] This estimate is by V. R. Garfias, and published in *World Petroleum* for March, 1933, p. 80. For the national ownership of petroleum production and reserves see " The Nationality of Commercial Control of World Minerals," by William P. Rawles, Secretary, *The Mineral Inquiry* (published by the American Institute of Mining and Metallurgical Engineers, and may be obtained from them at 29 West 39th Street, New York).

TABLE III.—PRODUCTION OF PETROLEUM AND ITS PRODUCTS IN THE UNITED STATES

(in thousands of barrels)

Year	Crude Petroleum	Gasolene	Kerosene	Gas and Fuel Oil	Lubricating Oil
1916	300,768	2,460	34,656	111,048	14,868
1922	557,532	160,920	54,912	254,916	23,304
1926	770,882	332,040	61,764	365,196	32,292
1930	898,008	484,800	49,212	372,504	34,200

Source: United States Department of Commerce, *Survey of Current Business,* Annual Supplement, 1932.

CHAPTER XII

THE INTERNATIONAL TIN RESTRICTION PLAN
by Oliver Lawrence

THE consumption of tin is insignificant compared with that of many other metals, but it is of vital importance in certain industrial uses and has given the remote and inaccessible areas which are its principal producers a definite function in the modern industrial world. Europe and North America, which habitually take nine-tenths of the world supply, contribute only 2 per cent. to it. The greatest producing area is the south-eastern corner of the Asiatic mainland, from Lower Burma eastwards to the south of China and southwards throughout the Malay Peninsula and its geological continuation in the East Indian islands. Between 1927 and 1930, 66 per cent., on an average, of the world's supply originated in this area within which Malaya, the Dutch Indies and, increasingly of late, Siam, were the most important individual producers. The only other developed deposits of first-rate importance are in Bolivia and Nigeria. Tin ore occurs widely in Central and South Africa, and the whole of this area may prove to be a continuous tin-field; but only in Nigeria, and latterly in the Belgian Congo, has output been organized on a large scale, just as Asiatic production has been mainly concentrated on the western slopes of the granite chain which forms the backbone of the Malayan Peninsula.

The form of occurrence is either in veins and lodes in the solid rock or as alluvial or detrital deposits derived from the disintegration or decomposition of the rock formation. Alluvial and detrital deposits are cheaply and easily worked and form the source of the bulk of the output in Malaya, the Dutch Indies, Siam, China and Nigeria; Bolivian tin, on the other hand, is mined from lodes. Alluvial tin-stone is easily separated by washing and, being a simple oxide, can readily be smelted by the most primitive methods. Consequently, tin-mining was an old-established industry in the Malayan Peninsula and the Dutch Indies under mainly Chinese ownership, long before the introduction of Western plants. Large-scale dredging and pumping merely represent a magnification of the old system without any fundamental alteration in technique, and the Chinese producer still survives and contributes as much as 35 per cent. of the output of the Federated Malay States. Smelting, however, has been reorganized on modern lines and centralized.

376

The Straits Trading Company and the Eastern Smelting Company handle most of the output of Burma, Siam, Malaya. Moreover, up till recently much of the output of the Dutch Indies was smelted in coal furnaces at Singapore and Penang, while the remainder of the Dutch output was reduced at Banka by means of modernized charcoal furnaces, producing a metal of very great purity. During 1933 the smelter which the Dutch had recently set up at Arnhem was greatly expanded. Figures for the last nine months of 1933 show that Dutch East India ore, most of which had previously been smelted in the Straits, was then being sent almost exclusively to Holland. The Bolivian and Nigerian output of ores is shipped almost in its entirety for smelting in Great Britain, where a number of independent plants were amalgamated at the end of 1929 as The Consolidated Tin Smelters, Limited, in which the Eastern Smelting Company also participates. Other smelters are of very minor importance; but reclamation from scrap material is important in the United States, where the output of " secondary " tin reached a figure as high as 32,000 tons in 1928, though the resultant product is by no means pure.

HISTORY OF TIN PRODUCTION

Western capital was slow to participate in Asiatic tin-mining. It was not until 1877 that the Straits Trading Company put up its first smelting plant, but it was thirty years before British interests concerned themselves with the actual extraction of the ore. Meanwhile the Chinese industry flourished and increased its output from 2000 tons in 1870 to over 50,000 tons in 1904, but in the process brought on its own decline as the richer surface deposits were exhausted. Simultaneously Cornish production began to decline, and Australian experiments did not justify first expectations, with the result that British capital began to participate in Malaya. Even by 1918 the output of the European companies represented only 32 per cent. of the total; but thereafter progress was rapid, and the proportionate share in British hands had doubled by 1931. Chinese producers, however, still survive and have adopted mechanical assistance on a small and inexpensive scale to supplement their own traditional methods. The development of Siamese tin took a very similar course and to a large extent is the product of British enterprise.

On the Nigerian plateau, tin-mining had also been a native industry before Western enterprise arrived, but for lack of communications development had been slow. The construction of a railway to the coast, in 1911, provided the necessary contact with civilization, and facilitated a more rapid expansion in the course of which the native producer has been entirely eliminated and dispossessed.

In the past the chief characteristic of British tin production, in strong contrast to Dutch and Bolivian practice, has been the predominance of small producing units. In 1929 the average number of dredges per company in Malaya was still only 1½, and there were few separate entities of any magnitude other than the Malayan Tin Dredging, the Pahang, and a few others. A unifying influence has been exerted, however, by financial grouping. Of the greatest importance is the Anglo-Oriental Mining Corporation, which participates in the control of producing companies not only in Malaya, Siam and Burma, but in Nigeria and Cornwall as well, and in Consolidated Tin Smelters. At the same time a movement towards the definite fusion of small working units, usually with adjoining leases, has not been entirely wanting; the London Tin Corporation, itself an offshoot of the Anglo-Oriental, has absorbed a number of Nigerian concerns, in addition to acting purely as a holding company; while the Consolidated Tin Mines of Burma represent an amalgamation of several smaller companies.

In sharp contrast to this complicated and in some ways wasteful system is the severely centralized Dutch industry. Geographically, also, the industry is concentrated, being confined to three small areas. Banka Island, lying off the south-eastern coast of Sumatra, has been exploited by a Government monopoly under an agreement made with the Sultan of Palembang in 1752. Singkep Island, to the north-west of Banka, has been privately exploited since 1927, but is of minor importance. Billiton Island, to the south-east of Banka, was worked by a private company on a lease obtained in 1860. In 1924 the lease expired. A new company was formed in which the Government obtained a 60 per cent. interest. Finally negotiations for the amalgamation of the Billiton and Banka mines were opened, and in September 1934 a commission was set up which is preparing the final amalgamation of the Billiton Maatschappij with the Government mines. It is reckoned that amalgamation will be an accomplished fact by the middle of 1935. This merger, taken in conjunction with the development of the Arnhem smelter, puts Dutch producers in a very strong position. As regards smelting, figures for the last nine months of 1933 show that Dutch East India ore, which had previously been reduced largely in the Straits, was being sent almost exclusively to Holland. Dutch East India ore, which accounted for 55 per cent. of Straits imports in 1930, accounted only for 9 per cent. in 1933. Thus the Dutch are now capable of forming an independent smelting policy instead of following the Straits. As regards actual production the Dutch Government, which up to now has owned nearly three-quarters of the industry, acquires in the Billiton Maatschappij a further 15 per cent. of the total industry. Some authorities give these deposits a relatively short life, though it is probably safe to say that others will be developed. Nevertheless, the tendency is everywhere towards the exhaustion of the secondary deposits, after which the Asiatic industry will have to turn increasingly towards the mining of lodes.

In Bolivia, tin-mining developed into a major industry from being a by-product of the silver-mining industry of the Bolivian Altiplano, and is controlled by a few strong combinations. The Patiño Consolidated was responsible for nearly half the Bolivian output in 1929, and about 85 per cent. of the whole is produced by Patiño and ten other large enterprises, the remainder being spread among a great number of small producers.

In short, the Dutch and Bolivian industries are subject to a relatively centralized control, with all that this implies, while the Malayan industry has always preserved a more democratic appearance, modified by financial groupings which have extended to Burma, Siam and Nigeria.

THE INDUSTRIAL POSITION OF TIN

As an industrial metal tin has aptly been compared to salt in cooking —insignificant but indispensable. Its major uses are for plating other metals; in alloys to make bearing metals, type metal and solder; and in the form of chemical compounds in the textile and pottery industries. The greatest demand for tin, therefore, comes from the canning industry, the manufacture of containers, and the automobile trade, but tends to be extremely inelastic in the face of even very severe price fluctuations. To take only two instances from important users of tin-plate: with the average price of canned foodstuffs around 1s. 6d., the cost of the pure tin employed represents only a small fraction of a penny, while in the automobile trade its cost does not amount to more than about 10s. in a finished product which sells for around £250. The technical position of the tin market has, therefore, little influence on the trend of demand, except in so far as a continued high level of prices discourages the extension of its uses and may even promote a search for substitutes—

as the employment of cellophane and aluminium for wrapping or packing food in preference to tinfoil or tinplate. The demand for tin depends more upon forces totally beyond the control of tin producers—the general state of industrial activity and, more particularly, the state of demand for semi-luxury consumption goods.

Price-swings are accentuated by the remoteness of tin-producing areas from consumers, which introduces a highly speculative element into the tin market. Moreover owing to the relative expensiveness of the metal and its small importance in determining final costs, manufacturers are habitually disinclined to carry more than minimum stocks, with the result that severe oscillations of price are apt to accompany the smallest divergence of supply and demand from the equilibrium level. Before large-scale methods were introduced, production followed closely the movements of demand, keeping prices fairly steady. Even in 1921 production reacted fairly readily to a very heavy fall in consumption. With the introduction of capitalist methods on a large scale much of this elasticity of production has been lost. Large-scale units in modern tin-mining cannot contract their output without substantially raising their costs; hence a failure of consumption to keep pace with production was bound to put them in a very awkward position —prices falling fast and costs rising fast—and one might expect that co-operation would suggest itself as an aid in facing the common difficulty.[1]

Between 1922 and 1927 the demand for tin rose steadily, and production was unable to keep pace with it; but in these years took place the rapid expansion of the industry's capacity which, by 1928, put production once again ahead of demand. Between 1900 and 1917 production and consumption had increased sedately and in unison— from about 100,000 tons per year to 130,000 tons. Following a period of disturbance, consumption rose once more—to 140,000 tons in 1922,

[1] The increasingly drastic nature of the restriction which was applied almost hints at the possibility that producers have been gambling on the results of a race. Given that the quantity taken varies very little with price increases, the vital consideration, from the point of view of producers' profits, in determining what degree of restriction to apply, is the *relative* rates of the *price* increase and the *cost* increase which restriction brings about. For example, if a 50 per cent. restriction of output involves a 40 per cent. rise in ton costs, will the accompanying rise in prices exceed or fall short of 40 per cent.?

It should be noticed that although this representation of the situation may suggest a monopolistic price-raising policy on the part of the producers, there is no proof in what has been said that the price and output attained through the above procedure would be less favourable to consumers than those which would have prevailed had the old system of small-scale production continued. Sub-capacity output of large-scale units, while more costly than full-capacity output of large-scale units, may be cheaper than small-scale production.

150,000 tons in 1925, 170,000 tons in 1928, and 180,000 tons in 1929. Production, having lagged behind from 1922-1927, equalled consumption in the latter year, exceeded it slightly in 1928, and was 10,000 tons ahead in 1929. The trend of prices reflected these movements accurately: a post-war peak of £315 per ton was reached in March 1927. Then came a sharp decline to £239 in March 1928, after which it remained fairly steady, though with a declining tendency for some months. The collapse of business activity during 1930 and 1931 carried consumption back to 160,000 tons and 140,000 tons; prices fell as low as £104 in December 1930, and production had to slow down in response, leaving an accumulation of stocks in the neighbourhood of 50,000 tons—approximately two and a half times as great as the amount normally required as a reserve against industrial consumption.

RESTRICTION BY VOLUNTARY AGREEMENT

There is every reason to believe that the tin producers appreciated the conditions of over-production in which they were living at an earlier date in its development than had the rubber growers in similar circumstances. It was brought home to them by the rapid fall in prices which began in the second half of 1927; but not until consumption began to fall away in the second half of 1929 was any constructive action taken. In July of that year the Anglo-Oriental group organized a meeting of representatives of about half the world's tin producers, which eventuated in the creation of the Tin Producers' Association, an organization designed to promote co-operation between producers and to further their interests. Its first action was to organize a voluntary restriction scheme for 1930, frankly predatory in intention towards the consumer, designed to curtail production by some 30,000 tons in 1930 by means of " holidays " and so to raise the price. The majority of Malayan and Nigerian producers, being largely members of the Tin Producers' Association, agreed to the scheme without delay. Moreover, the active participation of Patiño and Aramaya in Bolivia was secured by agreement with the President of Patiño (who became President of the Tin Producers' Association) and the Guggenheim interests; natural forces in the Bolivian industry were also working on the side of restriction, and many smaller producers were closing down owing to financial difficulties. Some measure of support was also promised by the Dutch. As far as curtailment of output was concerned, the scheme succeeded in so far as production was reduced by about 25,000 tons compared with the previous year. It is, however, interesting to note that the major contribution to this reduction came from Bolivia and the Dutch, who were only in the agreement by co-operation, and from various small producers who were not in it at all. The production of the membership of the Tin Producers' Association showed little change, though this does not necessarily imply evasion of the agreement, but is more a measure of the increase in their capacity. Circumstances, however, in the form of continually falling consumption, were working against the success of this scheme; and stocks continued to accumulate. So rapid was the deterioration that the price fell abruptly from £180 to £140 in the early spring, and once again to around £110 in the late autumn.

Although the Tin Producers' Association scheme was loyally supported, it met by no means with universal approval among producers— mainly because restriction raised working costs per ton. The problem of costs, as in all restriction schemes, has in fact tended to cause a split between high-cost and low-cost producers. Owing to technical improvements, a number of the larger alluvial producers could to-day make a very reasonable profit at a price of no more than £100 per ton—as some of them have admitted—but only provided that output is large enough to permit overhead costs to be adequately spread, in which case the resultant production would almost certainly exceed demand. At £150 unrestricted production would probably be profitable for the greater part of the Eastern industry; Nigeria seems to be in a similar position, especially since the introduction of hydro-electric power; in Bolivia, on the other hand, costs are very much higher. Any restriction in production in order to obviate the accumulation of excessive stocks of necessity narrows the volume of business over which fixed costs can be spread, and the marginal price is correspondingly raised. In 1930, before the suspension of the gold standard (which, however, affected only British territories), and in the absence of technical progress since achieved, average costs were undoubtedly higher than they are to-day. There were, nevertheless, a number of companies for whom, even then, a price in the neighbourhood of £110 was not in marked disparity with producing costs. It is understandable that they should have been lacking in enthusiasm for any scheme which might involve a 40 per cent. increase in their ton costs through a 50 per cent. output restriction, and possibly, if prices failed to respond equally to the increase in costs, a diminution in net profits, the more so if such a scheme tended to support competitors working on a high-cost basis.

INTERNATIONAL TIN RESTRICTION

By the end of 1930, however, it was generally realized that under-consumption added to over-production had produced circumstances which any voluntary effort, such as that sponsored by the Tin Producers' Association, was powerless to control. The Dutch, Bolivian and Nigerian governments would have been particularly embarrassed by a collapse in the tin industry, since it formed a major source of revenue, and with the two latter the most important national industry. When the idea of an international restriction scheme was put forward it was adopted with surprising rapidity—too rapid in fact for the approval of a number of producers in Malaya.

The restriction was to be enforced by the governments of the participating countries represented on an International Committee, and was to operate for two years from March 1, 1931, with a further extension if the participating governments so desired. Any government might, however, withdraw if any proposal that it made for an increase or decrease in the production quota was not unanimously accepted within six months. In this event the other governments were free to contract out of the scheme.

The express purpose of the scheme was to " secure a fair and reasonable equilibrium between production and consumption with the view of preventing rapid and severe oscillations of price." This object was to be achieved by allotting to each of the participants a standard tonnage and a percentage quota based on an agreed figure of production in 1929. World production in this year was assessed by the Committee at the following figures:

	tons
Malaya	69,366
Nigeria	10,412
Bolivia	46,338
Netherland Indies	35,730
Siam	9,939
Burma	2,443
Others	12,190
Total	186,518

It was agreed that any quotas imposed under the scheme should preserve the ratio of each producer to the total supply shown by these figures—37·19 per cent. for Malaya and 49·6 per cent. for the other participants. In the first instance, the Committee aimed at restricting world production to about 145,000 tons and imposed restrictions on the four participants amounting to about 22 per cent. of their joint production in 1929:

TABLE I.—RESTRICTION QUOTAS

	Tonnage	Per cent. of estimated World Supply		Per cent. of agreed 1929 Production
Malaya . .	53,925	37·19		77·74
Nigeria . .	7,750	5·34		74·43
Bolivia . .	34,260	23·63	49·60	73·93
Neth. Indies .	29,910	20·63		83·71

It was agreed that these quotas should operate for a period of not less than six months, with the proviso that delegations might propose an alteration during that period should circumstances urgently require it; but any change in a shorter period than three months was definitely excluded.

Each government undertook to control production so that it should correspond as closely as possible throughout the year with its export quota, and to prevent exports from exceeding the annual allotment, distributing them as uniformly as possible over the whole twelve months. The governments of Nigeria, Malaya and Bolivia undertook to pass legislation to ensure the enforcement of this control, but no legislative measures were required in the Dutch Indies, where only one small independent producer existed and the Government's control was already adequate.

The Committee was left with power to decide what statistics it would require, which were to be furnished by the participants; and provision was made for co-operative research with a view to increasing the consumption of the metal.

The possibility of extending the scheme to cover other producers was not excluded, and the governments of Siam and Burma were specifically invited to co-operate. This was the main outline of the scheme, which was pushed through in some haste so as to become effective on March 1, 1931. The methods by which it came into force were strongly criticized in Malaya; producers complained with some justification that they had not been consulted, and that the initiative had not come from them. Whatever justice one may find in these assertions—and it is true that the negotiations were carried on in Europe between governments which in the case of the Dutch Indies, Bolivia and Nigeria were far more representative of producing interests than the Colonial Office or the Malaya Government could claim to be of the more democratically constituted Malayan industry—experience of the initiation of the Stevenson scheme for the control of rubber shows that delay may be fatal in a matter of this kind. In fact, the postponement of the enforcement of the Tin Scheme from January 1, as first proposed, to March 1, to enable the Malayan Government to pass the necessary legislation, evoked a certain amount of " forestalling " which did not make the earlier months of restriction any easier. In these circumstances some disregard of democratic principles may be not unfavourable to producers in the long run.

Complaints from Malaya that her quota treatment was unfair, compared with that of the other participators, at first glance appear to have been without foundation, since the Malayan quota represented a restriction of only slightly more than 22 per cent. of the agreed 1929 output, compared with 26 per cent. for Bolivia and 25 per cent. for Nigeria. But it was objected, not without justice, that Malayan capacity had increased rapidly since 1929, and that in terms of current production the restriction was far more drastic than it appeared to be.

It was soon evident, however, that the restriction, as a whole, was not drastic enough, and, on May 16, 1931, a further cut of 20,000 tons in total output was recommended, reducing permissible production to about 66 per cent. of the 1929 standard. The new quota was accepted as from June 1, in spite of some dissatisfaction in Malaya. At about the same time, Siam announced her willingness to participate in the scheme, though on a rather different basis from that of the other participants, and was admitted in July. The quota for Siam was, in fact, fixed at a flat-rate basis of 10,000 tons per year—very favourable treatment in view of the fact that her output exceeded this figure by only 500 tons in 1929 and was no higher than 11,500 tons in 1930. The admission of Siam on these terms was, therefore, a move to prevent a dangerous increase in production in an important " outside " area, rather than a contribution towards the actual curtailment of output.

THE INTERNATIONAL TIN POOL

A further important development took place with the formation of the International Tin Pool, on August 12. The price of tin at the time was in the neighbourhood of £115, and no impression had been made on the level of stocks outstanding. Restriction had, in fact, only served to stabilize the position, and it was apparent that no material price improvement could come until the dead weight of surplus stocks had been removed from the market. A syndicate was accordingly formed with the object of holding up some 20,000 to 25,000 tons of the metal; it was essentially a private enterprise, formed with the object of ultimately raising prices; it was formed only after the International Committee had taken the decision to continue the quota agreement for at least three years, provided that the Pool had not previously been liquidated; and although it was to work in co-operation with the Committee, the co-operation seems only to have taken the form of " confidential communication " of the details of the Pool agreement to the governments and the appointment as chairman of the Pool of the representative of the Nigerian and Malayan governments on the International Committee. This constitution was severely criticized on the ground that the Pool was a private concern, working ultimately for private profit, and that a Government representative serving on it, even in a private capacity, was in an anomalous position. The nature of its operations was, however, strictly defined by a statutory scale of releases which provided, in its final form, for liquidation at the rate of 5 per cent. per month only when the price of tin had reached a level consistently above £165; the rate of liquidation could be increased to 10 per cent. per month at a price of £176 and to 20 per cent. at £198 or better.

By the end of the year, the Pool had succeeded in securing more than 20,000 tons of the metal for removal from the active market. It was expressly stated at the time that the stock was firmly held, being beyond the control of the actual participants, and could be dealt with only under the terms of the Pool agreement.

In spite of the restriction in output to 66 per cent., very little impression had been made on stocks, though it must be remembered that approximately 20,000 tons had by then been immobilized by the Pool. On the other hand, the price steadily appreciated from June to the end of the year, as far as £140, although the gain was subsequently entirely lost in the early months of 1932. There is no doubt that the annual production of 145,000 tons at which the Committee had aimed at the inception of the scheme was some way in excess of consumption during 1931. A further curtailment of production by 15,000 tons to 56 per cent. of 1929 production was therefore enforced on January 1, 1932; and with consumption and prices still declining, another cut of 8240 tons, later raised to 20,000 tons, was proposed for the period beginning June 1.

THE BYRNE RESTRICTION SCHEME

At this stage an independent proposal was laid before the Committee by the Tin Producers' Association. It submitted that, in view of the very unfavourable circumstances, the Committee's latest proposal was inadequate, and recommended that from June 1 onwards production should be restricted to 33⅓ per cent. only, compared with the Committee's restriction to 44 per cent. Moreover, it suggested that during the first two months of the plan there should be a complete export holiday, and that the permitted production should actually be spread over the succeeding ten months only.

This proposal, which is generally known as the " Byrne Scheme," was considered by the participants, and finally adopted, though not before the Committee's new quota had come into operation. It was therefore not possible to put it into effect until July 1. Though production continued during August and September, there were no exports during these months, but thereafter they were continued at the rate of one-tenth of the annual figure, which amounted in fact to 40 per cent. of the monthly production in 1929. In July 1933, when the monthly quotas again became one-twelfth of the annual figure, there was consequently a further actual decline in monthly production to 33⅓ per cent. of the 1929 figures, although the annual quotas were not changed.

After the adoption of the Byrne Scheme in July 1932, a noticeable improvement took place: stocks began to fall, and prices showed a rapid increase to over £150 in September. Since the improvement coincided with the beginning of business revival in many countries, it would be unwise to attribute it entirely to the Byrne Scheme, but the scheme at least performed the valuable service of preventing an expansion of production which might easily have offset the reduction in surplus stocks due to a revival in industrial demand. A slight recession in prices occurred in November and December 1932; but, as the decline in stocks became more rapid, a very remarkable recovery took place, for the price of tin jumped from £149 in March to £220 in June. At the same time, visible stocks fell below the 50,000 mark for the first time since 1930.

The movement of stocks at this time is particularly interesting, since it originated mainly in a revival of industrial demand in America. While world stocks as a whole had mounted during the depression, American stocks had actually declined from nearly 6300 tons in December 1931 to about 3500 in April 1932, as industrial users adopted a hand-to-mouth policy instead of keeping a considerable future supply. Therefore, as industrial demand increased in the middle of 1933 in America, there was a rise in American stocks, though it was accompanied by a decline in world stocks as a whole.

TABLE II.—VISIBLE STOCKS *

(thousand long tons)

Year		U.K.	U.S.A.	Afloat	Straits Carry-over	Total Visible
1932 Sept.	.	31·6	4·2	5·1	9·3	56·3
1933 Jan.	.	28·9	3·4	5·7	10·4	54·4
,, April	.	26·8	2·1	7·6	7·7	49·9
,, July	.	20·0	4·5	8·9	7·0	44·8
,, Sept.	.	14·0	6·0	7·3	4·7	35·8
1934 Jan.	.	8·7	8·3	4·4	3·6	28·3
,, April	.	5·1	5·6	6·1	2.7	22·4
,, July	.	3·6	6·5	5·7	2·5	20·5
,, Sept.	.	4·0	4·2	6·8	1·7	18·7
,, Oct.	.					20·4

* Moodys-Economist Services, *Industries and Commodities Bulletin*.

NEGOTIATIONS FOR FURTHER CONTROL

When the World Economic Conference met in London in the summer of 1933 and devoted a considerable portion of its energies to the discussion of production and marketing, an opportunity was presented to the tin industry to secure the solution of a problem that had begun to cause some anxiety, with good reason in view of the experience of rubber producers—the possible increase of production by non-participant producers stimulated by the greatly improved level of prices. As long as prices had remained low and unremunerative, this danger had been passive; but with their improvement during the spring and summer the restricting countries were, not unreasonably, disinclined to see other producers reap the benefits of their own abstinence. Producers of many other raw materials have had similar experiences; and, to cite a single instance, Brazil's unilateral action in restricting her coffee exports has been turned to full account by other growers in Colombia and elsewhere. The restricting countries, therefore, sought, through the agency of the 1933 Conference, to extend control of production to countries that had not hitherto participated. The restricting countries were also concerned as to the possibilities of the growth of large speculative activities in the stocks with the resumption of industrial demand.

The Committee's views were expressed to the Conference in a Memorandum submitted through the British delegation:

The International Tin Committee consider that the recent improvement in apparent consumption, which is most noticeable in America, is to some extent due to a reaction from the hand-to-mouth policy hitherto pursued by consumers —*i.e.* the increased demand for tin is not due, it would seem, solely to increased consumption, but it represents also in part speculation, and in part additions to stocks in the hands of manufacturers and intermediate holders. For this reason the current high level of prices may not last; and in any event, in view of the present great uncertainty of world conditions, and the very large excess of potential production over any demand that is probable for some time to come, the continuance of control is in their view essential to prevent the possibility of any relapse to the disastrous situation which led to the international agreement. During the period of control, producers in the signatory countries have had to endure, and continue to endure, the greatest hardship; for the past year they have been allowed to produce and export only one-third of their 1929 production, which is considerably less than their potential production; they have had to suffer all the risks and losses entailed by the drastic reduction of their experienced labour forces; and their overhead charges have, as a consequence of the great reduction of output, become very high. These heavy sacrifices they have borne in the interests of the industry; and they feel strongly that this burden should now be shared by all producers, for the reason that all producers participate in the benefits to the industry which have unquestionably been obtained as a result of the working of the control scheme. The wider the area over which that scheme operates, the more rapidly will the objectives it has in view be attained, and the lighter the burden will be on the individual producer.

The Committee estimated that the current production of non-participant countries was in the neighbourhood of 16,000 tons per annum, to which must be added 6000 tons of secondary tin recovered from scrap. Added to the current production of the restricting countries and Siam (64,056 tons), the total annual supply was estimated at 86,056 tons. Consumption during 1932 had not run above 100,000 tons, and a figure much in excess of this could not be counted on in future years unless a sustained improvement in consumption could be envisaged. Since the potential production of non-participants at £200 per ton was in the neighbourhood of 25,000 tons at least, and of secondary tin in the neighbourhood of 10,000 tons, the prospects for a further reduction in stocks or for an increase in quotas were not considered favourable.

TABLE III.—

TABLE III.—TIN OUTPUT IN NON-RESTRICTING COUNTRIES

(tons)

Country	Estimated Production in 1932	Potential Production
United Kingdom	1,192	3,000
Burma	2,534	3,000
Australia	854	3,000
Union of South Africa	541	1,300
Belgian Congo	683	2,000
Portugal	442	750
Mexico	782	1,000
Japan	582	1,500
China	4,992	10,000
French Indo-China	1,247	1,500
All Other Sources	1,061	1,000
Total	14,910	28,050

In any case, the existing scheme was due to expire on August 12, 1934, at the latest, and its renewal might be made difficult if the independent producers were to get all the advantages and none of the responsibilities. In fact, the draft scheme for the continuance of the control contained a clause specially designed to provide for the termination of the agreement if competition from the independent producers became too strong:

In the event of the committee being satisfied that the estimated production of non-participating countries has, for six consecutive months, exceeded 25 per cent. of the estimated world's production during that period, it shall be competent for any Government to give six months' notice of its intention to withdraw from the scheme. In the event of such withdrawal, the other signatory Governments may immediately abandon the scheme.

The sort of terms on which independent producers might be admitted to the scheme would probably involve their accepting a quota representing their 1932 production, and in any case one not exceeding the peak production in any of the years 1929-1933. The Committee were, therefore, willing to concede that new participants need not curtail their current production even where it represented a high percentage of capacity, and were prepared, as soon as it became possible to increase the quotas of the original participants, to increase the quotas of new participants *pari passu*. The Committee was obviously less concerned with restricting the current output of independent producers than with preventing a sudden increase.

Had the Conference not come to a rather premature conclusion it is possible that some constructive arrangement could have been made. As it was, the countries which were not members of the International Tin Committee were recommended to enter into negotiations with that body, as the Conference Sub-Committee considered that the existing scheme was " framed upon sound lines." It suggested that negotiations should be concerned with the agreement of an initial flat rate, a standard tonnage, and methods for the variation of the initial flat rate corresponding to quota increases in the signatory countries, and stressed the importance of early action in view of the imminent necessity of reviewing the original agreement. But it was a year before agreement with four countries was finally announced, and then only at a stiff price.

Consumption during 1933 belied the fears of the Tin Committee expressed in the summer that the improvement might prove to be ephemeral. Consumption rose from round about 9000 tons in the first four months, to 10,700 tons in May, 11,500 in June, and a peak of over 13,000 tons in July and August, the total for the year being 127,800 tons. The rapidity of the rise in demand seems to have been due partly to a re-stocking movement in the United States. In fact, the whole of the improvement in consumption during 1933 may be attributed with some certainty to American influences; it is estimated that in the course of the year American consumption increased from 41,000 to 60,000 tons, while demand from the rest of the world remained fairly stable round about the 1932 figure of 70,000 tons.

The holdings of the Pool, which had remained intact until July 1933, were then steadily liquidated at a handsome profit to the holders; by the end of November it was reported that they stood at 8000 tons only, compared with their peak level of 21,000 tons, and at the end of the year the last of the Pool's stocks were released.

The position had, therefore, substantially improved, and when the Committee met on October 27 it was able to agree to a new scheme of control, to operate for three years from January 1, 1934, involving an increase in permitted production to 40 per cent. of the assessment figure. The basic assessment also was slightly revised, and an additional quota of 4 per cent. during 1934 was agreed upon, allocated not proportionately, but arbitrarily, among the participants, to compensate for certain anomalies, and to adjust excess production in the past in certain areas. It was widely held that in raising the quota for January 1 to only 44 per cent. the Committee had taken an over-pessimistic view of the future of tin consumption and had opened the possibility of a shortage, should consumption continue in 1934 to run at levels approaching 10,000 to 11,000 tons per month. The quota was raised to 50 per cent. for the second and third quarters of the year, but on October 1 it was reduced once more to 40 per cent., which figure was to remain in force until April 1, 1935. The extra 4 per cent. allowed during 1934 expired on December 31. Table IV. shows permissible exports during 1934, together with actual exports for the first ten months of the year.

TABLE IV.—QUOTAS AND EXPORTS IN 1934

(tons)

	Dutch East Indies	Nigeria	Bolivia	Malaya	Siam	Total
Permissible Exports:						
1st Quarter . .	4092	1119	4668	7656	2448	19,983
2nd and 3rd Quarters .	5001	1392	5829	9456	2448	24,126
4th Quarter . .	4092	1119	4668	7656	2448	19,983
Actual Exports:						
1st Quarter . .	4240	995	4548	7707	2656	20,146
2nd ,, . . .	4853	1293	4918	8990	1880	21,934
3rd ,, . . .	5001	1486	5505	9565	3184	24,740
October . . .	1149	428	1919	2155	866	6,517

THE "BUFFER" STOCK POOL

Following the liquidation of the Pool stocks at the end of 1933, and the reduction of visible supplies to very low levels, the International Tin Committee in April 1934 recommended the creation of a " buffer " pool consisting of some 8000 tons of the metal.

The objects of the control, as reiterated by the Agreement of October 1933, were: " To secure a fair and reasonable relation between production and consumption with a view to preventing rapid and severe oscillations of price, and to ensure the absorption of surplus stocks."

As long as the third objective was not attained, the dangers of " rapid and severe oscillations of price " were not serious. With the reduction of the surplus, however, and the liquidation of Pool stocks, apprehension was expressed by the controlling authorities that the market would be increasingly open to the possibility of " cornering " and excessive speculation. For this reason, the proposal of a buffer pool was put forward, to act as a reservoir from which purely " market " movements could be drowned by the authorities. It was argued that this method offered more advantages than merely allowing stocks to reaccumulate in the market. It was contended in the first place that movements in market demand are not necessarily related to movements in manufacturers' consumption; in fact, if the estimate of dealers with regard to future consumption is inaccurate, the two may move in opposite directions. Alterations in production quotas with a view to equalizing price oscillations that might be entirely due to market vagaries would, it was contended, tend to defeat the primary object of the scheme—" the maintenance of a fair and reasonable level between production and consumption." The metal market was, not unnaturally, adversely inclined to any development that would restrict its opportunities, and consumers saw latent dangers in allowing representatives of producers permanently to exert a large proportionate influence in a small market. A strong suspicion seems to have been felt that the producing industry, having tasted the sweets of the first Pool, were anxious to repeat the experience. There was, moreover, a considerable inclination to doubt whether the creation of a new Pool would prove effective in its task of eliminating fluctuations. It has been observed by those in touch with the London metal market that speculators were more active during the life of the earlier Pool than at any other time during the past twenty years. Theoretically, at any rate, the introduction of a further imponderable influence in the market may well actually widen the field for speculation; speculation thrives on uncertainty, and the possible actions of the Pool authorities must be accounted an additional uncertain element. In any case it cannot be denied that the control authorities are undertaking grave responsibilities in attempting to disentangle " speculative " from " natural " price movements. It may also be found that the control of a rising market is an easier proposition than the support of a falling market; the experience of Copper Exporters Incorporated, to cite only one example, suggests that difficulties may lie in wait for the Pool in times of falling prices. In such periods, the existence of a pool may tend to depress rather than sustain prices.

But opposition was not only forthcoming from dealers and consumers, who were naturally predisposed to look upon a controlled market with disfavour. The scheme was by no means universally popular with producers, particularly in Malaya and among the Chinese small holders there, and a very sharp controversy arose, in which, incidentally, the Tin Producers' Association lost its chairman. The conflict was the old one between those who believe in permanent control and those who regard restriction as a necessary but temporary evil. It was the latter section that opposed the Buffer Pool scheme, maintaining that the objects for which the restriction scheme was set up—to tide the industry over the depression—had been fulfilled and that the process of de-control should begin. This opinion was most strongly held by small producers, who undoubtedly saw in the continuation of the Pool in the proposed form an attempt by the larger producers to dominate the market—a situation of which they had gained some experience in earlier unofficial pools. They were strong enough to extract a promise of a referendum on the subject, and had it ever been taken it is question-able whether the scheme would have gone through. But the opposition was very summarily overridden and the Pool agreement signed on July 10, 1934. A stock of 8282 tons was to be accumulated by a special export quota of 5 per cent. during the remainder of the year. A little later, presumably with the object of making permanent control more palatable to consumers, it was decided to invite consumers to form an advisory panel, whose members might attend meetings of the Tin Committee. The United States representative has already been appointed, but at the time of writing the United Kingdom consumers had yet to appoint theirs.

A REVIEW OF TIN RESTRICTION

The developments make 1934 an important date in the history of tin restriction. As far as machinery is concerned, the Tin Control scheme has been notably in advance of many other attempts to regulate raw-material production. The rapidity with which it was brought into operation naturally made the first six months a difficult period; and the assessment of individual Malayan producers was not at first very satisfactory. It says a good deal for the scheme that many producers who were formerly opposed to it have since modified their attitude; this has been due to a small extent to later legislation making permits exchangeable among producers, a system which also tends to con-centrate production in the most efficient plants. Further testimony to the efficient working of the scheme is provided by the small margins by which actual exports have deviated from the allotted quotas, though there was one large discrepancy in the summer of 1931, which is said to have been caused by an unexpected release of reserves from the Straits smelters. Bolivia has also shown a tendency, at times, to exceed her allowance.

One of the major sources of weakness has been materially reduced by the adhesion to the scheme of four more producing countries. The terms of agreement, which were announced during the summer of 1934, are shown in Table V.

TABLE V.—RESTRICTION QUOTAS FOR THE NEW ADHERENTS

(tons)

Year	French Indo-China *	Belgian Congo and Ruanda-Urundi *†	Portugal ‡	Cornwall ‡§
1934 . .	1700	4500	650	1700
1935 . .	2500	6000	650	1700
1936 . .	3000	7000	650	1700

* Should the export quota allotted to the original restricting countries rise above 65 per cent., these tonnages are to be raised by 25 tons for every 1 per cent. increase in the export quota over 65 per cent.

† For the twelve companies operating at the date of the agreement.

‡ Portugal and Cornwall have been given standard tonnages of 800 and 2615 tons respectively. Should the export quota allotted to the original restricting countries rise above 65 per cent. the flat rates are to be increased proportionately.

§ For the three important producers.

It is evident that the original restricting countries paid a heavy price for the co-operation of these four countries. The highest output hitherto achieved by the Belgian Congo was only 2225 tons (1933), and the Indo-Chinese output, though it has doubled since the inauguration of restriction, was still well below the 2000-tons level in 1933. Cornwall's quota represents a substantial increase over her output for recent years, though it is not much more than half her 1929 figure. When we remember that Malaya, Bolivia, Nigeria and the Dutch East Indies are producing only 40 per cent. of their 1929 output the extent of the concessions made to the Belgian Congo and French Indo-China is clear. The high price paid for their adherence was a measure of the original participants' anxiety to fix a limit to the decline in their own share of world production. The following figures illustrate the threat to restriction which was coming from " outside " production:

TABLE VI.—

TABLE VI.—OUTPUT OF FREE AND RESTRICTING COUNTRIES

(tons)

	Restricting Countries	Non-restricting Countries	Total Production	Percentage of Total Production by Non-restricting Countries
1924 . . .	123,237	12,196	135,433	9·0
1927 . . .	138,893	11,413	150,306	7·6
1931 . . .	172,107	14,879	186,986	8·0
1932 . . .	77,853	14,223	92,076	15·4
1933 . . .	66,641	17,201	83,842	20·5
1933—Dec. . .	4,987	1,705	6,692	25·5
1934—Feb. . .	6,268	1,665*	7,933*	21·0*

* Preliminary

To this extent, tin has had its " native problem " in the same way, though not to the same degree, as rubber. Nor is the problem finally disposed of while China remains outside the scheme. Tin deposits have been known and worked in the Kotchin district of Yunnan, on the Red River, for many hundreds of years, employing 50,000 to 75,000 people, and have yielded an output varying between 7000 (1924) and 14,000 tons (1922) in the period 1914-1928. Since then the output has been smaller—in the neighbourhood of 4000 to 8000 tons. But now that the Kotchin field has a good outlet by railway to Hanoi, the return of skilled Chinese labour from Malaya, displaced under the restriction scheme, coupled with the high current price of the metal, has made China potentially an important producer.

Otherwise, the resemblance between tin and rubber as subjects for control is not marked. In general, the control of tin production offers far fewer difficulties. The period of production is relatively short and the output largely independent of the weather. The difficulty of regulating the supply of rubber in the absence of any knowledge, first, of the quantity that will be needed seven years hence, second, of the number of trees which are in fact being planted, and, third, of the yield that will be obtained from each tree, has no real parallel in tin production. In the second place, the demand for tin has in the past been inelastic and relatively insensitive to changes in price. The control authorities are possibly gambling rather heavily on the chance that this characteristic will be permanent. In so far as tin is used to a large extent in luxury trades, for instance the automobile industry, the quantity demand does in fact fluctuate to some extent in accordance with the general state of trade. The American motor industry, which took a quarter of the total deliveries to the United States in 1928, took only one-eighth of the heavily reduced deliveries of 1931. There is also the possibility of a big development of the use of substitutes to be considered and the further advance of reclamation. As early as 1933 the American production of reclaimed tin increased by nearly 50 per cent. In order to meet this particular danger, the producers have set up a Tin Development Council, to extend the uses of tin, but it is doubtful whether propaganda will prove as successful a salesman as low prices.

In view of the fact that the big improvement in the tin position came in 1933 simultaneously with a big revival in industrial demand, it would be rash to attribute it entirely to the existence of control. Nevertheless, aided by trade revival, tin producers have succeeded in liquidating surplus stocks and tiding the industry over a period of intense depression, which was the primary object of the scheme. But it would cause little surprise if the past history of the scheme should prove to have been easy compared with the period that is to come. While there was a heavy accumulation of stocks there was a sufficient guarantee to the consumer against exploitation. Now that surplus stocks have been removed, the tin committee is faced with the far more difficult problem of preserving a fair and enlightened control in conditions where it has the power to squeeze the consumer, should it be unable to resist that temptation. To this extent, the control has arrived at the same cross-roads at which the authorities responsible for the Stevenson scheme chose the primrose path in preference to the straight and narrow way.

Notwithstanding that the authorities have frequently stated that they are not primarily concerned with prices but with securing a reasonable level of stocks and an approximate equilibrium of supply and demand, price must be an important consideration, for it has a definite influence on these other factors. As regards stocks, having effected the removal of more than two-thirds of the 1931 figure, the Committee has now to decide exactly what constitutes a surplus. Consumers would probably like to see visible stocks not below 25,000 tons, while the Committee appears to have a figure of around 17,000 tons, or less, in mind. This latter figure, which certainly represents a bare working minimum, was approached in September with visible stocks at 18,700 tons. It is, moreover, improbable that invisible stocks, mainly metal lying in private warehouses in Liverpool and the Straits, which once had to be reckoned with, are any longer important; they appear to have been very largely liquidated during 1933. The maintenance of any level of stocks, however, must involve the fixing of a " pivotal " price whether it is openly announced as such or not. Here the Committee is undoubtedly in perpetual danger of being caught between two fires. There is good reason to believe that, as long as costs do not rise substantially, an annual world demand of as much as 125,000 tons could be supplied for a reasonable profit by low-cost producers in Nigeria and the East at a price not much above £150 per ton. Such a price is definitely unpalatable to the high-cost producers, represented chiefly by Bolivia, but any higher price immediately raises the possibility of encouraging an expansion of production in " outside " areas and arousing the antagonism of consumers. The history of the scheme to date, however, suggests that a high rather than a low price is being aimed at, and possibly a higher one than was at first envisaged. It will be remembered that the original Pool's scale of releases was altered to make the first sales dependent on the attainment of a price of £165 instead of the original £150. Then a figure of £220 was mentioned unofficially during 1933 as that at which the control aimed under a restriction of 33⅓ per cent. But at the moment of writing, production is at more than 40 per cent. of standard, and the price has remained steady for some months just below £230. " The crux of the situation is the Committee's conception of a reasonable price," The Economist has accurately observed ; and has added: " In our view it is certainly below £200 per ton." It is to be hoped that the future history of tin restriction will allay the fears which the recent course of prices has inevitably aroused, and will not display the predatory characteristics which have hitherto ruined most schemes of artificial control.

CHAPTER XIII

THE INTERNATIONAL CONTROL OF RUBBER
by Oliver Lawrence

GOVERNMENT schemes for the control of production of certain raw materials have commonly been introduced with the motive of inducing a quick return to equilibrium of the forces of supply and demand, in circumstances where the action of the " automatic " process of adjustment has threatened the producing industry with widespread liquidation, which might well prove detrimental in the long period to consuming interests and to the community at large. A long period of acute depression where consumption runs continually below normal levels may result in the extinction of many producers with inadequate financial reserves, irrespective of their long-period efficiency. In this way productive capacity may be so reduced as to embarrass consuming industries when normal activity is resumed, besides involving producers and the community in general in severe financial losses and eventually opening the way to fresh over-expansion. In consequence, although under a system of complete *laissez-faire* depression eventually brings its own cure through the liquidation of what appears for the moment to be excess production, the process may be a long and painful one. Restriction schemes have been born of a desire to avoid the drastic social consequences of this deflationary process, which may be particularly severe in colonial areas where large native and sometimes immigrant populations are very much dependent on the prosperity of one or two raw-material producing industries, and where the standard of living is at all times not far removed from marginal existence. To this perhaps may be added the desire, inspired by a growing conviction that the " automatic " system itself has lost some of its old freedom of action through the growth of various frictional forces, to exercise a more or less permanent control with a view to prevention, as well as cure, of the worst excesses of the trade cycle.

Commodities in whose control the British Government has participated and which are produced largely in the East are two—rubber and tin.[1] Rubber production, following short periods of voluntary restriction in 1918 and 1921, came under Government control in Malaya at the

[1] See Chapter XII.

end of 1922 and continued to be restricted for six years before the scheme broke down. After an interval of five and a half years a comprehensive scheme of control, covering all the major rubber-producing areas, was inaugurated on June 1, 1934.

HISTORY OF PRODUCTION AND PRICES

Rubber production is one of the youngest of the plantation industries of the East, having been imported from the Amazon basin to Ceylon at the end of the nineteenth century, and developed on a commercial scale largely as a result of the devastation of the Singalese coffee industry by disease, spreading thence with great rapidity to Malaya and the Dutch Indies. Hitherto, the chief sources of supply had been the Amazon basin and Africa, where, however, rubber was not cultivated on commercial estates but collected from the wild tree in the forests. With the advent of the motor-car, the chief modern use for rubber—in tyres—was created; and in the period before the Eastern plantations came into bearing,[1] the wild-rubber collectors reached the zenith of their prosperity. By 1910, however, the plantations began to produce on a large scale, and the fate of the wild industry was sealed.

Being essentially of jungle growth, the rubber-tree flourishes only within a narrow belt bordering on the Equator; and it so happened that most of the areas suitable for its cultivation were under the British flag. British capital, therefore, aided by long experience in the management of tropical plantations, was mainly responsible for the development of the commercial estate, which proceeded rapidly up to 1914. The Malayan native and the Chinese immigrant were not slow to follow the lead of the British and the Dutch, and were never much above five years behind them. So great was the resultant expansion that the price of rubber had fallen in 1914 to a level around 2s. per lb from its highest point of 12s. 9d. in 1910 and talk of over-production arose and new avenues of bulk consumption—still one of the most pressing problems of the industry—were being sought. By the end of the war the estates planted in the boom period of 1910-1911 were reaching their full yield, and the price at Singapore had fallen to 1s. This was in part due to the shortage of shipping, which also considerably widened the margin between Singapore and London prices, and necessitated a temporary restriction of 20 per cent., which was, however, ineffective

---

[1] Plantations do not begin to yield until the fifth year from planting, and do not reach full bearing until eight to ten years.

in preventing an accumulation of stocks. But the immediate post-war demand was so great that when adequate transport became available a considerable increase in output was possible, and London prices rose still higher, to nearly 3s. The abrupt collapse of the immediate post-war boom in 1920 caused a sharp relapse—to 10d.; and a form of restriction (by 25 per cent.) was put into operation by the Rubber Growers' Association for one year. For a number of reasons—chiefly heavy over-stocking by American manufacturers during the previous boom and the increase of native production in Malaya as a result of plantings in 1914-1916—the scheme was not a success and failed to secure the requisite majority for its renewal at the end of 1921. The Rubber Growers' Association, however, supported by a large section of the industry in Malaya and Ceylon, considered the continuation of restriction essential and appealed to the Colonial Office to assume compulsory control. The outcome of their appeal was the appointment of the famous Stevenson Committee, on October 24, 1921.

The above brief and inadequate account of the growth of the industry will be better appreciated in connection with the following figures [1] for the years prior to the enforcement of the Stevenson scheme:

TABLE I.—WORLD PRODUCTION BEFORE RESTRICTION

(tons)

Year	Plantation Production				Wild Production	Consumption by Manufacturers
	British Malaya	Netherlands Indies	Ceylon	Total	Total	
1910 .	6,500	2,400	1,600	11,000	83,000	..
1914 .	47,000	10,400	15,800	75,700	46,000	..
1919 .	204,000	85,000	44,800	350,000	48,000	330,000
1920 .	181,000	80,000	39,000	316,000	37,000	270,000
1921 .	151,000	71,000	40,200	277,200	23,000	390,000
1922 .	214,000	94,000	47,400	373,700	26,000	435,000

America has always been the largest consumer of rubber, taking about two-thirds of the world's supply and utilizing by far the greater part of her imports for the manufacture of motor tyres. For this reason the state of activity of American business and of the motor industry in

[1] From *Studies in the Artificial Control of Raw Material Supplies*, No. 2, *Rubber*, by J. W. F. Rowe, published by the London and Cambridge Economic Service and Royal Economic Society, from which most of the material for this section has been drawn.

general is the most potent influence on rubber production from the demand side. While the phenomenal growth of the motor industry was the chief cause of the growth of rubber cultivation, economies and improvements in processing, particularly by way of securing a longer life for tyres, have tended to exercise a stabilizing influence on demand. At the same time, no very satisfactory progress has been made in developing new bulk uses. Rubber upholstery has gained some ground, but technical difficulties have prevented the widespread adoption of rubber for flooring and roads to which the industry has pinned its hopes for many years. America's dependence for her large needs entirely on the produce of areas under foreign control has also complicated the position of the Eastern estate, through the development of " reclamation " from waste and the stimulation of plantation industries under American control in Brazil and Liberia. Of still later origin, Soviet experiments with various wild plants from more temperate zones have received favourable reports and will possibly lead to important developments. The production of rubber from the Mexican *guayule* plant has been feasible for some time, but the Soviet experiments are concerned more with a new and superior species from Central Asia, which is said to yield a rubber of quality quite comparable with that of the Eastern product. The future of the Eastern industry can, therefore, by no means be considered assured, though their position will have been strengthened by the lowering of costs which they have achieved during the past few years.

WORKING OF THE STEVENSON SCHEME

The Stevenson Committee did not report until May 19, 1922. Early on, however, it had communicated with the Colonial Secretary to obtain permission to seek Dutch co-operation. These unofficial efforts were apparently unsuccessful, but in the first report strong emphasis was still laid on the necessity of securing this collaboration. The Committee estimated that world consumption had fallen behind production by 60,000 and 17,000 tons in the years 1920 and 1921, and that a still larger gap of 100,000 tons would be realized in 1922. Stocks at the beginning of 1922 were already at 310,000 tons (of which 200,000 were held in consuming countries), approximately 110,000 tons more than the normally necessary holding equal to eight months' consumption. In order to balance production and consumption, the Committee recommended a 25 per cent. restriction, but added that more drastic treatment would be necessary to remove the surplus stocks which would otherwise continue to hang over the industry. The distribution of production was estimated as follows:

								per cent.
Malaya	.	.	.	.	.	.	.	57·5
Ceylon	.	.	.	.	.	.	.	12·5
South India and Burma		.	.	.	.	.		2·0
Netherlands Indies		.	.	.	.	.		25·5
Other Countries .		.	.	.	.	.		2·5
								100·0

But although, according to this estimate, Malaya and Ceylon contributed as much as 70 per cent. of the world output, the Committee announced that it had never departed from " the conviction that it was impossible to deal with the problem as one affecting only the British Colonies and Dependencies in which rubber is produced. . . . This conviction formed the basis of the Committee's deliberations; and, in particular, they have throughout kept in view the fact that no scheme, however excellent in itself, could properly be recommended to you unless it commended itself to the authorities of the Dutch East Indies." The Committee put forward two schemes, the first being a combination of previous proposals involving the restriction of output, which the Committee preferred, the second Lord Stevenson's proposal for regulation through the control of exports by a scale of duties varying with the permitted volume of production and the trend of prices. But the final decision of the Committee was that further recommendations were impossible until the Dutch attitude was finally and officially known.

Official representations to the Netherlands Government were made unavailingly during the summer, in spite of support from the Dutch Rubber Growers' Association for a parallel investigation; and in August the Dutch refusal to take restrictive measures was finally communicated to the British Government.

The Stevenson Committee therefore returned to work, but with the appeal by the Rubber Growers' Association to the Colonial Office in September to impose control regardless of Dutch refusals to co-operate, the basis of its deliberations was radically altered. In the second report, issued on October 2, the original preferences were reversed, and export control was recommended as opposed to control of production. The Committee, in fact, went so far as to recant its decision that Dutch co-operation was essential—on three grounds: because production of rubber continued to increase at an excessive rate, because the Rubber Growers' Association had declared in favour of limited restriction, and because the Rubber Growers' Association was confident of securing the voluntary co-operation of British estates outside Malaya and Ceylon. The scheme was accepted by the Colonial Secretary and hurried through the various legislatures in time to begin operation November 1, 1922, its main provisions being as follows:

1. The percentage exportable at the minimum rate of duty ($\frac{1}{2}$d.—*i.e.* 2 cents Straits currency) was to start at 60 per cent. of standard production, which, in the case of mature areas, was to be the production in the year ending October 31, 1920.

2. For the purpose of the scheme, four restriction quarters of three months each were established, beginning November 1.

3. If during the second or any subsequent restriction quarter the price averaged less than 1s. per lb, the percentage exportable at the minimum rate of duty would be reduced to 55, and by a further 5 points every succeeding quarter unless and until the average price of the preceding quarter should reach 1s. 3d. (The percentage could not fall below 60 in the first instance unless the price averaged less than 1s.)

4. If and when in any restriction quarter the price averaged 1s. 3d. but less than 1s. 6d., the percentage exportable at the minimum rate of duty should be increased by 5 points for the ensuing quarter, but if in any quarter the average price exceeded 1s. 6d., by 10 points for the ensuing quarter.

5. Once the percentage had been lowered it could not be increased except on a basic price of 1s. 3d.

6. Any producer was able to export more than his quota on payment of higher export duties, beginning with 4d. for the first 5 per cent. above his quarterly export quota.

The main objective of the scheme may be put in a nutshell—the arbitrary determination of the largest producing group to raise the price to 1s. 3d., and to sustain this price-level artificially.

A considerable controversy has raged over the merits of this scheme which have been discussed by J. W. F. Rowe in greater detail than is possible here.[1] The reasons for the refusal of Dutch co-operation have always been obscure; the common explanation that the Dutch planters withheld support in order to reap the benefits of Malaya's sacrifices is untenable, as no Dutch planter can possibly have anticipated that the British Government would undertake restriction without Dutch co-operation. Suggestions that the Dutch Government could not undertake control on the lines envisaged for Malaya because it could not control native production, and did not wish to penalize European planters through its inability to do so, would be applicable to modern conditions but not to 1922, when the menace of native production had hardly arisen for serious consideration. The Dutch Government might, indeed, have

---

[1] See Rowe, *op. cit.*, pp. 14-60.

had some difficulty in exercising control over the European producers in 1922, owing to their innate hostility to Government intervention of any sort—which Rowe considers to have been the major factor influencing the Dutch refusal to co-operate at this time.

Having failed to secure Dutch co-operation, the British Government laid itself open to criticism by proceeding with a scheme applicable only to British territories. It is widely admitted that restriction for a short period from the end of 1921 might have prevented many of the industry's difficulties from arising. But during 1922 stocks had continued to accumulate at an alarming rate owing to the almost complete cessation of American buying, and the opportunity was lost. By the end of the year when the scheme actually came into operation consumption was picking up rapidly, and had reached something like equilibrium with production. The Committee, however, was concerned with equilibrium over a longer period. But although its fears of excess production in the future were actually justified, one may legitimately ask whether this excess production would have materialized had not the non-participant planters received the stimulus of high prices provided by the restriction scheme in its later stages. Had restriction come a year earlier—at the end of 1921—its effects could not have failed to be beneficial if it had merely succeeded in preventing the rapid accumulation of stocks. As it was, the twelve months from November 1921 were spent in negotiating, and stocks were allowed to pile up. Moreover, consumption was then increasing to such a degree that the disequilibrium between supply and demand began to disappear and only the burden of heavy surplus stocks remained. Had there been no restriction at all there is good reason to suppose that a slow recovery would have taken place, that excess stocks would gradually have been liquidated, and that much of the new productive capacity which was stimulated by the existence of restriction would never have been created. But recovery would doubtless have been delayed until 1924, and the continuance of low prices throughout 1923 might well have been disastrous to many European estates in Malaya, and would certainly have extinguished very many Chinese holdings.[1] It is not unlikely that the possibility of serious social consequences in the event of another year of depression, particularly on the Chinese population,[2] inspired the Colonial Office on

[1] Plantation costs at this time were probably in the neighbourhood of 10d. per lb on an unrestricted output. The price-level was around this figure at the beginning of 1922, but soon fell away to 7d. to 8d. in the autumn.

[2] Up to 20 per cent. of the planted area in Malaya was in Chinese ownership in 1922, representing most of the holdings from 25–100 acres and all the larger Asiatic holdings.

the advice of the Federated Malay States Government to approve the scheme. On these grounds some degree of temporary control does, indeed, seem to have been desirable, but only as long as the market was unduly depressed by the existence of huge surplus stocks and until the economic life of Malaya was restored to a reasonably safe condition. It is in the light of these considerations that the history of the scheme itself must be examined.

The announcement that the British Government intended to proceed with restriction, coming as it did in the face of most current forecasts, caused an immediate rebound in the price to 1s. 2d. by the end of 1922. The rise was reinforced by the misjudgment of American manufacturers who had bought lightly in anticipation of a fall during the autumn of 1922—with the result that the price averaged 1s. 5d. in the second restriction quarter, and a 5 per cent. increase in exports was allowed. With the price falling during the third quarter to 1s. 2d., the rise was cancelled, and at the end of the first year the quota remained at 60 per cent. with the price at slightly below 1s. 3d. Restriction had succeeded in keeping production down to the 1922 level; and, with the increase in consumption, stocks were reduced during the year by 30,000 to 40,000 tons. Production in Malaya and Ceylon had been considerably curtailed in spite of the maturing of new acreage, but the gap had been filled partly from stocks at Singapore and partly from increased production by other countries. The year was notable also for the beginnings of agitation from consumers: in Great Britain representations from manufacturers resulted in the appointment of a delegate to the Colonial Office Committee; in the United States the Secretary of Commerce had been most active in investigating the control of essential raw materials by foreign combinations, and a deputation of the Rubber Growers' Association had endeavoured to allay the fears of American consumers.

During 1924 [1] rubber prices continued to fall and in the third quarter averaged only 11d. per lb, with the result that output was reduced to 55 per cent. But though the price then recovered, it failed to reach the pivotal price of 1s. 3d. in the fourth quarter, and a further curtailment was impending. World exports during the year reached 429,000 tons. The assessment basis for Malaya and Ceylon had been revised, with the result that the Malayan standard production was considerably lower. Net exports, however, exceeded licensed exports by 15,000 tons,

---

[1] N.B.—The " restriction " year did not correspond exactly with the calendar year. Therefore, " 1924," " 1925," etc., refer to the twelve-month periods beginning on November 1, 1924, etc.

owing to smuggling and a further release of stocks from Singapore and Penang. Exports from the Dutch Indies showed an increase of 32,000 tons; the greater part of this—some 20,000 tons—represented an increase in native production. Fortunately, world consumption was 35,000 tons higher and exceeded exports by over 40,000 tons, and visible stocks were reduced by 60,000 tons.

The year 1925 opened with the export quota at 50 per cent. and with world stocks at about 180,000 tons, or, on the basis of the 1924 consumption, about 33 per cent. below the necessary eight months' consumption laid down by the Stevenson Committee. In the first quarter the price was just below 1s. 6d., and the quota was increased to 55 per cent.; in the second quarter it averaged 1s. 7d., and a 10 per cent. increase to 65 per cent. was permissible. Demand continued to overhaul supply, and by the end of June stocks had fallen to below 130,000 tons, with the result that prices rose sharply to 3s. 7d. for the third quarter, and a further 10 per cent. quota increase to 75 per cent. was allowed. The price continued to rise to over 4s. 6d. before the end of the year; but at this point the stock shortage began to fill up, and the movement was reversed. The world's exports for the year amounted to 517,500 tons against a consumption of 560,000 tons, allowing a further absorption of stocks. Dutch production increased by a further 40,000 tons of which a great proportion was native, and smuggling and evasion accounted for surplus Malayan exports over the quota and a certain part of the exports coming nominally from the Dutch Indies.

During the first quarter of 1925 the export quota was at 85 per cent., and the price averaged 2s. 8d. In addition to the 10 per cent. increase automatically due on this account, a special 5 per cent. increase was made for the second quarter, bringing permissible exports up to 100 per cent. of standard production. At this stage the scheme was amended by a provision stabilizing the quota for the third quarter at 100 per cent. which would be maintained unless the price fell below 1s. 9d. in that period, in which event exports were to be reduced to 80 per cent. In effect, this measure raised the pivotal price from 1s. 3d. to 1s. 9d. As prices averaged 2s. 4d. and just over 1s. 9d. for the second and third quarters, the year ended with exports still at 100 per cent. of standard, but the price declined further to 1s. 8d. During the year stocks increased once more from 160,000 to 245,000 tons, though even at this level they represented less than half-a-year's current consumption. The increase was due to a small decline in world consumption of *plantation* rubber, brought about mainly by the growing use of *reclaimed* rubber in the United States, which had risen from 76,000 tons in 1924 to 137,000 tons in 1925 and 164,000 tons in 1926. Production figures also showed a changed tendency. Malaya and Ceylon actually failed to produce to the full limits of their licence, but contributed 90,000 tons of the increased world supply. The remainder of the increase was mainly forthcoming from British estates in the Dutch Indies, which had been maintaining restrictions voluntarily while native rubber production showed a temporary stability.

Exports in the first quarter of 1927 were reduced to 80 per cent. of standard, but the price fell further to 1s. 7d. In February a new system of regulation, being a revision of the summary alterations of the previous April, came into force, whereby exports—

1. were to be stabilized at their existing figures as long as the price remained between 1s. 9d. and 2s., but were to be increased by 10 per cent. if such a price persisted for three successive quarters;
2. were to be increased by 10 per cent. (or from 80 to 100 per cent.) if the price exceeded 2s.;
3. were to be increased to 100 per cent. if the price exceeded 3s. irrespective of the existing level;
4. were to be reduced by 10 per cent. (or from 100 to 80 per cent.) if the price averaged 1s. 9d. to 1s. 3d.;
5. were to be reduced to 60 per cent. if the price fell below 1s. 3d. irrespective of the existing level.

The percentage in the second quarter was, therefore, reduced by 10 to 70 per cent.; and with prices declining to 1s. 7½d. the minimum rate of 60 per cent. became operative in the third quarter.

Even this further decrease failed to hold the price, which averaged only 1s. 4d. in the third period. Simultaneously, stocks, which had been stable up till June, began to increase slowly in the later months and finished 13,000 tons up on the year. World exports for the year totalled 607,300 tons, compared with 622,000 tons in the previous period—outside supplies having increased by 33,000 tons, while Malaya and Ceylon exported 47,000 tons less. The sluggish response to the very drastic tightening of restrictions can be attributed almost entirely to the number of unfilled export licences outstanding from the previous year when the whole of the permissible releases had not been filled. Consumption rose during the year to 590,000 tons, but remained below exports in spite of the tightening of restriction.

1928 opened with a further tightening of the restriction through a

TABLE II.—WORLD PRODUCTION, CONSUMPTION AND STOCKS

(1000 tons)

Year	World's Net Exports	World's Estimated Consumption	World's Visible Stocks
1922 . .	400	390	277
1923 . .	407	435	245
1924 . .	429	470	181
1925 . .	518	560	159
1926 . .	622	545	245
1927 . .	607	600	271
1928 . .	657	680	254

TABLE III.—PRICES AND EXPORT PERCENTAGES

Restriction Period	Pivotal Price		Average Price		Percentage of Standard exportable
	s.	d.	s.	d.	per cent.
1922–1923 I. . .	1	3	1	2·3	60
II. . .	1	3	1	4·9	60
III. . .	1	3	1	2·2	65
IV. . .	1	3	1	3·0	60
1923–1924 I. . .	1	3	1	2·2	60
II. . .	1	3	1	0·9	60
III. . .	1	3		11·0	60
IV. . .	1	3	1	2·6	55
1924–1925 I. . .	1	3	1	6·0	50
II. . .	1	3	1	7·4	55
III. . .	1	3	3	2·5	65
IV. . .	1	3	3	7·3	75
1925–1926 I. . .	1	3	3	10·7	85
II. . .	1	3	2	4·0	100
III. . .	1	9	1	9·0	100
IV. . .	1	9	1	8·2	100
1926–1927 I. . .	1	9	1	7·3	80
II. . .	1	9	1	7·7	70
III. . .	1	9	1	6·2	60
IV. . .	1	9	1	4·6	60
1927–1928 I. . .	1	9	1	7·0	60
II. . .	1	9	1	0·6	60
III. . .	1	9		9·2	60
IV. . .	1	9		8·9	60

reassessment of Malayan capacity, and prices rose to an average of 1s. 7d. in the first quarter, mainly on heavy buying by manufacturers, until the announcement was made that the Prime Minister had requested a report on the whole scheme from the Committee of Civil Research. Prices immediately began to decline and were no higher than 1s. at the beginning of April, when the Prime Minister, on receipt of the Committee's report, declared that the scheme would lapse on November 1, 1928. Prices oscillated violently before settling down at 9d., in view of the fact that manufacturers anticipated ample supplies at cheap prices with the termination of the scheme and were willing to back their opinion to the extent of living on their stocks for the remainder of the year. Manufacturing activity was high nevertheless, and consumption reached 680,000 tons, exceeding supply by 23,000 tons.

The approximate relation of supply to demand and the consequent effect on stocks during the course of the scheme may be summarized (see Tables on p. 409).

CONSEQUENCES OF THE STEVENSON SCHEME

It remains to trace the principal reactions set up by the scheme and the internal developments which radically altered the appearance of the industry.

In the first place, some antagonism was aroused among consumers, increasing as the scheme became more monopolistic in tendency. It centred in America, partly because American manufacturers are the most important consumers, partly because early opposition from British manufacturers was satisfied by the appointment of a representative of the Colonial Office Committee.

The scheme was inaugurated when American manufacturers were not expecting it and when they were mostly short of stocks. Nevertheless, there were ample stocks in existence; and although prices immediately rose abruptly, the report of the Rubber Growers' Association Committee which visited the United States early in 1923 shows that the majority of the American manufacturers, with the exception of Mr Firestone, were not antagonistic, that they appreciated the unenviable position of the producers, and that their only apprehension was in respect of the inelasticity of the scheme in the event of consumption expanding faster than the estimates on which the scheme was based. On this point they seem to have received an unofficial assurance from Lord Stevenson that the machinery of the scheme was not rigid, and might be stretched in this event. For two years, until prices began to rise in 1925, there were few objections, and American manufacturers were mainly engaged in competing with each other.[1] Mr Firestone, however, who had from the outset taken the view that the scheme was dangerously monopolistic in tendency, succeeded in raising the issue to a political level, with the result that President Hoover, then Secretary of Commerce, promoted an official investigation of foreign controls over raw materials essential to American industry, with particular reference to rubber, on the assumption that a serious shortage of supply might be expected between 1928 and 1930. Mr Firestone had failed to gain the active support of other manufacturers in his search for alternative sources of supply, but persisted in his own experiments in Liberia and elsewhere; Mr Ford had made similar experiments in the Amazon Valley. As the price began to rise steeply in the latter half of 1924, the manufacturers became more alarmed and sought to persuade the Colonial Office Committee, through the Rubber Growers' Association, to give the scheme that greater elasticity which they thought had been assured to them at the outset. This they were unable to secure, probably because Lord Stevenson's assurance was not meant to be perpetual but only to cover the period until the initial percentage of 60 per cent. should be tested as satisfactory.[2] Having failed to gain any satisfaction by this means, the industry requested the United States Government to make official representations, which was done, but with little effect. By the end of 1925, Mr Hoover had drawn up the main outlines of the defensive measures which America might take and gave them publicity in an open letter. They included the refusal of credits to foreign combinations (which was not important in the case of rubber), voluntary economy in use, the manufacture of substitutes, production in " free " areas, and centralized purchase.

A campaign for economy in use was actually put through, with the nominal support of manufacturers, and some of the decline of American consumption in 1926 is probably attributable to this measure. Of more importance was the development of rubber reclamation, which had assumed startling proportions by 1926 and was probably entirely unforeseen by producers of the crude product.

---

[1] This is important. The American rubber industry contains a few very large concerns and a number of smaller ones. The former habitually buy for requirements far further ahead than smaller firms, so that competition is very acute in times of fluctuating prices.

[2] See Rowe, *op. cit.*, pp. 49-50.

TABLE IV.—RUBBER RECLAMATION, 1922-1928

Year	American Absorption of reclaimed (tons)	Percentage of Total Absorption
1922 . . .	54,000	19·1
1923 . . .	70,000	22·8
1924 . . .	76,000	22·7
1925 . . .	137,000	35·2
1926 . . .	164,000	45·1
1927 . . .	190,000	50·5
1928 . . .	223,000	50·7

This development, though inspired to a great extent by considerations of price, must now assume permanent importance since reclaimed rubber, once the original prejudice towards it had been conquered, was found to possess certain manufacturing advantages; nor is it by any means non-competitive in price.

Efforts at stimulating independent production met with surprisingly little response beyond the isolated examples of Mr Ford and Mr Firestone. Some European estates have passed into American hands, but American capital was never widely employed in fresh planting, and probably never will be, as long as the American psychology contains an element of impatience which revolts at the idea of a long period of waiting before income can materialize.

Organized buying was also undertaken, but in circumstances and with objects which Mr Hoover can hardly have envisaged. For when prices collapsed at the beginning of 1926 many of the larger firms had already stocked themselves heavily at high prices, and were fearful of their competitive position vis-à-vis the smaller concerns adopting a less speculative policy in buying stocks. The raising of the pivotal price in 1926, openly attacked as a further example of monopolistic exploitation, was in fact not unwelcome, but it did not have the expected effect of raising the market price. Accordingly a buying pool was formed towards the end of the year by the principal rubber and motor manufacturers, with a capital of 50 million dollars. Its purpose was stated to be " to protect American manufacturers against excessive prices," which is a little hard to understand since the participants were at that time suffering from an excess of supply at too low a price relative to their own inventories and commitments. Had it lasted longer, it might have fulfilled its avowed function, but after buying heavily throughout 1927, it was liquidated with considerable losses following the announcement that restriction would be terminated, at a moment when its legality under the Constitution was being tested.[1]

No less important were the effects of six years of restriction on the producing end of the industry. With the termination of the scheme, consumers' stocks had been reduced, and consumption had reached high levels; but the price was about where it had been six years before, large accumulations awaited shipment, and production was at full capacity. Full capacity, however, meant something very different from the ideas of 1922, not only on account of the development of Dutch estates and the advance of reclamation in America, but more especially owing to the native production of the Dutch Indies.

When the scheme opened, producers under British control contributed 70 per cent. of the world's production, and costs in Malaya at about 10d. per lb were probably 1d. lower than the level on Dutch estates. At the termination of the scheme, the world's production had risen by 65 per cent., but the proportion under British control had fallen to under 60 per cent. In the same period the Dutch estates had approximately doubled their productive capacity and, by effecting continuous improvements in methods of planting and tapping, had reversed the cost relationship with Malaya.

TABLE V.—WORLD RUBBER PRODUCTION, 1920-1928 [2]

(1000 tons)

	1920	1921	1922	1923	1924	1925	1926	1927	1928
MIDDLE EAST									
British	226·4	201·2	271·7	235·8	233·7	281·8	367·6	324·0	385·5
Other	78·7	76·3	107·8	144·5	160·2	207·0	216·5	243·1	240·7
AMERICA									
Brazil	23·2	17·2	19·5	16·8	23·2	25·3	24·3	28·8	21·1
Other	6·3	3·3	4·1	5·0	2·0	2·8	3·0	2·5	1·5
Mexican Guayule	1·0	0·03	0·3	1·2	1·4	3·7	4·3	5·0	3·1
AFRICA	6·4	3·6	2·9	5·6	5·4	7·8	8·7	8·2	6·1
WORLD PRODUCTION	342·0	301·6	406·4	408·7	426·2	528·1	624·5	611·5	658·0
British Middle East as per cent. of total	66·20	66·72	66·85	57·70	54·84	53·37	58·90	52·98	58·59

[1] See Rowe, *op. cit.*, pp. 57-60.

[2] See E. G. Holt, *Marketing of Crude Rubber*, United States Department of Commerce. These figures are not quite consistent with those given in Table II. above, but the discrepancies are not serious.

TABLE VI.—ESTIMATED RUBBER ACREAGE IN THE NEAR EAST
(1000 acres)

End of Year	British	Non-British	Total
1920 . .	2868	1446	4314
1921 . .	2934	1507	4441
1922 . .	2977	1593	4570
1923 . .	3027	1683	4710
1924 . .	3076	1778	4854
1925 . .	3134	1987	5121
1926 . .	3294	2322	5616
1927 . .	3484	2679	6163

Of far greater importance was the enormous increase in native production in the Dutch territories, of which Table VII. gives some indication. This particular problem cannot be adequately appreciated without an understanding of the fundamental nature of native planting as it developed after the war. It is the accessory and aftermath of the system of rice culture which proceeds by the clearing of fresh tracts for cultivation and the abandonment of exhausted areas that have already borne one or two crops. The habit has grown up of planting the abandoned areas with rubber, which is largely left to take its chance with the jungle growth, and is eventually tapped if the current price makes it worth while. If the price is high enough tapping will be performed by hired (largely immigrant) labour, otherwise by the owner's family. Tapping is far more drastic than is practised on the European estates, and the trees are sooner exhausted if tapping is continuous; but thick planting, by conserving humidity and preventing soil erosion, as well as by increasing the actual stand of trees, makes for a high yield. And in practice, in spite of the drastic methods of tapping, the life of native plantings is not notably shorter than that of the estates, as the trees are fairly certain of rest periods when low prices tend to induce selective tapping only.

At the time when the Stevenson scheme was framed the significance of native rubber production was hardly appreciated. It was hardly even investigated until 1925, when the Dutch authorities intimately connected with native planting forecast a very rapid increase in production. The boom in prices during 1925 and 1926 went a long way towards making this a certainty, as in these years the native producer was so far stimulated by the high prices as to forsake his habitual methods and to plant tracts that had been abandoned two or three seasons before, in addition to those that had only just passed out of rice cultivation. By this time the Dutch had fully appreciated the gravity of the position, but similar enlightenment had not penetrated very far in London even in 1927. In fact, the action of the authorities in raising the pivotal price to 1s. 9d. early in that year shows that they at least cannot have fully understood the situation. This, indeed, was the action which, Rowe considers, " really turned the scheme into a mere attempt at monopoly and a more foolish one than most of the many which history records." Up till that moment the scheme had perhaps performed a valuable service in relieving the Malayan industry and Malayan society of the weight of a severe depression—at the cost of antagonizing consumers to a great degree and stimulating new planting in " outside " countries. Had there then taken place a gradual liquidation of the scheme, a return to more normal and reasonable price-levels and the prompt suppression of the tendency towards expanded planting—admittedly a difficult program—the popular verdict on the merits of artificial control as exemplified by this attempt might have been far different. As it was, the attempt to maintain prices at approximately twice the average cost of production gave rise to forces from which the industry still suffers.

At the termination of the Stevenson scheme, the menace of native production was very grave indeed; and it seemed not unlikely that estate production might succumb to it altogether, since a price-level sufficient to cover the costs of most European estates was sufficiently high to encourage a very great volume of native production. A radical change was not, however, long in coming; considerable improvements had been effected on Dutch plantations during the restriction period, and with the removal of the scheme developments of revolutionary importance have taken place in the technique of estate production everywhere. Without entering into details on this subject, it may be mentioned that the most important innovations have taken the form of rotational tapping, which greatly increases yields and conserves vitality (learned as a result of the enforced idleness of portions of estates from 1922 to 1928), the modification of clean weeding (resultant on the discovery that the haphazard native methods have certain definite advantages), and the improvement of plantation stock, mainly through the adoption of " bud-grafting," which in the long run may have the effect of doubling the yield per acre of estates. As a result, yields have shown a tendency to increase; and all-in costs, though by no means standardized, have progressively declined to levels between 4d. and 5d.—and in many cases below the former figure—though the validity of these figures as an indication of long-period costs may be called into question if every allowance is made for the maintenance of long-period efficiency and new development. The problem how to work the estates at a profit without encouraging an expansion of native production became less acute as the native technique fell further behind estate technique in respect of efficiency. It would, however, be quite erroneous to suppose that the problem is not still a very serious one, particularly as the native producers, so far as concerns productive capacity, are very much in the ascendant. For instance, it was estimated by the Rubber Growers' Association that at the end of 1930 estate acreage amounted to 4,180,982 acres, and that small holders had a total planted area of 3,702,424 acres; but while the proportion of " bearing " to " immature" acreage was 100 : 28 on Malayan estates and 100 : 55 on Dutch estates, it was estimated to be 100 : 129 for Dutch native plantings—ample evidence of the increasing significance of native acreage. Native cost of production depends on a number of different factors, mostly variable, such as for example the price of rice. It is always a very difficult matter to estimate at what price a substantial rise in Dutch native production will be encouraged. In 1929 1s. was the figure usually mentioned: Rowe, writing at the end of 1930 and noting that Javanese wages had been reduced and opportunities for normal employment had become less, thought that if these conditions remained and the price of rubber rose to 10d. the Dutch native output might increase substantially; but later events suggest a much lower figure. Dutch native exports rose from 61,000 to 113,000 tons in 1932-1933 under the influence of a price rise which began at $2\frac{1}{4}$d. in January 1933 and reached $4\frac{1}{8}$d. in December. The development of native rubber production can be seen from the following figures:

TABLE VII.—EXPORTS FROM THE NETHERLAND EAST INDIES, 1929-1933 *

(1000 tons)

Year	Estate Exports	Native Exports	Total Exports	Ratio of Native to Estate Exports
1929 . .	152·9	108·6	261·5	71 : 100
1930 . .	152·8	90·5	243·3	59 : 100
1931 . .	168·7	90·2	258·9	53 : 100
1932 . .	149·8	61·4	211·2	41 : 100
1933 . .	166·0	113·0	279·0	68 : 100

* Figures for all years except 1933 are taken from the *Indian Report, Statistical Abstract for N.I.* The 1933 figures are probably slightly too low in relation to the other figures, but the discrepancy is not large.

1929 was a not unhappy year for rubber producers. In spite of greatly increased production and the release of stocks accumulated in Malaya pending the conclusion of control, consumption continued to run at high levels, visible stocks were not rising at a dangerous rate, and prices continued to bear up moderately well at levels between 10d. and 1s. Even the Wall Street crash in October, which carried prices down to 8d. and caused an abrupt check in American business, did not cause undue pessimism; and the general tendency was to look forward to an early resumption of activity and the continuation of a much-increased demand. Early in 1930, however, it was becoming increasingly obvious that something more than a temporary business recession was in store, and the accumulation of stocks was regarded with some misgiving. Talk of artificial control immediately arose; and, mainly through the initiative of the Dutch, an Anglo-Dutch Liaison Committee, an unofficial body, was created, and a month's tapping holiday was eventually proposed and accepted for May. The scheme was voluntary but was well supported by the estates; native producers naturally did not participate at all; and this, supported by the rising tide of depression, rendered it entirely ineffective—with the consequence that rubber prices fell still further, to 6d. The significance of the attempt lies, however, in the fact that it was a co-operative effort: it provided the necessary evidence of the change of mind of a large section of Dutch opinion, and henceforth it is noticeable that the initiative in proposing restrictionist schemes tended to pass to the Dutch.

The Liaison Committee remained in being after the tapping holiday, but a series of events blocked all prospects of the immediate institution of control. At the end of June, the Rubber Growers' Association issued a statement in which it emphasized that restriction, though necessary, could not be effective if it were voluntarily applied; Government regulation was vital, but it must include native production and be based on a pivotal price of 9d. per lb, with the greatest possible degree of flexibility. A few weeks later, voting at a meeting of Dutch producers on the desirability of requesting Government intervention disclosed a large minority (in which American-owned estates formed a large block) opposed to restriction. In September Sir Cecil Clementi, the High Commissioner of the Federated Malay States, discussed the subject with the Dutch Governor-General on the occasion of a visit to the East Indies: a definite decision against interference was taken by the two Governments, and further prospects of control were for the moment dissipated. As this decision became more of a certainty, prices sagged and slumped and finished the year at 4½d., having been down at one time as low as 3½d.

This course of events was not wholly unwelcome to the low-cost producers who were concerned with improving efficiency and reducing costs to a point where the estates were really competitive with the natives. But progress was being blocked by many of the high-cost producers who preferred dissipating their sometimes extensive financial reserves, in the hope of something turning up, to going out of business or radically reorganizing their methods. As long as the price was in the intermediate—4d.-8d.—region this was a serious factor; for by producing at full capacity such producers could minimize their losses. Had the price risen above 8d., or thereabouts, they would have been able to afford to indulge in some voluntary restriction and conserve their supplies of bark; had it fallen below 4d. they would have found it less costly to shut down their estates on a care-and-maintenance basis. As it was, they were a factor in making total production extremely inelastic, reinforced as they were by small native producers, particularly in Malaya, who only tapped more frantically the lower prices fell, in an effort to equalize income. This latter tendency was not, incidentally, unwelcome, since it was assumed it would make for the complete exhaustion of native plantings in Malaya and would thereby strengthen the position of the low-cost estates even though it temporarily resulted in a large addition to current output. In short, low-cost producers foresaw that under conditions of *laissez-faire* a continued absence of demand would ensure a period of low prices, lasting perhaps into years, and reckoned that this would destroy or at any rate disarm the Malayan native producer and possibly liquidate the smaller and more uneconomic estates, or force them to amalgamate, and that the remaining capacity, operated at continually declining costs, and supplemented by new planting of very high-yielding properties, would be able to satisfy world demand at a price which was profitable to itself and not sufficiently high to call out extensive reserves of Dutch native capacity, which could never be extinguished by any means short of physical destruction.

The process of liquidation was, nevertheless, extremely slow; and fresh encouragement was given to producers of restrictionist tendencies when, early in 1931, the Dutch Colonial Government announced its participation in schemes for sugar and tin. Numbers of Dutch committees were immediately set up to study possible schemes and to organize support for restriction, since the Dutch Government had long since made it clear that it would not take action without an almost unanimous pressure from the industry. At the same time a Dutch deputation arrived in London, and the Liaison Committee again got to work to consider a scheme, submitted by Sir George Maxwell. By the autumn it was evident that the pressure from the Dutch producers was much stronger than it had been before. The swing of opinion may possibly be attributed to the surprising vitality of native production in the face of the continually low level of prices; but any such sentiments were undoubtedly reinforced by the prospects of British producers securing a differential advantage, following Great Britain's abandonment of the gold standard. At this juncture representations by British producers caused the opening of direct negotiations between the British and Dutch Governments, in conjunction with their Colonial authorities. After some months the inevitable decision was reached, in August 1932, that the Governments were convinced of the impossibility of framing and operating " an international scheme which would guarantee the effective regulation of the production or export of rubber." The ruling factor had been the apparent inability of the Dutch Government to exercise any control over native production, without which, it was agreed, no restriction would be effective.

Following this announcement, the price of rubber, which had already declined to $2\frac{1}{8}$d. on a statement of opposition to restriction by Mr Lutyjes, the Netherlands East Indies Minister of Agriculture, slipped further to $1\frac{7}{8}$d. The pace of liquidation and reorganization was, in consequence, somewhat accelerated; but estate companies were everywhere reluctant to take this step, or even to close down temporarily, in order to avoid the dispersion of expert staff and the loss of coolie labour that had in some cases been imported at considerable expense from India.

In spite of their rebuff in the autumn of 1932—by which time 144 schemes of control in one form or another had been put forward—the advocates of restriction again became active in the early months of 1933. The British growers again approached the Government at the instance of Dutch producers and, finding the British authorities, as usual, willing to consider any scheme that was workable and carried Dutch support, settled down to negotiation. Sir Cecil Clementi, however, speaking in October, for the Malayan Government, made it quite clear that the initiative must come from the Dutch, and the centre of activity was necessarily in the Dutch Indies. The accession of M. Colijn as the Netherlands Prime Minister in the early summer accelerated discussion.

Rubber prices during 1933 not unnaturally reflected current rumours of restriction prospects, but the fluctuations on this account took place against a background of rising demand. In 1932 production had more nearly descended to the level of consumption than for some years past; in 1933 consumption increased by nearly 130,000 tons and exceeded the 1929 level, but rumours of restriction and the rise in price, partly on this account, held up the process of liquidation and amalgamation in European estates and rather surprisingly stimulated a great increase in native output. For the price improvement was of comparatively modest dimensions, a move from 3d. in May to $3\frac{1}{2}$d. in June and $3\frac{3}{4}$d. in July, reaching 4d. after a relapse, at the end of September, and 5d. in February 1934. Under these conditions, where the price in the first half of the year averaged $2\frac{1}{2}$d. and in the second half nearer 4d., estate production of Malaya and the Netherlands showed the same inelasticity as in the falling market and increased by a mere 12,000 tons over 1932. On the other hand native production in these countries, which amounted to 130,000 tons in the first half-year, increased to 190,000 tons under the influence of the higher price. The increase in world production, therefore, exceeded the revival in demand; and by the end of the year stocks were once more accumulating at an alarming rate. The burden of those stocks overhanging the market, economies in the use of rubber, and the greatly increased productive area under rubber indeed promised an inauspicious future for the rubber industry for some years to come, unless some halt could be called in the rate of production. Dutch officials might well doubt their ability to enforce any restrictive regulations among a native population in an area as extensive and in part difficult of access as Sumatra; many authorities considered that the only effective way of dealing with native production was by expropriation and destruction at the ports, while if due regard was to be paid to long-period considerations, control had to be exercised over new planting as well. In these circumstances it is not surprising that the Dutch Government hesitated to commit itself to any of the paper schemes that were constantly being submitted. However rumours of an impending scheme became more and more persistent, and at the end of April it was announced that agreement had been reached and control would be inaugurated on June 1, 1934.

THE 1934 RESTRICTION SCHEME

The new agreement runs till December 31, 1938, and covers between 95 and 100 per cent. of world crude-rubber resources. The quotas, based not on past production as under the Stevenson scheme but on potential production, are as follows:

TABLE VIII.—THE NEW QUOTAS, 1934-1938

(tons)

	1934	1935	1936	1937	1938
Malaya . . .	504,000	538,000	569,000	589,000	602,000
N.E.I. . . .	352,000	400,000	443,000	467,000	485,000
Ceylon . . .	77,500	79,000	80,000	81,000	82,500
India	6,850	8,250	9,000	9,000	9,250
Burma . . .	5,150	6,750	8,000	9,000	9,250
N. Borneo . .	12,000	13,000	14,000	15,500	16,500
Sarawak . . .	24,000	28,000	30,000	31,500	32,000
Siam	15,000	15,000	15,000	15,000	15,000

Provision was made for an exceptional increase in Siam's basic quota if the maturity of her recent plantings necessitated it, and French Indo-China was accorded special treatment for her exports to France.

New planting, except for experimental purposes, was prohibited for the duration of the scheme and replanting limited to 20 per cent. of the existing planted area of any estate. The export of planting material was prohibited in order to discourage the development of " outside " production.

The scheme is administered by the International Rubber Regulation Committee, on which are represented the producing interests of the participants. An invitation was also extended to European and American manufacturers to nominate a panel which should tender advice to the International Rubber Committee on matters affecting manufacturers' interests—such as, for example, stocks and exportable percentages —and should attend those of the Committee's meetings which concern such interests. This panel was completed only at the end of October, when the United States representative, Mr A. F. Townsend, was appointed. It remains to be seen whether it will exercise any real influence over the producers' policy. It must be remembered that its powers are purely advisory.

The stock and commodity markets of the world had for some time anticipated the return of control, and had discounted it on the basis of a measure of restriction sufficient to enforce at once a pivotal price of 8d. or 9d. The details of the scheme were not known until May 8, when it came out that the Committee had discarded the method of regulation by means of a pivotal price, and had adopted a relatively gradual scale of restriction, with export quotas as follows:

June and July 1934	100 per cent. of standard quotas
August and September	90 " " "
October and November	80 " " "
December	70 " " "

The rubber market's disappointment at the news is reflected in the course of prices.

TABLE IX.—AVERAGE PRICE OF RIBBED SMOKED SHEET
(pence per lb)

April 26	27	28	30	May 1	2	3	4	5	7	8	9	10	11	12	14
$5\frac{7}{8}$	$6\frac{1}{32}$	$6\frac{3}{32}$	$6\frac{9}{16}$	$6\frac{1}{4}$	$6\frac{15}{16}$	$6\frac{7}{8}$	7	$7\frac{3}{16}$	$7\frac{3}{8}$	$7\frac{1}{8}$	$6\frac{11}{16}$	$6\frac{1}{2}$	$6\frac{9}{16}$	$6\frac{7}{16}$	$5\frac{1}{16}$

After this reaction prices recovered. During September they rose to $7\frac{1}{2}$d. There was a reaction in the middle of the month on reception of the news that Siam had refused to ratify the restriction agreement, which her representative in London had signed only subject to ratification by the Siamese Assembly. The incident did not, however, cause a serious crisis, as the Committee was confident of its ability to come to terms with Siam.

At the end of October a more serious crisis occurred. The Committee, which had met in order to fix the export quotas for 1935, broke up the meeting without having been able to come to any agreement on the subject. News of this fact produced a sharp reaction in prices, ribbed smoked sheet falling to $6\frac{1}{4}$d.; and the market was anything but reassured by the details concerning the disagreement which gradually became available. The *impasse* reached at the Committee meeting was due to the fact that the Dutch were finding themselves unable to control their native producers. During the first four months of restriction native exports exceeded their quota by about 30 per cent., and this in spite of an export tax so heavy as to threaten grave political unrest. Faced with this situation the Dutch representatives on the Committee demanded an increase of the export quota to 80 per cent., while the British apparently favoured a 65 or 70 per cent. quota. Since the latter do not hold the necessary three-quarters of the votes they were unable to override the Dutch demand. On November 3 it was agreed to fix the quota at 75 per cent. for the first quarter of 1935. The change of export quota from 70 to 75 per cent. represents an increase from 70 to about 81 per cent. of the 1934 standard quotas, since the 1935 standard is higher than that of 1934.

This crisis, coming only five months after the inauguration of the new control scheme, was instructive. It brought back the rubber industry with a rude shock to the fact that up to the present the control of native production has shown itself to be both essential to the success of a restriction scheme and by no means certainly capable of realization. At the present time the Dutch are engaged on a large-scale scheme for the assessment of individual native plantations. They have partially or wholly assessed districts covering about one-sixth of native production, and hope to institute restriction on the basis of individual assessment throughout these districts by the spring of 1935. But expert opinion is sceptical of the prospects of extending this method to a larger proportion of native production in the near future. One has only to remember that native rubber comes largely from scattered up-country plantations, often entirely concealed by jungle, to appreciate the reason of this scepticism. And if the control of native production is still to depend largely on the export tax method, then there remains the double risk that the administrative organization will not be strong enough to enforce control, or that the political organization will not be strong enough to enforce an efficient administrative system, supposing one to exist.

An interesting incident in the recent crisis was the dispatch of a cable by the Chairman of the Trade Association of Palembang (Sumatra) in which he said that a further rise in rubber prices was unnecessary, as even at half the ruling price the population would be able to produce on a remunerative basis. This statement, written under the strain of native dissatisfaction with the restriction scheme, once more raises the doubt whether the new scheme is calculated primarily to smooth out excessive fluctuations in supply and maintain a price satisfactory to both producers and consumers, or whether it is designed to raise prices monopolistically.

At the London Economic Conference in 1933 it was laid down, at the instance of Sir Philip Cunliffe-Lister, that producers' agreements designed to raise the price of commodities to reasonable levels and to obtain equilibrium of supply and demand should conform to the following tests:

1. The commodity must be one of world importance where an excess of stocks or productive capacity calls for special concerted action.
2. The agreement should be comprehensive as regards the commodities regulated and should even include related or substitute products.
3. It should be comprehensive as regards producers, commanding a general

measure of assent among exporting countries and producers within them, and providing for the co-operation of non-exporting countries with a considerable production.

4. It should be fair to all parties, producers and consumers, and worked with the co-operation of the latter, who are equally concerned with producers in the maintenance of regular supplies at fair and stable prices.

5. It should be administratively practicable as regards machinery and the ability of governments to enforce its operation.

6. It should be of sufficient duration, even if a merely temporary expedient, to give an adequate assurance to all concerned that its object can be achieved.

7. Due regard must be had to the desirability of encouraging efficient production.

The new restriction agreement does at any rate conform more nearly to these principles than did the Stevenson scheme. Most of the major mistakes of the latter have been avoided. The 1934 scheme covers the high percentage of total production which is essential to the success of such control, although the wide scope of the scheme has introduced severe administrative difficulties. It is fairly elastic: unlike the Stevenson scheme, which was based on a pivotal price, and involved the fixing of prices for periods of three months, it stipulates no definite price; further, its quotas are based on potential instead of past production. Lastly, it makes some provision for co-operation with rubber manufacturers. But it has not solved the question of native production. Native exports from the Dutch East Indies were 65 per cent. lower in October than in September 1934, and remained low during November. But this fall—if due, as it is believed, largely to the accumulation of stocks in the hands of Chinese dealers—does nothing to solve the problem. Again, reclaimed rubber is not included in the scheme, and the proportion of reclaimed to crude rubber used in America has been rising since June.

The recent statistical history of the rubber industry is summarized in Table X. Liquidation of surplus stocks, which was a main aim of the control plan, has not yet begun. Stocks have in fact continued to increase, and stood at 687,000 tons at the end of August, in spite of the fact that consumption for 1934 is estimated at about 100,000 tons above the 1933 level. They are now not very far off 300,000 tons above what is generally regarded as " normal." Nevertheless, given a continued expansion in world crude-rubber consumption, these stocks should not constitute an insurmountable barrier to prosperity.

TABLE X.—WORLD PRODUCTION, CONSUMPTION AND STOCKS [1]

(1000 tons)

Year	Production (World crude shipments)	Consumption (Est. World)	Stocks			Average Price
			U.S.A.	U.K.	World	
						(pence per lb)
1929 . .	861·4	807·0	122·1	73·3	366·4	10·25
1930 . .	819·8	716·0	202·2	118·6	488·4	5·91
1931 . .	796·8	678·2	322·8	127·1	628·5	3·17
1932 . .	708·3	658·4	379·0	92·7	630·0	2·30
1933 . .	851·2	813·6	364·5	86·5	654·0	3·25
1934 . .	677·2*	641·5*	362·6†	105·3†	687·5†	5·99†

* First eight months.   † End of August.

Reviewing the first five months of its existence, one cannot say that the International Rubber Regulation Committee has yet achieved any very positive results. It is, however, to be congratulated on resisting the advice of those who believe in rubber at 9d. or 1s. That the attempt to enforce such a price would defeat itself by drawing forth additional supplies of native and reclaimed rubber should be abundantly clear in view of the demonstrated tendency for native rubber to exceed its quota with rubber at 7d. In these circumstances progress cannot be made on other than a modest scale, and the fact that the Committee has not been over-ambitious at the outset is possibly the strongest influence in favour of the ultimate achievement of its aims.

[1] Moody-Economic Services, *Industries and Commodities Bulletin.*

CHAPTER XIV

INTERNATIONAL CONSERVATION OF FISHERIES IN THE NORTH PACIFIC

by Robert A. Mackay

INTRODUCTION

FISH, always an important item in man's food, has assumed a new importance with the progress of science and invention. New methods of canning and refrigeration have combined with railway development to make fish available to inland peoples as it has never before been. Extended markets have in turn stimulated the application of machinery and industrial methods to the fishing industry itself, as for example, the steam trawler, and these have added to man's skill as a fisherman so greatly that certain species have approached, or are approaching, exhaustion. Where fishing is prosecuted wholly within one country, as is the case with many fresh-water fisheries, the control of the industry and the conservation of the species in question are relatively simple. A much more complex situation, however, arises in the case of fisheries on the high seas.

The high sea, unlike the land, cannot be appropriated but remains the common property of the family of nations. Similarly, the products of the high sea are *res nullius* until captured by man. State ownership of the sea and of its products in their natural state stops with the marginal belt around the coasts.[1] While the ships of a state beyond territorial waters are still within the jurisdiction of their own state, no state can in time of peace exercise jurisdiction over the ships of any other state on the high seas except with the consent of the state concerned. Thus, while a state can control its own fishermen and fishing vessels while on the high seas, it can exercise no jurisdiction over foreign fishermen or foreign ships without the consent of their own state or states. Nor has a state any proprietary right to fish for sea animals on the high seas, even though they from time to time resort to or live in its territorial waters. Nor has it any right to exercise any protective jurisdiction over such fish or sea animals when on the high seas.[2]

[1] Oppenheim, *International Law*, vol. i., p. 441 ff. The jurisdiction exercised by Great Britain over the pearl fisheries as far as twenty miles off the coast of Ceylon would appear to be an exception established by prescription (*ibid.*).

[2] Question 5, submitted to arbitrators in Behring Sea Arbitration. " Has the United States any right, and if so, what right of protection or property in the fur seals fre-

It sometimes happens that a state may accidentally control fishing on the high seas when, for example, a fishery is used only by its own nationals or prosecuted only from its ports, in which case municipal regulations may be adequate to protect or control the fishery in question [1]; but such control is only accidental and gives the state no ownership or jurisdiction over the fishery, except possibly by prescription.

Again, fishing for sea fish may occur almost exclusively within territorial waters, as in the case of the Pacific salmon, in which case the territorial Power may regulate the fishery as it sees fit. Certain difficulties may, of course, occur where the fishery is distributed between the territorial waters of two or more countries, in which case joint action may be necessary, but even here municipal regulations for territorial waters largely meet the case. In this connection the convention, negotiated but still unratified, between Canada and the United States to protect the sockeye salmon is worthy of study, and we shall examine it later.

Two instances of international action to protect and regulate fishing on the high seas have occurred in the North Pacific Ocean. These— the protection of the fur seal, and of the halibut—two outstanding examples of international co-operation to conserve animal life on the high seas, are worthy of careful study. In addition the Convention for the Regulation of Whaling applies to the Pacific Ocean as well as to other seas.

THE FUR SEAL OF THE NORTH PACIFIC [2]

Life-History [3]

The fur seal of the Pacific Ocean (*Callorhinus*) is believed to come to land only in summer, for the purpose of breeding and rearing the young; the rest of the year is spent entirely at sea. The breeding males are called bulls, the females, cows, and the young, pups. Males just approaching full maturity are termed half-bulls; the youngest males are

quenting the islands of the United States in Behring Sea when such seals are found outside the ordinary three-mile limit? " *v.* Argument of the United States, Moore, *Arbitrations*, p. 831. On both counts the arbitrators answered in the negative. See Moore, *Digest*, vol. i., p. 911 ff.; *Arbitrations*, p. 4761.

[1] *E.g.* the pearl fisheries, covering about 700,000 sq. miles of high seas off the Australian coast, have, in fact, been controlled in this way (*Bulletin, U.S. Bureau of Fisheries*, xxviii. (1908), p. 109).

[2] For assistance in preparing this section of the paper I am indebted to Mr George H. Crouse, B.A., of Dalhousie University.

[3] See in this connection *Bulletin, U.S. Bureau of Fisheries*, vol. xxxiv. (1914), pp. 17-105. This account is confined to the Alaska Fur Seal (*Callorhinus alascanus*) which frequents the Pribilof Islands.

called bachelors. The breeding-ground is called a rookery, while the place resorted to by the bachelors is called a hauling-ground. Each autumn the seals migrate southward, returning the following spring to the Pribilof Islands and other rookeries to breed. The older animals return first and the youngest last. The adult males begin to arrive at the Pribilof Islands around May 1; the adult females and older bachelors come mainly in June; the two-year-olds in July; and the yearlings late in August and early in September.

When the old bulls have reached the islands they choose a place on the rookery-ground and await the arrival of the females. They stay in the same place during the whole breeding season without eating. Seals are very polygamous animals, and a harem of as high as a hundred cows may be served by one bull, but the harems vary from this number to two or three females. After June 1 the females of three years and over begin to arrive, and within a few days the pups are born, one pup to each pregnant female; the majority of the pups are born between June 20 and July 20. On arrival the females at once land and join a bull, and the harems grow rapidly. Within a few days after the birth of her pup the female is impregnated, so that the period of gestation is very little short of a year. After this the cows take journeys to sea for the purpose of feeding, returning at intervals to suckle the young pups. These journeys are kept up until November, when all the seals leave the islands.

The male seal normally begins to breed at the age of six or seven years; the female normally gives birth to her first pup at three years of age. Both males and females live about twelve to fourteen years.

From these facts it will be apparent that there would normally be in the herds a considerable surplus of bulls over the number required for the propagation of the species. Indeed, it has been estimated that 90 per cent. of the males are unnecessary for this purpose.

The fur seal of the Pacific Ocean has long been known as a valuable fur-bearing mammal and extensive sealing operations have been carried on since early in the last century. The habits of the seal in migrating yearly during the breeding season to the same rookeries and in living on the rookeries during the season of bearing the young and breeding make its capture comparatively easy. The first commercial method of capturing seals was to take them on the rookeries during this season, a method so easy that the seal was all but extinguished in the South Pacific. In the north its survival has been due largely to the policy of conservation begun about 1840 by the Russian Government, which prohibited indiscriminate slaughter on the rookeries on the Pribilof

Islands and instituted a system of Government control of the industry. Under this females were protected, while a proportion of the males from two to three years old were selected and driven off the rookeries like sheep for slaughter.[1] Under this system the seal herd of the North Pacific increased to the extent that when the islands passed to the United States on the purchase of Alaska the herd on the islands numbered from 3 to 4 million seals.[2] After Alaska passed to the United States in 1867 a monopoly of the fishery on the Pribilof Islands was granted to a private company, which was limited, however, to a catch of 100,000 male seals annually under the system instituted by Russia.[3]

From time immemorial the Indians had captured seals at sea on their migrations to and from the rookeries or when they left the rookeries for food. This method was not, however, particularly destructive until white men conceived the idea of using the Indians with their canoes from large vessels on the high seas to follow the migrating herds or to hover off shore from the rookeries, where the seals could be captured when they left the rookeries for food. The method of capturing seals at sea, known as " pelagic sealing," now became very destructive. No discrimination was shown by the fishermen between males and females. Mature females captured while migrating to the rookeries were ordinarily pregnant and near to delivery; if captured while feeding from the rookeries their young pups remained to die of starvation; if captured on their migrations from the rookeries they were ordinarily again pregnant. Further, in view of the fact that at the same time the surplus males were being slaughtered on land, from 60 to 80 per cent. of the seals captured in pelagic sealing were females. In addition, it is estimated that from three to five seals were killed for every one retrieved. Pelagic sealing became an important factor in Behring Sea about 1881, and by 1891, it is estimated, one hundred and fifteen vessels were engaged in it, each with from five to twenty canoes.[4] The destructive nature of the methods employed is seen in the dwindling of the land catch on the islands. Prior to 1886 the company was able to obtain its allowance of 100,000 male seals, but in 1891 it obtained only 12,040.[5] " In every season since 1890," says the *United States Bureau of Fisheries Bulletin* for 1914, " the recorded pelagic catch exceeded the land catch, so that during this period of steady decline of the herd even the primary losses due to pelagic sealing were greater than those of land killing.[6] Under

[1] Stevenson, *Bulletin, U.S. Bureau of Fisheries*, vol. xxviii. (1908), Proceedings Fourth International Fisheries Congress, p. 124.

[2] *Ibid.*   [3] *Ibid.*, p. 125.   [4] *Ibid.*   [5] *Ibid.*   [6] *Ibid.* p. 74.

these circumstances the company enjoying concessions to take seals on the islands lost all incentive to preserve the herds, and resorted also to indiscriminate slaughter.[1] The fur seal of the North Pacific thus rapidly approached extinction.

Early Attempts at Conservation

The fur seal industry first assumed international importance in 1821, when Russia prohibited, except in case of distress, the landing of foreign vessels on its mainland, or islands, or approach thereto within one hundred miles. Great Britain and the United States immediately protested against this assumption of jurisdiction beyond ordinary territorial limits, with the result that Russia acceded to their protests and agreed by treaty to permit to the nationals of both parties commerce with the natives and fishing, subject to restriction as regards inshore fisheries.[2]

In 1867 Alaska was ceded to the United States. The growth in pelagic sealing after 1880 seemed to presage the extinction of the herds on the American islands, and accordingly in 1886 the Government of the United States proceeded to enforce its municipal regulations against pelagic sealing throughout the whole water area of the territory ceded by Russia. In short, Behring Sea was declared a *mare clausum* for the purposes of seal-fishing. In the same and the following years several Canadian sealing vessels were taken and condemned.[3] The British Government protested vigorously against these seizures, with the result that in 1887 the President directed the release of all vessels or persons held and the quashing of all pending proceedings resulting from this application of American law beyond the three-mile limit. This, however, did not prevent further seizure, and the controversy with Great Britain still continued.

On August 19, 1887, the American Government instituted negotiations for international co-operation " for the better protection of the fur seal fisheries of Behring Sea." All questions as to the legality of the measures taken by the United States to protect the fishery were, however, expressly excluded from the negotiations. The governments of France, Germany, Great Britain, Japan, Russia, Norway and Sweden

---

[1] Stevenson, *Bulletin, U.S. Bureau of Fisheries*, vol. xxviii. (1908), Proceedings Fourth International Fisheries Congress, p. 76.

[2] Moore, *Digest of International Law*, vol. i., p. 890 ff.

[3] *Bulletin, U.S. Bureau of Fisheries*, xxviii. (1908), p. 125; Moore, *Digest*, vol. i., p. 896; *British and Foreign State Papers*, vol. lxxix. (1887-1888), p. 1240 ff.; *United States Foreign Relations*, 1886-1887.

were approached on the matter, and of these the governments most concerned in the protection of the fishery—France, Great Britain, Japan and Russia—replied favourably. A convention was virtually agreed upon, when negotiations were broken off by Great Britain because of the opposition of Canada to restrictions on pelagic sealing, Great Britain being unwilling to enforce the convention against Canadian wishes. Since pelagic sealing was at the time largely a Canadian industry, any attempt at international control was now out of the question.[1] This attempt having failed, the United States in 1889 again began to enforce its municipal regulations throughout Behring Sea alleging, among other reasons, a property right in the seals even on the high seas, in view of their remaining a part of the year on American coasts and being semi-domesticated like the honey bee, and further that Russian jurisdiction had extended over Behring Sea, and that this jurisdiction had passed to the United States with the purchase of Alaska. Great Britain vigorously protested and offered to arbitrate the matter, to which the United States agreed.[2]

With the arbitration award in general we are not directly concerned. Suffice it to say, that on the questions both of jurisdiction in Behring Sea and a property right in the fur seals beyond the three-mile limit, the American claims were denied.[3] Article VII. of the treaty of arbitration provided, however, that should the American claims fail the arbitrators should determine what concurrent regulations were needed for the preservation of the fur seal outside the three-mile limit.

Regulations provided under the Arbitration Award of 1893[4]

The principal methods of control provided by the Arbitration Award were as follows[5] :

1. A closed area of sixty miles around the Pribilof Islands in which pelagic sealing should be forbidden to their nationals by both countries.
2. A closed season from May 1 to July 31, in which pelagic sealing on the high seas should be forbidden to their nationals by both countries in the area

[1] Moore, *Digest*, vol. i., p. 897.
[2] For a fuller account of the arguments on both sides, see Moore, *Digest*, vol. i., pp. 897-904.
[3] Moore, *Digest*, vol. i., p. 910 ff., gives a fairly complete account of the arbitration. Also Moore, *History and Digest of International Arbitration* (hereafter cited *Arbitration*), p. 755 ff.
[4] Printed in full, *ibid.*, pp. 914-916, also in *Bulletin, U.S. Bureau of Fisheries*, xxviii. (1908), p. 173.
[5] Indians, except when employed for seal-fishing, or when fishing outside territorial waters under contract, were excepted from the prohibitions.

north of the 35th parallel N. latitude and eastward of the 180th degree of longitude north to the water boundary of the treaty between Russia and the United States of 1867, following that line to Behring Straits.

3. Use of firearms, nets and explosives forbidden.

4. Only licensed sailing vessels and qualified seal-fishermen to be permitted to fish for seals during the open season.

5. Statistics of sex of seals and places where captured to be kept by masters of vessels engaged in the fishery.

The regulations were to remain in force until abolished by mutual agreement, but were to be re-examined every five years in the light of experience.

The regulations were to be enforced jointly by appropriate legislation. The enforcing legislation provided for the policing of the area by the cruisers of both countries, and arrest of persons and vessels suspected of violating the regulations by the public vessels of either country, suspects to be handed over, however, to their own country for trial and punishment.[1]

The regulations provided under the Arbitration Award of 1893 proved disappointing. For example, in 1894, the year in which the regulations went into force, the pelagic seal catch amounted to 61,838, exceeding that of any previous year.[2] In the first place, due to insufficient knowledge of the life-history of the seal, the closed season and the closed area around the Pribilof Islands were inadequate. The sixty-mile area around the islands had been intended to protect the female while feeding from the islands, whereas the female often went farther afield than this. The closed season, moreover, was too short, and did not protect the seals migrating later to the islands nor the migrations southward from the islands.

Secondly, nationals of countries other than Great Britain or the United States were not affected by the regulations, and the numbers of fishermen from the countries engaged in pelagic sealing increased when the restrictions were put on American and British vessels. Efforts to induce other countries to accept voluntarily the regulations provided by the Award proved unavailing. Japan and Russia, the countries most interested, declined to accept them unless similar protection should be given to their own seal fisheries.[3] Under such conditions it was quite possible for nationals of countries other than the United States and

[1] For disputes as to U.S. Statute, see *U.S. For. Rel.* 1896, p. 255 ff.; *B. and F. State Papers*, vol. lxxxix. (1896-1897); Neilson, *Brit. Am. Claims Com. Report*, 1922, " In the matter of the *Wanderer*."

[2] *Bulletin, U.S. Bureau of Fisheries*, xxviii. (1908), p. 130; xxxiv., p. 22.

[3] Moore, *Digest*, vol. i., 922.

Great Britain to take seals outside the three-mile limit at any season of the year and by whatever method they pleased.

The restrictions as regards pelagic sealing in the eastern section of the Pacific Ocean and Behring Sea tended also to encourage seal-fishing off Russian and Japanese coasts. As a result, Russia attempted to prohibit seal-fishing within ten miles of her mainland and within thirty miles of the Commander and Robbin Islands. Great Britain refused to concede such right of extra-territorial jurisdiction, but agreed to co-operate with Russia to prohibit fishing by her nationals in this area, and an order in council to this effect was issued November 21, 1895. A similar agreement had already been effected between Russia and the United States, Russia agreeing to limit the land catch on her islands in return for the loss of fishing rights to the United States.[1]

The rapid decline of the seal herds, even under the regulations agreed to by the three Powers, Russia, Great Britain and the United States, induced Great Britain and the United States to appoint in 1896 a joint scientific commission to study the question. This commission, known as the Jordan-Thompson Commission, concluded that pelagic sealing was the cause and recommended its abolition. In 1897 the United States, Russia and Japan signed a convention agreeing to abolition over the whole North Pacific for the period of one year, the convention to take effect on acceptance by Great Britain. Great Britain, at the instance of Canada, however, refused to accept without compensation.[2] Again and again after 1897 negotiations for abolition of pelagic sealing were instituted by the United States, but until 1911 they bore no fruit owing to the conflicting interests of the different Powers. The United States, Russia and Japan were agreeable to abolition since it would enhance the value of the herds on their rookeries. Great Britain, or rather Canada, the only part of the Empire really interested in the matter, with no rookeries of her own benefited by pelagic sealing, and would not agree to abolition without adequate compensation. The United States consented to handing over a share of the annual land catch. Canada, however demanded in addition pecuniary compensation for

---

[1] *Bulletin, U.S. Bureau of Fisheries,* xxviii., p. 130 ; *B. and F. State Papers,* vol. lxxxvii. (1894-1895), p. 1058; Moore, *Digest, ibid.*

[2] *Bulletin, U.S. Bureau of Fisheries,* xxviii., p. 131; xxiv., p. 22. Also *U.S. For. Rel.* 1896, 1897, *passim*; *B. and F. State Papers,* vol. lxxxix. (1896-1897), p. 786 ff. for correspondence. For the views of the Canadian Government, see *Canada, Sessional Papers,* vol. xlvi. (1912), No. 84, pp. 25-26. For the Convention between U.S., Japan and Russia, *v. Can. Sess. Pap., ibid.,* p. 12. The U.S. prohibited pelagic sealing to its own nationals, Dec. 29, 1897. Canada and Japan were thus the only important interested states after this date.

the loss of a vested right in the fishery. To this the United States would not consent, since it would give grounds for similar claims from Russia and Japan and since the herds were rapidly becoming of little commercial value in any case.[1]

Ultimately in 1911 an agreement was reached between the four Powers interested and two conventions were agreed to, one between the United States and Great Britain, the other between the four Powers. Since the latter superseded the former as regards the methods of international control, it will be sufficient to analyse its terms.

Control under the Treaties of 1911 [2]

The essential principles of the treaties were:

1. Absolute prohibition of pelagic sealing anywhere in the high seas in the Pacific Ocean north of the 30th parallel of North latitude by the nationals of the four contracting Powers, except by natives when not fishing under contract or as employees. The public officers of all four parties were given authority to arrest and hand over to their respective countries persons or vessels suspected of violating the regulations on the high seas. Japan, Russia and the United States agreed to maintain patrols for police purposes. Further, all four Powers agreed to prohibit the use of their ports or territories for the purpose of pelagic sealing, and the importation of seal skins taken illegally and of all seals of certain species taken under authority of the Power owning the rookery.

2. Compensation: (a) The countries owning the rookeries were to give compensation as follows: The United States, 15 per cent. of the seals taken annually on rookeries to Canada and Japan each; Russia, 15 per cent. annually to Canada and Japan each; and Japan, 10 per cent. to the United States and Russia each. Should the seals resort to British territory, Great Britain should give 10 per cent. to each of the other three Powers. (b) Pecuniary compensation: The United States should pay immediately to Great Britain and Japan the sum of 200,000 dollars each in lieu of seal skins to that value to which they would be entitled under the treaty. Moreover, Great Britain and Japan should receive a minimum of not less than 1000 skins per annum whatever the total catch of the United States might be, provided that the United States might in any year prohibit entirely the taking of seals, but if so, Great

[1] *Can. Sess. Pap., ibid.*

[2] Text of the Treaties—*Treaties and Agreements affecting Canada in force between His Majesty and the United States of America, 1814-1925,* pp. 374, 391. Also U.S. Treaty Series.

Britain and Japan should each receive 10,000 dollars for each year the prohibition continued.

The convention was to go into effect on December 15, 1911, and to continue in force for fifteen years, and thereafter until twelve months' notice given by any of the parties. At any time after termination a conference to consider modification or extension might be called by any of the parties. The treaty is still in force.

As to the effectiveness of this convention in protecting the fur seal there can be no question. The following Table compiled from reports of the U.S. Bureau of Fisheries [1] shows how rapidly the seal herd of the Pribilof Islands has been rehabilitated. The count carried on by officials of the Bureau is no doubt sufficiently accurate for practical purposes:

1912	.	.	215,738	1922	.	.	604,962
1913	.	.	268,305	1923	.	.	653,008
1914	.	.	294,687	1924	.	.	697,158
1915	.	.	363,872	1925	.	.	..
1916	.	.	417,281	1926	.	.	761,281
1917	.	.	468,692	1927	.	.	808,870
1918	.	.	496,432	1928	.	.	871,513
1919	.	.	524,235	1929	.	.	971,527
1920	.	.	552,718	1930	.	.	1,045,101
1921	.	.	581,443				

Thus from 1912 to 1923 the herd increased from 215,738 to 653,008, or was more than tripled; in 1930 the herd was five times as large as in 1912.[2] For this phenomenal increase two factors outweigh all others in importance—the careful control of land slaughter under the system instituted by Russia almost ninety years ago, and carried on under direction of the officials of the Bureau themselves, and secondly, the virtually complete cessation of pelagic sealing.[3] This has been made

[1] *U.S. Bureau of Fisheries—Alaska Fishery and Fur Seal Industries*, 1923, and later issues.

[2] Indeed so numerous is the seal herd now that frequent complaints are heard that it is becoming highly destructive of fisheries on both Asiatic and Alaskan coasts. These charges are, however, denied on competent authority. See complaints, *Pacific Fisherman*, vol. xxviii., No. 5, p. 26, and No. 6, p. 19. For denial, No. 6, p. 18. The recovery of the American herd is apparently in striking contrast to the condition of the Russian herd, which was reported in 1922 to be still badly depleted. The reasons for the difference stated were (a) general lawlessness following the Revolution, (b) abuse of the clause permitting killing by aborigines, and (c) the fact that the herd in moving northward was more vulnerable than the American herd (L. Stejneger, " Fur Seal Industry of the Commander Islands, 1922," *Bulletin, U.S. Bureau Fisheries*, vol. xli. (1925), pp. 289-332).

[3] While the Indians are still permitted to carry on pelagic sealing their operations are relatively insignificant. Statistics of captures by Indians indicate a much greater abundance of seals than formerly. See statement of fur seal skins taken and landed in British Columbia 1912-1927 (*Ann. Rep. Dept. Marine and Fisheries*, (Can.) Fisheries Branch, 1928, p. 97).

possible only by the treaty, which has given the United States authority to police the waters in question, and has provided a means of punishment for offenders.

THE PACIFIC HALIBUT

The halibut (*Hippoglossus*) is a " bottom " or demersal variety of sea fish—that is, it inhabits the bottom rather than the surface of the sea and is not migratory but spends its life in general in the same locality.[1] It attains to maturity slowly. Professor W. F. Thompson, a well-known authority on the halibut, estimated some years ago that at twelve years only about 50 per cent. are mature. A recent investigation estimates that at six years the halibut weighs only 4 lb; at fourteen years 28 lb, while at forty years it weighs about 80 lb.[2] At about 20 lb the female is sufficiently mature to begin reproduction. The size to which the fish attains makes the halibut commercially profitable long before it has reached maturity, a fact which has hastened the destruction of the species, since many fish are caught before they reach the age of reproduction.

Like most fish of demersal or " bottom " variety, the halibut apparently does not range far afield for food, but contents himself with the food he finds on his own bank. This fact, coupled with the size of the fish, means that in general halibut are spread thinly over the fishing-grounds and do not run in thick schools as do the migratory fishes. This in turn influences the methods of the fishery; nets are of little use, the ordinary method of fishing being by hook and line anchored and buoyed, several lines being attached together in what is called a " skate."

One important geographical factor must also be borne in mind. The continental shelf on the Pacific side of the North American continent is comparatively narrow, much narrower, indeed, than the shelf on the Atlantic. The area of the shelf from Juan de Fuca Strait to the islands off the north-west corner of Alaska has been estimated at only about 80,000 square miles, or much less than the North Sea. Of this, only a small portion contains fishing banks. Nor are the banks connected; on the other hand, they lie scattered on the shelf along the coast, some near

[1] For the life-history of the halibut see the *Report of the International Fisheries Commission*, appointed under the Northern Pacific Halibut Treaty 1923 between the United States and Canada, for 1927; also J. P. MacMurrich in *Trans. Roy. Soc. Can.*, III. ser. (1913), vol. vii., sec. 4; W. F. Thompson in Report of Commissioner of Fisheries, British Columbia, *Sessional Papers*, 1916.

[2] International Fisheries Commission according to *Canadian Annual Review*, 1927-1928, p. 642.

shore, some a considerable distance out to sea. Further, the shelf is, for the most part, narrow and can thus be " combed " for fish more easily than could a wider area.[1] Further, the isolation of the banks in the case of the halibut means that there is little if any interchange of life between banks.

The Fishery

The following sketch of the halibut industry and its history from the report of the International Halibut Commission made to the governments of the United States and Canada in 1927 explains admirably the progressive decline which has taken place in the abundance of the halibut due to commercial fishing.[2]

Fisheries for halibut are prosecuted in the North Pacific and the North Atlantic oceans, and yield about 90 millions of lbs annually. The Pacific halibut fishery, which is covered by the terms of this convention (*i.e.* of 1923), is the greatest in the world. The annual catch exceeds 50 millions of lbs, which represents about 60 per cent. of the world's catch. Of the remainder about 30 millions are credited to European countries and 6 millions to the Atlantic coast of this continent. The value of the Pacific halibut catch to the fishermen is about 7 million dollars annually, and it is consequently one of the most important fisheries in North American waters. The Pacific halibut is, therefore, one of the most important species of food fishes indigenous to the waters of the North American continent. . . .

The Pacific halibut fishery originated soon after the first railway communication was established between the two coasts of the United States. It is, therefore, comparatively young. It had its inception in 1888 near Cape Flattery, at the entrance to Juan de Fuca Strait. The fishery expanded rapidly and by 1910 it had extended to grounds off Cape Ommaney, Baranof Island, 600 miles to the north. Subsequent expansion has extended the fishery until it now covers about 1800 miles of coast. Formerly as many fish were taken from the 600-mile stretch as are now procured from the entire area of 1800 miles. The banks on the eastern side of the Gulf of Alaska, which yield spawning fish, were first exploited in 1913. In 1926 the larger boats made by far the greater part of their catches in the vicinity of Kodiak Island, on the western side of the Gulf of Alaska, about 1200 miles beyond the original fishery. The catch on the older grounds south of Cape Ommaney has decreased from a total in excess of 50 million lb in 1910 to about 21 millions in 1926, and much greater effort was exerted in making the catch in the latter year. It is evident that the present level of production has been maintained by extending fishing operations to new areas, as the catch on

---

[1] For a brief description of the " shelf " see W. F. Thompson, Report Commissioner of Fishery, British Columbia, *Sessional Papers*, 1916, p. 132.

[2] *Report of the International Fisheries Commission appointed under the Northern Pacific Halibut Treaty of 1923*, Ottawa, 1928; Thompson and Freeman, *History of the Pacific Halibut Fishery*, Report of the International Fisheries Commission, No. 5 (Vancouver, 1930).

the older grounds decreased, and by increasing the intensity of the fishing effort.

The amount of gear now used on the older banks is about two and one-half times the quantity formerly used, yet the present catch is only about 40 per cent. of the former yield from these grounds. Under the stress of this great intensification of fishing effort the abundance of fish on the older banks has fallen enormously, to 16 per cent. of the abundance in 1906. Where in 1906 the catch per set of a unit of fishing gear was nearly 300 lb, in 1926 it was below 50 lb. Expressed in another way, it required six units of gear to catch as many fish as one unit caught in 1906. The decline has gone on at an even rate and shows no tendency to slacken. Accompanying this fall in abundance there has been a decrease in the average size of the fish landed, and a great increase in the percentage of undersized fish. For example, between 1919 and 1926 the percentage of undersized fish from the older banks increased from 20 to 30 per cent.

The more recently exploited banks to the westward show the same trend, the catch having fallen from 160 lb per unit of gear in 1923 to 100 lb in 1926, and was still lower in 1927, while at the same time there was an increase in the number of fish under $11\frac{3}{4}$ lb.

The rapidity of decline is regarded as especially serious because of the very slow rate of growth of the halibut, an adult being from twelve to twenty-five years, or over, in age. Hence the present decline has taken place within the lifespan of one halibut of ordinarily large size. As nearly all the fish which are being caught now were spawned eight or ten years ago, the abundance of the younger fish, which will annually be available for capture in the next ten years, has already been established. If these are greatly reduced in numbers, and the intensity of the fishery is maintained, the outlook for a future stock of spawning fish sufficient to maintain the supply presents a hopeless picture. In fact the commission's investigations indicate that relatively few mature halibut are now found on the older banks.

This situation obviously could not be dealt with by either Government acting alone. Most of the fish were being taken beyond territorial waters. While either country might have laid restrictions on its own nationals or vessels as regards fishing on the high seas, such restrictions could not be applied to nationals or vessels of the other country. Restrictions by Canada, for example, would only have driven fishing companies to register their ships in the United States and to operate from American ports, thereby benefiting the American side of the industry. Co-operation between the two governments was thus the only possible remedy.

The first attempt at co-operation occurred in 1918, when a conference on fisheries was held between representatives of the two countries. It reported in favour of a closed season of three months from November 15 to February 15, and joint scientific investigation to obtain further data on the life-history of the halibut. It drew up, in addition, a draft treaty dealing with the halibut reciprocal port privileges and the tariff on fish.[1] The treaty, however, failed to pass the Senate, apparently because of its omnibus character. In 1922 Canada suggested that the halibut be dealt with alone,[2] and a draft convention dealing with the halibut fishery was submitted by the Government of the United States. This, with minor changes, was ultimately agreed to by both governments.

The Treaty of 1923

The treaty of 1923 provides for the following methods of conservation:

1. An annual closed season from November 15 to February 15 inclusive, in which " the nationals, inhabitants and the fishing vessels and boats " of both countries are prohibited from fishing in the territorial waters of either, and the high seas off the western coasts of Canada and the United States, including Alaska. The closed season may be modified at the end of the third season on the recommendation of the International Commission provided for in the treaty. Halibut caught incidentally while fishing *bona fide* for other fish in this area may be used for food of the crew, and any additional must be turned over to the properly constituted authorities of either country on landing, the same to be sold and the proceeds thereof to be turned into the public revenue of the country concerned.

2. " Every national, inhabitant, vessel, or boat " of either country violating the closed season may be seized by the public officers of either country except within the territorial waters of the other, offenders to be turned over to their own country for trial and punishment.

3. A scientific commission of four members, two from each country, is provided for, to exist so long as the convention remains in force, to study the life-history of the halibut and to make recommendations as to its preservation and the development and control of the industry.

The convention was to remain in force five years and thereafter until two years after notice of desire to terminate by either party. Both parties agreed to implement the treaty by appropriate legislation. This legislation in both instances provides for [3] : (*a*) Closing of ports of both countries for fishing illegally, preparing to fish illegally, leaving or permitting a vessel to leave port for illegal fishing, or landing halibut

[1] See *Report of American-Canadian Fisheries Conference of 1918*, Washington, 1920. See also discussion of various proposed methods of conservation, W. F. Thompson in *Sess. Pap. B.C., Report of Commissioner of Fisheries*, 1917, p. 28 ff.

[2] *Canada Bureau of Statistics, 1927—Fisheries Statistics*, 1926, p. 9.

[3] *U.S. Stat. at Large*, 1923-1925, pp. 648-650 ; *Revised Statutes of Canada*, c. 75.

illegally caught; (*b*) Patrolling of the fishing-grounds; (*c*) Severe penalties for infractions.

The closed season provided in the treaty of 1923 has not, it is clear, proven an adequate means of preserving the fisheries. On the contrary, the catch has increased.[1] The closed season, November 15 to February 15, was formerly the least profitable season for fishing owing to winter weather conditions. During this period much gear was often destroyed, losses in the fishing fleet were more numerous, and weather conditions often prevented continuous fishing. Further, the fish taken during this season were frequently of poor quality. The closed season was, therefore, an economic benefit to the industry, making it more profitable to fish during the remainder of the year. The closed season protected the fishermen but not the fish.

The treaty, however, proved of great advantage, in that it provided for an international scientific commission, as mentioned above. This Commission, after careful and extended study both of the life-history of the halibut and of the industry, recommended a revision of the treaty,[2] These recommendations were finally embodied in a new treaty which became effective May 9, 1931.

The Pacific Halibut Convention of 1931 [3]

The Convention of 1931 made several radical changes:

1. It extended the closed season, but empowered the international commission to alter or suspend it as deemed necessary (Article I.).

---

[1] *Report of the International Fisheries Commission*, 1928, p. 14, reports the following landings:

Five years' average, 1919 to 1923 .		.	.	.	51,595,000 lb
1924	.	.	.	.	.	57,691,000 ,,
1925	.	.	.	.	.	53,170,000 ,,
1926	.	.	.	.	.	56,278,000 ,,
1927	.	.	.	.	.	56,899,000 ,,

[2] *Ibid.*, p. 9. The Commission recommended as follows:

(1) A progressive limitation of the catch yearly by a predetermined percentage in certain areas where the fishery has become greatly depleted, until the yield has become stable. This percentage reduction should be frequently revised as occasion warranted.

(2) The establishment of two " nursery " areas in which fishing should be prohibited, investigation showing that these two areas were populated apparently permanently by immature fish. Such other grounds as found by the Commission to be similarly populated should also be closed.

(3) The prohibition of gear found unduly destructive.

(4) The extension of the closed season by two weeks at its beginning as an aid to the industry. Future alteration in the closed season to be provided for.

(5) Licensing of all vessels fishing for halibut in treaty waters under conditions necessary for the purpose of the treaty.

[3] Canada, *Treaty Series*, 1931.

2. It empowered the Commission (Article III.):
   (*a*) to divide the halibut fishing banks into areas;
   (*b*) to limit the catch permitted in each area;
   (*c*) to fix the size and character of fishing appliances;
   (*d*) to make regulations for the collection of statistics;
   (*e*) to close entirely to halibut-fishing such areas as it found populated by small or immature halibut.

   No regulations were, however, to be valid until affirmed by the Governor-General in Council of Canada and the President of the United States.

3. The treaty was to remain in force five years and thereafter subject to denunciation on two years' notice.

Provisions for policing the areas remained the same as in the previous treaty.

The treaty of 1931 is indeed unique. Under it the International Fisheries Commission was given effective legislative and administrative control over a fishery which extends along some 1800 miles of coast, and includes both territorial waters and the high seas. While regulations of the Commission must be approved by the two governments, this amounts to little more than formal ratification of the Commission's decisions. The Commission is not, however, a police authority; this function is left to the two governments concerned as in the treaty of 1923.

The function of the Commission is primarily that of conserving and improving the fishery. The satisfactory fulfilment of this function must be based on scientific knowledge of the life-history of the halibut, of ocean currents, and of other matters affecting the natural increase of the halibut. It entails also accurate statistical knowledge of fishing activities over the whole area, and of the methods and practices of the industry. The Commission's activities are carried on from two centres—scientific from Seattle, and statistical at Prince Rupert. Its regulatory methods are, roughly, as follows. The fishing-grounds from Washington to the Aleutian Islands are divided into consecutively numbered areas. In some areas, or parts of areas, where the halibut are immature, fishing is prohibited. A closed season still operates for other areas, with, in addition, a quota or total number of halibut that may be taken yearly in each. The quota is fixed by the Commission on the basis of the condition of the fishery. In order to enforce the quota all halibut ships are licensed and the continuance of the licence is conditioned on the prompt reporting to the appropriate fisheries officers of either country by the master on landing of the quantity of halibut taken, and the area. The Commission is thus able to estimate in advance the probable date when the quota will be reached in any area. The date estimated is announced, sometimes as far as a month in advance, as the closing date for fishing in the area. On the whole this method has proved remarkably successful.[1]

In co-operation with the fishing industry regulations as respects gear and methods of fishing have been developed. Indeed the Commission appears to be to a considerable extent a means of promoting the self-regulation of the industry.[2]

The success of the Commission in conserving and improving the fishery seems assured. Already there are indications of improvement in the fishery, although, owing to the slow growth of the halibut, it will be some years before any substantial increase in the quantity of fish can be evident.[3] Further, Commission control has eliminated the possibility of international friction over the decline of the fishery. It seems to have won the support both of the fishing interests and of their governments.

THE SOCKEYE SALMON CONVENTION

The protection of the sockeye salmon constituted another problem turned over to the International Fisheries Commission of 1918. This choice species of salmon once constituted the bulk of the take on Puget Sound, but it has been progressively declining. From 1913 to 1929 it declined from 60 to 10 per cent. of the catch. Again, in the four years, 1921, 1923, 1925, 1929 the total catch in Puget Sound was only 471,884 cases, whereas it was 1,673,099 in 1913 alone.[4] The sockeye spawns in the Fraser river and its tributaries. To reach the Fraser it must go through American waters. It is therefore impossible for either country to regulate the fishing adequately alone. Moreover, much of the fishing for sockeye is done outside the three-mile limit.

Attempts to secure protection of the fishery by reciprocal legislation have been made from time to time since 1904 but without success. A treaty for regulation was negotiated in 1907 but was finally rejected by the American Senate in 1913.[5] A conference between the two govern-

---

[1] W. F. Thompson: " Halibut Study," *The Pacific Fisherman*, 31: 2 (Jan. 1933), p. 159; also Canada, Department of Fisheries, *Annual Report*, 1932-1933, pp. 22-25.

[2] *The Pacific Fisherman*, 32: 2 (Jan. 1934), p. 166.

[3] An increase in the catch per skate, or unit of gear, from 49 lb in 1930 to 64 lb in 1932 is noted by the Commission, but with the warning that this was due to less fishing rather than more fish (Canada, Department of Fisheries, *Annual Report*, 1932-1933, p. 25).

[4] *The Pacific Fisherman*, vol. xxix. (Jan. 1931), No. 1, pp. 14-16; *Congressional Digest*, 1930, p. 1068 ff.

[5] *Congressional Digest, loc. cit.*

ments in 1921-1922 again recommended a treaty but no results were forthcoming until 1929 when a treaty was finally signed between the two governments.[1]

The treaty proposed to cover the Fraser river and all its tributaries, as well as a portion of the high seas around the mouth of the river where salmon-fishing was extensively carried on. Like the Halibut Convention it provided for an international commission—six members, three from each country. The Commission was empowered to make a thorough investigation into the natural history of the sockeye salmon, into hatchery methods, spawning-grounds and other matters. To that end it was to be empowered " to improve spawning-grounds, acquire, construct and maintain hatcheries, rearing-ponds and other such facilities for the propagation of sockeye salmon . . . and to stock the waters with sockeye salmon by such methods as it may determine to be most desirable." In addition it was empowered to recommend to the two governments the removal of obstructions to the ascent of the fish (Article III.). It was further empowered to limit the catch, or prohibit fishing (unlike the halibut treaty without the necessity of approval by the two governments). It could also regulate fishing gear. It was required, however, to so regulate the fishing that an equal portion of the catch might be taken by the fishermen of each of the High Contracting Parties. Regulation by the Commission was to require the affirmative vote of at least two commissioners from each country. Expenses were to be borne equally by the two governments.

The treaty received wide support in both countries, but unfortunately it was vigorously opposed by the purse-seine fishermen of the State of Washington, who appear to be politically powerful. As a result, the Governor of the State of Washington waged an active campaign against the treaty, which has so far failed to pass the American Senate. The grounds of opposition seem to be that the treaty would enable the commissioners to discriminate against the purse-seine fishermen, that it assured to Canada a larger share of the fishery than she was at the time enjoying, and that the treaty was an invasion of state's rights by the Federal Government of the United States.[2] Meantime, the sockeye salmon industry seems to continue to decline.[3]

[1] Canada, *Treaty Series.*

[2] *Congressional Record*, December 9 and 18, 1930, pp. 454 aod 1068 ff.; *Pacific Fisherman*, xxvii., No. 10 (September 1930), p. 16 ; xxix., No. 1 (January 1391), pp. 14-16.

[3] *New York Times*, December 14, 1933.

COMMODITY CONTROL IN THE PACIFIC AREA

CONVENTION FOR THE REGULATION OF WHALING

Whaling has long been of commercial importance, the oils, whalebone and other products abstracted from the whale being important industrial products, while in certain countries, notably Japan, whales have been, and still are to some extent, used for human food. The North Atlantic, particularly the Greenland coasts, were formerly important whaling areas, and the North Pacific to a lesser extent. In both these areas extensive operations have greatly reduced the supply and indeed have virtually exterminated certain species. The Antarctic is still, however, an important whaling area.

Improved methods of whaling such as the use of explosive shells rather than the old harpoon methods, the use of " floating factories," and power-driven vessels have greatly increased the catch.[1]

The growth of the industry and the declining catch in northern waters have raised grave fears lest whales become extinct. Suggestions for international control of the industry have been made from time to time, but not until recently has any definite progress been made. In 1924 the Assembly of the League of Nations initiated an inquiry into subjects possible and desirable of regulation by international agreement. Among subjects recommended was that of the exploitation of the riches of the sea, with special recommendation of the whaling

[1] The following Table, adapted from the *Statistical Yearbook of the League of Nations*, 1931-1932, p. 83, illustrates the increase in the catch in recent years:

WHALING STATISTICS

(Number of whales caught)

	1921-22	1922-23	1923-24	1924-25	1925-26	1926-27	1927-28	1928-29	1929-30	1930-31
Geographical distribution—										
Antarctic and West Australia	7,023	9,910	7,271	11,157	14,959	13,664	14,809	20,341	30,167	40,201
Coast of Africa	2,335	3,105	3,649	4,384	4,646	4,144	3,835	3,362	3,498	823
Coast of Spain and Portugal, North Atlantic and Arctic	1,518	2,320	3,034	3,171	3,068	1,826	1,561	1,159	1,472	703
Pacific (North)	1,356	1,363	1,102	1,892	1,804	2,064	1,412	1,241	975	..
Coast of Chile and Peru	202	..	257	774	1,568	931	300	330	250	..
Japan and Corea	1,506	1,422	1,526	1,875	2,148	1,546	1,607	1,463	1,312	1,147
Total Catch	13,940	18,120	16,839	23,253	28,193	24,175	23,524	27,896	37,674	42,874
Of which—										
Norwegian whaling	6,157	8,738	7,180	12,460	14,727	12,754	11,791	14,996	21,609	25,952
British whaling	4,105	5,675	5,759	6,835	8,735	7,248	7,095	8,230	12,204	13,019
Whaling of other countries	3,678	3,707	3,900	3,958	4,731	4,173	4,654	4,670	3,861	3,903

industry.[1] The first practical step was taken by Norway, which forbade the taking of certain types and regulated the industry generally in the interests of conservation. The legislation could, of course, apply only to Norwegian ships or nationals.[2] Meantime the question of conservation was under investigation by the Economic Commission of the League and by a sub-committee of experts. In 1930 these committees produced a draft convention based largely on the Norwegian legislation. This convention was opened for signature at the Twelfth Assembly of the League, and was immediately signed by representatives of South Africa, Australia, Canada, Great Britain, France, India, New Zealand and Norway, and shortly thereafter by Columbia and Spain.[3] It was to go into effect ninety days after ratification by eight countries, including Norway and Great Britain, which together control close to 90 per cent. of the industry. As yet not sufficient countries have ratified to make the convention effective.

The convention applies to all waters of the world, both territorial waters and high seas, though it does not prevent additional regulations by any state over its territorial waters. It applies only to baleen or "whalebone" whales. It prohibits the killing of right whales, of cows accompanied by calves and of calves. It requires that the fullest use of carcases must be made. It requires that the remuneration of crews shall not be based only on the number of whales caught. The High Contracting Parties agree to require the licensing of all whaling vessels, to require licensees to keep accurate biological data of all whales taken, of the number, and of the amount of whale products. Statistics are to be forwarded to the International Bureau of Whaling Statistics at Oslo. Other states are to be invited to accede to the convention, which is to continue in force for three years, subject to denunciation on six months' notice. Any two parties to the convention may call a conference for revision. Each member undertakes to carry the convention into effect by appropriate legislation and to enforce its provisions as against its own nationals or ships of its own registry.[4]

The convention is a unique attempt to regulate an industry on all seas of the world. It has, however, certain serious defects. So long as all countries where the whaling industry is or can be carried on are not included, it will not be completely effective, since it will be relatively

---

[1] Monthly Summary of the League of Nations, vol. xi. (1931), p. 234.

[2] Science, lxx., No. 1819 (November 1929), x.

[3] Monthly Summary, loc. cit.

[4] Text of the convention in Monthly Summary, vol. xi. (1931), pp. 278-280, or League of Nations Publications, C. 642M. 256, 1931, 11B.

easy for nationals of one of the contracting parties to circumvent the convention by registering their ships with a non-contracting state. Under modern methods of floating factories, and all-year-round or long-term operations, whaling interests are moreover relatively independent of port facilities. Under such conditions it would seem relatively easy for the whaling interests to avoid control, especially so when there is no provision for policing of whaling areas. A self-denying ordinance without some machinery of administrative supervision or control does not promise to be very effective. The convention is, however, a step forward, since it at least provides a method of collecting information necessary for any adequate system of control.

CONCLUSIONS

The high seas and their products are the heritage of all nations, though, of course, most particularly of those nations advantageously located to harvest the sea most economically. As the supply of fresh agricultural land diminishes, the sea is likely to become of increasing importance as a source of man's food-supplies. It is probable that the sea may be tapped for food far more abundantly than at present without endangering the continuity of supply. It is indeed possible that Nature may be assisted (as she has long been on land) to increase her supplies of the products for man's growing needs. Possibly the application of industrial methods to fishing may endanger Nature's powers of recuperation, as indeed it has in the case of the fur seal and the halibut. The great need, in any case, is to see whither we are tending, to discover whether the supply of any particular species is being endangered, and if so to invent remedies for its conservation and, if need be, its recovery. Some remedies may be scientific, others must be political, involving co-operative effort and the development of administrative machinery between states interested. Each case must be dealt with individually, according to the habits of the species involved, the methods and location of the fishery, and other peculiar factors. As yet, no method of conservation or control appears to be of general application. The point of departure in any case must be minute scientific inquiry into the branch of the fishing industry involved. Only thus can we discover whether Nature needs assistance in the preservation of such forms of marine life as are valuable to man.

Certain general conclusions from the experiments we have examined appear to be warranted:

1. Protective measures are effective only when based on adequate scientific data, as regards (a) the life-history of the fish or mammal to

446

be protected; (*b*) the history of the fishing industry. The regulations of the Award of 1894 for the protection of the fur seal appear to have failed because of inadequate knowledge both as regards the life-history of the seal and as regards the pelagic sealing industry. The Halibut Treaty of 1923 did not prove entirely satisfactory primarily because of inadequate knowledge of the life-history of the halibut.[1]

Scientific knowledge and accurate statistics are thus the basis of successful international regulation. As regards studies in the life-history of commercial fishes, great strides have been made in recent years by Government bureaus, private organizations, and scientists, notably by the fisheries bureaus of the United States, Great Britain, Japan, Norway and Canada, by such semi-official bodies as the International Council for the Exploration of the Sea,[2] the North American Committee on Fisheries Investigations which is composed of representatives of the United States, Canada, Newfoundland, France and Portugal, as well as by individual scientists.

Great gaps remain, however, in our knowledge of the fishing industry.

On this point a report of the United States Bureau of Fisheries for 1926[3] has the following to say, which though concerned with the conditions in the United States is equally applicable to other countries:

Undoubtedly the most serious handicap to the proper development of effective fishery conservation in the United States is the almost uniform lack of adequate statistics of the fisheries. While there has always been a more or less general realization of the economic value of records of total annual yield, the number of persons engaged, and the amount of investment in the fisheries, less attention has been given to the need for determining the relative abundance of the fisheries stock, year by year, as an indication of the state of the fisheries. It has been announced repeatedly that the aim of the division of scientific inquiry is to study fluctuation in the fisheries and to determine their immediate causes; but in nearly every case it has been impossible to attack the problem from a quantitative standpoint, which is by far the most important aspect, because of the lack of suitable statistical data. The yield per unit of effort, such as the boat catch per day, has long been recognized as a useful index of abundance of fish in the sea, but the present records cannot be analysed on that basis. Suitable statistics must contain these essential details: they must be uniform throughout the range of a fishery, continuous, free from bias, and stored in central places in such a way that they may be preserved for subsequent analysis by fishery investigations.

---

[1] That is, on the part of the framers of the treaty, who seem to have largely ignored Professor Thompson's excellent reports for the Government of British Columbia cited above.

[2] Formed at Copenhagen, 1902, by representatives from Great Britain, Germany, Russia, Denmark, the Netherlands, Norway, Sweden. Its activities are practically confined to European waters.

[3] No. 1029, entitled *Progress in Biological Studies*, 1926.

2. In view of the fact that fishing on the high seas is ordinarily carried on by private rather than public enterprise, international regulation obviously entails in most cases some form of international police for enforcement. So far the police measures in the Fur Seal Treaty and the Halibut Treaty seem to be tolerably adequate. These, it will be remembered, are: patrolling by the public ships of the countries concerned, the right of visit, search and seizure of ships of the parties to the respective treaties, but trial and punishment by the flag state of vessels seized. Since 1882 this method has been in vogue in the North Sea, and has proven satisfactory there as well.[1] The same method was also used in the suppression of the slave trade at sea in the nineteenth century.[2] Indeed, the convention for the suppression of the slave trade and certain conventions for the protection of fisheries are the only instances where states have consented to police action on the high seas against their nationals by the public vessels of other countries.

3. Although each case of regulation must be dealt with separately and on its merits, the commission method of administrative control worked out in the halibut treaties is a highly suggestive method. It provides for flexibility; it takes the subject out of politics; it permits the development of an administrative technique so badly needed in international affairs; and, above all, it permits the development of international institutions according to function, rather than according to the outworn canons of national sovereignty.

[1] See Appendix for extract on police measures from North Sea Convention.
[2] *E.g.* General Act of Brussels, 1890, *v.* Moore, *Digest*, vol. ii., p. 948.

INDEX

2 F